PREFACE

A FTER CURIATIUS MATERNUS had recited his drama on the subject of Cato, not without disapprobation in high places, his friends paid him a visit. Discovering the author with the scroll in his hands, they opined that he might be going back and purging the text to make it safe for publication—'non quidem meliorem, sed tamen securiorem'. The response of Maternus dispelled the pleasing illusion: he already had in mind a second piece that would leave his opinions about rulers and government in no kind of doubt. In fact nothing less than a *Thyestes*.

Coming so soon after *Ammianus and the Historia Augusta* (1968), a book on a similar theme may arouse curiosity as well as disquiet. Let it at once be said that no retreat is conveyed, or any abatement. Rather a firm stand on the better cause, which I have long believed to be the 'victrix causa'. That is, not six biographers composing the Historia Augusta at different times in the epoch of Diocletian and Constantine, but one man's work and a date in the last decade of the fourth century. Such was the thesis of Hermann Dessau, long contested or evaded, but affirmed once again in this volume. The subject is vast, with multiple repercussions on the study of literature and history. It was the main purpose of the previous book to estimate the habits and quality of the artful impostor, to assign him a literary personality and put him in a recognizable milieu and reading public. Other aspects of the HA, such as the structure and sources of the earlier biographies, were less on show, being subordinate to the inquiry.

The present collection of studies will offer some compensation. The case is stated for *Ignotus*. That is, the basic and sober source of the nine biographies of emperors from Hadrian to Caracalla (Ch. III). At the same time, attention goes to the 'secondary *Vitae*', as they are called, which reveal significant links of language and ideas with later productions. They were not secondary in the conception of the author, who discloses haste and fatigue in mere compilation, his bent and delight being historical fiction (Ch. IV). Discussion of sources evokes the biographer Marius Maximus, whose contribution is put under scrutiny, not without paradoxical appreciation of his merits (Ch. VII). Maximus is set in confrontation with the historian Cassius Dio. Since they were close coevals, and each survived to hold a second consulship in the reign of Severus Alexander, a comparison of their careers, adducing detail about other senators of the time, is variously instructive (Ch. VIII).

Biography or history, the inevitable theme down to the last days is good emperors and bad. The potency of the Antonine name is therefore exemplified (Ch. V), and the fame of Trajan through the ages (Ch. VI). Those themes foreshadow a brief glance at the idealized figure of Severus Alexander. The fraudulence of the *Vita* is exposed (no novelty), and, more important, the obscurity of the long reign, with indication of sundry elements of continuity, notably the chief men in the Senate (Ch. IX). In sequel, because of evidence or theories about a 'senatorial revival', the emperors of the year 238: Gordianus, Pupienus, Balbinus (Ch. X).

By a convention both ancient and modern, the year 235 marks the end of a 'sub-Antonine' age and an abrupt break in history: Severus Alexander murdered and the proclamation of a crude and barbarous soldier. Maximinus, however, is due for rehabilitation. He was not, as Herodian alleged, a shepherd from some remote Thracian village. Rather, it can be argued, a Danubian and a Roman citizen by birth (Ch. XI).

The line of rulers deriving their obscure origins from the martial provinces of Illyricum is generally held to begin with Claudius in 268. Maximinus and Decius are potent precursors. The sequence which leads forward to Diocletian and Constantine is examined in detail: links existed in fact, and others were duly created by the HA in an unexpected mastery of technique (Ch. XII and Ch. XIII). Detail about the local provenance of Danubian emperors brings up the problem of the historical sources, both Latin and Greek, for the middle of the third century (Ch. XIV). In appendage, the *Vita Taciti*, among the most revealing since it is all but total fable. This emperor is alleged to be a frugal and benevolent scholar, chosen after long and edifying negotiations backward and forward between the army (anonymous) and the Senate. The hypothesis is here advanced that Claudius Tacitus was in fact the nominee of the generals—and a veteran survivor from their company (Ch. XV).

So far the Danubian Emperors, better thus styled than 'Illyrian'. Those whom the HA fatigues may find history and facts in those chapters. Yet the fabrications of the HA, introduced in the theme of Ch. I ('The Bogus Names'), being pervasive, are seldom out of sight for long. In equity to the ingenious author, an appraisal is essayed of that literary talent which few seem to discern or concede (Ch. XVI). Next, and in consonance, some remarks on the development of fictional history from Ctesias to

EMPERORS
AND BIOGRAPHY

EMPERORS
AND BIOGRAPHY

STUDIES IN THE
HISTORIA AUGUSTA

BY

SIR RONALD SYME

OXFORD
AT THE CLARENDON PRESS
1971

Oxford University Press, Ely House, London W. 1

GLASGOW NEW YORK TORONTO MELBOURNE WELLINGTON
CAPE TOWN SALISBURY IBADAN NAIROBI DAR ES SALAAM LUSAKA ADDIS ABABA
BOMBAY CALCUTTA MADRAS KARACHI LAHORE DACCA
KUALA LUMPUR SINGAPORE HONG KONG TOKYO

PRINTED IN GREAT BRITAIN
AT THE UNIVERSITY PRESS, OXFORD
BY VIVIAN RIDLER
PRINTER TO THE UNIVERSITY

Geoffrey of Monmouth. They lead to a definition of the principles of authenticity that apply to the HA, with select specimens to show what can happen when proper criteria are neglected (Ch. XVII, 'Fiction and Credulity').

A brief epilogue (Ch. XVIII), alluding to the controversy about the HA, sets out the order in which the problems are best approached. That is to say, structure and sources; authorship; the author; the genre and purpose. Finally the date. That question was touched on in Ch. I and in Ch. II. No fresh argument is here adduced to confirm the theory that the HA was composed in the close vicinity of 395, that convenient 'annus mirabilis'.

A number of these essays were written separately, before a design began to emerge. It was the intention that each should be self-contained and intelligible without recourse to the others. The same practice obtains in subsequent pieces. Hence a certain amount of repetition. Since the argument entails a plethora of detail and is built up on recurrent and interlocking themes, a plea of condonation may be put in. Moreover, the matter falls outside the field of many historians; and the *Vitae* are in scant favour with classical scholars, although the author was a word-fancier.

The first four chapters are in fact papers that were delivered in the *Colloquia* at Bonn, from 1965 to 1968.[1] They are here printed without any change. I am grateful for the permission to republish. Furthermore, and for the second time, I am happy to acknowledge a debt to the erudition and judgement of Mr. T. D. Barnes, who redressed many imperfections. Others subsist. But enough has been said. As the Emperor Otho observed in comment on his own exit, 'plura de extremis loqui pars ignaviae est.'

R. S.

Oxford
11 March 1969

---

[1] Ch. I: *Bonner Historia-Augusta-Colloquium 1964/5* (1966), 257 ff. Ch. II and Ch. III: ib. *1966/7* (1968), 119 ff. and 131 ff. Ch. IV: ib. *1968/9* (1970), 285 ff.

CONTENTS

I · THE BOGUS NAMES

SEVENTY-FIVE YEARS have passed. Much erudition was thrown into the battle, some of it in vain; and a long sequence of rearguard actions has been fought. Perhaps an epoch is now coming to a close. A broad measure of agreement about some at least of the problems that the Historia Augusta presents may at last be within reach. Not that there is an end to labour and vexation.

The decisive blow for freedom was struck in 1889, when Hermann Dessau published his classic and revolutionary paper. Not the six named authors, writing over a long tract of years in the reigns of Diocletian and Constantine. Instead, one man, towards the end of the fourth century, such was the thesis of Dessau.[1]

It is worth asking how he came to that notion. Not, it appears, from criticism of historical sources. Dessau did not set out from the disturbing parallels between the HA and Aurelius Victor (or even Eutropius). Nor did his incentive come from detailed studies in the history of the late imperial age. The point of departure is clear—nothing but his work for the *Prosopographia Imperii Romani*. Dessau had charge of Vol. II, of which the printing began in 1892; and he took over Vol. III.

The HA offers a mass of invented speeches, letters, and documents. Also more than two hundred characters not elsewhere attested, most of them highly suspect. Among them are no fewer than thirty-five historians or biographers, cited as 'authorities', from the ineffable 'Aelius Junius Cordus' downwards. Confronted with these names, the conscientious editor of a work of reference had to make decisions, or at the least register a proper word of warning. Furthermore, his investigations showed that some of the spurious characters ostensibly belonging to the third century reflected the nomenclature of a later age. They evoked families high in prominence at Rome in the second half of the fourth century. There were other suspicious features. Dessau saw no alternative: the HA was composed in the reign of Theodosius (379–95).

Dessau was a sober scholar, averse from paradox. His action provoked

---

[1] H. Dessau, *Hermes* XXIV (1889), 337 ff.; XXVII (1892), 561 ff.

scandal and alarm. It was necessary to face or evade the argument which he based on the damaging names. How could that be done? Mommsen was therefore constrained to conjure up an editor in the age of Theodosius.[1]

That concession in fact undermined the 'traditional' date, but it failed to impose conviction. The ominous names subsisted. Nor was it possible to demolish Dessau's main contention, that the HA was not written when it purported to have been written. However, a modification seemed admissible. The names and families (it was argued) might be held consonant with a slightly earlier date of composition, under Julian (in 361–3). That was the thesis of Baynes, powerfully argued and enlisting notable adherents.[2] None the less, his theory lapses, since nothing demands that the HA must belong precisely then and not later.

Caution is therefore prescribed, and it is expedient that the problem be carefully defined and delimited. A recent survey comes out with a firm pronouncement: the point at issue is to determine whether the collection of imperial *Vitae* was composed before or after the death of Constantine. Until that is decided, no progress can be made, so it is implied.[3] At first sight, the notion appears to correspond with sound and scientific method. If, however, the question be asked why that date and term be selected, a doubt arises. What is its source and validity? Mainly the dedications to Diocletian and Constantine or the references to those rulers, and to Constantius. Therefore, since the HA is patently an imposture, because of the fraudulent documents, it does not deserve credence for other and unsupported claims.[4]

The corollary one would like to see is a full and proper restatement of the traditional date, with or without the multiple authorship. That would be instructive, on various counts. What is to be made, for example, of one of the six ('Lampridius'), in address to Constantine? The Emperor, he says, has constrained him to write the *Elagabalus* against his will (*Elag.* 35. 1). That product is a farrago of cheap pornography.

---

[1] Th. Mommsen, *Hermes* xxv (1890), 228 ff. = *Ges. Schrift.* vii (1909), 302 ff.

[2] N. H. Baynes, *The Historia Augusta. Its Date and Purpose* (1926). He was followed by Hohl, Ensslin, and Seston.

[3] A. Momigliano, *Journal of the Warburg and Courtauld Institutes* xvii (1954), 22 ff. = *Secondo Contributo alla storia degli studi classici* (1960), 105 ff. The paper has had notable repercussions. Observe A. H. M. Jones, *The Later Roman Empire 284–602* iii (1964), 1: 'A. Momigliano . . . has to my mind conclusively demonstrated that there is no valid reason for doubting that the *Historia Augusta* could have been written at the date its authors profess to have written it.'

[4] It will be instructive to quote Baynes: 'in discussing Dessau's article it is, of course, unnecessary for me to waste words on his proof that the biographies cannot have been written at the time when they purport to have been composed' (o.c. 12).

The first and necessary action is to estimate the quality of the HA. That task should not be beyond the powers of literary and historical scholarship. Next, the motives behind the writing. Not so easy, yet not hopeless, if mischief and mystification be admitted in their own right. As with other pseudepigrapha, it may not be wise to aim at extreme precision.

When the attempt is made to expose a fraud, attack on all fronts is to be commended. Since, however, the grand assault on the HA started from the bogus names, it will be appropriate to revert to that approach, but with a different emphasis, not seeking in the first instance to establish a date for the compilation.[1]

How an author of fictitious narrations proceeds in the selection of personal names is a topic of instruction and entertainment in any age. As concerns the HA, two paths offer. First, one might put two or three choice passages under rigorous scrutiny. For example, the assertions about the family and relationships of Clodius Albinus or the Emperor Gordian; or the nine names of the dignitaries present at Valerian's council of state held in the Thermae at Byzantium (*Aur.* 13. 1). Any one of these items is revealing and damning. Second, classify the procedures of the HA under various heads. Some conclusions ought to emerge about the tastes and interests of the author—and also about his reading matter. That path will here be followed, with brief exemplification: the complete list would take too long. Though the notion of some team work need not wholly be dismissed, it will be assumed for convenience that a single author is in cause.

I. Indistinctive names. If a writer wishes to cover up his tracks, he will tend to operate with names that pass easily and excite no suspicions. Thus 'Junius Severus', sent by Commodus to replace Clodius Albinus, the governor of Britain (*Clod. Alb.* 14. 1), or 'Junius Balbus' the consular, married to the daughter of the Emperor Gordian (*Gord.* 4. 2).[2]

II. Imperial *gentilicia*. By the nature of things most of these are safe and

---

[1] The study of the names has been unduly neglected. There was, to be sure, A. v. Domaszewski, 'Die Personennamen bei den Scriptores Historiae Augustae', *Heidelberger S-B* 1918, Abh. 13. That contribution, valuable on certain details, was wholly unmethodical; and it was marred by all manner of wild fancies. Hohl in his survey was unduly severe (*Bursians Jahresberichte* CC (1924), 167 ff.). In general, he attached little importance to the bogus names. He was prepared to admit only two categories as useful to the historical inquirer, viz. 'die redenden Namen', such as 'Lampridia', and 'Suetonius Optatianus', and the few names of eminent families that pointed to the age of Theodosius (ib. 192). That was a harmful restriction.

[2] Both were registered with no sign of warning by Riba, P–W x. 966; 1084. 'Junius Balbus' and his wife were admitted by Ensslin in *CAH* XII. 79.

inconspicuous from 'Ulpius' down to 'Annius' and 'Aurelius'. Some perhaps occurred to the author unconsciously, such as 'Annius Fuscus', the parent of Pescennius Niger (*Pesc.* 1. 3), or 'Aurelius Verus', who wrote a history of Trajan (*Alex.* 48. 6). But 'Fulvius Boius, dux Raetici limitis' (*Aur.* 13. 1), looks deliberate.[1] It need not be added that he can invent a number of descendants of the Antonine dynasty, with portions of suitable nomenclature. Among them are 'Ulpia Gordiana', mother of Gordian, his wife 'Fabia Orestilla', her parent 'Annius Severus' (*Gord.* 2. 2; 17. 4; 6. 4). There is also 'Junia Fadilla', betrothed to the son of Maximinus the Thracian (*Maximin.* 27. 6), and that paragon of the virtues, 'Ulpius Crinitus, dux Illyriciani limitis' (*Aur.* 13. 1), who adopted Aurelian.[2]

III. Names from earlier *Vitae*. First, 'Palfurius Sura'. He was mentioned by Marius Maximus in his *Nerva*, according to the scholiast on Juvenal IV. 53. It is a fair inference that the lost *Vita* did not neglect this colourful character—and 'Palfurius Sura' turns up as an author (*Gall.* 18. 6). Second, 'Baebius Macer', *praefectus urbi* in 117 (*Hadr.* 5. 5). He is also the Prefect of the Guard, present at Byzantium in the year 258 (*Aur.* 13. 1).[3] Third, 'Lollius Urbicus', governor of Britain *c.* 140 (*Pius* 5. 4): 'Lollius Urbicus, in historia sui temporis', is cited for a detail concerning letters written by the son of Macrinus (*Diad.* 9. 2).[4]

IV. Recurrent and favourite names. The author, exploiting 'Baebius Macer', produces the *rhetor* 'Baebius Macrianus', one of the ten teachers (all suspect) who educated Severus Alexander (*Alex.* 3. 3); also a 'Baebius Maecianus' related to Clodius Albinus (*Clod. Alb.* 6. 1). Further, he took a fancy to 'Maecius'. He invented 'Maecius Marullus', the father of Gordian, 'Maecia Faustina', his daughter, and another member of the family, 'Maecius Gordianus', Prefect of the Guard in 244 (*Gord.* 2. 2; 4. 2; 30. 1). Then he went on to 'Maecius Brundisinus, praefectus annonae Orientis' (*Aur.* 13. 1), and 'Maecius Faltonius Nicomachus', a consular who delivers an oration at the accession of the Emperor Tacitus (*Tac.* 5. 3). The *cognomen* 'Maecianus' therefore comes under suspicion. Not merely 'Baebius Maecianus' (*Clod. Alb.* 6. 1), but 'Cereius Maecianus', written to

---

[1] Antoninus Pius was by birth an Aurelius Fulvus; and his maternal grandmother was a Boionia (*Pius* 1. 4).

[2] That character may owe his existence to the Emperor 'Ulpius Crinitus Traianus, natus Italicae in Hispania' (Eutropius VII. 2. 1).

[3] The name may have had an added appeal—a Baebius Macer cited by Servius on *Ecl.* IX. 46 and *Aen.* V. 556 (*PIR²*, B 21). Presumably the man who wrote on *fastalia sacrorum* (Fulgentius, *Serm.* 6).

[4] Of ephemeral notoriety in the present age, for he was accepted and acclaimed as a great imperial historian by E. Kornemann, *Kaiser Hadrian und der letzte große Historiker von Rom* (1905), 124 f.

by 'Claudius Sapilianus' (*Tac.* 19. 3), and the 'Maecianus' who receives a letter from the usurper Proculus (*Quadr. tyr.* 12. 7).[1]

v. The names of the 'six authors'. The mother of Pescennius Niger is called 'Lampridia' (*Pesc.* 1. 3); a 'Cornelius Capitolinus' is an authority on Zenobia (*Tyr. trig.* 15. 8); and 'Trebellius Pollio' perhaps lends his own name as label for a usurper who may never have existed (*Tyr. trig.* 26).[2]

vi. Names of classical authors. For more ample information about the Emperor Tacitus, one is referred to 'Suetonium Optatianum, qui eius vitam adfatim scripsit' (*Tac.* 11. 7).

vii. Names from literature. Wide reading, curious erudition, and a retentive memory—the theme would repay a thorough investigation. In the present place it will be enough to take three sources only, viz. Cicero, Suetonius, and the scholiasts.

First, Cicero. The author's familiarity comes out in various ways. He reports that the Emperor Balbinus claimed descent from Balbus Cornelius Theophanes, the historian, who got the Roman citizenship from Pompeius (*Max. et Balb.* 7. 3). The item is significant. The historian Pompeius Theophanes took Cornelius Balbus as his son in adoption, a fact known on extant evidence only from two passages in Cicero (*Pro Balbo* 57; *Ad Att.* VII. 7. 6). The author has muddled the item. Perhaps that also is significant.

Again, he shows awareness of the Calpurnii Pisones. The usurper Piso, to be sure, was supposed of that lineage, 'vir summae sanctitatis et temporibus suis Frugi dictus et qui ex illa Pisonum familia ducere originem diceretur, cui se Cicero nobilitandi causa sociaverat' (*Tyr. trig.* 21. 1). The allusion is to the marriage between the orator's daughter and C. Calpurnius Piso Frugi (quaestor in 58 B.C.). Another usurper, Titus, had for wife a Calpurnia, 'sancta et venerabilis femina de genere Caesoninorum, id est Pisonum' (*Tyr. trig.* 32. 5). What follows indicates that the author has Caesar's wife in mind, the daughter of L. Piso Caesoninus (*cos.* 58 B.C.)—there is a peculiar statement about that lady's statue in the temple of Venus Genetrix, about the pearls of Cleopatra which she possessed.[3]

Cicero (and Ciceronian *scholia*) may be divined. That being so, no surprise if characters from Cicero come into employ. In the first instance, Quintus Ancharius in the year 258, described as 'praeses Orientis' (*Aur.* 13. 1). It would be anomalous at that time, or later, to find a person bearing

---

[1] It is superfluous to point out that 'Capitolinus' and 'Vopiscus' each have a predilection for the names 'Maecius' and 'Maecianus'.

[2] For the alleged usurper 'Trebellianus' see A. Stein, P–W VI A. 2262.

[3] Again, confused erudition. It was Cleopatra's statue that stood on show in the temple according to Cassius Dio LI. 22. 3.

a style of nomenclature that lacked a *cognomen*.[1] Is he not Q. Ancharius, succeeding L. Piso as proconsul of Macedonia in 55 B.C. (*In Pisonem* 89)?[2]

Further, 'Autronius Tiberianus' who writes a letter to his parent 'Autronius Justus' (*Tac.* 19. 1). The name evokes the notorious associate of Catilina, consular candidate for 65 B.C. The annals of the Empire disclose no Autronius of any consequence. Another item from the Catilinarian context is 'Mallius Chilo', recipient of a dispatch from Aurelian (*Aur.* 23. 4). Now Q. Mallius Chilo is named by the manuscripts of Cicero, *In Cat.* III. 14. That raises a problem of no small interest. Editors alter the text, replacing him by Q. Annius Chilo, who stands in Sallust as 'Q. Annius' (*Cat.* 17. 3; 50. 4).[3]

Second, Suetonius. The HA produces as wife for Severus Alexander 'Memmia, Sulpicii consularis viri filia, Catuli neptis' (*Alex.* 20. 3). The source is clear. Observe the wife of Sulpicius Galba in Suetonius, 'Mummiam Achaicam, neptem Catuli' (*Galba* 3. 4).[4] Next, two persons called 'Arellius Fuscus'. The one is a consular who sponsors a decree of the Senate deifying the deceased usurper Piso (*Tyr. trig.* 21. 3), which would be strange enough, if Piso had ever lived. The other is a proconsul of Asia, the predecessor of 'Faltonius Probus' (*Aur.* 40. 4). Now there was a famous rhetorician of that name, mentioned several times by the elder Seneca.[5] The HA may have got him from the lost work of Suetonius, *De rhetoribus*.

Third, scholiasts. The HA has its habitation in the close vicinity of that tribe. It reproduces their philological erudition (or fancies), their confusions due to hasty compilation—and their lack of historical sense. Certain of the Ciceronian items bear witness. Parallels have properly been sought and found in Servius.[6]

One of the points of contact deserves especial attention. The HA reports uncertainties about Saloninus, the son of Gallienus. On one report he had that name because he was born at Salonae, a city of Dalmatia (*Gall.* 19. 3). There is an ominous parallel.[7] Servius, commenting on the miraculous child of the *Fourth Eclogue*, boldly produces Saloninus, a son of Asinius Pollio, born at Salonae. The child duly smiled at birth, and soon died. There is no reason to believe that the infant ever existed.[8]

---

[1] Hence, if necessary, cause to disallow 'Titus Veturius', the preceptor of an emperor (*Alex.* 3. 2), and 'Marcus Fonteius, amator historiarum' (*Quadr. tyr.* 2. 1).

[2] Domaszewski, o.c. 4.   [3] Domaszewski, o.c. 56.

[4] Pointed out by E. Groag, P-W III. 1796.   [5] *PIR*[2], A 1030.

[6] H. Dessau, *Hermes* XXIX (1894), 415; E. Hohl, *Hermes* LV (1920), 307. Among the instances is the etymology of 'Caesar' as the Moorish word for an elephant (*Ael.* 2. 3, cf. Servius on *Aen.* I. 286). Note also the writer Baebius Macer (above, p. 4, n. 3). The subject is a long way from being exhausted.   [7] A. Alföldi, *Num. Chron.* IX (1929), 265.

[8] R. Syme, *CQ* XXXI (1937), 39 ff.

The item is instructive. Does it show the HA drawing on the commentary of Servius? Not quite. There were earlier commentators (not worse or better), such as Aelius Donatus, who was one of Jerome's instructors.

A scholiast on another author, however, can be brought into play, perhaps disclosing the source of a fabricated name in the HA. The commentator on Juvenal iv. 81 amalgamates two characters, viz. C. Passienus Crispus (*cos. II 45*) and C. Vibius Crispus (*cos. suff. III*, ? 83). Now the HA comes out with Vibius Passienus, proconsul of Africa in the time of Gallienus, who supported the usurper 'Celsus' (*Tyr. trig.* 29. 1).[1]

The scholia on Juvenal were composed subsequent to 353 (the note on x. 24 mentions Cerealis, *praefectus urbi* in that year). How much later, it is not clear. One theory incautiously supposes that they were the work of a pupil of Servius.[2] Given the presumed age of that scholar, a young man at the dramatic date of Macrobius' *Saturnalia* (? 383), the theory is most implausible.

Juvenal (it appears) was a recent discovery to men in the second half of the fourth century—almost forgotten for long ages.[3] The HA does not name him; but traces of the satirist have recently been detected in the compilation.[4] That is a cruel blow to the credulous. The proconsul 'Vibius Passienus' now lends a hand and reinforces the impact.

VIII. Names of fun and fantasy. The author delights in etymology. The bogus parent of Pescennius Niger, namely 'Annius Fuscus', is equipped with a *cognomen* corresponding to that of his son (*Pesc.* 1. 3). One may note in passing that the grandfather was 'curator Aquini'. That is to say, the residence of the satirist Juvenal. Comment is superfluous.[5]

Nor need words be wasted on the author called 'Maeonius Astyanax'

---

[1] J. Schwartz, *Ant. class.* XXXIII (1964), 423. The above remarks on the Juvenalian *scholia* were in fact written before I had cognizance of this valuable article. Let that be stated not as a claim to merit but in independent support of a good cause.

[2] G. Highet, *Juvenal the Satirist* (1954), 186. The pupil is designated 'a well-trained pagan scholar'.

[3] G. Highet, o.c. 184 ff. Jerome never names him, but cites one passage (1. 15) three times. That is strange, but significant. By contrast, Persius occurs no fewer than twenty times, cf. H. Hagendahl, *Latin Fathers and the Classics* (1958), 284.

[4] A. D. E. Cameron, *Hermes* XCII (1964), 363 ff.

[5] J. Hasebroek was inclined to admit the notice as authentic (*Die Fälschung der Vita Nigri und Vita Albini* (1916), 41 f.). It was Dessau in his review who detected the reference to Juvenal and to the interests of the author (*Wochenschrift für kl. Philologie* 1918, 389 ff.). This item was missed by A. D. E. Cameron, o.c. 363 ff., as by many other scholars.

For a parallel, though incomplete and proving nothing, observe that the scholiast on Juvenal 1. 20 has a satirical poet called Silius, otherwise not on record (some identify him with the Silius Proculus of Pliny, *Epp.* III. 15), and allegedly from Suessa Aurunca (i.e., the home of Lucilius).

(*Tyr. trig.* 12. 3). Doubly a Phrygian, for he is endowed with a *cognomen* from Homer. Another Maeonius occurs, the murderer of the Palmyrene ruler Odenaethus (*Tyr. trig.* 15. 5; 17. 1). The *nomen* does not happen to be attested—but there was a Paeonius among the correspondents of Symmachus (*Epp.* II. 45).

Reference has already been made to some of the counsellors of Valerian in solemn conclave at Byzantium—'Baebius Macer', 'Quintus Ancharius', and others. The list exhibits two men with *gentilicia* nowhere on the remotest record: 'Murrentius Mauricius' and 'Avulnius Saturninus'.

In the close vicinity of that scene belongs 'Aelius Xiphidius', the *praefectus aerarii*. Valerian by letter instructed him to furnish money and equipment (a curious enumeration follows) for the impoverished Aurelian (*Aur.* 12. 1). The name 'Xiphidius' evokes a weapon of war. It puts one in mind of 'Toxotius' the ostensible senator *c.* 240 (*Maximin.* 27. 6). Now 'Toxotius', as will be shown, points to a later age, in which the most peculiar *cognomina* or *signa* had come to proliferate among the aristocracy.[1] Indeed, there is a clue to the fabrication of 'Xiphidius'. Symmachus happens to mention a lady of the senatorial class called Fasgania (*Epp.* I. 74); and there was Phasganius, an uncle of Libanius (*Or.* X. 19, etc.). That name speaks for itself: deriving from the old Greek word for a sword, familiar from Homer and the tragedians. Therefore 'Xiphidius' falls into its proper time and epoch.[2]

IX. Perverted names. One example is clear. Using Suetonius, the author changed 'Mummia' to 'Memmia' (*Alex.* 20. 3, cf. above). That is a mere trifle in the devices of the HA. If an author is anxious to be plausible, he may try to convey an impression of novelty (and hence of authenticity) by names that look original because different. Thus 'Avulnius' and 'Murrentius' (*Aur.* 13. 1).

One trick is to modify the shape of familiar names. Several instances have been detected. As consul in 258, the HA produces 'Nemmius Fuscus' (or 'Memmius Fuscus'). Editors have emended to 'Nummius Tuscus'. Perhaps they were on the wrong track. Again, 'Faltonius Probus', proconsul of Asia (*Aur.* 40. 4). The name 'Faltonius' is distinctive—and it happens to possess no small significance for alert students of the HA (see below). Yet it might be better to keep the 'Falconius' of the manuscripts. The name exists, though portentously rare.[3]

---

[1] Thus 'Lampadius', 'Phosphorius', 'Asterius', etc.

[2] *Addendum.* 'Xiphidius' is on attestation, see below, p. 216. It was not a creation of the author.

[3] 'Falconius' occurs in *CIL* VI. 12533; VIII. 5404. Relevant are the *cognomina* of Fidiculanius Falcula (Cicero, *Pro Caecina* 28) and Q. Pompeius Falco (*cos. suff.* 108).

As has been shown, the author employs 'Arellius Fuscus' on two occasions (*Tyr. trig.* 21. 3; *Aur.* 40. 4). What is one to make of the writer called 'Dagellius Fuscus' (*Tyr. trig.* 25. 2)? Should one emend? And if so, to 'Arellius'?[1] Perhaps rather to 'Vagellius', in view of Juvenal XVI. 23, 'declamatoris mulino corde Vagelli'. But it would be better to retain 'Dagellius' in his own right, as deliberate fabrication. Similarly, the Pisidian brigand 'Palfuerius' (*Prob.* 16. 4). There is no point in improving the name to accord with 'Palfurius Sura' (*Gall.* 18. 6, discussed above).

One can proceed on this line. A dispatch of Septimius Severus refers to 'Statilius Corfulenus', who in the Senate had proposed honours for Clodius Albinus and his brother (*Clod. Alb.* 12. 11). The *nomen* 'Corfulenus' lacks attestation. It is not beyond credence. The Corfidii were a reputable family in the Sabine country, known to Cicero and to Varro;[2] and a Corfonius happens to be on record as a senator in 376.[3] But the true source is surely the D. Carfulenus whom the author encountered in the writings of Cicero. Commanding a legion, D. Carfulenus played a notable role in the autumn of 44 and in the spring of the following year.[4]

That is not all. Specimens can be adduced that appear hitherto to have escaped notice. First, 'Aradio'. In Africa Probus fought in single combat 'contra quendam Aradionem' (*Prob.* 9. 2). 'Aradio' succumbed, but was honoured for his valour by a tumulus two hundred feet high, 'quod adhuc exstat'. Fiction, but Cicero once again, and abstruse knowledge. P. Sittius was killed in battle by a Numidian chieftain, much to the delight of Cicero—'Arabioni de Sittio nihil irascor' (*Ad Att.* XV. 17. 1).

Second, 'Claudius Sapilianus'. He indites a letter to his uncle 'Cereius Maecianus', exulting in the liberty and dignity newly acquired by the Roman Senate (*Tac.* 19. 3). Now 'Cereius' is not impossible as a *nomen*.[5] Nor is 'Sapilius', though nowhere attested. One observes, however, that there was a Sapidianus, *vicarius* of Africa in the year 399 (*C.Th.* XVI. 2. 34). Symmachus wrote a letter to this man (*Epp.* IX. 16).

Two or three instances of malformation might be put down to errors in the manuscript tradition. This accumulation engenders distrust. The perversions are clearly a device and habit of the author. Hence valuable clues. The names 'Corfulenus' and 'Aradio' disclose his freakish erudition.

[1] As does Hohl in his edition.
[2] See Schulze, *LE* 156 and *TLL, Onom.*
[3] *CIL* VI. 751 b II. Otherwise only in *CIL* VI. 16095.
[4] Cicero, *Phil.* III. 23; *Ad Att.* XV. 4. 1; *Ad fam.* X. 33. 3; cf. *Bell. Alex.* 31. 1; Appian, *BC* III. 66. Noted by Domaszewski (o.c. 117), who, however, preferred to emend the name in the HA.
[5] It happens to be attested, once (*CIL* XIII. 1996: Lugdunum).

'Sapilianus', however, encourages a further step (which accords with other indications).

On the specimens so far presented, the author appears, like the prophet Habakkuk, 'capable de tout'. And the frequentation of this 'farceur' is an incitement to the worst excesses of scholarly fantasy. There are dire warnings.[1] None the less, one more example occurs of a personal name that may have been deliberately perverted. So portentous are the repercussions that it can only be adduced with due and extreme diffidence.

Reference has already been made to the senator with the startling name of 'Toxotius'. He took over 'Junia Fadilla', who had been the bride destined for the son of Maximinus; and, like her, he belonged to the family of the Antonine Caesars—'eiusdem familiae senator' (*Maximin.* 27. 6). That is a patent fraud, and the whole context is suspect.

The author chronicles those who taught the son of Maximinus: the items about the ten educators of Severus Alexander warn one what to expect (*Alex.* 3. 2 f.). First, there is a Greek scholar called Fabillus, 'cuius epigrammata Graeca multa et extant', among them a version of a passage in Virgil (*Maximin.* 27. 3). The name 'Fabillus' lacks attestation. Second, a Latin *grammaticus*, Philemon, who may have existed.[2] Third, the jurist Modestinus: he is a historical character, viz. Herennius Modestinus, a pupil of Ulpian.[3]

The list proceeds with 'oratore Titiano, filio Titiani senioris'. At once a perplexity. There is a Julius Titianus on clear record, a contemporary of Fronto. Sidonius says that he wrote letters 'sub nomine illustrium feminarum'. They called him 'oratorum simiam'.[4] Now the HA has the phrase 'simiam temporis sui, quod cunctos esset imitatus'. So far so good. But it is not clear that one has to admit the existence of his son, the ostensible tutor of the boy; and no other source betrays awareness of two Julii Titiani. To this invention there is a disturbing parallel: two *grammatici* called 'Scaurinus'. The HA produces as the teacher of Verus 'Scaurinum grammaticum Latinum, Scauri filium, qui grammaticus Hadriani fuit' (*Verus* 2. 5). Also, however, 'Scaurinum Scaurini filium,

---

[1] That is, certain operations of Domaszewski.

[2] See Strzelecki, P–W xix. 2152 ff.

[3] One authentic name is no support for any of the others. The author possessed no evidence about the education of the youth—and he is not aware of the mother, Caecilia Paulina (*PIR²* C 91). Maximinus' son was not much younger than Severus Alexander, who was born *c.* 208. Each, it is implied, enjoyed the best education the age could produce; but they managed to avoid having the same teachers.

[4] Sidonius, *Epp.* I. I. 2, cf. *PIR¹*, J 391. The two Julii Titiani are accepted without misgivings in *PIR* and by Diehl in P–W x. 892 f.

doctorem celeberrimum' (*Alex.* 3. 3).[1] To be rejected, along with the other teachers of Severus Alexander. And further, one will therefore conceive doubts about the second Sammonicus Serenus, who gave his father's library to the younger Gordian (*Gord.* 18. 2).[2]

That is not the worst. The text goes on to mention 'Graecum rhetorem Eugamium sui temporis clarum' (*Maximin.* 27. 5). The person is not elsewhere attested. 'Eugamius' is rare indeed. The author may have had another name in mind. The rhetorician Eugenius leapt into notoriety in the year 392. Eugenius was put up as emperor by Arbogast. He perished in September of 394 when the cause of the old faith, renascent for a season, was destroyed in the battle fought beside the river Frigidus.

'Eugenius' modified to 'Eugamius', that might seem too good to be true. Yet perversions of this kind belong to the normal practices of the author. For discretion and safety one might waive 'Eugamius'. But, if a date be sought, one is not entitled to neglect 'Claudius Sapilianus', who evokes the Sapidianus who was *vicarius* of Africa in 399.

x. So far, nine categories. The most significant has been reserved for the climax, the fictitious characters who by their names reflect families eminent in the Roman aristocracy in the second half of the fourth century: Ceionii, Faltonii, Ragonii, etc. It will not be necessary to recapitulate the arguments of Dessau, which many have doubted, nobody has demolished.[3]

There happens to be no Anicius in the HA. But a clear allusion has been detected to the great Sex. Petronius Probus, who styled himself 'culmen Aniciorum'.[4] Probus was consul in 371, his sons shared the *fasces* in 395. The author alleges that the descendants of the Emperor Probus went away and lived near Verona. A prophecy announced the future glory of the family—'tantae in senatu claritudinis fore ut omnes summis honoribus fungerentur' (*Prob.* 24. 3). After which, the author neatly covers up his traces by saying: 'adhuc neminem vidimus.' Now Sex. Petronius Probus in fact came from Verona.[5] The prophecy duly fulfilled thus points not only to his multitudinous public honours but perhaps to the joint consulship of his young sons.

[1] The *grammaticus* Q. Terentius Scaurus (*PIR*[1], T 71) flourished in the time of Hadrian, cf. Gellius xv. 11. 3. Only the HA produces Scaurinus his son and Scaurinus his grandson, educators of princes.

[2] The scholar Sammonicus Serenus (*PIR*[1], S 122) referred to by Arnobius, Macrobius, Servius, and Sidonius, flourished in the Severan period, and was put to death by Caracalla (HA, *Carac.* 4. 4). The ostensible son (*Gord.* 18. 2, cf. *Alex.* 30. 2), lacks other attestation.

[3] H. Dessau, *Hermes* xxiv (1889), 351 ff. Baynes, it will be observed, assumed that they were anachronistic, notably 'Toxotius' (o.c. 22 ff.). Add, for 'Maecii', below, p. 12.

[4] *CIL* vi. 1753 = *ILS* 1267.

[5] *CIL* v. 3344 = *ILS* 1266.

Perhaps the prime exhibit is the senator 'Toxotius', whose bride 'Junia Fadilla' brought with her the betrothal gifts (duly specified) which she got from the son of Maximinus the Thracian (*Maximin*. 27. 6 ff.). With the name 'Toxotius' one is at once transported into the circle of pious ladies frequented by Jerome when he sojourned at Rome from 382 to 385. Paula, that famous *dévote*, was the widow of Julius Toxotius. Her son, the younger Toxotius, married Laeta, daughter of Ceionius Caecina Albinus (one of the pillars of the pagan cause). Jerome comes out with startling asseverations about the ancestry of several aristocratic families. While Toxotius traced his descent from Agamemnon and Aeneas, Paula was 'stirps Gracchorum'.[1] That item is important. Paula was close kin to a man called Furius Maecius Gracchus, who, when *praefectus urbi* in 376, destroyed a shrine of Mithras.[2]

It is welcome to have the name 'Maecius' cropping up in this season. It concerns the Historia Augusta, very closely. Not only because of the fabricated 'Maecius Faltonius Nicomachus' (*Tac*. 5. 3), all three details of which name are damnatory.[3] The item has a wider repercussion.

According to the HA, the Emperor Gordian was descended from the Gracchi on the father's side (*Gord*. 2. 2). How could that be? Some might be tempted to invoke as explanation the 'Sempronianus' in his nomenclature: he was M. Antonius Gordianus Sempronianus Romanus.[4] But there is no sign that the author was thinking of the 'Sempronianus'. The *Vita* registers the father of Gordian as 'Maecius Marullus' without bothering to furnish any elucidation about the Gracchan descent. The clue can now be supplied, a Maecius with the *cognomen* 'Gracchus'. That is to say, Furius Maecius Gracchus, Prefect of the City in 376.

A fresh item thus goes to the dossier. It was not needed. Enough damaging items had already piled up. Either 'Toxotius' or 'Maecius Faltonius Nicomachus' was good enough.

A question could not fail to arise. The author has projected names into the past. What was his motive? He was not inadvertent. 'Toxotius' was striking—and perhaps it inspired him to employ 'Xiphidius'. And 'Faltonius' was uncommon, of fairly recent emergence in the aristocracy.

---

[1] *Epp*. 108. 1.

[2] *Epp*. 107. 2.

[3] Domaszewski proclaimed that the name was indubitably authentic (o.c. 7). According to Momigliano, 'Domaszewski, if often strange, was never foolish' (*Secondo Contributo* 114).

[4] So Domaszewski (o.c. 82). He there argues that Gordian's Gracchan and Trajanic ancestry is correct. The item is registered by Ensslin without any expression of doubt (*CAH* XII. 77).

In senatorial houses, it finds its first attestation with Anicia Faltonia Proba, the aunt of Sex. Petronius Probus.[1]

The thing was deliberate. An easy explanation offers—the author wished to pay a delicate tribute to birth and rank, furnishing ancestors already illustrious in an earlier century. That is not the whole truth. It is not certain that this author, making play with genealogies, is sincere in devotion to the aristocracy. His portrayal of the Emperor Gordian might suggest a doubt. That ruler, the son of 'Ulpia Gordiana' and married to an ostensible descendant of Marcus ('Fabia Orestilla'), looks like an ideal Antonine emperor put on exhibit as a figure of amicable parody, with a variety of humorous exaggerations. One might wonder whether he was not exercising gentle malice at the expense of those genealogical pretensions which were so impudently paraded by the aristocracy, with loyal support from the intemperate zeal of friends or clients, some perhaps credulous, others artful.[2] One of those clients cannot evade scrutiny—Jerome, a master of guile and eloquence.

Even on the present restricted type of inquiry, the lineaments of the author begin to take shape. 'Capitolinus' or 'Vopiscus' (or any one of the other four), the same methods and habits emerge, likewise the same language.[3] He forges documents, invents names, and (most significant) alters names. He can invoke a medley of recondite erudition; and he declares an especial interest in the history as well as the processes of classical scholarship, to the point of inventing *rhetores* and *grammatici* (observe the teachers of Severus Alexander and of Maximinus' son). Other passages declare the *grammaticus*—the portentous lists of equipment and clothing and wild beasts. And there is the wanton profusion of details about food and drink and sex. Those things were not meant to be taken seriously. And he has his own silly or elaborate jokes. This man is a kind of rogue scholar.[4] Almost, one might say, a scholiast on a holiday from the routine of pedestrian tasks.

Therefore, for fun, the author claims to be a serious researcher, vindicating biography against the ostensibly superior genre of history. In documentation and in personal details, there resides the truth, he implies, not in

---

[1] For the stemma, see A. Chastagnol, *Les Fastes de la préfecture de Rome au Bas-Empire* (1962), 292. The first Faltonius of consequence was Faltonius Restitutianus, equestrian governor of Mauretania Caesariensis in 240 (*PIR*², F 109). The *nomen* is infrequent in Italy: *CIL* v (none); ix (2); x (2); xi (4). But observe Africa: viii. 854 (Thuburbo Maius); 16010 (Sicca); 17346 (Thabraca); 18065 (Lambaesis).

[2] I hope to develop that theme in another place.

[3] H. Dessau, *Hermes* xxiv (1889), 378 ff.

[4] E. Hohl, *Hermes* lv (1920), 302 ff.; 308 ff. Cf. J. Straub, *Studien zur Historia Augusta* (1952), 11.

style and eloquence. He will write 'non tam diserte quam vere' (*Prob.*
2. 7).[1] Such is the noble profession. From time to time the deceiver lowers
the mask. For example, when scourging the follies and fraudulence of
other biographers (whom he invents), notably 'Aelius Junius Cordus'.[2]
The prime revelation occurs in the exordium of the *Vita Aureliani*.
The Prefect of the City, after friendly and encouraging discourse on the
high themes of history and veracity, tells the author to write as his fancy
dictates. All the classical historians were liars, and he can join their company with a clear conscience—'securus, quod velis, dices, habiturus mendaciorum comites quos historicae eloquentiae miramur auctores' (*Aur.* 2. 2).

Historians, as they acquire skill in their art, sometimes become bold and
free. That was the happy fortune of Cornelius Tacitus. He produces an
interchange of letters between Tiberius Caesar and his minister; while
Seneca and Nero confront each other, in private conclave, with elegant
orations.[3]

This writer, of a very different order, also gets better and better, achiev-
ing mastery in his genre, which is plain fiction. Dealing with the earlier
rulers, he was hampered and constrained by facts. The lives of pretenders,
such as Clodius Albinus, encouraged him to invent lavishly. With Maximin
and Gordian, though constricted by sources such as Herodian and Dexippus, he was able to break loose and furnish all manner of novelties. As
'Capitolinus' on Gordian he enjoys himself enormously; and as 'Vopiscus'
he rises to his peak when writing on Aurelian and Tacitus.

The impostor deserves credit for a kind of original talent. Not only does
he invent some thirty-five 'authorities'.[4] He passes himself off as a whole
school and epoch of imperial biography, extending over many years.
Parading the apparatus of erudition, with documents, polemics, and
scholarly dubitations, he reduces taste and learning to absurdity. He knows
what he is doing. And, though he may not have set out to deceive all his

---

[1] Cf. *Probus* 1. 6: 'neque ego nunc facultatem eloquentiamque polliceor sed res gestas quas
perire non patior.' Also *Tyr. trig.* 1. 1; 33. 8. He uses the language of researchers—'non satis
comperi' (*Tyr. trig.* 18. 12); 'sed ego senatus consultum ipsum non inveni' (*Prob.* 7. 1). And
he has a discussion with 'Marcus Fonteius, amator historiarum', at which coins of the usurper
Firmus are produced to prove an argument (*Quadr. tyr.* 2. 1).

[2] Mommsen rejected this 'authority' in a vigorous phrase—'der Biograph hat . . . in
diesem Pseudo-Cordus sich zugleich einen Gewährsmann und einen Prügelknaben ge-
schaffen' (*Ges. Schrift.* VII. 343).

[3] Tacitus, *Ann.* IV. 39 f.; XIV. 53 ff.

[4] H. Peter duly registered them (*HRR* II (1906), 129 ff.), with erudite comment (ib.
CLXXXVIIII). Momigliano eschews the whole topic: 'I avoid on purpose the question whether
the H.A. claimed to have used literary sources that never existed' (*Secondo Contributo* 110).
That was unfortunate, on various counts.

readers, he succeeded in the end where he might least have expected: he has been able to take in heavy cohorts of sober scholars. That he did simply because he is a humorist. The performance engenders a reluctant sympathy.[1] It is a welcome relief to discover such a phenomenon in the last days, in the age of dull Symmachus and the dreadful Jerome. Not indeed that Jerome's talent for satire should be underestimated; and Jerome was no mean expert in impudent fiction, as witness his Life of Paulus, the desert hermit whom he invented as the predecessor of Antony.[2]

For the understanding of that age, a passage in Ammianus is enormously instructive. The historian, enamoured of Rome and the Roman tradition, found little to applaud in the aristocracy.[3] He solemnly and bitterly indicts their neglect of serious studies—they kept their libraries shut up like sepulchres (xiv. 6. 18). And their choice of reading was deplorable—'quidam detestantes ut venena doctrinas Iuvenalem et Marium Maximum curatiore studio legunt' (xxviii. 4. 14). Few have failed to see the relevance of this passage.[4] Like the satirist, the biographer Marius Maximus may have been a recent discovery, suddenly in fashion.[5] Now the HA, after having cited Marius Maximus often, passes severe censure on him—'homo omnium verbosissimus, qui et mythistoricis se voluminibus implicavit' (*Quadr. tyr.* 1. 2). That is delicious. It recalls the repeated flagellation of 'Aelius Junius Cordus', whom the HA invented as an authority, and as a warning. With feigned deprecation of the trivial and the fabulous, the author in his impudence goes further than did Marius Maximus and makes a mock of biography.

The prime requisite in the study of the HA is to discover the character and quality of the author. That seems to come out easily and clearly—and he was not at great pains to disguise himself all the way. What is the next step?

To embark on anxious inquiry about the design of an impostor is often to labour in vain.[6] All manner of motives are in play: the desire to

---

[1] Thus E. Hohl, *Bursians Jahresberichte* cc (1924), 208.

[2] For the talents of this author see the excellent and entertaining book of D. S. Wiesen, *St. Jerome as a Satirist*, Cornell Studies in Classical Philology xxxiv (1964).

[3] For Ammianus' alleged friends in the aristocracy, see now A. D. E. Cameron, *JRS* liv (1964), 15 ff. They were not numerous.

[4] And indeed some hold firmly that the HA itself shows signs of being later than Ammianus. Thus J. Straub, *Heidnische Geschichtsapologetik in der christlichen Spätantike* (1963), 53 ff.

[5] Ammianus, the scholiast on Juvenal iv. 53, and the twenty-six citations in the HA: that is the total evidence for the biographer Marius Maximus.

[6] A number of scholars are unduly worried by the famous question 'cui bono?' Similarly

fill gaps in knowledge, the parade of science, the exercise of technique, the delight in deception for its own sake. Other pseudepigrapha offer guidance. Speeches and letters abounded in antiquity; and forged inscriptions, in any age, will not be left out of the reckoning. Mere profit in money, or even the aspiration to literary fame, need seldom be invoked, still less the purpose of influencing opinion and advocating some political end. Pseudo-Cicero and Pseudo-Sallust are a deterrent.[1]

The HA discloses a number of themes and attitudes—reverence for the Senate, fervour for 'good emperors', dislike of military despotism or the regiment of eunuchs, and so on. Furthermore, though pagan, it seems crypto-pagan, unobtrusively suggesting a plea for tolerance. That is important. It indicates a date towards the end of the fourth century.[2] But it is hazardous to bring the HA into immediate relation with any historical transactions, so as to fix its composition within the limits of a year or two.[3] The present inquiry, based on the bogus names, permits and perhaps encourages a dating in the vicinity of the year 400.[4] That concords with other types of evidence, many and varied—and convergent.[5]

The time may now have come to reverse the question. Let the assumption be made that the HA was composed towards the year 400. What arguments avail to impugn it? How can one go on maintaining that the compilation might have been produced before the death of Constantine? All too many rearguard actions were fought in the long warfare that began in 1889.

as concerns another product of this period, the correspondence between St. Paul and Seneca, the expert in the matter says that the ultimate motives for it are hard to perceive (Momigliano, *Secondo Contributo* 117).

[1] R. Syme, *Mus. Helv.* xv (1958), 46 ff.; *Sallust* (1964), 297 ff.

[2] As a *terminus post quem* the Battle of the Frigidus in 394 has found much favour. See A. Chastagnol in his recent survey of the problem, *Actes du VIIᵉ Congrès, Aix-en-Provence, 1-6 avril, 1963* (1964), 193 = *Bonner Historia-Augusta-Colloquium 1963* (1964), 49. That is the view of Alföldi, cf. *A Conflict of Ideas in the Late Roman Empire* (1952) 126 f. The *terminus ante quem* is another matter. Chastagnol opts for 398.

[3] *Addendum.* For an advance from this position, see now *Ammianus and the Historia Augusta* (1968), 79.

[4] Indeed, perhaps nothing impedes going down to about 405.

[5] The items and aspects have become fairly numerous. Momigliano's recent estimate is an understatement—'one or two passages may point to a post-Constantinian date either for the whole collection or at least for the passages themselves' (*The Conflict between Paganism and Christianity in the Fourth Century* (1963), 96).

II · *IPSE ILLE PATRIARCHA*

SOME WRITERS get bolder as they go on, and therefore better, discovering talent and a true vocation. The author of the Historia Augusta belongs to that happy company. Having already put on abundant show his virtuosity in the art of historical fiction, he introduces the *Vita Aureliani* with a scene that conveys an avowal.

It is his most elegant piece of fooling so far. In amicable discourse the Prefect of the City incites 'Flavius Vopiscus' (for that is the name the impostor now assumes) to undertake a noble and patriotic task. He shall compose biographies of emperors. No inhibitions. The four historians of classic rank and fame (Livy, Tacitus, Sallust, Trogus) each and all stand convicted of mendacity: 'securus, quod velis, dices, habiturus mendaciorum comites quos historicae eloquentiae miramur auctores' (*Aur.* 2. 2).

What emerges bears out the hint and forecast. As witness all the paraphernalia in the imperial council at Byzantium, when that great soldier, 'Ulpius Crinitus' (a descendant of Trajan), takes Aurelian as his son by adoption (13 f.). Or again, the consular orator 'Maecius Faltonius Nicomachus', deprecating hereditary succession and solemnly denouncing boy princes—'dii avertant principes pueros' (*Tac.* 6. 5).

Disquisition on historians and biographers recurs deliciously in the preface of the *Probus* (1 f.). It is reinforced in the *Quadrigae tyrannorum*, that team of four usurpers whom the author yoked together by fraud and artifice. This time he goes on to stage a debate with five friends who, like himself, are 'amatores historiarum'. They gravely discuss criteria of historical authentication, not without appeal to coins (*Quadr. tyr.* 2). The *Quadrigae* exhibits the ingenious operator at the high peak of his performance. Apart from the bare names of the four usurpers (Firmus, Saturninus, Proculus, Bonosus) hardly a fact can be found to mar the harmony of the narration.[1] Fiction almost total. That is a benefit. To study the fabrications is the best way to understand the HA. The *Quadrigae* occupies a position of predilection and delight.

[1] Firmus falls in the time of Aurelian (*Aur.* 32. 2), the other three under Probus (*Prob.* 18. 4 ff.). That is no impediment to the cynical author. In his exordium he puts all four under Aurelian (*Quadr. tyr.* 1. 4). But later he has Saturninus, Proculus, and Bonosus each destroyed by Probus (11. 1; 13. 4; 15. 2).

Firmus leads off, insurgent in Egypt, with a suitable allusion to the fanaticism of the natives—'Aegyptiorum incitatus furore' (3. 1). Firmus was a merchant prince of great opulence, who said that he could maintain an army from his supplies of paper and glue. He constructed a palace of glass cubes, he traded with the Blemmyes and the Saraceni, he sent argosies to India.

Various engaging particulars are vouchsafed about Firmus, his habits and physique—huge of build, with protuberant eyes, curly hair, scarred forehead, and a swarthy complexion. So strong was he that, lying on his back, he could hold up an anvil. Voracious, he would eat an ostrich a day; and, though temperate in drink, he had a strong head, being able to vanquish in competition the 'notissimus potator' called 'Burburus' (4. 4).

Further items are added on the authority of 'Aurelius Festivus', a freedman of Aurelian. Firmus used to swim among crocodiles, anointed with their fat; he rode the elephant and the hippopotamus; he was conveyed, or rather flown, by huge ostriches (6. 2).

Next in the *Quadrigae* comes Saturninus. The HA brings him to Egypt, without warrant and wantonly. He is also alleged to be a Gaul by extraction, which is false.[1] Aurelian, so the HA proceeds, gave to Saturninus a great command, the 'limitis orientalis ducatus', with the injunction that he must never set foot in Egypt (7. 2). Aurelian was a 'vir prudentissimus'. He feared what would happen should Saturninus go there, 'si praeturbidam civitatem vidisset'. When brought together, the Gallic temperament and the Egyptian would wreak havoc (7. 3, cf. 9. 1). The Gauls are a 'gens hominum inquietissima et avida semper vel faciendi principis vel imperii' (7. 1).

A digression now intervenes. The author turns aside to delineate the Egyptian character in a string of vigorous epithets: 'ventosi, furibundi, iactantes, iniuriosi atque adeo vani, liberi, novarum rerum usque ad cantilenas publicas cupientes, versificatores, epigrammatarii, mathematici, haruspices, medici' (7. 4).

And there is a further aggravation of their iniquities. Namely, Christians, Samaritans, and other inveterate malcontents: 'nam in eis Christiani, Samaritae et quibus praesentia semper tempora cum enormi libertate displiceant' (7. 5).

Such is Egypt, in the author's estimation. He proffers an apologia, in mock humility and scholarly conscience. Lest any of the Egyptians

---

[1] For the facts about (Julius) Saturninus, attested by other authors and by coins, see A. Stein, P–W II A. 213 ff.

conceive anger, there is a document. Nothing less than a missive of Hadrian, from a good source—'ex libris Flegontis liberti eius' (7. 6).

The *Letter of Hadrian* (8. 1 ff.) exhibits marked virtues of style and spirit. And, not so common, it has structure and coherence. Too good therefore for 'Vopiscus', that was at one time the opinion of Hohl, a scholar second to none in his understanding of the HA.[1] On the contrary. This piece of humour and malice exemplifies the mature talent of the impostor, comparable in its way to the prefaces of *Aurelianus* and *Probus*.

'Vopiscus' achieved a palmary exploit. It has earned the supreme compliment in the recent age. One scholar argues the *Letter* authentic: erudite analysis declares the very manner and idiosyncrasies of Hadrian.[2] Another, after eloquent and ingenious ratiocination, affirms that the *Letter* is genuine in substance.[3] It only needs to be cleared of accretions, such as the references to Christianity. Hence testimony of unique value subsisting about Hadrian and Hadrian's son. The Alexandrians, according to the *Letter*, 'in filium meum Verum multa dixerunt' (8. 8). That statement (the Emperor's own words) is used to support the notion that the man whom Hadrian took in adoption was in truth Hadrian's own son, but illegitimate, the fruit of adultery.

That need not detain. Only the HA assigns to the Ceionius Commodus whom Hadrian adopted the additional *cognomen* of 'Verus'. It is plainly false.[4] The item serves to damn the 'document'.

Anachronism is patent. Hadrian in his peregrinations went to Egypt in 130. From Egypt he indites the epistle to Servianus, his brother-in-law—'Hadrianus Augustus Serviano consuli salutem' (8. 1). Servianus, however, was consul in 134 (for the third time); and it was not until the end of 136 that Hadrian adopted Ceionius Commodus.

Nor need words be wasted on the *libri Flegontis*. The only other evidence for a work of Phlegon on Hadrian happens to occur in the HA itself, in a suspicious context of the *Vita Hadriani*.[5]

Not that it is idle to ask about the source and inspiration of 'Vopiscus'. Ammianus Marcellinus has a long digression on Egypt (XXII. 15. 1–16). That might have influenced the HA. The notion was worth canvassing.[6]

[1] E. Hohl, *Hermes* LV (1920), 305.

[2] H. Bardon, *Les Empereurs et les lettres latines* (1940), 400.

[3] J. Carcopino, *Rev. ét. anc.* LI (1949), 304 f. The whole article (262 ff.) is reproduced without acknowledgement in *Passion et politique chez les Césars* (1958), 143 ff.

[4] For the facts, *PIR*², C 605.

[5] The Emperor instructed his 'liberti litterati' to publish his Autobiography under their names: 'nam et Phlegontis libri Hadriani esse dicuntur' (*Hadr.* 16. 1). The author of the HA was familiar with the notion of literary impersonation—who more so?

[6] J. Schwartz, *Bulletin de la Faculté des Lettres de Strasbourg*, 1961, 169 ff.

Furthermore, the trace of Juvenal has recently been detected, precisely in the *Letter of Hadrian*.[1] The satirist, sunk for long ages, was a new discovery, on sudden notoriety in the age of Theodosius.[2]

Not Hadrian therefore, but 'Vopiscus'. The *Letter of Hadrian* is variously noteworthy.[3] What it reports about religion in Egypt engages attention of scholars ever and again. Hadrian in the exordium is at pains to confute the all too favourable estimate that Servianus had formed. The natives, Hadrian says, are frivolous, totally devoid of any sincere beliefs: 'Aegyptum ... totam didici levem, pendulam et ad omnia famae momenta volitantem. illic qui Serapem colunt, Christiani sunt, et devoti sunt Serapi qui se Christi episcopos dicunt. nemo illic archisynagogus Iudaeorum, nemo Samarites, nemo Christianorum presbyter non mathematicus, non haruspex, non aliptes. ipse ille patriarcha, cum Aegyptum venerit, ab aliis Serapidem adorare, ab aliis cogitur Christum' (8. 1–4).

It would be a temptation to go into all the detail—or linger on the alleged equivalence of Serapis and Christ among the Egyptians. Such have been the preoccupations of many scholars. The last sentence in the passage tends to be neglected or evaded. It contains a puzzle and a clue.

Who is 'ipse ille patriarcha'? The bishop of Alexandria, so the earliest commentators took it. But they were bothered, and rightly, by the phrase 'cum Aegyptum venerit', which implies that the person was normally absent, and not resident in Egypt. How was that to be got over? Casaubon supposed that Hadrian in his ignorance had made a mistake. Salmasius went one better: before Hadrian turned up in Egypt the bishop had prudently left the country.

The bishop of Alexandria: some scholars in the recent age have made the same assumption. Thus Geffcken, in a valuable study of religion in the HA—but briefly, without elucidation, and taking the thing for plain and obvious.[4] Hohl also was of that opinion, and he put up an argument: since Alexandria is not the same as Egypt, the reference is to journeys of

---

[1] A. D. E. Cameron, *Hermes* xcII (1964), 365. He adduces Juvenal III. 76 f. to explain *Quadr. tyr.* 8. 3 'non mathematicus, non haruspex, non aliptes'. Add J. Schwartz, on the usurper 'Celsus', *Ant. Class.* xxxIII (1964), 419 ff. The proconsul of Africa, 'Vibius Passienus' (*Tyr. trig.* 29. 1) is damning and revealing: the scholiast on Juvenal IV. 81 confuses Passienus Crispus and Vibius Crispus. Compare, independently, R. Syme, discussing the bogus names in the HA (*Bonner Historia-Augusta-Colloquium 1964/5* (1966), 263 = above, p. 7).

[2] G. Highet, *Juvenal the Satirist* (1954), 184 ff.

[3] See the proper and thorough analysis of Wolfgang Schmid, *Bonner Historia-Augusta-Colloquium, 1964/5* (1966), 153 ff.

[4] J. Geffcken, *Hermes* LV (1920), 288. For Geffcken, that resulted from 'eine ruhige Lektüre'.

the bishop outside the metropolis.[1] Baynes imported a refinement. The allusion is to Athanasius, and not in a friendly way: 'the one Alexandrian patriarch of whom the West of Europe had any intimate knowledge'.[2] That suited his dating of the HA—which, after receiving rapid and notable support, has lapsed in the sequel. Not many students of the HA care to venture an opinion. Silence is safer. Momigliano, however, has frankly avowed that he cannot understand the passage.[3]

It is expedient to look at it—'ipse ille patriarcha, cum Aegyptum venerit, ab aliis Serapidem adorare, ab aliis cogitur Christum' (8. 4). Now compulsion is brought upon the patriarch. One lot forces him to worship Serapis, the other Christ. Therefore, it is patent, he cannot belong to either faith; and the HA has already referred to the votaries of Serapis and of Christ (alleging them interchangeable). The third category of religions in Egypt remains, Judaism. The identity of 'ipse ille patriarcha' therefore emerges unsolicited.[4]

The Jewish patriarch: that was taken for granted some time ago in the standard work dealing with the position of the Jews in the Roman Empire. No argument was thought necessary.[5] However, three more recent writers on that subject have ignored or discarded the HA passage.[6] That was unfortunate, on various counts.

The Jewish patriarch, a high dignitary, deserves brief inspection. The facts are not remote or in any dispute; they come from Jewish, Christian, and pagan sources; and they have been put on adequate register.[7]

The patriarch had charge and authority over all Jews everywhere. Not only Palestine, but the Diaspora. He was at the same time the head of a religious community and a vassal prince without territorial dominion.

[1] S-B der deutschen Ak. der Wissenschaften zu Berlin, 1953, 2. 53.

[2] N. H. Baynes, The Historia Augusta. Its Date and Purpose (1926), 66. Followed (with an aberrant dating) by H. Stern, Date et destinataire de l'Histoire Auguste (1953), 67 f.

[3] A. Momigliano, Journal of the Warburg and Courtauld Institutes XVII (1954), 41 = Secondo Contributo alla storia degli studi classici (1960), 131.

[4] That is the plain meaning of the Latin. Observe, for example, J. B. Lightfoot, The Apostolic Fathers II, S. Ignatius and S. Polycarp (1889), I. 481: 'the words . . . show plainly that the person so designated did not live in Egypt and did not profess to be a Christian.' It was unfortunate that Lightfoot took the letter for genuine.

[5] J. Juster, Les Juifs dans l'Empire romain I (1914), 394. However, a little lower down Juster, in addition to his notes, conceived a doubt: 'il y a peut-être lieu d'y voir une allusion au patriarche chrétien d'Alexandrie et à ses déplacements dans le pays' (404 f.).

[6] H. Zucker, Studien zur jüdischen Selbstverwaltung im Altertum (1936); M. Simon, Verus Israel (1948); M. Avi-Yonah, Geschichte der Juden im Zeitalter des Talmud (1962).

[7] See the works cited in the preceding footnote. For most purposes the thorough and methodical exposition of Juster is good enough. Add the mosaic recently discovered at Tiberias. Among the inscriptions on it occurs a $\theta\rho\epsilon\pi\tau\delta\varsigma$ $\tau\hat{\omega}\nu$ $\lambda\alpha\mu\pi\rho\sigma\tau\dot{\alpha}\tau\omega\nu$ $\pi\alpha\tau\rho\iota\alpha\rho\chi\hat{\omega}\nu$ (B. Lifschitz, Zeitschr. des deutschen Palästina-Vereins LXXVIII (1962), 181 f.).

Hence the patriarch might suitably bear the traditional title of 'ethnarch', as on his earliest non-Jewish attestation, in one of the writings of Origen.[1]

The post went back to the aftermath of Hadrian's war against the Jews. As in the earlier client kingdoms, succession was hereditary. That produced abuses (patriarchs youthful, incompetent, or immoral), which Christian writers were not slow to seize upon. Eusebius invoked a menacing prophecy in Isaiah, and Jerome improved upon it.[2] The Latin text runs 'et dabo pueros principes eorum, et effeminati dominabuntur eis.'

Jerome was writing in or about the year 409. The words, so it happens, fit the recent condition of the Empire under the sons of Theodosius—and the phrase would have been much to the liking of 'Vopiscus' and other enemies of boy princes.[3] Jerome, however, duly sees the prophecy manifested in the patriarchate, 'consideremus patriarchas Iudaeorum et iuvenes sive pueros, effeminatosque ac deliciis adfluentes, et impletam prophetiam esse cernemus.'[4]

Along with boys or voluptuaries, the dynasty of the patriarchs exhibited another deleterious feature, namely great wealth. Revenues accrued from the communities abroad. The patriarch sent out envoys each year, *apostoli*, to bring in the *aurum coronarium* (as the term is designated in the imperial enactments).[5] The Fathers of the Church waxed indignant. Thus Jerome—'principes Iudaeorum qui supra arguti sunt in avaritia'.[6]

Revenues and a dynasty, that was not all. The Roman government had accorded privilege, status, and titles. The patriarch had a *praefectura honoraria*, he bears the title of *vir illustris*. As such he is styled in the *Codex Theodosianus* in enactments of 392, 396, and 397.[7] When the title was first conferred, there is no clear sign. Perhaps by Julian, who for his own designs showed especial favour to the Jews.[8] Perhaps later, by Theodosius.

However that may be, the patriarch, still *vir illustris* in 397, suffered a quick and sharp demotion. A law of Honorius in 399 confiscated the *aurum coronarium*. It uses terms of no amenity, referring to 'depraedatio';

---

[1] Origen, *Ep. ad Africanum* 14: *PG* XI. 84.

[2] Eusebius, *In Is.* 3. 3 f.: *PG* XXIV. 109; Jerome, *PL* XXIV. 64.

[3] cf. HA, *Tac.* 6. 5, on 'pueri principes', quoted above. For that general theme, W. Hartke, *Römische Kinderkaiser* (1951), 57 ff. To have 'Maecius Faltonius Nicomachus' denouncing boy princes was a genial and diabolical invention. The nomenclature is a figment, and revealing. The aristocrat Nicomachus Flavianus was the paladin of the old faith, defeated along with Arbogast and Eugenius at the Battle of the Frigidus in September 394.

[4] Jerome, *In Is.* 3 f.: *PL* XXIV. 64.

[5] *C.Th.* XVI. 8. 14. For the full details, J. Juster, o.c. 388 ff.

[6] Jerome, *In Is.* 2. 18 ff.: *PL* XXIV. 86.   [7] *C.Th.* XVI. 8. 8; 11; 13.

[8] M. Avi-Yonah, o.c. 199.

and the patriarch himself is either mentioned curtly, without any title
of honour, or denounced as an exploiter—'ille depopulator Iudaeorum'.[1]

The patriarch next occurs in the *Codex* in 404. He now has a title, it is
true, but he is only *vir spectabilis*.[2] The government restores the honours
and privileges the patriarch had got from Theodosius and from earlier
emperors.[3]

They were revoked in 415. The patriarch, here given a personal
name for the first time (he was previously anonymous, or even lurking
under a plural), is sternly rebuked for various transgressions, among
them the building of synagogues—'quoniam Gamalielus existimavit se
posse impune derelinquere, quo magis est erectus fastigio dignitatum',
etc.[4] He therefore forfeits the 'codicilli honorariae praefecturae'. Several
years later, the dynasty lapsed, and the office. An enactment of 429 has
the phrase 'post excessum patriarcharum'.[5]

To sum up. Towards the end of the fourth century, the Jewish patriarch
enjoys the prestige of wealth and ancestry, also a title of high eminence
in the imperial administration. Hence a public personage, 'erectus fastigio
dignitatum'. Be he an infant or a nonentity, he is none the less the prince
of the Jews.

In any age mere birth or rank may acquire strength and notoriety—
by the man's own attainments, by favour of a ruler, or by sheer accident.
Three pieces of evidence converge, indicating a patriarch of no small
consequence in the days of Theodosius.[6]

First, Libanius. Eight of his letters, between 388 and 393, are addressed to a patriarch.[7] One of them (in 393) shows his son among the
pupils of the Antiochene sophist.[8]

Second, the medical author Marcellus, writing in the vicinity of the
year 400. He registers a remedy recently demonstrated efficacious by
the patriarch Gamaliel—'ad splenem remedium singulare quod de ex-
perimentis probatis Gamalielus patriarcha proxime ostendit'.[9]

Third, an episode in Jerome. It occurs in the letter to Pammachius
(the Roman senator who became a monk), written in 395 or 396: 'dudum
Hesychium, virum consularem, contra quem patriarcha Gamalihel
gravissimas exercuit inimicitias, Theodosius princeps capite damnavit
quod sollicitato notario chartas illius invasisset.'[10]

[1] *C.Th.* XVI. 8. 14.   [2] *C.Th.* XVI. 8. 15.   [3] *C.Th.* XVI. 8. 15 (cf. 17).
[4] *C.Th.* XVI. 8. 22.   [5] *C.Th.* XVI. 8. 29.
[6] O. Seeck, *Die Briefe des Libanius* (1906), 162; P–W VII. 690. Seeck assumed him identical
with the Gamaliel who was degraded in 415 (*C.Th.* XVI. 8. 22). That is not certain—and
perhaps wrong.   [7] viz., *Epp.* 914 (Förster), 917, 973, 974, 1084, 1097, 1098, 1105.
[8] *Epp.* 1098.   [9] Marcellus, *De med.* XXIII. 77.   [10] Jerome, *Epp.* LVII. 3.

That is to say, Theodosius executed Hesychius for suborning the patriarch's secretary. Gamaliel triumphant over his enemy and the destruction of a Roman provincial governor, the incident must have had a wide resonance.[1] Jerome happens not to be lavish in allusions to contemporary events in the world.

When did Gamaliel's victory occur? 'Not so long ago' says Jerome ('dudum'). That cannot be pressed.[2] But the neighbourhood of 390 is not excluded, a season critical for the relations between Jews and the Roman government. With Christians for emperors, the Jews were in for trouble, but not all at once or in any regular rhythm. Those emperors had a dual role or personality. As the successor of pagans in exercise of the supreme power, the ruler had a plain duty to maintain rights and privileges that had been guaranteed by law and tradition. On the other side, he might prove unable to restrain the zeal of bishops or curb his own convictions; and in the end he might go the easy way against justice and the dictates of humanity.

In 388 occurred an action of wide and fateful repercussions. The bishop of Callinicum on the Euphrates mustered his flock and set fire to a synagogue.[3] Theodosius ordered him to rebuild the edifice, but the potent influence of Ambrose intervened on the side of the bishop. Two years later, as the result of an incident of a different nature (the massacre at Thessalonica), the Emperor fell completely under the dominance of Ambrose, being reduced to do public penance (December 390). Not but that Theodosius still made an effort. In 392, though measures were enacted against conversions and mixed marriages, he expressly safeguarded the jurisdiction of the patriarch.[4] Further, in 393, protecting synagogues from robbery or destruction, Theodosius affirmed the legality of Judaism— 'Iudaeorum sectam nulla lege prohibitam satis constat.'[5]

The episode of Gamaliel and Hesychius may therefore belong about 390. However, it is enough to demonstrate a patriarch brought into high prominence in the days of Theodosius. He can be identified without discomfort as the correspondent of Libanius, hence extant as late as 393. How long he survived is uncertain—the chronology of these patriarchs

---

[1] Some neglect it. Thus M. Simon, *Verus Israel* (1948).

[2] The preceding sentence in Jerome registers an incident in Livy (the story of the treacherous Faliscan schoolmaster). One may observe, for what it is worth, the phrase 'dudum iusseramus' in the enactment of Honorius in 404, referring to what had been decreed five years earlier (*C.Th.* xvi. 8. 17, cf. 8. 14). For the employment of 'dudum' in Symmachus, compare W. Hartke, o.c. 287 ff.

[3] Ambrose, *Epp.* 40. 6 ff.: *PL* xvi. 1103 ff.

[4] *C.Th.* xvi. 8. 8.   [5] *C.Th.* xvi. 8. 9.

is in dispute.[1] Gamaliel's successor may have been young, so some suppose, going by Jerome's comment on the text 'pueri principes'.[2] However, the last of the line was the Gamaliel named and degraded in 415.

It remains to draw the consequence for the HA. If the author was writing towards the end of the fourth century, he had in mind not merely the Jewish potentate but a known personage of public renown. 'Ipse ille patriarcha', that is, *the great Gamaliel in person*, is put under constraint, when he comes to Egypt, to pay homage now to Serapis, now to Christ.[3] That is a joke against Gamaliel. Insistent on deriding Egypt, the author spares none of the cults. He even brings in the Samaritans.[4]

The HA betrays a certain knowledge of Jewish matters. The preface of the *Vita Claudii* carries a curious item. As the 'doctissimi mathematicorum' averred, 120 years was the span of mortal life, and nobody exceeded it. They added a story about Moses who raised complaint because he had to die when only 125 years old: 'Mosen solum, dei, ut Iudaeorum libri locuntur, familiarem, centum viginti quinque annos vixisse; qui cum quereretur quod iuvenis interiret, responsum ei ab incerto ferunt numine neminem plus esse victurum' (2. 4). It is anomalous that Moses, after being described as 'dei familiaris', should receive his admonition from an 'incertum numen'. However, let that pass. This story is not in the Old Testament, where Moses in fact dies at 120. But a parallel exists. A Talmudic legend can be adduced.[5] Moses at the age of 120 refused to pass on, obdurate against a whole sequence of celestial envoys, until the Almighty intervened and promised to make due provision for his obsequies.

The extreme term of 120 years for human existence was a standard notion, probably going back to Varro.[6] It turns up a little later in the HA. The *haruspices* foretold a great emperor in the line of Tacitus—'victurus annis centum viginti et sine herede moriturus' (*Tac.* 15. 2). That is one

[1] And not here relevant. Seeck assumed that the Gamaliel involved with Hesychius (Jerome, *Epp.* LVII. 3) was identical with the Gamaliel degraded in 415 (*C. Th.* XVI. 8. 22). Avi-Yonah registers a Gamaliel VI, patriarch from 400 to 425, yet holds him the same as Jerome's Gamaliel in the days of Theodosius (o.c. 230). That will not do.

[2] Thus J. Juster, o.c. 395.

[3] Whether in fact the patriarch was in the habit of coming from Tiberias to Egypt for pastoral visitations is another matter. Implausible—and irrelevant. The Roman government would not have liked the intrusion of a *vir illustris* in Egypt.

[4] The mention of the Samaritans in HA (also in *Elag.* 3. 5) is significant, cf. the pertinent observations of Dessau, *Janus* I (1921), 124 ff. In the *Codex Theodosianus* the Samaritans appear for the first time as a distinct community in an enactment of 390 (XIII. 5. 18).

[5] Noted by Geffcken, *Hermes* LV (1920), 294.

[6] Lactantius, *Inst. div.* II. 12. 23; Servius on *Aen.* IV. 653. Lactantius refers to 'idonei auctores', and he has criticism of Varro in the near context.

of the impostor's most amusing fabrications, and variously instructive. In the matter of Moses, why did he choose 125, not 120? This too may be play: he likes to create wilful variants, parading science or scholarly dubitation.[1]

Elsewhere, nothing of any great significance crops up about Jews. Few in this late season are likely to accord credence to Severus Alexander and his domestic chapel: images of four *animae sanctiores*, Abraham standing in the company of Christ, Apollonius, and Orpheus (*Alex*. 29. 2).

Again, it is only malice and the author's congenial manner when he alleges that the people of Antioch called Alexander an 'archisynagogus' (28. 7). Humour at the expense of a Syrian emperor (albeit one embellished and transfigured by the author) is quite in keeping. And, a deliberate refinement, Alexander blends an appeal to the god of Gaza with a tag from the Catilinarian orations of Cicero: 'o Marna, o Iuppiter, o di immortales! Arabianus non solum vivit, verum etiam in senatum venit' (17. 4).[2]

Further, the author invents the converse of a food taboo for the benefit of the Jews. According to Elagabalus, Jews were under positive injunction to eat ostriches (*Elag*. 28. 4). The author himself is not devoid of interest in that bird: observe the daily diet of the usurper Firmus (*Quadr. tyr*. 4. 2).

Finally, another piece of humour, occurring suitably in the *Quadrigae tyrannorum*. Who can resist 'Vituriga', married to the usurper Proculus, the 'uxor virago' who impelled him? This powerful lady acquired the name of the Jewish Hercules. Not that the author uses that phrase, only the equivalent—'nomine Samso, quod ei postea inditum est' (12. 3).[3] The impostor goes on gaily to put on show another woman with a masculine name: 'Hunila', a Gothic princess allocated for wife to Bonosus by the Emperor Aurelian (15. 7).

The concern of the HA with Jews was not, it appears, either sustained or notably malevolent. Fun and oddities rather than any preoccupation

---

[1] Observe the birthplace of Geta, Mediolanum (*Geta* 3. 1), against Rome (*Sev*. 4. 2); or the fraudulent dubitations about the age of Gordian III, with appeal to 'Junius Cordus' (*Gord*. 22. 2); or the origin of Carus, with many fictions (*Car*. 4. 1 ff.).

[2] For the god Marnas, cf. J. Straub, *Bonner Historia-Augusta-Colloquium 1963* (1964), 165 ff. He was under menace in the nineties, his shrine was finally demolished in 401.

[3] Cf. Domaszewski, *Heidelberger S-B* 1918, Abh. 13, 20: 'Samso ist der biblische Samson.' There is something more in the passage, and a valuable clue. No reader of Ammianus in any age could forget the vivid picture of the Gallic female, more savage than the male in conflict—'tum maxime cum illa inflata cervice suffrendens, ponderansque niveas ulnas et vastas, admixtis calcibus emittere coeperit pugnos' (xv. 12. 1). A reminiscence of this passage produces in the HA the 'uxor virago' of Proculus, called 'Vituriga' (a name patently Celtic). The allusion seems so far to have escaped notice.

with cult and race and nationality. As the author avows, 'sum enim unus ex curiosis' (*Prob.* 2. 8). What then shall be said of his religious persuasions, in so far as conveyed (or disclosed) by the *Letter of Hadrian*? Perhaps not much.

The HA had mentioned Serapis when the Emperor Septimius Severus paid a visit to Egypt. The notice is sympathetic. Severus (the author says) showed afterwards that his 'peregrinatio' had been sheer pleasure. For several reasons: 'propter religionem dei Serapidis', also for the antiquities and the sight of novel animals and monuments (*Sev.* 17. 4).

After that, nothing about the god for a long space, until the *Letter of Hadrian*: the worshippers of Serapis are 'Christiani', whereas those who call themselves 'episcopi Christi' are pledged to Serapis (8. 2).

The scandalous allegation that the two cults are equivalent and interchangeable is not just an isolated piece of slander. Something similar comes out in a story that acquired currency not long after the destruction of the Serapeum (in the summer of 391). It is first attested in the *Historia Ecclesiastica* of Rufinus, composed about 405.

As follows. A portentous discovery was made in the vaults of the Serapeum: a hieroglyph, in the shape of a cross. Being interpreted, it meant 'vita ventura'. For which reason, many pagans were induced to pass over.[1] Slightly different versions occur later in Sozomenus and in Socrates.[2] According to Socrates, the pagans argued that the hieroglyph was something which the religions of Christ and Serapis possessed in common.

The item is entertaining. It may with propriety be adduced to illustrate the passage in the HA.[3] But it cannot quite be adopted as the source and origin of that fancy picture.

The author is a pagan, to be sure. How devout, that is a question. The *Letter of Hadrian* must be contemplated as a whole, and taken in its full context. That is to say, the fictions about Saturninus and about Firmus. On a cool inspection, what then emerges?

First, the author is possessed by a general hostility towards Egyptians. After the remarks about the patriarch he reverts at once to that topic of predilection, with violent superlatives,—'genus hominum seditiosissimum, vanissimum, iniuriosissimum' (8. 5).

Second, he denies sincerity to the religions professed in Egypt. Serapis or Christ, it is all one—yet, by paradox, the Jews benefit from an apparent indulgence, for compulsion has to be brought upon their patriarch.

Third, and in consonance. Egypt knows only one true divinity. It is

---

[1] Rufinus, *Hist. Eccl.* XI. 29. [2] Sozomenus VII. 15. 10; Socrates V. 17.
[3] J. Schwartz, *Bulletin de la Faculté des Lettres de Strasbourg* (1961), 172 f.

money: 'unus illis deus nummus est. hunc Christiani, hunc Iudaei, hunc omnes venerantur et gentes' (8. 7).

If these points be held valid, a consequence follows, of no small significance. Egypt (as has been shown) is wantonly dragged into the narrative about the usurper Saturninus. He was never there. What might be the purpose of that elaborate operation? Perhaps, so some opine, to enable the author to insert a damaging attack on Christianity. That notion depends upon an assumption: he was hostile from persuasion and of set purpose, any device availing. On the contrary, his interest seems casual and sporadic, no trace of design or system. The character of the references to Christianity, and their distribution, calls for careful scrutiny.[1]

Egypt is another matter. That ancient land had a general and pervasive appeal, because of the exotic and the fabulous, as witness all the fictions about Firmus. Add to that the author's dislike of Egyptians, especially for their 'furor'.[2] Yet a further question arises, pertinent to the character of the author. How far is that aversion personal, how far literary and traditional? If the latter stands in preponderance, his attitudes may owe something to influences from Juvenal and from Ammianus.[3]

The personality and tastes of the author come in. Not a devoted advocate, taking up the pen to support (however covertly) some cause of religion or politics. Rather a kind of scholiast who debases the techniques of erudition and turns imperial biography into a travesty. Also a mystifier, delighting in deceit, and a humorist not wholly negligible.[4]

To conclude. It was the purpose of this paper to demonstrate that 'ipse ille patriarcha' is the prince of the Jews. In fact, the Gamaliel who flourished in the days of Theodosius was a personage, involved in an incident of notoriety. Serapis was also on the lips of men—the battles in Alexandria and the destruction of his shrine in 391.

If the HA was composed in the sequel of those momentous transactions, the author's observations acquire point and relevance. And something more: satire and malice. Serapis or Christ, what did it matter? There is no religion in Egypt, only frivolity or rabid violence.

---

[1] A. Momigliano, *Secondo Contributo* (1960), 129 f.

[2] Not only Firmus 'Aegyptiorum incitatus furore' (*Quadr. tyr.* 3. 1). The Egyptians are 'furibundi' (7. 4). Further (and previously) the usurpation of Aemilianus is introduced with 'furiosi ac dementes' (*Tyr. trig.* 22. 1). Instances of their quarrelsomeness are adduced— and a trivial incident excites their 'familiaris furor' (22. 3), out of which arises the proclamation of Aemilianus.

[3] Above, p. 19. For an anthology of hostile opinions about Egyptians, see O. Seeck, *Geschichte des Untergangs der antiken Welt* iv[2] (1923), 503 f.

[4] E. Hohl, *Bursians Jahresberichte* cc (1924), 208; J. Straub, *Studien zur Historia Augusta* (1952), 15.

The date of the HA cannot be evaded—or discussed in this place. Suffice it to say that two paths offer—the impact of contemporaneous events and the potent influence of another writer, namely Ammianus.[1] It would be good fortune should they converge. If they do, the vicinity of the year 395 will become more than merely plausible.[2]

[1] The influence of Ammianus has been detected by Schwartz, and also by Straub, *Heidnische Geschichtsapologetik in der christlichen Spätantike* (1963), 53 ff. A number of other items can be adduced. I have recently brought to completion (May 1966) a study entitled 'Ammianus and the Historia Augusta'. (*Addendum*: published in June 1968.)

[2] This paper was presented at the Bonn Colloquium on June 3, 1966. It was composed before I had knowledge of the article of Professor Wolfgang Schmid on the *Letter of Hadrian* (since published in the *Bonner Historia-Augusta-Colloquium 1964/5* (1966), 153 ff.). Through his courtesy, I saw the proofs; and I am happy to acknowledge our agreement about 'ipse ille patriarcha'.

III · *IGNOTUS*, THE GOOD BIOGRAPHER

1. *Introduction*

DATE AND PURPOSE of the Historia Augusta, that has been the chief pre-occupation in the recent age, with exacting scrutiny brought to bear upon items of anachronism or clues to the time of writing. Much erudition therefore and acumen, but the results have not enforced conviction everywhere; and caution or scepticism comes into play on the other side, scoring easy successes in a small field.

Something was lost in the process. First, the HA as a whole. This is a literary product. It was expedient to go into composition and structure, style and language (in their various and revealing types).

Second, the idiosyncrasy of the author. Where he compiles or abbreviates a source, not much can be gleaned. The paramount advantage comes from his fabrications—as, on a higher level, from speeches or digressions in the historians of antiquity. If those fabrications are segregated (it is not a hard task), and arranged by their type and by the stages of their emergence, the tastes and habits of the author will not be beyond an estimation. Fiction is a better guide than fact.

Third, the subject of the present inquiry. As he goes on, the author wins liberation and develops his talent. He produces long stretches of sheer invention. By contrast, the *Vitae* of the earlier emperors down to Caracalla. What the author presents is compilation, and hasty at that, various strands or additions being evident.

It was an old fashion to dissect those imperial biographies, and easy enough in the operation, which disclosed a framework of facts unimpeachable beneath the accretions. Hence a basis for hypotheses about the character of the main source, some still valid, others lapsing in the sequel after they had produced an annalistic historian writing in Latin not long after the year 217.

That fashion has long been in abeyance. For various reasons. One of them is patent—a general discredit or fatigue ensuing on the excessive addiction to 'Quellenforschung'. The results often failed to recompense the effort. And some of the adepts were guilty of ignorance or delinquency. They omitted to reckon, for example, with the industry of a conscientious historian or the resources of information about recent transactions available to a senator and consul (i.e., Cornelius Tacitus).

It is high time to revert to the older habit and give some thought to the ultimate source of the early *Vitae* in the HA. Facts can be established; and a modest measure of conjecture is enjoined. The inquiry has a limit, but it transcends the composition of those *Vitae*. It bears ultimately upon a large subject—the design and procedures of the impostor who passed himself off as six biographers writing in the age of Diocletian and Constantine.

II. *The early* Vitae

In the first place, some definitions are needed. The biographies can be classified according to accuracy, composition and structure, type of source. Also, though that habit is passing, by the names of the ostensible authors and by the imperial dedications or invocations. The prime criterion is accuracy and value. Hence the standard modern notion of 'main *Vitae*' and 'subsidiary *Vitae*' (or 'Nebenviten'). It goes back to Mommsen, but draws justification from various phenomena or express statements in the collection itself.

In the sequence from Hadrian to Macrinus and his son Diadumenianus (sixteen biographies) which because of the dedications he styled the 'Diocletianic series', Mommsen ordained nine main *Vitae*, seven subsidiary.[1] The latter comprised Caesars, short-lived rulers, and usurpers, viz. Aelius Caesar, Verus, Avidius Cassius, Pescennius Niger, Clodius Albinus, Geta, Diadumenianus. Poor stuff, taking their material for the most part from the main *Vitae*, or just inventing. As Mommsen said, 'nicht etwa eine getrübte Quelle, sondern eine Kloake'.[2]

That classification was variously defective and vulnerable. First, it is not safe to go by the labels and dedications—and special pleading intervened.[3] Second, between the *Caracalla* and the *Macrinus* a change is apparent, and a contrast: structure, source, quality (of which more below). As Mommsen himself conceded, the *Macrinus* bears a damaging resemblance to those 'Nebenviten' he so imperiously derided.[4] It is better to make the series end with Caracalla, as various arguments enjoin. Third, nothing compels the relegation of the *Vita Veri* to the category of 'bad lives'.

---

[1] Mommsen, *Ges. Schr.* VII (1909), 316 ff. = *Hermes* XXV (1890), 243 ff.

[2] o.c. 324.

[3] In Mommsen's 'Diocletianic series' the *Clodius Albinus* and the *Geta* have invocations of Constantine.   [4] o.c. 323.

Indeed, another criterion avails, quite simple and straightforward: rulers assigned and not assigned a separate biography in the basic source. A clue offers, to more things than one.

III. *The* Vita Veri

This biography opens with a brief statement. Not, as in most of the Lives of princes and pretenders, a programmatic preface carrying a justification for their inclusion. The author is merely explaining a point of arrangement, why he treats Verus after Marcus and not before. He says: 'scio plerosque ita vitam Marci ac Veri litteris atque historiae dedicasse ut priorem Verum intimandum legentibus darent, non imperandi secutos ordinem sed vivendi: ego vero, quod prior Marcus imperare coepit, dein Verus, qui superstite perit Marco, priorem Marcum dehinc Verum credidi celebrandum' (*Verus* 1. 1 f.).

How many biographers in fact narrated the life of Verus before that of Marcus is a question that need not detain. Let it be supposed that the plural *plerique* denotes a single writer, and the answer is *Ignotus*.[1]

Turn to the *Verus*. The matter of that biography confirms. Brief inspection will suffice. This *Vita* is accurate. It furnishes many names and particulars not deriving from the *Marcus*. For example, the birth date of the prince and his extraction: 'natus est Lucius Romae in praetura patris sui XVIII. Kal. Ianuariarum die, quo et Nero, qui rerum potitus est. origo eius paterna pleraque ex Etruria fuit, materna ex Faventia' (1. 8 f.).[2]

Further, names. Observe a general in the Parthian War, Martius Verus (7. 1); or Libo, the cousin of the Emperor Marcus, whom no other written source discloses (9. 2);[3] and on a lower level, the actors and dancers (8. 7 and 10; 9. 3).

Moreover, fabrications are absent. No speeches and documents, no bogus characters, no Virgilian quotations or Latin verses, or any of the other regular devices of the impostor as exhibited in the 'Nebenviten'. Much of the content, to be sure, is trivial. The contrary would surprise, given the known tastes and predilections of Lucius Verus. But Verus was an *Augustus*, he reigned for nearly eight years sharing the supreme power

---

[1] For the postulate of *Ignotus* as the basic source down to Caracalla, see, in brief statement, R. Syme, *Ammianus and the Historia Augusta* (1968), 92 f.

[2] Nothing impugns Faventia: his maternal grandfather C. Avidius Nigrinus (*suff.* 110) was killed there (*Hadr.* 7. 2). As for the paternal ascendance, Etruria is reasonable for the ultimate *origo* of the Ceionii, given their *nomen*. Perhaps from Bononia, not far from Faventia along the Aemilia, for it was an ancient foundation of the Etruscans. Cf. R. Syme, *Athenaeum* XXXV (1957), 315.

[3] i.e. the son (consulate not attested) of M. Annius Libo (*cos.* 128).

with Marcus. No excuse was needed for his inclusion in a sequence of imperial biographies. *Ignotus* (so it appears) offered none, the compiler added none.

The *Vita Veri* therefore regains its proper rank and estimation.[1] The consequences are valuable. In this one category (i.e. biographies furnished by the source), nine *Vitae* from Hadrian to Caracalla inclusive. In the other, one Caesar (Aelius, the adopted heir of Hadrian), and one prince of the dynasty, namely Geta, who happens to be an *Augustus*, although the author of the HA ignores (or rather denies) that fact;[2] and further, three pretenders, viz. Avidius Cassius, Pescennius Niger, Clodius Albinus. *Ignotus* passed over these five persons. To supply their biographies is one of the impostor's avowed claims to originality.

IV. *The Nine* Vitae

In the quest for *Ignotus*, brief comment is expedient. Though marred by error, abbreviation, and the intrusion of scandal or ineptitudes, the information is proved excellent. Thus the ancestry of Pius and of Marcus. Again, the official careers of Hadrian, of Pertinax, of Didius Julianus, and of Severus: for two of those rulers, epigraphic evidence enables dates and details to be sorted out.[3]

The basic text has been roughly handled. It underwent two operations, of a contrary nature. First, curtailment. In narrating the last journey of Hadrian, the compiler takes him rapidly from Syria to Egypt in 130 (*Hadr.* 14. 4), and leaves him there, to proceed (after a brief note on Antinous) to a disquisition on his literary pursuits and personal character (interrupted by a passage about his friends). Similarly, Severus is deposited in Egypt in 199 (*Sev.* 17. 4), and the compiler turns to a new source, which resumes his whole reign. Again, the actions of Caracalla from the suppression of Geta to his own murder in Mesopotamia, five years of the reign, are abridged in an intolerable fashion, so as to be barely intelligible (*Carac.* 5 f.). Second, expansion. The *Vitae* exhibit insertions and appendages of various types and extent. Of some the origin happens to be registered or can plausibly be surmised, viz. a number of the scandalous and trivial items.[4] Further, and of crucial significance, two passages from other authors have been interwoven in the middle of *Vitae*, in *Marcus* (15. 3–18. 1) and in *Severus* (17. 5–19. 4). From Eutropius and from Aurelius Victor, so Dessau declared.[5]

---

[1] For the full statement and proof, T. D. Barnes, *JRS* LVII (1967), 65 ff.
[2] *Geta* 1. 2: 'qui prius rebus humanis exemptus est quam cum fratre teneret imperium'.
[3] Below, p. 42.   [4] i.e. Marius Maximus.
[5] H. Dessau, *Hermes* XXIV (1889), 363 ff. There is no point in chronicling dissidents.

The second passage is instructive. Taking leave of Severus, in Egypt, the compiler goes on to use Victor, with the introductory phrase: 'et quoniam longum est minora persequi' (17. 5). His energies flag and fail; haste and impatience are elsewhere undisguised.

An important consequence follows. Whether or no the compiler of the nine *Vitae* is the same person as the author of the whole HA, those *Vitae* are subordinate to his main design and preoccupations. That general theme cannot be discussed in this place—nor can that other question, how many stages have to be assumed in the editing and compiling of the early *Vitae*.

Before that, it is expedient to define the character of *Ignotus* and indicate his quality. Given the signs of abbreviation, a source of reasonable bulk was requisite. Not, therefore, the 'Kaisergeschichte' which Enmann postulated in 1884—and which still must be accepted in any event as the common source of Victor, of Eutropius, of the *Epitome*.[1] Whether or no it was employed by the HA (and some now incline to doubt)[2] need not concern the present inquiry. Something else obtrudes, however. It will be necessary to clear the ground and dispose of other candidates who have enjoyed a certain favour.

v. *An alleged annalist*

The main source was excellent: sober, precise, and addicted to facts. It could be disengaged by dissection of the *Vitae*. The early years of this century witnessed notable efforts.[3] Also premature conclusions. An annalistic historian was discovered and put on show, with affirmations about the scope of his work and its quality; and the author was duly equipped with a personality and a local origin.

Domaszewski ordained the conclusion of his history at the year 197.[4] For Schulz, it ended with the death of Caracalla.[5] Kornemann, however, carried it into the early years of Severus Alexander, but not as far as the death of the great jurist Ulpian (which he put in 228).[6] And, to be sure,

---

[1] A. Enmann, *Philologus*, Supp. IV (1884), 337 ff.

[2] Thus T. Damsholt, *Class. et Med.* XXV (1964), 147.

[3] J. M. Heer, 'Der historische Wert der Vita Commodi in der Sammlung der S. H. A.', *Philologus*, Supp. IX (1904), 1 ff.; O. Th. Schulz, *Leben des Kaisers Hadrian* (1904); *Das Kaiserhaus der Antonine und der letzte Historiker Roms* (1907); E. Kornemann, *Kaiser Hadrian und der letzte große Historiker von Rom* (1905).

[4] A. v. Domaszewski, *Neue Heidelberger Jahrbücher* X (1900), 233. Followed by J. Hasebroek, *Untersuchungen zur Geschichte des Kaisers Septimius Severus* (1921), 107.

[5] Schulz, o.c. (1907), 4.   [6] Kornemann, o.c. 82 f.

some date other than the decease of a ruler may attract a historian. Thus, in the reign of Severus, the end of the civil wars with the defeat of Clodius Albinus. Or, for that matter, 202; or 204 (the year of the *Ludi Saeculares*), when prospects seemed fair for family and dynasty, and a catastrophe soon to ensue (the destruction of Plautianus). Again, after Elagabalus, a historian of the time might take pleasure in expatiating on the felicity of the new reign, with the Senate restored to pristine honour and wise counsellors in the entourage of the young prince. Not for long, however. The murder of Ulpian ensued soon after.[1]

More important, the quality of the work. For Schulz, without question better than Cassius Dio, better than anything that the written testimony supplied for any period of the Roman Empire.[2] Similarly Kornemann, who, ignoring Ammianus, styled his annalist 'the last great historian of Rome', superior in many ways to Tacitus—who, with appeal to Leo, is designated 'dieser große Rhetor und Dichter unter den Historikern'.[3]

Third, the person. Schulz assumed that he came of an old aristocratic family—but also from Egypt, perhaps Egyptian by parentage, and having got some of his schooling at Alexandria.[4] But further, in close relation to the 'inner circle' of the *condiscipuli* of Marcus, hence not likely to have been born later than 122 or 123. Therefore, since he described the reign of Caracalla, he died *c.* 220, in extreme old age.[5]

Kornemann was able to furnish much more in the way of useful particulars.[6] For example, the annalist exhibited a special interest in Egypt and in Africa. Not much concern for military transactions, however, and no sympathy for the soldier. Rather civil administration and *praefecti urbi*. Perhaps a senatorial jurist, to be sought in 'the circle of Ulpian'.[7] Kornemann's annalist was also an old man when he wrote, being over eighty at the beginning of the reign of Severus Alexander.[8] Necessarily, because of his identity—being none other than the Lollius Urbicus who is cited by the HA as authority for a letter sent by Macrinus' son to his mother (*Diad.* 9. 2). The historian is therefore a son of Lollius Urbicus (*suff. c.* 136) who won the victory in Britain early in the reign of Pius. Being African, the historian thought well of the African dynasty.[9]

---

[1] M. Aurelius Epagathus (*PIR²*, E 67), responsible for the murder of Ulpian, is now attested as Prefect of Egypt in 224, cf. *P. Oxy.* 2565.

[2] Schulz, o.c. 3; 213.

[3] Kornemann, o.c. 119.

[4] Schulz, o.c. 212, cf. 118 (where Pelusium is suggested as his place of birth).

[5] Schulz, o.c. 212 f.   [6] Kornemann, o.c. 82–128.

[7] ib. 118.   [8] ib. 125.

[9] ib. 121 ff.

By age and the privilege of experience, 'ces terribles vieillards' who have thus been conjured up (one of them all but a centenarian) were no doubt well qualified to write history, if they ever existed. They are figures of fantasy, worthy to rank with figments of the HA—and a warning of the dire perils attendant on the frequentation of its author. Hence a lesson for any who venture to make conjecture about *Ignoti* such as the main source of the earlier *Vitae*, or the arch-impostor himself.

Despite flagrant excess, the 'great annalist' enjoyed long favour and acclaim. In 1926 Baynes accepted him, with some due reservations;[1] and he was still flourishing in the middle thirties.[2]

Meanwhile, voices of protest had been heard. Good sense spoke there, and plain truth. Although large patches of certain *Vitae* (e.g. *Hadrianus* and *Marcus*) exhibit a pattern of narration in chronological order, it is not possible to draw the line in the HA between historical and biographical material.[3]

The death blow was delivered in 1934.[4] No Latin writer of annalistic history existed in the age of the Severi. Since Suetonius, biography held the field. Indeed, the Greek Cassius Dio is much under the influence of that pattern and tradition—observe his treatment of Hadrian.[5]

The ostensible dichotomy between good history and trivial biography, an easy expedient, has now perished. The 'great annalist' is relegated to the 'history of the problem'. *Ignotus* composed biographies. He is disclosed in body and lineaments on an inspection, however cursory, of one of the less conspicuous among the *Vitae*, and least involved in past controversies.

VI. *The* Vita Pii

Allowing for some displacements and additions, this biography exhibits a structure corresponding to the Suetonian model: ancestry, career, accession, actions and comportment of the ruler, decease, and deification.[6] Nobody has doubted the excellence of the information, which stands out clearly in a pair of recent studies, devoted the one to the personal names in the *Vita*, the other to the foreign policy of Antoninus Pius.[7]

---

[1] N. H. Baynes, *The Historia Augusta. Its Date and Purpose* (1926), 69.

[2] P. Lambrechts, *Ant. class.* III (1934), 177; W. Hüttl, *Antoninus Pius* I (1936), 18.

[3] E. Hohl, *Neue Jahrbücher* XXXIII (1914), 198; A. Rosenberg, *Einleitung und Quellenkunde zur römischen Geschichte* (1921), 241.

[4] G. Barbieri, *Annali della R. Scuola Normale Superiore di Pisa*[2] III (1934), 525 ff.

[5] F. Millar, *A Study of Cassius Dio* (1964), 61.

[6] H. Peter, *Die Scriptores Historiae Augustae* (1892), 106 ff.

[7] H.-G. Pflaum, *Bonner Historia-Augusta-Colloquium 1964/5* (1966), 143 ff.; K. F. Stroheker, ib. 241 ff.

The text carries errors, to be sure. Not many, and they can be put down to faulty transmission. 'Lamia Silanus', the husband of Pius' elder daughter (1. 7), is patently a Lamia Silvanus (cf. *PIR²*, A 206); one must correct 'curatorem' (9. 6) into 'Eupatorem' (*PIR²*, J 300); and the *gentilicia* of two Guard Prefects, Cornelius Repentinus and Furius Victorinus, have been inverted (8. 8). In the list of the jurisconsults the second name is 'Salvius Valens' (12. 1). Something has gone wrong. Though there existed a Salvius Valens, on solitary attestation as a provincial governor (*Dig.* XLVIII. 2. 7. 2), he is ruled out. One misses the great jurists P. Salvius Julianus (*cos.* 148) and L. Fulvius Aburnius Valens (*PIR²*, F 526). Mommsen therefore read 'Salvio ⟨Juliano, Fulvio⟩ Valente'.[1] That is clearly the solution. Finally, an error of another type. The text gives the age of the Emperor at decease as 'anno septuagesimo' (12. 4). He was seventy-four, as is proved by the date of birth which had duly been supplied (1. 8).

That does not amount to much in view of the mass of facts. At the outset the *Vita* retails the extraction and kinsfolk of Antoninus Pius. Precious details, among them Nemausus as the *patria* of the Aurelii Fulvi. Also Boionia Procilla, the wife of his maternal grandfather Arrius Antoninus (1. 4). Now the future emperor, i.e. T. Aurelius Fulvus (*cos.* 120), had taken over the *cognomen* 'Antoninus'.[2] No inscription happens also to assign him 'Boionius'. The HA, however, introduces him as 'Titus Aurelius Fulvus Boionius Antoninus' (1. 1). The 'Boionius', by no means impossible, is perhaps illicit. But, occurring in the ultimate source (one may conjecture), it was transmitted to the epitomators in late Antiquity.[3]

Moreover, without giving names, this source refers to two sons of Pius (1. 7), to cousins from whom he inherited (1. 9), to 'fratres' who died before he came to the power (5. 2). Only the sons stand otherwise attested.[4] Further, the *Vita Pii*, it is claimed, furnishes a sagacious selection of the personages most prominent in the reign.[5] Only one *praefectus urbi*, it is true. That is, Orfitus, who resigned, allegedly by his own choice (8. 6). And only one of the generals, Lollius Urbicus (5. 4). But it was Lollius

---

[1] Mommsen, *Ges. Schr.* II (1905), 13 f.

[2] *PIR²*, A 1513. Only one inscription appears to give him the *nomen* as well, viz., the consular date (120) in *CIL* VIII. 8239: 'Tito Aurelio F[ulvo Arrio] Antonino'.

[3] Eutropius, VII. 8. 1; *Epit.* 15. 1. Not in Victor, who, however, calls Marcus 'M. Boionius'. The channel of transmission is Enmann's KG.

[4] *ILS* 350 f. (in the Mausoleum of Hadrian).

[5] Pflaum, o.c. 149.

who won the signal distinction in this peaceful age: his victory in Britain gave Pius his sole imperatorial acclamation. On the other hand, this *Vita* registers four of the five attested *praefecti praetorio*, viz. Gavius Maximus, Tattius Maximus, Cornelius Repentinus, Furius Victorinus (8. 7 f.). And five jurists are named (12. 1, amended, cf. above).

There is something else, and very precious. Two senators came to grief, on charges of high treason: Atilius Titianus and Priscianus (7. 3 f.). The *Fasti Ostienses* confirm. The name of T. Atilius Rufus Titianus (*cos.* 127) has been erased (*FO* xxvi); and the rubric of the year 145 carries the notice 'de Cornelio Prisciano in sen. [iud. pal]am factum quod provinciam Hispaniam hostiliter inqu[ietaverit]' (*FO* xxvii).

Finally, the name of another senator that has been invoked to commend this *Vita*, but not on secure grounds. To illustrate the 'civilitas' of Antoninus Pius, the *Vita* inserts an anecdote. Visiting the mansion of Homullus, the Emperor admired the marble columns and asked where they came from. Homullus answered with a rebuke—'cum in domum alienam veneris, et mutus et surdus esto.' As for the Emperor, 'patienter tulit', like other *ioca* of Homullus (11. 8). This man can be identified as M. Valerius Homullus (*cos.* 152).[1] Valerius Homullus crops up in the *Marcus*, the subject of an anecdote most hostile to the dynasty. When the mother of Marcus was at prayer, Homullus whispered to Pius 'illa nunc rogat ut diem tuum claudas, et filius imperet' (*Marcus* 6. 9). Both items, it is clear, do not belong to the basic source. So far names and facts. And one will suitably add the catalogue of buildings at Rome and elsewhere (8. 2 f.), accurate and valuable, albeit incomplete.[2]

By contrast, the various inventions are missing which show the impostor's hand and habits, such as spurious documents and letters, Greek verses in translation, oracles in the form of Virgilian quotations, and so on. With a single exception. One of his devices makes a sporadic appearance, the bogus character. To the list of the five jurists (each rendered with two names) is appended 'et Diaboleno'. Genuine characters from earlier *Vitae* sometimes turn up in the sequel as figments in a new role;[3] and the author of the HA likes to distort the shape of names.[4] There was a great jurist, Javolenus Priscus (*suff.* 86): he may well have been registered in the lost *Vita Traiani*.

---

[1] Pflaum, however, argues for the consul's unattested father (o.c. 147 f.).

[2] W. Hüttl, *Antoninus Pius* I (1936), 338 ff.; Fr. Pöschl, *Wiener Studien* LXVI (1953), 178 ff.

[3] R. Syme, *Bonner Historia-Augusta-Colloquium 1964/5* (1966), 260 = above, p. 4. Thus 'Homullus' in the *Vita Alexandri*, giving admonition to Trajan (65. 5).

[4] R. Syme, o.c. 264 f.

Nor is trivial or scandalous gossip much in evidence. This *Vita* carries four anecdotes (4. 8; 10. 4; 10. 5; 11. 8). Like various ineptitudes or other palpable additions they may all be insertions from other sources.

Regarded as a whole, the *Vita Pii* is a sober prosaic piece of work. The original source has not been much tampered with. It now remains to examine what the compiler did to *Ignotus*.

First, the compiler was rough and careless, as is evident in other *Vitae*. He displaces and transposes a number of items from the source.[1] His abbreviation produces inconsequences. And he leaves out certain transactions which have been transmitted through the common source of Victor, Eutropius, and the *Epitome*.[2] Victor has the nine-hundreth anniversary of Rome (15. 3), which was celebrated in 147 or 148; and the *Epitome* registers embassies from India, Bactria, and Hyrcania (15. 4), also the bread riots at Rome when the mob threw stones at the Emperor (15. 9).

One might make further surmise. The text registers only one *praefectus urbi*, viz. Orfitus, on the occasion of his demotion (8. 6).[3] It fails to name his successor. An author who is deemed careful to set on record the most conspicuous public personages in the reign of Pius ought not to have neglected the Prefects of the City. That post generally implies an iteration in the *fasces*. In fact, the reign exhibits only two *bis consules*, viz. Bruttius Praesens (139), Erucius Clarus (146), and perhaps a third, Bellicius Torquatus (143).[4] Erucius, *praefectus urbi*, died during his second consulship, early in the year 146 (*FO* xxvii). There is a chance that the successor of Orfitus at the outset of the reign was not Erucius but Bruttius Praesens.[5] Otherwise the only *praefectus urbi* on attestation is Lollius Urbicus (*suff. c.* 136), not consul again; and the beginning of his tenure evades all conjecture.[6]

Second, after compilation and abbreviation, the manner of the writing. None of the rhetoric or flowery words that occur in the subsidiary *Vitae* (such as *Avidius Cassius*) or in later portions of the HA. But the compiler here and there uses the idiom and vocabulary of his own epoch. For example, 'rebellio' in the sense of 'insurgent' (5. 5). That is one of the peculiar words which Dessau singled out.[7] Designating Atilius Titianus

---

[1] H. Peter, o.c. 107; Ch. Lécrivain, *Études sur l'Histoire Auguste* (1904), 121.
[2] i.e. Enmann's KG.
[3] i.e. Ser. Scipio Salvidienus Orfitus (*cos.* 110).
[4] Groag in *PIR²*, B 104, cf. 99.   [5] R. Syme, *Historia* ix (1960), 375.
[6] For the evidence, *PIR¹*, L 240. A *praefectus urbi* probably died in 160, cf. *FO* xxxiiia.
[7] Dessau, *Hermes* xxiv (1889), 389 f.

and Priscianus each as 'affectatae tyrannidis reus' (7. 3 f.), the writer implies that they were armed usurpers. Again, 'iudex' for a magistrate or provincial governor (8. 6) is an anachronism. And there is a late odour in the phrase describing material help given by Pius to 'senatores urbis ad functiones suas' (8. 4). It suggests Rome of the fourth century.[1]

Third, the additions. Most of them are fairly clear. They betray their nature on various criteria. What is here presented is a brief statement, eschewing argument; and not everybody may be in agreement about each item.[2]

Pius 1. 8: 'cuius hodieque reliquiae manent' (the note on his palace at Lorium).

2. 1–10. Most of this is suspect, except for the magistracies (9). Comparison with Numa (2) would be appropriate at the end of the *Vita*— where it in fact occurs (13. 4).[3] The disquisition on the name 'Pius' is bad material, like *Hadr.* 24. 3–5.

3. 1–5. Some of the portents might be accretions.

3. 7. Discord with his wife.

4. 2–3. Reasons for the adoption (cf. *Hadr.* 24. 3). He is here called 'Arrius Antoninus', as in *Hadr.* 24. 1. Not in any other written source.

4. 5: 'qui postea Verus Antoninus dictus est'. Erroneous.

4. 8. What Pius said to his wife when he was adopted.

5. 3. Governors in office for seven or nine years. That is refuted by the facts. But it may be an authentic misconception of the biographer.[4]

6. 9–10. The quaestorships of Marcus and of his brother by adoption. The HA persistently and wrongly attached 'Verus' to the name of L. Aelius Caesar (cf. *PIR*[2], C 605)—and his son did not acquire it until 161. The latter is here styled 'Annius Verus', as in *Hadr.* 24. 1.[5]

10. 3. The consulship of that man, here styled 'Verus Antoninus', cf. 4. 5.

10. 4. Anecdote about Apollonius the teacher of Marcus, with 'Calchis' as his origin: it was Chalcedon.

---

[1] Victor calls Pius 'senator urbis' (15. 2). For *functiones*, Symmachus, *Epp.* VII. 1: 'post magnificam ludorum consularium functionem'.

[2] For a parallel treatment, cf. Schulz, o.c. 10 ff. (at some length); Lécrivain, o.c. 121 (not adequate).

[3] The comparison with Numa occurs in Eutropius VIII. 8. 1; *Epit.* 15. 3. Not in Victor. The item its relevant to Enmann's KG.

[4] Against the fact, R. Syme *JRS* XLIII (1953), 149; *Gnomon* XXIX (1957), 518 and elsewhere. For the full statement, A. R. Birley, *Corolla memoriae Erich Swoboda dedicata* (1966), 43 ff.

[5] Observe also Eutropius VIII. 9. 1: 'L. Annius Antoninus Verus'; 10. 1: 'Verus Annius Antoninus'; *Epit.* 16. 5: 'Lucius Annius Verus'. Not in Victor. Again, relevant to KG.

10. 5. Another anecdote on the same theme.

11. 3. 'orationes plerique alienas dixerunt quae sub eius nomine fe-runtur: Marius Maximus eius proprias fuisse dicit.'

11. 8. Anecdote about Pius and Homullus (cf. above). Probably from Marius Maximus, as also the story in *Marcus* 6. 9.

12. 1: 'et Diaboleno' added to the list of jurists (cf. above).

Abridgement, rewriting in his own language and additions, that is what the compiler did. He dealt in a more drastic fashion with the *Marcus* and the *Severus*, interpolating shorter versions of events from Eutropius and Victor. These *Vitae* were too copious for his purposes. The *Pius* was probably fairly short anyhow, like the *Pertinax* and the *Didius Iulianus*, which show few signs of interference.

Some *Vitae* have appendages at the end, the result of revision. Thus *Marcus* (28. 10–29. 10) and *Verus* (10 f.). Not so the Pius. Likewise no invocation of an emperor. That suspicious feature occurs in three of the nine *Vitae*, each time in an added context (*Marcus* 19. 12; *Verus* 11. 4; *Sev.* 20. 4).

The *Vita Pii* has prime significance on two counts. First, to establish the character of the ultimate source, a biography. Second, what was done to that biography. A clear result emerges. Whatever might be supposed the treatment of some other *Vitae*, only two operations need here be assumed, viz. abridgement and additions. And no call to postulate an interval of time, or different agents.

VII. *The quality of* Ignotus

Examination of the *Pius* has thrown up a guiding line. The *Pertinax* is also remunerative.[1] It would not be a long or delicate task to clear it of accretions. And the *Didius Iulianus* has hardly any. The author of the nine *Vitae* begins to acquire shape and definition through the *Pius*. It will be expedient to give a selective summary of his merits, drawn from the other biographies.

1. Sources. Two autobiographies offered, those of Hadrian and Severus. Conjecture about other written sources would not be profitable. However, like Suetonius, he could no doubt consult archives, documents, inscriptions. The habit of erudite inquiry was nothing novel.

2. Facts and dates. The author was careful to supply the day and the month for births and deaths of emperors (e.g. *Pert.* 15. 6). Several of those dates are missing from the text in its present condition (there

[1] The *Pertinax* was wrongly impugned by R. Werner, *Klio* XXVI (1933), 283 ff. Against, G. Barbieri, *Stud. it. fil. class.* XIII (1936), 183 ff.

is no point in specifying). He is to be presumed accurate, though he may have gone wrong on the birth year of Severus—146 (*Sev.* 1. 3), whereas Cassius Dio indicates 145.[1] For the error in the day of the month, April 8 instead of April 11, the transmission may take the blame.[2] Other transactions are registered precisely, e.g. the Battle of Lugdunum (*Sev.* 11. 7); and one short section of the *Vita Commodi* (11. 13–12. 9) carries no fewer than seven dates.

3. The ancestry of rulers. As has been shown, the section at the head of the *Vita Pii* is excellent. The *Hadrianus*, however, is brief and scrappy. No grandparents, yet at the end, after Hadrian's wife follows the strange item 'atavus Maryllinus qui primus in sua familia senator populi Romani fuit' (*Hadr.* 1. 2).[3] In the *Marcus*, the text has to be emended in three places. First, and patently, 'Domitia Lucilla' for 'Domitia Calvilla' (1. 3). Second, continuing with this lady, the text should be supplemented 'Domitia Lucilla, Calvisi Tulli ⟨filia, avia materna Lucilla Domiti Tulli⟩ bis consulis filia'.[4] Third, the maternal grandfather of Marcus (1. 4) can be converted with advantage into 'Rupili ⟨Li⟩boni⟨s⟩'.[5] Again, the ancestry of Didius Iulianus is sound if one expunges the phrase beginning 'proavus fuit Salvius Iulianus, bis consul, praefectus urbi', etc. (*Did.* 1. 1).

4. The previous careers of emperors. Valuable and unimpeachable information was provided; and independent evidence (or good sense) can generally straighten out the products of abbreviation and confusion. Two inscriptions corroborate or correct items about Hadrian and about Didius Iulianus.[6] The career of Severus can be explained and interpreted.[7] Nor were the military occupations of Pertinax beyond the reach of expert inquiry (cf. *PIR²*, H 33). The recent discovery of an inscription on the Rhine, disclosing several of his equestrian posts, brings welcome confirmation.[8]

5. Personal names. The teachers of Marcus are put on record, both the *grammatici* (*Marcus* 2. 3 ff.) and the philosophers (2. 7 ff.). Some of

---

[1] Dio LXXVI. 17. 4, supported on astrological grounds by J. Guey, *Bull. Soc. nat. ant. France* (1956), 33 ff.

[2] For the evidence, see the Feriale Duranum in *Yale Class. Stud.* VII (1940), 253. Similarly 'idibus Augustis' (*Sev.* 5. 1) for his proclamation at Carnuntum. In fact April 9 (ib. 100).

[3] An addition, yet possibly authentic: i.e. from the basic source.

[4] R. Syme, *JRS* XLIII (1953), 150; *Tacitus* (1958), 793.

[5] A. R. Birley, *Historia* xv (1966), 249 ff.

[6] *ILS* 308 (Athens); 412 (Rome).

[7] See now T. D. Barnes, *Historia* xvi (1967), 91 ff.

[8] H. G. Kolbe, *Bonner Jahrbücher* CLXII (1962), 407 ff., whence *AE* 1963, 52.

the names in the first category have incurred suspicion.[1] Yet it appears that the basic text was sound.[2] Nor is there cause to incriminate any of those who gave instruction to Verus, not even 'Scaurinum grammaticum Latinum, Scauri filium' (*Verus* 2. 5).[3]

Elsewhere, in the *Commodus*, no fewer than forty names are registered, not to be found in the other sources (Dio and Herodian).[4] But several of the forty-one senators put to death by Severus, a portentous catalogue (*Sev.* 13), should be challenged.[5] Notably 'Ceionius Albinus', compare 'Ceionius Postumus', the alleged parent of Severus' rival (*Clod. Alb.* 4. 3); and there are six Pescennii, culminating in 'Pescennius Albinus'.

6. Odd persons. Observe, for example, the architect Decrianus (*Hadr.* 19. 12); Valerianus, a friend of Pertinax from the old days when they were schoolmasters together (*Pert.* 12. 7); and Tausius the Tungrian soldier, who struck the first blow (11. 9).

7. Roman topography. The author liked precise detail. The mansion of Marcus' grandfather was 'iuxta aedes Laterani' (*Marcus* 1. 7). Hadrian for his mausoleum chose a site 'iuxta Tiberim et aedem Bonae Deae' (*Hadr.* 19. 11). Inscriptions confirm this shrine of *Bona Dea*, which no other author mentions.[6] Likewise unique is the part of the Imperial Palace called 'Sicilia et Iovis cenatio' (*Pert.* 11. 6). As for the 'aedes Vectilianae' on the Mons Caelius, where Commodus passed the last night of his life (*Comm.* 16. 3, cf. *Pert.* 5. 7), that item had a long perpetuation, for it is registered by Jerome in his Chronicle and by Orosius (VII. 16. 4).[7]

8. Law and administration. *Ignotus* not only gave catalogues of jurists (*Hadr.* 18. 1; *Pius* 12. 1). He furnishes full detail, not eschewing technical language, about the enactments of several rulers (*Hadr.* 22; *Marcus* 9. 7–11. 10; *Pert.* 7. 2 ff.; 9. 1 ff.). The long passage in the *Marcus* is remarkable on various counts. This author, who elsewhere seems chary of expressing opinions of his own, pronounces a verdict—'ius autem magis vetus restituit quam novum fecit.' There speaks the writer of the Severan age.

9. Emperors and Senate. That is the central and passionate theme for a political historian. The biographer evinces little emotion. His views are

---

[1] E. Birley, *Bonner Historia-Augusta-Colloquium 1964/5* (1966), 36 f.

[2] A. R. Birley, *Bonner Historia-Augusta-Colloquium 1966/7* (1968), 39 ff.

[3] But 'Scaurinus, Scaurini filius, doctor celeberrimus' (*Alex.* 3. 3) is bogus, like his nine colleagues.   [4] Heer, o.c. 132 f.

[5] E. Birley, o.c. 37.

[6] Platner–Ashby, *A Topographical Dictionary of Ancient Rome* (1929), 75. That work missed the item from the HA.

[7] Perhaps transmitted from *Ignotus* by Enmann's KG.

conventional and predictable. He is on the side of moderation and morality. He regards with favour rulers who respect the dignity and privileges of the Senate—what writer entertained contrary notions?

In one particular, *Ignotus* exhibits noteworthy independence of judgement. The senatorial tradition, as represented by Cassius Dio, was bitterly hostile towards Didius Julianus. *Ignotus* makes some defence of the usurper. According to Dio, Didius on the evening after the murder of Pertinax, indulged in a sumptuous banquet in the Palace (LXXIII. 13. 1). *Ignotus* is at pains to refute the calumny—'quod falsum fuisse constat' (3. 8). He makes appeal to the frugal habits of Didius, who would often make a dinner of vegetables alone.[1] Again, in Dio's account of a riot, Didius lost patience and ordered the soldiers to kill (13. 4). For *Ignotus*, Didius maintained composure—'haec omnia Iulianus placide tulit, totoque imperii sui tempore mitissimus fuit' (4. 8). The senator Cassius Dio saw and shared the experience of the year 193. The biographer may also have been there.

The account adds up. What emerges is not sharp, vivid, personal. Only a conscientious scholar, averse from style and rhetoric, with no doctrine or fantasies, but addicted to facts and dates. Can one go further? The confident pronouncements attendant upon the resurrection of the 'great annalist' are a deterrent. Caution is in place, and boldness earns no profit here.

None the less, a modest surmise need not mislead. *Ignotus* had some legal competence and an interest in learning. He wrote at Rome—and may well have witnessed the momentous transactions of 193 (his exposition becomes more lively).[2] A knight rather than a senator, and not necessarily in one of the high equestrian posts. In short, a recognizable successor of Suetonius.

Ignotus, however, did not follow the master-biographer in his appetite for drink and sex, anecdote and scandal. Readers in any age of imperial Rome would rate him dull and pedestrian. Abridgement did not make the product more exhilarating. On the contrary. To enliven it, other devices and sources were requisite. In the first place, a writer who took delight in the trivial and indecorous.

---

[1] The elaboration may belong to the author of the HA.

[2] Also valuable details. Thus 'Vespronius Candidus, vetus consularis, olim militibus invisus ob durum et sordidum imperium' (5. 6, cf. Dio LXXIII. 17. 1) and Valerius Catullinus, sent by Didius to replace Severus in his governorship (5. 7). The latter person is not elsewhere on record.

VIII. *Marius Maximus*

This biographer took up where Suetonius left off. He wrote the lives of the emperors from Nerva to Elagabalus, the twelve in his selection corresponding in their total to the *De vita Caesarum* of the classic exponent. Maximus is cited no fewer than twenty-six times in the HA, and his name occurs for mention three times.[1] Moreover, on various criteria, his presence may be surmised in a number of other passages. Otherwise no mention anywhere of Maximus, save by felicitous coincidence in two other writers of late Antiquity: Ammianus (XXVIII. 4. 14) and the scholiast on Marius Juvenal IV. 53. Like Juvenal himself, Maximus was probably a recent rediscovery.[2]

It was easy to assume that his *Twelve Caesars* is the main source of the early *Vitae* in the HA. The step was early taken.[3] Nor did the notion lose appeal with the new turn of inquiry inaugurated in the year 1889. Peter, that erudite and conservative scholar, was a firm proponent.[4]

In the sequel, interest lapsed, and for a time Maximus languished under the shadow of the 'great annalist'. He began to revive with encouragement from Hohl, who in 1934 briefly stated that Maximus was the ultimate source of such portions of the earlier *Vitae* as have historical value.[5] The thesis was re-affirmed some twenty years later.[6] Hohl's formulation must be carefully noted: the basic source of the *Vitae* from Hadrian to Elagabalus was not Marius Maximus in his entirety, but that biographer as transmitted by Enmann's 'Kaisergeschichte'. The latter work, so he suggested, was little other than an abridgement of Maximus.

In the most recent season, Maximus benefits from a total resuscitation. Half a dozen names can be cited.[7] But no arguing of the case, only an assumption.

---

[1] For the *fragmenta*, H. Peter, *HRR* II (1906), 121 ff. Apart from them the name of the biographer occurs in *Probus* 2. 7; *Quadr. tyr.* I. 1 and 2.

[2] For the rediscovery of Juvenal, cf. G. Highet, *Juvenal the Satirist* (1954), 181 ff.; A. D. E. Cameron, *Hermes* XCII (1964) 367 ff.

[3] J. J. Müller, 'Der Geschichtsschreiber L. Marius Maximus' in *Büdingers Untersuchungen zur römischen Kaisergeschichte* III (1870), 19 ff.; J. Plew, *Marius Maximus als direkte und indirekte Quelle der S. H. A.* (Prog. Straßburg, 1878).

[4] H. Peter, *Die Scriptores Historiae Augustae* (1892), 98, cf. 108; *HRR* II (1906), CLXXXVIII.

[5] E. Hohl, *Klio* XXVII (1934), 156; *Bursians Jahresberichte* CCLVI (1937), 144. That is, by the channel of Enmann's KG.

[6] E. Hohl, 'Das Ende Caracallas', in *Misc. Ac. Berol.* II. 1 (1950), 276 ff.; cf. *S-B der Ak. der Wiss. zu Berlin* 1953, Abh. 2, 17: 'wie in der Tat in der ersten Hälfte des Corpus die für den Historiker brauchbare Substanz letzten Endes dem Marius Maximus verdankt wird.'

[7] A. D. E. Cameron, *Hermes* XCII (1964), 373; W. Seston, *Mélanges Carcopino* (1966), 881; A. R. Birley, *Marcus Aurelius* (1966), 20; H.-G. Pflaum, *Bonner Historia-Augusta-Colloquium 1964/5* (1966), 144; W. Seston, ib. 218; K. F. Stroheker, ib. 255.

Before a doctrine forms and hardens into accepted truth, it will be well to take a look at the claim. Weight and numbers need not be allowed the predominance. Where then should we be? The past history of the HA before and after 1889 is a due deterrent.

One must follow where the argument leads. In fact, a whole sequence of reasons can be set forth that tell against Marius Maximus.

1. Inspection shows that the citations of Maximus have been grafted onto the main source. Not always with skill. Observe, for one example, the insertion about the ultimate ancestry of Marcus Aurelius (*Marcus* 1. 6). This conclusion was stated in 1904, as obvious, and again demonstrated in 1954.[1] No refutation appears to have been attempted.

2. Many of the citations are trivial in content or scandalous. From their close context (or without that support) other deleterious items or anecdotes can be surmised. Thus, in the *Pius*, not long after an opinion of that biographer (11. 3), follows a story about a certain Homullus (11. 8).[2]

3. Orations in biography. The HA mentions two imperial speeches furnished by Marius Maximus, viz. Marcus to his counsellors, after the suppression of the pretender Avidius Cassius (*Marcus* 25. 11) and Marcus in laudation of Pertinax (*Pert.* 2. 8). An innovation, and not reassuring. *Ignotus* stood by his model, Suetonius.

4. Marius Maximus appended documents, cf. *Comm.* 18 f. (the *senatus consultum*); *Pert.* 15. 8 (a letter of Pertinax). There is no sign that the basic source adopted this practice.

5. Opinions expressed by Maximus clash with the basic text. The main trend of the *Vita Hadriani* is favourable to that ruler, or neutral. Maximus, three times out of four, is hostile—Plotina's influence and Trajan's lack of sympathy (2. 10); Hadrian's congenital cruelty (20. 3); his acting 'per simulationem' (25. 4).

6. The *Vita Veri*. As has been shown above, this biography must no longer be left among the 'Nebenviten'. It belongs to the main series. Now a *Verus* written by Maximus will not concord with the total of twelve rulers from Nerva to Elagabalus. The life and actions of that person (it follows) were recounted in the *Life of Marcus* by Maximus. That biography, so at least the HA asserts, comprised two volumes (*Avid.* 6. 7; 9. 5).

7. The *Vita Macrini*. If the HA had been using Maximus, there was no reason to drop him at this point. On the contrary. Yet the *Vita* reveals no trace of the particulars which Maximus was in a position to furnish,

---

[1] Heer, o.c. 152; G. Barbieri, *Riv. fil.* xxxii (1954), 36 ff.; 262 ff.
[2] cf. above, p. 38.

for example, the origin and career of Macrinus (see below). The consular biographer was appointed *praefectus urbi* by this emperor (Dio LXXVIII. 14. 3); and later, after his defeat, received a dispatch from him (36. 1; LXXIX. 2. 1). Maximus, pursuant to his practice (*Comm.* 18. 1; *Pert.* 15. 8), would hardly fail to subjoin such a document to his *Vita Macrini*. The HA happens to quote an *epistula Macrini* sent to the Senate after his proclamation (6. 2 ff.). It is pure invention.

Internal evidence thus subverts and destroys the case for Marius Maximus. His quality as a biographer also comes into question. To that estimate, two items are relevant.

1. Ammianus, adverting on the frivolity of aristocrats, condemns their choice of reading:—'quidam detestantes ut venena doctrinas Iuvenalem et Marium Maximum curatiore studio legunt, nulla volumina praeter haec in profundo otio contrectantes' (XXVIII. 4. 14). Golden words. The collocation of the two detrimental authors is instructive. The satirist exposed luxury and vice in its high season; the biographer dwelt with predilection on the shady sides of the Antonine dynasty. The austere and embittered Ammianus would not have condemned a sober chronicler of imperial *Vitae*.

2. A verdict in the HA. After long silence, the HA reverts to Maximus towards the end. 'Vopiscus', as the author now styles himself, furnishes a brief catalogue of good biographers: 'Marium Maximum, Suetonium Tranquillum, Fabium Marcellinum, Gargilium Martialem, Iulium Capitolinum, Aelium Lampridium ceterosque qui haec et talia non tam diserte quam vere memoriae tradiderunt' (*Probus* 2. 7).

The artifice is delicious. As elsewhere, genuine names and false interlaced. The author adduces two figments ('Fabius Marcellinus' and 'Gargilius Martialis'), and two of his own ostensible predecessors ('Julius Capitolinus' and 'Aelius Lampridius'), thus lending them authentication. A little later, Suetonius and Maximus recur. He notes their practice— neither wrote separate lives of usurpers (*Quadr. tyr.* 1. 1). He duly praises Suetonius, 'cui familiare fuit amare brevitatem'. Then he rounds on Maximus, 'homo omnium verbosissimus, qui et mythistoricis se voluminibus implicavit' (1. 2).

The truth at last, so it might seem. Caution is prescribed. Why give credit to the virtuous indignation of 'Vopiscus'? Marius Maximus was something better than a mere verbose romancer. Though prone to the trivial and scandalous, though admitting orations, he used documents and could not help transmitting a great deal of accurate and useful information. Further, the testimony of Ammianus is not the whole truth either. The historian writes in angry censure, no mean satirist himself when portraying life at Rome.

What matters is the internal evidence. Advocates of the consular biographer must be left to meditate upon the seven points of argument. A further consideration is not out of place. If the main source down to Caracalla was dull and factual, the author of the HA had every reason to enliven it. Maximus offered, writing with zest and spite about bad emperors and good, not sparing their consorts and eager to insinuate, even when he dealt with the sanctified Marcus, that all was not well within the house.

The author had his ambition. Not only to supersede earlier biographers (while compiling or looting them), not only to furnish the *Vitae* they had disdained,[1] but to surpass Maximus by the long extension of his work, and no less by the range and variety of his inventions, producing romance and a parody of the biographic art.

Indeed, Maximus himself may have derived from *Ignotus* the impulsion to compose biographies of a different kind, calculated to capture the favour of the reading public. *Ignotus* would have furnished help and a useful framework—and no need for many of his facts and dates. Nothing forbids that notion, if it be supposed that the unknown biographer belongs to the early years of Severus Alexander.[2]

The emergence of *Ignotus* imports a new factor into the writing of biography and history in the twenty years subsequent to the death of Caracalla. Cassius Dio comes into the reckoning, a close coeval of Marius Maximus. The time of this writing is relevant. A recent study argues that he had completed in 219 the books down to the death of Septimius Severus.[3] Perhaps that date is a little too early.[4] Even so, it is legitimate to conjecture that Marius Maximus composed his biographies to emulate or supplement the history of the Greek senator. Further, the problem might now arise of the relationship in time between *Ignotus* and Dio—and the sources which each employed.[5]

Let that pass. The theme of debate concerns the basic source of the nine *Vitae*. Marius Maximus must give way before a writer of more

[1] viz. *Aelius* and *Geta*; *Avidius, Pescennius, Clodius*: not in *Ignotus* or Maximus. Then *Diadumenianus*.

[2] Hence consequences of some interest for 'Quellenforschung'. The KG could draw material from *Ignotus* both directly and indirectly (through Marius Maximus).

[3] F. Millar, *A Study of Cassius Dio* (1964), 30.

[4] G. W. Bowersock, *Gnomon* XXXVII (1965), 471 ff.

[5] Some scholars have supposed that the HA used Cassius Dio. Not a useful hypothesis. Having *Ignotus* down to 217, the author did not need the Greek sources (i.e. Herodian and Dio).

modest rank and pretensions. Senator, consul, and commander of armies, the friend of emperors and their traducer, 'cadit Maximus'.

In this investigation it has so far been assumed that *Ignotus* elected as the term for his sequence of biographies the end of the House of Severus in 217. A suitable parallel to Suetonius, who concluded with the decline and fall of another dynasty that had issued from civil war. It remains to see how far the assumption can be corroborated.

ix. *Where* Ignotus *ended*

The notion of the unknown biographer happens to be no novelty. It was advocated by Lécrivain in 1904. Unfortunately, in extreme brevity —only two pages in a long book.[1] Lécrivain assumed that the work went as far as to include Macrinus. He was also emboldened to add conjecture about the author—from Egypt, probably Alexandria, and in any event 'un homme politique'.[2]

There ought perhaps to have been other outspoken advocates of this theory. They are not easy to discover. Yet it was the logical consequence for any who rejected both the 'great annalist' and Marius Maximus. Quite recently, Schwartz has entertained the idea of a continuation of Suetonius, perhaps going as far as Severus (inclusive).[3] But his remarks were brief indeed, and of extreme diffidence. He was ready to concede that this author might not have been a direct source of the HA.

For *Ignotus* and his point of termination, light comes from the *Vita Macrini*; and, as so often in the HA, from fiction, not fact. A line can be drawn between the *Caracalla* and the *Macrinus*.

The previous nine biographies scrupulously registered at the outset the facts about family and extraction, not omitting dates of birth (day and month and year). Precise and valuable. The introductory remarks in the *Commodus* and *Caracalla* happen to be curt. These were sons of emperors, the relevant particulars had already been stated, so the compiler explains (*Comm.* 1. 1; *Carac.* 1. 2).

By contrast, the *Vita Macrini*. It leads off with a programmatic preface, variously instructive and permitting sundry suspicions (see below). Brief remarks follow about the accession of the new ruler, 'humili natus loco et animi atque oris inverecundi' (2. 1). Then is inserted a disquisition about the name 'Antoninus' which Macrinus assigned to his son (2. 5–3. 9):

[1] Lécrivain, o.c. 191 f.

[2] ib. 192: 'Les détails si précis que beaucoup de textes donnent sur l'Égypte font croire qu'il était originaire de ce pays, sans doute d'Alexandrie. Mais ce fut un homme politique qui a certainement habité Rome.'

[3] J. Schwartz, *Bonner Historia-Augusta-Colloquium 1963* (1964), 159 f.

appeal to a prophecy made by the 'vates Caelestis' at Carthage will indicate the quality of the material.

And, after long delay, opinions are vouchsafed about the origin and career of Macrinus, purporting to come from later statements in the Senate: 'verba denique Aurelii Victoris cui Pinio cognomen erat, haec fuerunt' (4. 2). The item is significant, for more things than one, but it seems not to have been accorded much value by scholars preoccupied with the date of the HA. The 'Aurelius Victor' here cited as an authority is not one of the bogus writers in the HA: he is a bogus character. The name is taken from one of the not named sources of the HA, viz. Aurelius Victor: a known character, who was *praefectus urbi* in 389. Furthermore, a man from Africa, as he stated in modest pride (20. 5 f.).

To continue. On the statement of 'Aurelius Victor Pinius', Macrinus was of libertine stock, and a 'homo prostibilis'.[1] Severus banished him to Africa, where, among other things, he took up the study of rhetoric—'lectioni operam dedisse, egisse causulas, declamasse, in ludo postremo dixisse' (4. 3). These and other particulars the author refuses to vouch for, 'sed et haec dubia ponuntur, et alia dicuntur ab aliis.' He therefore proposes other versions. Macrinus had been a gladiator, but on retiring from the profession, 'accepta rudi', he went to Africa, to various occupations—a huntsman, a courier, and finally *advocatus fisci* (4. 6).

The author's procedure deserves a word in passing. First, the scholarly dubitation (with or without some named authority) about an emperor's origin and early pursuits. It evokes for comparison the prime exhibit later on, when the impostor has mastered the technique of circumstantial fraudulence, namely the disquisition about the Emperor Carus. There, after sundry contrasted opinions, he cites 'ephemeris quaedam' according to which that ruler came from Mediolanum but was enrolled in the town council of Aquileia (*Car.* 4. 4). Second, the interest in Africa and its schools of rhetoric. The author also adduces a letter written by the son of Macrinus, or, as some hold, by his tutor—'quidam magistri eius Caeliani ferunt, Afri quondam rhetoris' (*Diad.* 8. 9). Various signs suggest (nothing avails for proof) that the author of the HA may be African by origin.[2]

That need not detain. We are in the realm of historical fiction. To return to facts—the predilection of *Ignotus*, the source of the nine *Vitae*. The author of the HA has not bothered to ascertain the precise origin of Macrinus. It was not beyond research, had he cared. He makes play with invented African occupations of Macrinus, twice. In fact, Macrinus came

---

[1] The word is Plautine (cf. *Persa* 837), hence a clue to the tastes and habits of the author.
[2] R. Syme, *Ammianus and the Historia Augusta* (1968), 198 ff.

from Caesarea in Mauretania Caesariensis. Cassius Dio bears witness; and he gave the year of birth.[1]

That should suffice. *Ignotus* ended with Caracalla. However, for confirmation may be added sundry features of the *Macrinus* not manifest hitherto in the series of the nine *Vitae*.

1. The programmatic preface, with disquisition on princes, usurpers, or short-lived emperors—'vitae illorum principum seu tyrannorum sive Caesarum qui non diu imperarunt in obscuro latent' (*Macr.* 1. 1). That bears a resemblance to prefatory matter in three of the five 'Nebenviten', viz. *Aelius*, *Pescennius*, and *Avidius* (the last is embedded in the text, 3. 1 f.). Further, high professions about the biographer's vocation—'ea quidem quae memoratu digna erunt'. That looks forward to the author's later assertions of scruple and veracity, with castigation of inferior performers who, writing about emperors, expatiate on details of diet and dress and so on.

2. A bogus authority. One predecessor only, viz. 'Helius Maurus', freedman of Hadrian's freedman Phlegon, cited for some rubbish in the *Vita Severi* (20. 1), and to be presumed an insertion in the final revision. In the preface of *Macrinus* emerges 'Junius Cordus', who is duly censured (1. 3 ff.), and who incurs chastisement in the sequel.

There was a reason for the invention. *Ignotus* had terminated, and another Latin source, Marius Maximus, would soon run out. The author needed an equivalent scandal-monger and romancer. And, in fact, there is a link of idea and word between Maximus and 'Cordus'. Maximus, as is disclosed towards the end, was guilty of 'mythistorica volumina' (*Quadr. tyr.* 1. 2). The preface of *Macrinus*, denouncing 'Cordus', says 'libros mythistoriis replevit' (1. 5). The relation is patent—and in fact the only occurrence of those two words in Latin.

3. A Greek source. Herodian is used and summarized but not named.[2] The author had become aware that he would have to turn to Greek sources (Dexippus as well as Herodian) for Alexander and later emperors.

4. The composition of the *Macrinus*. Fluent but untidy. Not resembling the impatient compression in the *Caracalla*. Even in his later evolution, the author of the HA is no good on structure.

5. The fabrications. Certain types now emerge. Namely an emperor's letter to the Senate (6. 2 ff.); Latin verses allegedly translated from a Greek original (11. 4 ff.; 14. 2); a quotation from Virgil (12. 9), though not one

[1] Dio LXXVIII. 11. 1; 40. 3.
[2] *Macr.* 8. 3–10. 3, a brief summary of Herodian v. 3. 1–4. 12.

of the notorious emissions from oracles.[1] These features will all be discovered in the 'Nebenviten', and in later biographies. None of them had occurred in the *Vita Caracallae*.

x. *Conclusion*

The case for *Ignotus* has been stated, and for present purposes the dossier is now closed. More could have been said.

Intricate problems subsist, inherent in the present condition of the nine *Vitae* from Hadrian to Caracalla. They demand careful analysis, and comport no hope of an easy and agreed solution. It may be of some use to set forth the different themes to be investigated.

1. The compilation and abbreviation of *Ignotus*
2. Additions from Marius Maximus
3. Additions from other sources
4. The composition of the five 'Nebenviten'
5. The revision of the nine *Vitae*
6. The insertion of imperial dedications
7. The labels of four authors added.

That is a forbidding total. Should not the thing be given up? And why yearn for the unverifiable? Yet it is not as bad as it looks.

First, how many operations have to be inferred? Not many perhaps— and for the *Pius*, it can be argued, only two.

Second, at what intervals of time? There is no logical necessity to postulate additions and revisions long years after. An editor in the last years of Constantine (the latest clear date is the end of Licinius in 324) is only a phantom or mechanism of defence.[2] The 'Theodosian Redactor' (Mommsen's refuge under the impact of Dessau) may also depart.

Third, how many hands in the game? Possibly two, on a faint conjecture. The author, it might be supposed, used an assistant for the first task of compiling the nine *Lives*, holding himself in reserve for the congenial pursuits of fiction and romance in his 'Nebenviten' and in the later *Vitae*.[3]

That notion is a luxury, or a harmless concession. It does not amount to collaboration, or entail belief in the six biographers (or somewhat fewer, as the clever or credulous ordain); and in fact, none of those six anywhere asserts that he is writing as member of a team.[4]

---

[1] On revision one of those oracles was even inserted in *Hadr.* 2. 8.
[2] The device of Peter, Lécrivain, and others.
[3] R. Syme, o.c. 182 f.
[4] To be sure, 'Vopiscus' praises 'Pollio' (*Aur.* 2. 1; *Quadr. tyr.* 1. 3); and he includes two

Taken as a whole, the HA should be assigned to one author. What alternative subsists? His character, education and tastes can be surmised from his own original work: the fiction and fabrications. His design admits a conjecture. The motives are another matter.

of the others in his catalogue of sterling biographers (*Probus* 2. 7). From that it is a far cry to the statement of Momigliano, 'some at least of the alleged biographers claim to have written in collaboration' (*The Conflict between Paganism and Christianity in the Fourth Century* (1963), 96). At the most, 'Vopiscus' implies that he is continuing the work of 'Pollio'. No hint that he is a friend or ally.

IV · THE SECONDARY *VITAE*

1. *Introduction*

AT FIRST SIGHT the imperial biographies are disconcerting in their variety. As was said of an encyclopedia, 'opus diffusum, eruditum nec minus varium quam ipsa natura'. Nature in all her freaks and sports never brought forth anything like the Historia Augusta. It is a monster. Bewilderment does not abate when the components are analysed, when one *Vita* is set against another, when different sections of the work are mustered for comparison. The HA is an unremitting challenge. To be understood even partially, it must be surveyed as a whole.

The earliest portion (as extant) discloses the central problems in all their complexity. The run of emperors from Hadrian to Caracalla is reinforced (if that is the word) by secondary *Vitae* of princes or pretenders, derivative and largely fictional. Having slight value as history, these products tend to be condemned and discarded. Yet they furnish precious clues to the nature and authorship of the HA, foreshadowing the long tracts of fiction in the later *Vitae*. For that reason, those secondary *Vitae* should be segregated for separate appraisal. That is the main theme of the present investigation.

With the primary *Vitae*, the inquirer confronts a clear issue. A basic source can be detected, excellent and unimpeachable on facts. It has been abridged and mutilated; it is overlaid and interlaced with heterogeneous material; and most of the *Vitae* have suspicious appendages. Of which type is the source: history or biography? There was controversy, most of it now obsolete. For a time the persuasion held of a great annalistic historian, not inferior (in accuracy at least) to Cornelius Tacitus. That fancy has been dissipated. The source, it is clear, was biographical. A known author therefore comes into play, the consular Marius Maximus, writing in the time of Severus Alexander. He narrated the lives of twelve Caesars, from Nerva to Elagabalus.

That seemed good enough in the past, and Marius Maximus wins advocates in the recent season. Why look further? And the addiction to 'Quellenforschung' engenders fatigue and distaste. However, inspection counsels against. There are powerful objections. To cut a long story short:

the citations of Maximus in the HA betray their nature. They are additions, grafted on the original text. Maximus lapses. One is left with the postulate of an unknown biographer.[1]

Therefore *Ignotus*. Many things speak for him. If he is accepted, that is not the end of trouble and vexation. It is still necessary to examine the accretions and revisions that have brought the primary *Vitae* to their present unlovely condition. As if that were not bad enough, there is a further problem: the interrelation in design and composition between primary and secondary *Vitae*. Genesis and structure of the early *Vitae* (both types), such is the formidable proposition. It would entail searching inquiry and a heavy volume. In any event, some sort of working hypothesis cannot be evaded. In the course of what follows, a hypothesis will be presented—in extreme brevity.

II. *Primary and Secondary* Vitae

The distinction is indicated and declared in the first biography belonging to the category of princes and pretenders, viz. that of Hadrian's ill-starred heir. The reader of the work will learn about those who were 'nec principes nec Augusti'; and also about a number of other persons who 'quolibet alio genere aut in famam aut in spem principatus venerunt' (*Ael.* 1. 1). The prefatory remarks are supported by a note in epilogue (7. 4 f.). Moreover, five similar statements of a programmatic nature occur in the sequel.[2] There are some variants of definition. For example, the notion of short-lived emperors obtrudes. A problem for the conscientious biographer, because 'in obscuro latent' (*Macr.* 1. 1).

That is not all. The ingenious author invents predecessors in the genre. To begin with, they are an anonymous company, writing biographies of one prince only (*Ael.* 5. 3). Then, as is suitable, names emerge: a pair of prolific biographers. First, 'Aemilium Parthenianum, qui adfectatores tyrannidis iam inde a veteribus historiae tradidit' (*Avid.* 5. 1). Second, 'Junius Cordus', who is honoured with a full and formal introduction in the preface of the *Vita Macrini* (no other of the spurious 'authorities' gets so handsome a treatment). His plan was 'eorum imperatorum vitas edere quos obscuriores videbat' (*Macr.* 1. 3). Nothing more is heard of 'Aemilius Parthenianus', but 'Junius Cordus' is employed several times and castigated for his delinquencies.

---

[1] As argued in *Bonner Historia-Augusta-Colloquium 1966/7* (1968), 131 ff. = above, Ch. III; *Hermes* XCVI (1968), 494 ff. See also brief indications in *Ammianus and the Historia Augusta* (1968), 34; 92 f.; 177; 182.

[2] *Avid.* 3. 1 ff.; *Pesc.* 1. 1 f.; 9. 1 f.; *Macr.* 1. 1 ff.; *Quadr. tyr.* 1. 1 ff.

So far the author in his professions. A different criterion offers. The earlier *Vitae* in fact divide by source and accuracy. Regarded as history, the secondary biographies are poor stuff. When not sheer fiction, they take their material either from the primary *Vitae* or from the sources of those *Vitae*. Thus the biography of Aelius Caesar. Except for an item from the *Vita Veri* (*Ael.* 2. 8 f.) and two citations of Marius Maximus (3. 9; 5. 5), everything genuine derives from the *Vita Hadriani*.[1]

Double evidence, therefore, for a dichotomy. Scholarship lives on and from signal achievements in the past. Definitions and themes of argument about the HA go back to Dessau's paper in the year 1889—and, with less advantage, to some of the reactions which his audacious act provoked. Mommsen in 1890 segregated the first sixteen biographies (from Hadrian to Macrinus and his son inclusive) and styled them 'the Diocletianic series'.[2] Nine emperors supply the primary biographies. That left seven, reckoned as secondary, as 'Nebenviten'. Such was the standard classification, accepted with no dissent (or not much). It labours under grave defects and must now be modified in vital particulars.[3]

First, the whole definition of a 'Diocletianic series'. Two of those seven 'Nebenviten' in fact carry dedications to Constantine (*Clod. Alb.* 4. 2; *Geta* 1. 1). There was a larger fallacy. Dessau dismissed the dedications or invocations as a fraudulent device to convey a fraudulent dating for the imposture. Mommsen, who acknowledged some of Dessau's other arguments, was not able to give up the dedications. He clung to the ostensible date for the main bulk of the HA and put up in defence the notion of a 'Theodosian editor'—to no good result.

Second, the *Vita Veri* was relegated to the category of the 'Nebenviten'. That was premature, and an error. Verus was in fact an 'Augustus', he reigned for nearly eight years as partner of Marcus in the supreme power. Introducing Verus, the author presents no justification for giving that person a separate treatment, as he does in all but one of the secondary *Vitae*. He merely states that he will narrate Verus after Marcus, not before. He reverses (so he says) the order of other biographers—'scio plerosque ita vitam Marci ac Veri litteris atque historiae dedicasse ut priorem Verum intimandum legentibus darent' (1. 1).

Though much of the material in this biography may appear trivial, the information is excellent. Observe the names and facts that do not

---

[1] One passage is instructive—'statuas sane Aelio Vero per totum orbem colossas poni iussit' (*Ael.* 7. 1). Patently an invention. The word 'colossus' as an adjective recurs in *Alex.* 25. 8; 28. 6—and nowhere else in Latin, cf. *TLL*.

[2] Mommsen, *Ges. Schr.* VII (1909), 316 ff. = *Hermes* xxv (1890), 243 ff.

[3] *Bonner Historia-Augusta-Colloquium 1966/7* (1968), 132 f. = above, p. 30.

derive from the *Marcus*. The *Avidius* stands in sharp contrast. Moreover, the accretions are not more numerous than in others of the main *Vitae*, such as the *Marcus*; and the various types of invention favoured by the impostor (set out below) are absent. Inspection and dissection of the *Verus* has now restored this biography to its proper place and estimation.[1]

The consequences are momentous. Another biography goes to the account of the basic source, *Ignotus*, and helps to round him off. Next, the assumption that the source was none other than Marius Maximus (it has recently been gaining ground) receives a mortal blow. Two arguments combine to reinforce the impact. First, on internal evidence. The life and habits of Verus were retailed (so the HA asserts) by Marius Maximus in his biography of Marcus, which comprised two books, the first of them terminating with the decease of Verus (*Avid.* 6. 7; 9. 5). The consular biographer did not write a separate *Vita Veri*. Second, on external evidence. Maximus wrote in continuation of Suetonius—his *Nerva* stands on attestation.[2] And he went down to Elagabalus, so all concede. For the total of his imperial biographies Ausonius brings confirmation. To his *XII Caesares* are appended twelve more, describing a second and post-Suetonian set of twelve, from Nerva to Elagabalus. Verus is not on the list.

Third, the *Vita Macrini*. As Mommsen ordained the matter, the 'Diocletianic series' took in the biography of this emperor. Mommsen was under no illusions about its quality. Indeed, he suggested that it might better belong with the next *Vitae* (those of Elagabalus and Severus Alexander). A pertinent observation, though thrown out casually in a brief note.[3] Mommsen should have prosecuted the idea. The *Macrinus* proclaims a break with what went before: composition and sources as well as accuracy. It is diffuse as well as careless and cynical. In fact, longer for a brief reign than the *Vita Caracallae*, where the author, tired with the task of compiling, compresses six years ruthlessly.

The contrast between the two *Vitae* points to a painless conclusion. The source used hitherto had run out. In default of which, the writer need not have been at a loss. Adequate information was to hand if he cared to look. Marius Maximus had been made *praefectus urbi* by Macrinus, he had received dispatches from that emperor, as Cassius Dio attests (LXXVIII. 36. 1; LXXIX. 2. 1). This biographer was in a position to supply facts such as Dio registers, for example the origin of Macrinus (from Caesarea

---

[1] As demonstrated by T. D. Barnes, *JRS* LVII (1967), 65 ff.
[2] In the scholiast on Juvenal IV. 53.
[3] Mommsen, o.c. 323.

in Mauretania) and the year of his birth (LXXVIII. 11. 1; 40. 3). Nothing of the kind is reflected in the HA. Instead, wilful ignorance and a welter of inventions, conveyed under the mask of scholarly dubitation—'sed et haec dubia ponuntur, et alia dicuntur ab aliis' (*Macr.* 4. 5). That is one of the tricks and diversions, on abundant show in the sequel.

The miserable *Macrinus* is in fact to be estimated one of the prime documents for the understanding of the HA, structure as well as authorship. This biography presents sundry phenomena not so far manifest in any of the primary *Vitae*.

1. A programmatic preface, resembling sections in the 'Nebenviten', but longer and more explicit. The author opens with the remark 'vitae illorum principum seu tyrannorum sive Caesarum qui non diu imperarunt in obscuro latent' (1. 1). He goes on to observe how arduous is the task to ascertain facts about those rulers or usurpers of brief duration. He will do his best, drawing 'ex diversis auctoribus'. But only 'memoratu digna'. There follows an attack on 'Junius Cordus' (1. 3 ff.), with examples of the sort of trivial detail a serious biographer will eschew. 'Cordus' was a romancer, he filled his books with 'mythistoriae' (1. 5).

2. The employment of a Greek source for the first time. A piece of the *Macrinus* (8. 3–10. 3) is an abridgement of Herodian (v. 3. 3–4. 12). That historian, however, is not named.

3. Various fabrications. Thus a bogus authority, 'Junius Cordus'. (There is 'Helius Maurus' of *Sev.* 20. 1, but it is a late insertion in that *Vita.*) Also, an emperor's letter to the Senate (6. 2 ff.); Latin verses allegedly translated from anonymous Greek (11. 4 ff.; 14. 2); a Virgilian quotation (12. 9).

The *Macrinus* thus exhibits a revealing kinship to the 'Nebenviten', and a new departure in the main series. *Ignotus* ended with Caracalla, and there is no trace (that is a surprise) of Marius Maximus in the *Macrinus*: in the *Elagabalus* he is cited once (*Elag.* 11. 6) and several times in the *Alexander*, in reference to earlier reigns (*Alex.* 5. 4; 21. 4; 30. 6; 48. 6; 65. 4).[1] After the *Caracalla* the HA has recourse to Greek sources—and a plethora of invention. Before he reached that point, the author had become aware of their existence. Herodian happens to be used not only in the *Macrinus* but in a short passage of the *Clodius Albinus* (8. 1–4, cf. Herodian III. 5. 8). Moreover, Herodian is twice named in that *Vita* (1. 2; 12. 14). There must also be mentioned another Greek writer, Quadratus, i.e.

[1] There are various puzzles in the employment of Marius Maximus by the HA. The accurate piece of narrative in *Elag.* 13–17 may derive from this source, cf. *Hermes* XCVI (1968), 500.

the historian Asinius Quadratus who gets mentioned twice (*Verus* 8. 4; *Avid*. 1. 2), though he can hardly be reckoned a source. The eastern campaigns (of Severus, of Caracalla, and of Macrinus) may have brought his *Parthica* to the cursory notice of the author. These phenomena bring up the interrelation between primary and secondary biographies.

Ignotus was the basic source of the 'Nine *Vitae*', Hadrian to Caracalla (including the *Verus*). There remain five 'Nebenviten', viz. the biographies of Aelius Caesar, Avidius Cassius, Pescennius Niger, Clodius Albinus, and Geta. As for the last of those, the author for his own design covers up the fact that the younger son of Severus was an 'Augustus' with the mendacious allegation 'prius rebus humanis exemptus est quam cum fratre teneret imperium' (*Geta* 1. 2).

For present purposes no account need be taken of the *Vita Diadumeni*, one of the 'Nebenviten' in Mommsen's scheme. But the son of Macrinus was an 'Augustus' in truth—and in the conception of the HA. And nothing needs to be said about a similar product, the account of Maximinus' son which forms the second part of *Maximini Duo*. The five 'Nebenviten' are best defined as biographies that had no precedents either in *Ignotus* or in Marius Maximus. That is important. They will now be put under brief scrutiny.

III. *The composition of the Secondary* Vitae

The five should be studied in conjunction. Not that they are all of one piece. Divergences are clear in structure and manner. The *Aelius* happens to be reasonably well shaped, but the *Avidius*, after appearing to peter out, picks up again and goes on to quote a number of letters (9. 5–13. 7), and ends with a second supplement (13. 8–14. 8). The *Clodius Albinus* also has an appendage (13. 3–14. 6), the *Pescennius* an even longer continuation (9. 5–12. 8).

The untidy composition of the 'Nebenviten' has given rise to theories that invoke different strata or rewriting. Peter supposed them built up in the same way as the primary *Vitae*: an original core with conflations and accretions. And in some he was able to distinguish two main sources.[1] Another scholar, Lécrivain, put out the notion that, while three of them (*Aelius, Avidius, Pescennius*) were revised by 'Julius Capitolinus', the other two were his own unaided production.[2]

[1] H. Peter, *Die Scriptores Historiae Augustae* (1892), 199 (the *Avidius*); 206 (*Clodius Albinus*). Peter was willing to admit 'Aemilius Parthenianus' (*Avid*. 5. 1) as the second source in that biography. Two sources have also been postulated by J. Schwartz in an elaborate study, *Bonner Historia-Augusta-Colloquium 1963* (1964), 141 ff., cf. 162.
[2] Ch. Lécrivain, *Études sur l'Histoire Auguste* (1904), 267.

Efforts of this order are superfluous. They neglect the obvious.[1] As is evident in some of the later *Vitae*, the author for all his talents is no good on structure. Observe, for example, the appendages to the *Tacitus* (15–19). And there is no need to admit any revision going beyond an addition of a few sporadic items, if at all. The 'Nebenviten' are free composition.

Differentia of subject will also be taken into account. The *Aelius* gives a picturesque rendering of the perfect voluptuary, but the *Geta* lacks life and colour. By contrast with both, the biographies of the three pretenders (which accord well together) show great ease and freedom and richness of invention, extending to the exposition of political doctrines.

The type and incidence of fabrications also varies. Again, the biographies of the three pretenders stand out. Neither *Aelius* nor *Geta* contains, for example, any of the principal types: bogus characters and invented documents. For that matter, in the series opened by the *Vita Macrini*, the *Elagabalus* has none, in sharp contrast to its sequel and pendant, the *Alexander*. No scholar seems to doubt that they are by the same hand.

So far differences. Certain common features must be assigned primacy of esteem. First, statements of a programmatic nature in the preface or elsewhere. They occur twice in the *Aelius*, at beginning and end. The *Avidius* postpones (to 3. 1), whereas the *Pescennius* is equipped with a second and longer preface (9. 1 ff.). None was required in the *Clodius Albinus*: it belongs so closely with the *Pescennius*, where the relevant themes already had an iterated exposition. The last of the five opens with a brief statement to explain 'cur etiam Geta Antoninus a me tradatur' (1. 1). The question, it may be conceded, was not idle. The author answers it in his own fashion. He retails the reasons which induced Severus to confer on his second son the name 'Antoninus'. Severus did no such thing.

The primary *Vitae* eschew prefaces and excuses. The opening remarks of the *Verus* are not of that sort. They merely explain the order in which two *Vitae* are presented to the reader.

Second, a cognate matter. Each of the five secondary *Vitae* carries a dedication or invocation. In two it opens the preface (*Aelius* and *Geta*), in the others it occurs in the body of the biography. The first three invoke Diocletian, the others Constantine (*Clod. Alb.* 4. 2; *Geta* 1. 1). There is no reason for supposing that these invocations are a subsequent

---

[1] The author's habits come out clearly in the *Pescennius*. Having exhausted his main themes, he reverts to them in order to fill space, and starts again with a second preface (9. 1 ff.).

addition. By contrast, only three of the nine primary *Vitae* are equipped with this device. Diocletian is invoked, twice in 'bad passages' generally reckoned as additions (*Marcus* 19. 12; *Sev.* 20. 4), and once in an appendage (*Verus* 11. 4).

Third, the use of the first person singular. It occurs a number of times in the secondary *Vitae*, in the explanatory sections registered above and elsewhere (e.g. *Avid.* 1. 7; *Pesc.* 9. 3; *Clod. Alb.* 4. 1; 14. 3). That was only to be expected. Apart from the 'scio plerosque' introducing the *Verus*, the primary *Vitae* show seven instances. Their distribution may be instructive. Two are in reference to Marius Maximus: a document inserted from that biographer (*Comm.* 18. 2), and a speech deliberately not inserted (*Pert.* 15. 8). Of the other five, three occur in the notoriously bad passage in the *Severus* (20. 1; 4; 9), the other two in an accretion on the *Caracalla* (8. 1; 9. 10). The personal note in those five instances points to the same author as the author of the 'Nebenviten'.

iv. *The fabrications*

Specimens of inventive fancy have already been indicated. As elsewhere in the HA, fiction is a better guide than fact. The secondary *Vitae* offer a straight path towards authorship. It will be expedient to catalogue the main types of fabrication in those biographies, each by its first emergence.

A. Characters. Avidius Severus, centurion, father of the usurper. *Avid.* 1. 1.
Authors. Aemilius Parthenianus, biographer. *Avid.* 5. 1.
Letters. Verus to Marcus. *Avid.* 1. 7 ff.
Speeches. Oration of Marcus. *Avid.* 12. 2 ff.
Acclamations in the Senate. *Avid.* 13. 2 ff.
Date by day and month. *Clod. Alb.* 4. 6.
Date by *consules suffecti* as well. *Geta* 3. 1.

B. Official posts. 'Ragonius Celsus Gallias regens'. *Pesc.* 3. 9.
Regiments. Albinus commands 'equites Dalmatae'. *Clod. Alb.* 6. 2.
Mixed corps. Armenians, Sarmatians, and 'mille nostri'. *Pesc.* 4. 2.
Topography. The 'campus Iovis' at Rome. *Pesc.* 4. 1.
Edifices. Niger's mansion there, 'hodie Romae visitur'. *Pesc.* 4. 1.
Statues. Hadrian ordains 'statuas per totum orbem colossas'. *Ael.* 7. 1.
Paintings. Niger depicted in an Isiac procession. *Pesc.* 6. 8.

C. Quotations from Virgil. *Ael.* 4. 1 ff.
Oracles that quote Virgil. *Pesc.* 8. 3.
Omina imperii. *Clod. Alb.* 5. 3 ff.
Greek verses in translation. *Pesc.* 12. 7.

Literary productivity. Albinus wrote *Georgica*, perhaps also *Milesiae*. *Clod. Alb.* 11. 7 f.

Extant speeches. One of Aelius Caesar, 'hodieque legitur'. *Ael.* 4. 7.

'Litterati' as friends of rulers. *Ael.* 4. 2.

Antiquarian digressions. *Ael.* 2. 3 f.

Grammarians' fantasies. *Geta* 5. 4 ff.

D. Parentage. Avidius Severus, father of the usurper. *Avid.* 1. 1.

Relatives. Aelius Bassianus, proconsul of Africa, related to Albinus. *Clod. Alb.* 4. 5.

Genealogy. Descent from Postumii, Albini, Ceionii. *Clod. Alb.* 4. 1.

Physical appearance. *Pesc.* 6. 5.

Self-contradictory and vapid characterizations. *Avid.* 3. 4.

Luxurious habits. *Ael.* 5. 6 ff.

Gluttony. A portentous consumption of fruit. *Clod. Alb.* 11. 3.

v. *The Author*

The items registered above reveal a writer developing a native gift for deceit. Fresh devices accrue later on, and well before the end the ingenious impostor comes out as a notable practitioner in the art of historical romance. His tastes and habits are already manifest in the secondary *Vitae*. Six features stand out.

1. The parade of erudition. It may be genuine, as in the learned digression on the name 'Caesar' (*Ael.* 2. 3 f.). But it is also a joke. Geta puts to the *grammatici* questions about the proper terminology of animal noises— 'velut agni balant, porcelli grunniunt, palumbes minurriunt', etc. (*Geta* 5. 4 f.).

2. Literary tastes. Hadrian liked to have 'litterati' about him (*Ael.* 4. 2; 5). He quotes Virgil (4. 1 ff.). So does one of the pretenders (*Clod. Alb.* 5. 2). Marcus appeals to Ennius and to Horace (*Avid.* 5. 7; 11. 8).

Severus with 'si ulla vena paternae disciplinae viveret' (*Pesc.* 3. 11) exploits a tag from Persius (i.e. 1. 103 f.); and the author, assigning to Niger a grandfather who was 'curator Aquini' (*Pesc.* 1. 3) slips in an allusion to the domicile of the other satirist. And there are several reminiscences of Sallust (most clearly in *Avid.* 14. 8).

Princes themselves perform as writers. Aelius Caesar was 'eloquentiae celsioris, versu facilis' (*Ael.* 5. 2); and he delivered 'orationem pulcherrimam, quae hodieque legitur' (4. 7). The favourite authors of this voluptuary were Ovid, Martial, and the cookery book of Apicius (5. 9). Clodius Albinus wrote *Georgica*; and, as some say, *Milesiae*—'quarum fama non ignobilis habetur, quamvis mediocriter scriptae sint' (*Clod.*

Alb. 11. 8). Severus in a dispatch to the Senate denounces the frivolous occupations of his rival—'inter Milesias Punicas Apulei sui et ludicra litteraria' (12. 12).

Finally, the most idiosyncratic of inventions: a novel type of 'sortes Vergilianae'. They do not emerge from consultation of the sacred book, a practice which arose in late Antiquity. They are emitted by oracles at Delphi and at Cumae (*Pesc.* 8. 3 ff.; *Clod. Alb.* 5. 4).[1]

3. Style and vocabulary. There is the same blend of incongruities as in the later *Vitae*: stylish or archaic words, technical terms, and the language of the author's own time. Observe the archaic 'indipiscor' (*Ael.* 2. 3), the rare 'excaldo' (*Avid.* 5. 1). On the other side, 'buccellatum', the soldiers' bread (*Avid.* 5. 2; *Pesc.* 10. 4); 'papilio', a tent (*Pesc.* 11. 1); 'stellatura', a type of military graft (*Pesc.* 3. 8).

Of primary value are the peculiar, if not unique, words and expressions that crop up in different sections of the HA.[2] For example, 'rebellio' (*Avid.* 9. 11); 'speciatim' (*Avid.* 6. 5; *Clod. Alb.* 12. 1); 'conflictu habito' (*Clod. Alb.* 8. 4); 'in litteras mittere' (*Avid.* 3. 3; *Pesc.* 1. 1); 'necessarius rei publicae' (*Avid.* 1. 2; 2. 7; *Pesc.* 3. 5). Nor will the rhetorical effects be neglected. For example, Avidius denouncing the philosophical emperor (*Avid.* 14. 2 ff.), or Severus in derision of his rival (*Clod. Alb.* 12. 6 ff.). Vigour, skill, and variety are on show. Though the author lacks command of structure, he is able to bring out contrasts.

4. Wit and humour. The dreadful puns that evoke a schoolboy (or his instructor) make an early start in an epistle of Verus—'Avidius Cassius avidus est . . . imperii' (*Avid.* 1. 6). However, a certain grace is revealed in the tastes and pastimes of Hadrian's heir—his voluptuous repose under an awning, 'unctus odoribus Persicis', the light literature he preferred (Martial was his Virgil), and so on (*Ael.* 5. 3 ff.). The description ends with the prince's apophthegm—'uxor enim dignitatis nomen est, non voluptatis' (5. 12). No doubt a traditional witticism, like Caracalla on his brother—'sit divus dum non sit vivus' (*Geta* 2. 8). But 'philosopha anicula' and 'luxuriosus morio' for Marcus and Verus (*Avid.* 1. 8) might be his own invention.

Further, Pescennius Niger shows point and spirit. He rebukes the troops in Egypt—'Nilum habetis et vinum quaeritis' (*Pesc.* 7. 7); and when the natives of Palestine raised complaint about taxation he exclaimed, 'ego vero etiam aerem vestrum censere vellem' (7. 9). Again, comic

---

[1] This peculiar device was first shown up by Dessau, *Hermes* XXVII (1892), 582 ff.
[2] Emphasized by Dessau, *Hermes* XXIV (1889), 386 ff.; XXVII (1892), 594 ff.

exaggeration. Monstrous details that are vouchsafed for by 'Cordus' document another pretender's addiction to fruit: five hundred figs he ate when hungry, a hundred Campanian peaches, ten melons of Ostia, etc. (*Clod. Alb.* 12. 14).

5. Mendacity and perverse variants. To render a character, the author invents contrary traits that add up to precisely nothing. Thus 'saepe religiosus, alias contemptor sacrorum, avidus vini item abstinens, cibi adpetens et inediae patiens, Veneris cupidus et castitatis amator' (*Avid.* 3. 4). Nor is he loath to contradict himself. Niger, after being introduced as 'libidinis effrenatae ad omne genus cupiditatum' (*Pesc.* 1. 4), turns out to be 'rei veneriae nisi ad creandos liberos prorsus ignarus' (6. 6).

There are other wilful tricks. According to Marius Maximus, Hadrian invented a game-pie of four ingredients, the 'tetrafarmacum' (*Alex.* 30. 6, cf. *Hadr.* 21. 4, where Maximus is not named). The *Vita Aelii* serves up a different version. It is really a 'pentafarmacum', the credit belongs to Hadrian's heir. The author must therefore correct the account which, following Maximus, he gave in the *Vita Hadriani* (*Ael.* 5. 4 f.).[1] Next, another exhibition of scholarship. Geta was born at Rome (*Sev.* 4. 3). Mediolanum is now substituted (*Geta* 3. 1), with a date by month and day (May 27), and by consuls: *suffecti*, however, which is implausible and damning. Further, as has been already indicated, the author both denies that Geta was an 'Augustus' and alleges that he was called 'Antoninus'.

6. A biographer's profession. He is truthful and serious. If you want 'frivola', read 'Aelius Cordus' (*Clod. Alb.* 5. 10). This is the deleterious biographer who, as 'Junius Cordus', is solemnly taken to task in the preface of the *Vita Macrini*. Another and a bolder attitude will be advertised later on when the HA exalts the plain style and honesty of biographers and decries the 'eloquentia' of the historians.

VI. *His political opinions*

Hadrian's heir and young Geta had little to offer. The three pretenders were more promising. Views about good and bad emperors belonged to the theme; and doctrines of government are expounded, or at least adumbrated.

Avidius Cassius is put on parade as a model military man, intent on discipline. Also, the soldier and practical man is set against the philosopher.

---

[1] In *Alex.* 30. 6 the game-pie was still a 'tetrafarmacum'. The item could be used to support an argument that the *Aelius* was written later than the *Alexander*.

In a vigorous harangue (presented in the form of a letter) Avidius denounces the unworldly preoccupations of Marcus as encouraging incompetence and corruption among the administrators (*Avid.* 14. 2 ff.).

A general who curbs the soldiery may have to be stern and ferocious. Virtue can be practised to excess, 'severitas' may be termed 'crudelitas' (4. 1). Savage examples are vouchsafed (4. 2 ff.). Yet the rigour of Avidius was salutary. The soldiers on the Danube were chastened, the barbarians begged for a peace of one hundred years (4. 9).[1] And he converted to good habits the licentious legions of Syria, 'diffluentes luxuria et Dafnidis moribus agentes', as Marcus testifies in a dispatch (5. 5 ff.).

Discipline is the keynote, recurring in the other two *Vitae*. The author has not bothered to register a single military exploit of the greatest general the Parthian War produced. And something more. The habits of the usurper were harsh, 'ad censuram crudelitatemque propensiores'. But empire would have made him a better man, 'non modo clemens sed bonus' (13. 10). Next, Pescennius Niger. On a special mission in Gaul to round up deserters when Septimius Severus was governor of Lugdunensis, he earned especial praise, as Severus testified in a letter to the Emperor Commodus (*Pesc.* 3. 5). And in truth Pescennius checked sundry abuses of which the military were guilty (3. 6 ff.). Testimony is also quoted in a later letter of Severus 'ad Ragonium Celsum Gallias regentem (3. 9 ff.). Indeed, Marcus had written about him to 'Cornelius Balbus' (4. 1). Again, in Egypt (where he never was) Pescennius sternly rebuked the idle and pretentious 'milites limitanei' (7. 7 f.).

As if that were not enough, the author goes on in his continuation of the biography after it seemed to stop. He reverts to military discipline (and its corollary, the protection of civilians) at some length and with suitable use of technical terms such as 'papilio' and 'buccellatum' (10 f.).

Clodius Albinus was also savage—'atrox circa militem' (11. 6). Other features are brought into greater prominence. Albinus was reluctant towards taking power—'invitum me, commilitones', etc. (3. 3). He was liked by the Senate (12. 1), and he advertised a more than normal deference to the high assembly. In his harangue to the troops in Britain he condemned bad emperors and enounced a novel and paradoxical doctrine: 'senatus imperet, provincias dividat, senatus nos consules faciat' (13. 10). The invention is significant. It foreshadows the policy and even the measures attributed to 'good emperors' in a later epoch. Tacitus ordained a 'senatorial restoration'. So did Probus, soon after. Even were the iteration

---

[1] It need not be added that nothing shows Avidius anywhere near the Danube.

not suspect, the particulars are rhetorical or vague and enigmatic (*Tac.* 18. 3; 19. 2; *Prob.* 13. 1).

The opinions disclosed in these three secondary *Vitae* add up to something. How much? That is a question. Caution is enjoined.

The author is in favour of discipline, clemency, and respect for the Senate. The contrary would surprise, in any age. The opinions are conventional and inevitable. But not without some value. These *Vitae* look forward to the treatment of later emperors in the sequence from Aurelian to Carus both in this respect and in the use of 'iudicia principum': that is to say, the device whereby a ruler produces a testimonial to the merit of a general destined (or worthy) to be his successor.[1]

Emperors strong but clement, who could gainsay that ideal? It represented a combination of the great archetypes, Trajan and Marcus. Two further considerations come in, relevant both to the later *Vitae* and to the surmised date of the HA.

First, the three pretenders benefit from a favourable presentation. That is not enough to constitute an apologia for usurpation. Nor is it any surprise. Contrasts existed. They were enhanced by the author for dramatic effect. Setting Avidius against Marcus, he is not proposing to depreciate that lay-saint. Indeed, the *Vita* (it has been claimed) is not so much a panegyric of Avidius as an illustration of the clemency of Marcus.[2] Similarly, since Severus was cruel and hostile to the Senate, it was natural and easy to discover virtue in his defeated rivals. Again, like Avidius Cassius, Pescennius would have turned out an excellent emperor. In fact, the potential author, so all affirm, of the reforms that Severus could not, or would not, make; and he would have proceeded 'sine crudelitate, immo etiam cum lenitate' (*Pesc.* 12. 3).

Second, legitimacy and hereditary succession. Avidius, as befitted one ostensibly descended from the Cassii of the Republic, was an enemy to the imperial system—'oderat tacite principatum nec ferre poterat imperatorium nomen.' But he recognized that it could not be abolished (1. 4). Manifestations of hostility to the succession of sons are another matter. They occur. Not many, however, or in sharp prominence. Marcus, to be sure, is made to say 'plane liberi mei pereant, si magis amari merebitur Avidius quam illi' (2. 8). But, if that theme was already an urgent preoccupation with the author, he was sadly oblivious. Denouncing

---

[1] In the sequence of emperors between Decius and Carinus the device is employed with great skill—and to link rulers at more than one remove, cf. R. Syme, o.c. 135.

[2] N. H. Baynes, *The Historia Augusta. Its Date and Purpose* (1926), 84. He concludes that the biography is 'in a word, Zeitgeschichte' (85). Klebs, discounting 'politische Ideen', had seen only stale rhetoric (*Rh. Mus.* XLIII (1888), 342). The antithesis is imperfect.

Marcus, Avidius Cassius failed to advert upon the promotion of the boy Commodus.

The author implies, it may be said, that Niger or Albinus would have been better rulers for Rome than the sons of Severus. Severus in his autobiography announced an intention of making them his heirs (*Pesc.* 4. 7). That does not amount to much. The notion is not a fancy of the HA, hence a useful clue. It goes back to Marius Maximus (cf. *Clod. Alb.* 3. 4). However, a violent attack on the dynastic policy of Severus crops up elsewhere, in a 'bad passage' in the *Vita* of that emperor (20. 4 ff.). The supreme exposition of the theme comes much later, when 'Maecius Faltonius Nicomachus' (revealing nomenclature) delivers a solemn and passionate harangue before the Senate. 'Dii avertant principes pueros', so he exclaims (*Tac.* 6. 5).[1]

To sum up. If a writer has decided to compose fictional biographies, he cannot evade 'good' and 'bad' emperors. In the nature of things, standard opinions are reflected, not much subject to variation through the centuries and appropriate under Trajan or Severus Alexander no less than in the days of Diocletian or Theodosius. Marius Maximus would no doubt have furnished some guidance—were it needed. The doctrines discoverable in these secondary *Vitae* do not suggest that they belong to a plan of propaganda. The author had elected to write about usurpers and pretenders. Dramatic propriety explains many features—also a sense of equity or his own native perversity.[2]

The 'Nebenviten' disclose a literary personality—and a progression in the art of fraudulence. On sundry signs and symptoms they also look forward to the later *Vitae*.[3] That theme would be variously remunerative. The next step, however, entails an inquiry of a different order, highly complex and much more hazardous: inception and design of those five 'Nebenviten', and their relation to the 'Nine *Vitae*'.

VII. *Interrelation with the Primary* Vitae

The five 'Nebenviten' were designed to form pendants or supplements to the primary *Vitae* on which they follow. Thus *Aelius* after *Hadrianus*, *Avidius* after *Marcus* and *Verus*, and so on. Each also written in that order of time, such appears to be the general assumption. It is natural and obvious; and it may indeed hold for the *Geta* (i.e. composed at once after the *Caracalla*).

---

[1] 'Nicomachus' evokes Nicomachus Flavianus, the paladin of the pagan cause; and the other two members of the name also suggest his period.   [2] R. Syme, o.c. 212.

[3] The relevance of the *Avidius* to the *Tacitus* was well brought out by Hohl, *Klio* xi (1911), 318 ff.

Otherwise, one might not be so sure. The manner of composition differs. In the one category, compilation and abridgement, a prosaic task. In the other, fluent discourse with much creative fantasy. In the received order, the biographies of four emperors separate the *Avidius* from *Pescennius Niger* and *Clodius Albinus*. But those products exhibit a strong family resemblance.

A doubt therefore arises, and the chance of another explanation. Perhaps the author, after compiling the *Vitae* down to Caracalla, added his *Geta* and then turned back to compose the other four, one after another. It will be necessary to see whether there are indications that conflict with the received order or show items in 'Nebenviten' taken from primary *Vitae* that now stand later in the sequence. The enterprise is delicate, but not to be evaded. Several items may now be put under inspection.

1. In the *Avidius* the author says of Marcus 'de Pertinace et Galba idem sentiebat' (8. 5). That will not do. Editors have recourse to excision.[1] Not the best explanation. Perhaps the author had already written the *Vita Pertinacis*. Otherwise, haste and inadvertence. The two names came to mind together, inevitably, as once again: 'eo genere quo Galba, quo Pertinax interemptus est' (*Claud.* 12. 5).

2. A letter of Marcus in the *Avidius* conveys the bogus character 'Caesonius Vectilianus' (5. 8). Why and whence the *cognomen*? Commodus was assassinated in the *domus Vectiliana* (*Comm.* 16. 3; *Pert.* 5. 7). That mansion is attested in the HA and it occurs in the standard tradition of late Antiquity.[2]

Perhaps the author had already narrated the assassination of Commodus, and so the *domus Vectiliana* stuck in his mind. A bogus character taking his name from an edifice, that seems too much. Stranger associations may operate when the HA invents nomenclature.[3]

3. The extraction of L. Verus is precisely reported—'avi ac proavi et item maiores plurimi consulares . . . origo eius paterna pleraque ex Etruria fuit, materna ex Faventia' (*Verus* 1. 8 f.). The first item indicates the Ceionii, the second the maternal grandfather C. Avidius Nigrinus (*suff.* 110). He was a friend of Hadrian and one of the four consulars executed for an alleged conspiracy in the first year of the reign: he was

---

[1] Thus both Peter and Hohl.

[2] For the *testimonia*, R. Helm, *Die gr. christ. Schriftsteller* XLVII (1956), 424; R. Hanslik, P–W VIII A. 1778 f. Jerome and Orosius have 'in domo Vestiliani,' which Hanslik is disposed to regard as the correct form, 'Vectilius' not being on attestation as a *nomen*.

[3] For example, the thought of a Gallic 'virago' produces 'Vituriga'—who changes her name to 'Samso' (*Quadr. tyr.* 12. 3).

killed at Faventia (*Hadr.* 7. 2). Now the *Vita* of Aelius Caesar, the father of Verus, says 'maiores omnes nobilissimi, quorum origo pleraque ex Etruria fuit vel ex Faventia' (*Ael.* 2. 8). On the face of things, that looks like a garbled version of the passage in the *Vita Veri*—although, to be sure, some might argue that both derive from a common source.

Furthermore, the *Vita Aelii* goes on to state that its author will in due course provide fuller details when he comes to narrate the life of L. Verus: 'et de huius quidem familia plenius . . . disseremus' (2. 9). At first sight that statement would be decisive for the priority of the *Aelius*. Yet it may merely reflect the author's awareness that the *Aelius* was to be inserted earlier in the series than the *Verus* (which had already been composed). Cross references in the HA deserve careful attention. A parallel can be adduced to support the above interpretation. The *Marcus* has a reference forward to the *Commodus* for the gladiatorial pursuits of that emperor—'ut in vita eius docebitur' (*Marcus* 19. 5). Natural enough, it should seem. But the reference in the *Marcus* is embedded in a chapter which betrays itself as an addition, on various criteria (including the invocation of Diocletian, 19. 12). Therefore perhaps a piece composed later than the *Vita Commodi*, and the forward reference is delusive.

Not much emerges, it must be confessed, to corroborate the notion that the 'Nebenviten' were written after the main series from Hadrian to Caracalla. However, another factor may be brought in, though it is by no means conclusive. It concerns cross references. The 'Nebenviten' have them, both to others of their category and to primary *Vitae*. But, apart from the indication about Geta in the *Vita Caracallae*, 'ut in vita eius exponemus' (11. 1), none of the primary *Vitae* to which a secondary biography is attached betrays awareness that anything of the kind is to follow. They carry no forward reference from a *Vita* to its pendant. That is suspicious. Were they closely linked by their time of writing, some such sign would be natural and even expedient. For example, the *Marcus* or the *Verus* might have alluded to the full treatment of Avidius Cassius soon to ensue; and the author of the *Vita Severi* could have explained that much more was going to be said about Pescennius Niger and Clodius Albinus, at once, before the *Caracalla*.

The argument is adduced, for what it may be worth. Another question now obtrudes, not wholly idle. Why were those products written at all? Introducing his *Geta* the author confesses that the Emperor Constantine and other readers may well ask 'cur etiam Geta Antoninus a me tradatur'. The reasons, as has been shown, are fraudulent. In epilogue on the biography of Aelius Caesar he proffered the justification for all the

'Nebenviten'—'meae satisfaciens conscientiae, etiamsi multis nulla sit necessitas talia exquirendi' (7. 5).

That is to say, he does it from a sense of duty. Which recalls a biographer's noble professions elsewhere. Further, there was no necessity to write those *Vitae*. The author himself makes the admission. How and why did the idea take shape? Is it an afterthought, or does it belong to the original design?

Coming to deal with Septimius Severus, a compiler of imperial biographies might wonder whether Niger or Albinus did not deserve separate treatment—the latter had in fact been associated in the power with Severus for the space of three years, bearing the title 'Caesar'. Again Geta, who was an 'Augustus'. The two pretenders might have carried his thoughts back to Avidius Cassius. Then the events of the year 217. Macrinus after his campaign against the Parthians conferred on his son the title of 'Caesar' and the name 'Antoninus'; and Diadumenianus became 'Augustus' shortly before the defeat of Macrinus in the next year.

However, on the face of things there was no great call to narrate either Niger or Albinus, unless a man happened to be interested in war and campaigns. Which is not the case with this author. Nor could Geta with ease or advantage be segregated from the context of father and brother: the execution of the *Vita Getae* shows it. And there was nothing new or true to be said about the heir of Hadrian.

There lies the clue. It was the author's ambition to outdo his predecessors both by the compass of his work and by the variety of his inventions. Hence, in the first instance, biographies that had not been attempted by *Ignotus* or by Marius Maximus. The thing could not be achieved without the lavish use of fiction. No drawback. That was his bent and delight. Creative writing, not compilation.[1]

The secondary *Vitae*, it appears, were not an afterthought. That they were composed subsequent to the compilation of the 'Nine *Vitae*' may not quite be susceptible of proof. None the less, the notion was worth canvassing; and it may happen to accord with a larger hypothesis about the stages by which both categories acquired their present shape and order.

VIII. *Genesis and revision of the primary* Vitae

The basic text and structure can be disengaged. It had been subjected to two contrary operations: abridgement and expansion. The source, it is

[1] That is to say, the primary *Vitae* from Hadrian to Caracalla (which historians must study) were the secondary concern of the author.

clear, was too long for the purposes of the compiler. He curtails drastically, even where the matter ought to have carried some appeal to the reader. For example, when both Hadrian and Severus are brought to Egypt. To the brief account of Severus' visit is appended the remark 'quoniam longum est minora persequi' (*Sev.* 17. 5). It serves to introduce a summary of the whole reign, taken from a shorter source (17. 5–19. 4).

That is significant. Dessau here detected a piece of Aurelius Victor, woven into the account. Few will now care to dispute. Dessau also pointed to a parallel phenomenon in the *Vita Marci* (16. 3–18. 1). This time, Eutropius. Mommsen concurred in both discoveries. But not everybody accepted Eutropius. There was a way out. The passage might go back to the common source of Victor and Eutropius. That is to say, the 'Kaisergeschichte' postulated by Enmann in 1884. His KG must stand, for all that some play it down or even deny its use by the HA. For present purposes it need not matter.

The basic source (i.e. *Ignotus*) was too long. It had a second defect, being sober and factual, as is shown by texts that have not been much tampered with, such as the *Pius* and the *Didius Julianus*. Marius Maximus offered remedial aid. The consular biographer, while presenting facts of value (and even documents), was addicted to scandalous revelations about the Antonine dynasty.

From these sources therefore the abridged *Ignotus* was both enlarged and enlivened. The problem becomes complex. First, material from Marius Maximus was transmitted to Victor and Eutropius by the channel of Enmann's KG. Second, it is not at all clear how much was added at this stage, how much accrued later, on the revision of the 'Nine *Vitae*'. Third, compilation and the first additions: one operation or two? For simplicity and convenience, let them be supposed to be more or less simultaneous.

Next, the five secondary *Vitae*. As has been suggested above, they were composed after the series of the primary *Vitae* down to Caracalla.[1] When not inventing, they drew both on the 'Nine *Vitae*' and on their sources. Notably Marius Maximus. For example, what the *Vita Hadriani* reports about Hadrian's skill in astrology and the 'tetrafarmacum' (16. 7; 21. 4) is expressly attributed to Maximus in the *Aelius* (3. 9; 5. 4) and Maximus mentioned Severus' intention of naming Niger and Albinus as his successors (*Clod. Alb.* 3. 4 f., and, anonymous, *Pesc.* 4. 7).

Finally, the revision of the 'Nine *Vitae*'. It may have been largely

---

[1] They might, it is true, fall even a little later. That is, after the series *Macrinus–Alexander*. Cf. above, p. 64, n. 1.

inspired by the 'Nebenviten', the influence of which can be detected. And more material is brought in from sources already employed. Select and summary examples may be cited.

1. Invocations of an emperor. Present in each of the 'Nebenviten', but in three only of the 'Nine *Vitae*'. Each time Diocletian is invoked, in late and bad passages (*Marcus* 19. 12; *Verus* 11. 2; *Sev.* 20. 4).

2. An oracle in the form of Virgilian verses has been added to the *Vita Hadriani* (2. 8). On that follows the reference to an oracular response 'ex fano Niceforii Iovis'. It is reported on the authority of 'Apollonius Syrus Platonicus' (2. 9). No evidence attests this type of activity at the shrine, or the existence of 'Apollonius'. The whole context is suspect. The author had begun merely by quoting Virgil. The oracles are a later refinement, first emerging in the *Vita Pescennii* (8. 3; 6).

3. The story that Verus was poisoned. Obscurely alluded to in the *Vita Veri* (10. 2) with a cross-reference to the *Marcus* (i.e. 15. 5), it now becomes explicit in the appendage (*Verus* 11. 2).

4. The appendage to the *Marcus*, obviously (29); also the chapter of scandal (19), proceeding to the invocation of Diocletian (19. 12); further, most of the latter part of the *Vita Caracallae* (8. 1–11. 7). Perhaps it seemed that the abbreviation of the *Caracalla* had been overdone.

5. Some names in the *Vita Severi*. The list of forty-one senators put to death by Severus (13. 1–7) contains suspicious names. Observe 'Ceionius Albinus'. He derives from the faked Ceionian ancestry (*Clod. Alb.* 4. 1 f.), which also produced the pretender's father 'Ceionius Postumus'. And there will be no confidence in a run of six Pescennii, ending with nothing less than a 'Pescennius Albinus'. Another passage serves up a 'Clodius Celsinus', described as 'Adrumetinus et adfinis Albini' (11. 3). He spoke for Albinus in the Senate, incurring the anger of the Emperor. Incident and person are a figment.

6. The rubbishy chapter in the *Severus*, introduced by 'legisse me memini apud Helium Maurum Phlegontis Hadriani libertum', etc. (20. 1). This fellow is the first (and last) invented 'authority' to occur in the 'Nine *Vitae*'. There follows a long and tedious declaration about hereditary succession, with invocation of Diocletian; and, before the end, a reference to Micipsa's 'divina oratio' in Sallust.[1]

So far, a brief statement of the case. As concerns the 'Nine *Vitae*', three stages might in theory be defined: compilation, additions, revision. It is

---

[1] *Sev.* 21. 10, cf. 23. 4. On which, see J. Straub, *Bonner Historia-Augusta-Colloquium 1963* (1964), 171 ff.

simplest to combine the first two and regard them as one operation. In any event, for a *Vita* like the *Pius*, which has few accretions, no more than two operations need to be postulated.

Further questions now come in. First, and subsidiary. Is the abbreviator of *Ignotus* the same person as the creative author of the 'Nebenviten'— and of the rest of the collection? The master-hand might have employed secretarial aid for the crude work of compiling. That notion is admissible. It does not do much harm—or good.[1] Nor does it entail belief in a plurality of authorship or anything that deserves the name of collaboration.[2]

Second, the stages of composition as indicated above. There is no logical necessity to postulate any great intervals of time. The first act of compilation was hasty and impatient, likewise the revision.

A hypothesis has been presented, in outline. It is reduced, for convenience, to the most simple terms. Perhaps too simple, given the messy condition of most of the 'Nine *Vitae*'. The advocate of a general hypothesis can hardly expect to gain ready assent, since in the past so many elaborate constructions have foundered. It would be a temptation to give up, leaving the HA as 'a question above antiquarism, not to be resolved by man, nor easily perhaps by spirits'.

IX. *Labels of authorship*

There remains one artifice of a different dimension: the pseudonyms attached to the biographies. It is a matter which in this late season has little more than an antiquarian interest, for it belongs to sad and early episodes in the 'history of the problem'.

Having exercised his talents in the secondary *Vitae* (and revised the whole product) the author could proceed to another series of biographies. The preface of the *Macrinus* declares a new turn. Also a grave scholar's dedication to 'digna memoratu' and distaste for petty detail, with castigation of 'Junius Cordus'. It was now, or perhaps a little further on, that the impostor's fancy for bogus names, combining with his delight in any manner of deception, engendered a novel device. He would pass himself off as a plurality.

The fourteen *Vitae* (both categories together) are labelled with the names of four authors. Aelius Spartianus takes seven for his portion, Julius Capitolinus five, while Vulcatius Gallicanus and Aelius Lampridius have one each. There is no point in specifying. Then, Gallicanus

---

[1] R. Syme, o.c. 182.
[2] And in fact no one of the 'six' asserts that he is writing in concert with any of the others. The notion of their collaboration (e.g. Baynes, o.c. 147) is a modern assumption or expedient.

and Spartianus having fallen out, Capitolinus writes the *Macrinus*, Lampridius the next three (the biographies of Diadumenianus, Elagabalus, and Severus Alexander). Capitolinus takes up the tale again with *Maximini Duo*, and at a later stage two fresh names emerge, Trebellius Pollio and Flavius Vopiscus, carrying in succession the collection to its term with Carus and his sons.

So far so good. Unfortunately, label and book are not always in accord. A biographer may fail to get the appropriate *Vita* to which his previous performances entitled him; and attributions clash with evidence in the text. Two instances may suffice. Capitolinus proposes to write the *Commodus*, reasonably enough (*Marcus* 19. 4): Lampridius does it. Spartianus intends to deal with Clodius Albinus (*Pesc.* 9. 3): that biography bears the label of Capitolinus, who thinks that he has written the *Pescennius* (*Clod. Alb.* 1. 4).

The conclusion is clear. The labels are an afterthought, and were casually attached. Therefore to be discarded. Yet, like other fabrications, these four pseudonyms might repay scrutiny. Writers of fiction in any age tend to select names that are either very common or very rare. The former disarm suspicion, the latter insinuate authenticity. The HA duly conforms. *Nomina* like 'Aelius' and 'Junius' appeal. Of the eleven Aelii, all are spurious or suspect, even 'Aelius Celsus' in the list of senators put to death by Severus (*Sev.* 13. 2). Likewise nine of the eleven Junii.[1]

Two of the first four pseudonyms are Aelii, viz. Spartianus and Lampridius. Now the archetypal bad biographer 'Junius Cordus' first appears in the guise of 'Aelius Cordus' (*Clod. Alb.* 5. 10). An 'Aelius Corduenus' had been registered a little earlier in a letter of Commodus (*Pesc.* 4. 4). 'Corduenus' happens to lack other attestation as a *cognomen*. 'Cordus' would be familiar to a reader of Juvenal—at least it comes in the opening lines (1. 2).

As for Aelius Lampridius, observe 'Lampridia' not far away, the mother of Niger (*Pesc.* 1. 3). That name is rare and striking. It is first attested about the year 400, borne by a senator.[2]

The name of Julius Capitolinus carries no clues. The other, Vulcatius Gallicanus, is styled 'v(ir) c(larissimus)'. He enjoys a double distinction. The only one to bear a title of rank and be allocated a single biography (the *Avidius Cassius*). The name recurs once in the HA with an alleged historian, 'Vulcatius Terentianus' (*Gord.* 21. 5), but the *cognomen* is

---

[1] R. Syme, o.c. 166 f.

[2] *CIL* III. 14239 (Salonae). It is next on show with an orator and poet named by Sidonius (VIII. 11. 3, etc.).

a favourite. Three of the four instances belong to patently spurious characters, viz. 'Moesius Gallicanus' (*Tac.* 8. 3) and 'Mulvius Gallicanus' (*Prob.* 4. 3), both Guard Prefects, and that delightful old man 'Turdulus Gallicanus'. This 'vir honestissimus ac sincerissimus' had composed a memoir of much service to his friend the author (*Prob.* 2. 2).

As has been noted, the deleterious 'Cordus', introduced as an 'Aelius' (*Clod. Alb.* 5. 10), becomes a 'Junius' in the preface of the *Vita Macrini*.[1] The author forgot. In the present order, *Macrinus* comes not long after *Pescennius*. But in the interval of time fell the revision of the primary *Vitae*, so it may be conjectured. In the sequel, Cordus reverts to 'Aelius', once only (*Maximin.* 12. 7), quickly becoming a 'Junius' again (27. 7; *Gord.* 12. 1, etc.).

Uncertainty about the nomenclature of a character, even if he is of some importance, that is one of the normal hazards of prose fiction.[2] But the casual fashion in which the author-labels have been attached is hard to parallel. The phenomenon extends to the next four biographies as well, although they form a clearly-defined unit. Capitolinus has the *Macrinus*; but the son of Macrinus, Elagabalus, and Severus Alexander are the work of Lampridius; and Lampridius assumes that he has written the *Macrinus* (*Diad.* 6. 1). The notion of affixing the labels may therefore have come to the author a little later than the inception of the *Macrinus*. Which does not matter at all.

x. *Epilogue*

Like the invocation of emperors, the labels of the 'six biographers' in the HA are only a trick. That was at once evident to Dessau. Few were willing to follow. Desperate attempts ensued to save and vindicate those precious authentications. To bring them into line and establish some credible order of authorship and writing much effort was needed—and juggling with the attributions. Hence theories of intolerable elaboration.[3]

However, 'hoc artificium periit.' For those who accorded credence to the miracle of the Thundering Legion Gibbon could devise no worse

[1] It is assumed in this paper that the *Clodius Albinus* is later than the *Caracalla* but earlier than *Macrinus*. But it is still open to argue that the five 'Nebenviten' were composed after the *Vita* of Severus Alexander, cf. above, p. 71, n. 1. In that case the 'Junius Cordus' in the exordium of the *Macrinus* would be prior to 'Aelius Cordus' in the *Clodius Albinus*.

[2] Readers of Proust will recall the uncertainty about M. Verdurin: was he 'Gustave' or 'Auguste'? Nobody invokes the type of remedy which is implicit in the entry 'Aelius Junius Cordus' in *PIR*², A 198.

[3] Thus Peter, o.c. 49. In his theory, the *Vitae* were composed at different times, beginning in the reign of Diocletian; and, towards 330, one of the biographers, 'Capitolinus', reverts to authorship and edits the collection. Similarly Lécrivain, o.c. 27; 395 ff.

fate than that they should also believe in the Thebaean Legion; and if anyone still clings to the 'six biographers' (or a selection of them) he may be recommended to accept 'Junius Cordus'.[1] As has been stated more than once, the fabrications furnish the clue to author and authorship. Enough is already on show in the secondary *Vitae*.[2]

The education, habits, and tastes of the impostor are disclosed. He was a kind of rogue scholiast. As he went on, he got bolder and better, ending with elegant parody of erudition and polite letters. Whereas in the *Macrinus* he was content to defend good biography against bad, towards the end he comes out with an attack on history and the high style. 'Eloquentia' is one thing, truth another. To get the truth, you must apply to biographers, who write 'non tam diserte quam vere' (*Prob.* 2. 7). That is an audacious posture. It may have a reason and a meaning—perhaps evoked by a work of abnormal pretensions. That is, the History of Ammianus Marcellinus.[3]

Facts and documents therefore, not style. Impressed by the parade of documentation in 'Flavius Vopiscus', Ranke saw a genuine researcher— 'er ist seiner Natur nach ein Forscher'.[4] Scholars in later ages have dubbed him a 'Fälscher'. The label lacks amenity. And some find it inadequate. How far did the ingenious contriver hope to deceive—or even intend? The thing is a hoax.[5]

In the *Vita Aureliani* the mask is lifted for a moment. In epilogue on amicable discourse about history and biography, the Prefect of the City bids 'Vopiscus' be of good cheer. He shall write as he pleases; he will have as companions in mendacity the classic models of 'historica eloquentia' (*Aur.* 2. 3). The author needed no encouragement in the art. He had rebuked 'Junius Cordus' for 'mythistoriae' (*Macr.* 1. 5); and towards the end he accuses Marius Maximus of composing 'mythistorica volumina' (*Quadr. tyr.* 1. 2). The collocation is instructive.[6] He was writing romance himself.

[1] 'Cordus', accepted by Peter and by Klebs, still finds champions. Among them, E. K. Rand in *CAH* xii (1939), 599; E. Manni, *L'impero di Gallieno* (1949), 112; H. Bardon, *La Littérature latine inconnue* ii (1956), 273; A. Bellezza, *Massimino il Trace* (1964), 35; S. Mazzarino, *Il pensiero storico classico* ii. 2 (1966), 224, cf. 285.

[2] The common features of the 'six' all through and the arguments against plurality of authorship have recently been catalogued, at some length, by P. White, *JRS* lvii (1967), 115 ff.

[3] R. Syme, o.c. 103.

[4] Cited by Hohl, *Bursians Jahresberichte* cclvi (1937), 139.

[5] As Dessau declared, 'eine Mystification liegt vor' (*Hermes* xxiv (1889), 392). After the long years of controversy (much of it misguided and sterile) Dessau's main contentions emerge unimpaired.

[6] Neither word occurs in any other Latin author (according to the *schedae* of TLL).

The epoch of Symmachus and Jerome witnessed the rediscovery of forgotten texts and a renascence of Latin letters. Season and society at Rome fostered fraud and imposture as well as erudition. Combining both, the author of the great hoax concords with his time. He is also a comic writer. The notion may come as a surprise and a strain on belief. One can see Symmachus, for example, in the role of a scholiast: he was an editor of classical texts. But Symmachus would not have warmed to the fun in the game. Jerome, however, had in him the makings of a great humorist, though not of the kindly sort: scholarship, satire and invective, a gift for inventions, and no kind of scruple.

V · THE *NOMEN ANTONINORUM*

'DURING A HAPPY PERIOD of more than fourscore years the public administration was conducted by the virtue and abilities of Nerva, Trajan, Hadrian, and the two Antonines.' Thus Gibbon, in his opening paragraph. The terminal point was unavoidable. With the death of Marcus, the age turned to rust and iron, so Cassius Dio declared.[1]

Historians in the recent time, under other influences and preoccupations, extend the felicitous years to cover Septimius Severus and his son Antoninus Caracalla. For Mommsen it was a question 'whether the domain ruled by Severus Antoninus was governed with the greater intelligence and the greater humanity at that time or in the present day'.[2] And further, beyond Caracalla. Though Severus Alexander dispensed with the appellation 'Antoninus', the 'Antonine Monarchy' can be carried forward as far as 235, for convenience and utility.[3]

1. The *cognomen* 'Antoninus' had a paradoxical destiny. Aristocrats often show a predilection for nomenclature from the maternal side of the family. Examples abound.[4] T. Aurelius Fulvus (*cos.* 120), who, after the decease of father and grandfather, had been brought up in the household of old Arrius Antoninus, duly inherited the name (along with a part at least of the ample fortune). An inscription dated by his consulship reveals it.[5] Indeed, on tiles of the year 134, he is merely styled 'Arrius Antoninus'.[6]

When adopted by Hadrian, he dropped the *gentilicium* but retained the *cognomen*, which, when he died, passed to his heir. So the young Marcus, originally an Annius Verus, but M. Aelius Aurelius Verus when the adoptive son of Pius, changed his name on his accession to M. Aurelius

---

[1] Dio LXXI. 36. 4.

[2] Mommsen, *The Provinces of the Roman Empire* I (1886), 5.

[3] M. Hammond, *The Antonine Monarchy* (1959).

[4] Thus C. Ummidius Quadratus (*suff.* 118), the grandson of Ummidia Quadratilla (Pliny, *Epp.* VII. 24). Testamentary adoption is not the sole or necessary explanation. For this case, and for parallels, cf. *Historia* XVII (1968), 83 f.

[5] *CIL* VIII. 8239. For 'Boionius' as a part of his nomenclature (not on official record), see above, p. 37.

[6] *CIL* XV. 32; 92 f.; X. 8043³². On XV. 94 he is 'Ful(vus) Ant(oninus)', on XV. 95 'Antoninus' only.

Antoninus. Marcus, repairing an injustice, associated with himself in the power L. Aelius Aurelius Commodus, i.e. the son of Aelius Caesar (the ill-starred Ceionius Commodus whom Hadrian had designed to succeed him). Marcus transferred his own original *cognomen* 'Verus' to his partner, who is henceforth styled 'L. Aurelius Verus'. That person, it is important to note, was not an Antoninus. Marcus was holding the *cognomen* in reserve for a son, or sons, of his own. It was in fact given to the twin brother of Commodus, born on August 31, 161, but dying at the age of four (*Comm.* 1. 2 ff.). In the event, Commodus himself, though sharing the supreme power from the end of 176, and soon after 'Augustus', had to wait until the death of Marcus.

'Antoninus' had become a potent name. The usurper Septimius Severus was anxious to attach himself to the dynasty. Various devices availed. As early as 195 he annexed Marcus and all the imperial titulature back to Nerva, styling himself 'divi Marci filius, divi Commodi frater'. And in the next year, making his elder son a Caesar, Severus conferred on him the name 'M. Aurelius Antoninus'.

The process goes on. After the murder of Caracalla in 217, Macrinus, taking 'Severus' for his own *cognomen*, honours his son Diadumenianus with 'Antoninus'. Then comes Elagabalus, passed off as a son of Caracalla. He takes the name from the outset. Hence six Antonini, but no more thereafter: the cousin, Severus Alexander, though likewise a 'son' of Caracalla, does not bear the dynastic name. Only a pair of usurpers testify: the shadowy Antoninus, insurgent in Syria against Severus Alexander, and (more tangible through coins) the man who proclaimed himself emperor in 248 or soon after: L. Julius Aurelius Sulpicius Uranius Antoninus.[1]

11. Accident sometimes creates for historians or biographers a subject of ideal compass. Writing under Severus Alexander, the consular Marius Maximus found that he had twelve Caesars precisely for his portion, if he left out Verus (though Verus had been an 'Augustus' for eight years). The rulers of the high Antonine prime, the transference of the power to unworthy sons, and the decline of dynasties, that was the given theme, terminating with Elagabalus. As Ausonius exclaims,

> tune etiam Augustae sedis penetralia foedas
> Antoninorum nomina falsa gerens?[2]

---

[1] For the well-attested pretender *c.* 248, see *PIR*[2], J 195. The evidence about the usurper (or usurpers) in the time of Severus Alexander is confused and conflicting. See G. Barbieri, *L'albo senatorio da Settimio Severo a Carino* (1952), 400.

[2] Ausonius, *De Caesaribus* 97 f.

Elagabalus was not only the spurious Antoninus who defiled the consecrated name. By dramatic convenience, he was the last ruler to bear it. One may compare the HA: 'hic finis Antoninorum nomini in re p. fuit, scientibus cunctis istum Antoninum tam vita falsum fuisse quam nomine' (*Elag.* 33. 8).

Elsewhere the author in four places designates Elagabalus as 'ultimus Antoninorum' (*Macr.* 7. 8; *Elag.* 1. 7; 18. 1; 34. 6). The label was obvious enough, yet he might have taken it from Marius Maximus.

That biographer, as various signs indicate, was not the basic text of the nine *Vitae* of emperors from Hadrian to Caracalla inclusive. A writer of a different order has to be postulated, the *Ignotus*. None the less, the HA may have drawn on him for Elagabalus, notably the full and accurate account of his last days (*Elag.* 13–17).[1] What other Latin source availed?

There was the 'Kaisergeschichte' which Enmann detected long ago as the common source of Victor and Eutropius (also, be it noted, of the *Epitome* of Pseudo-Victor). The KG itself, however, was a brief and scrappy compilation.

III. Epitomators are prone to error and confusion. The KG can furnish palmary specimens, exhibiting the scarcity of exact historical knowledge.[2] Variants or changes in dynastic names are a fruitful source of misconceptions among the unscholarly in any age. The treatment of L. Verus furnishes melancholy instruction. Victor happens to be correct, but the *Epitome* styles him 'Annius Verus' (*Epit.* 16. 5). For Eutropius, he is 'L. Annius Antoninus Verus' (VIII. 9. 1), then 'Verus Annius Antoninus' and 'Verus Antoninus' (10. 2 f.).

The HA follows suit. L. Verus is twice introduced as 'Annius Verus' (*Hadr.* 24. 1; *Pius* 6. 10). Further, he is styled 'Antoninus' a dozen times. That is not all. The author suitably imports an aberration all his own. If L. Verus was an Annius Verus, what about his parent, L. Aelius Caesar? The author in twenty places assigns him 'Verus' for *cognomen*. Which has not misled most students of the HA.[3]

The author had a precedent for enrolling L. Verus among the 'Antonini', namely the KG (as extant in Eutropius). It was welcome, and it fitted general fantasies about the *nomen* which he developed later on. Further, he invents another of them, Geta. Hence the explicit catalogue of eight, ending with 'octavus Heliogabalus' (*Macr.* 3. 4).

---

[1] Below, p. 121.   [2] Below, pp. 231 f.

[3] For the detail, *PIR*[2], C 605. The fraudulent 'Verus' attached to Hadrian's heir was exploited by Carcopino, illicitly. See above, p. 19.

IV. Addressing the Emperor Constantine, the author concedes that he and many others may well wonder why a Life of Geta is being offered; and, as a preliminary, he expounds (at some length) the reasons which induced Severus to confer the name 'Antoninus' on his second son (*Geta* I. I–2. 5).

To Severus it was revealed in a dream that an Antoninus would succeed him. Without delay therefore, he made Bassianus an Antoninus; and further, on a parent's thought or wifely admonition, he did the same for Geta. But there was a second reason. Severus was a devoted admirer of the philosophic emperor whom he always called his father or his brother (2. 2); and it was his design that all rulers in the sequel should be Antonini.[1] But again, 'dicunt aliqui', he wished to honour Pius rather than Marcus, for Pius, appointing him *advocatus fisci*, opened up the 'primi gradus vel honoris auspicium' (2. 4).

That silly fabrication, by the way, happens to be highly instructive on several counts. Only Victor (20. 30) and Eutropius (VIII. 18. 2) have the detail that Severus held the post of *advocatus fisci*. Victor, registering his devotion to the memory of Marcus, states that he assigned to Caracalla for that reason the dynastic name: 'Bassianoque Antonini vocabulum ad-diderit, quod ex illo post multos dubiosque eventus auspicia honorum cepisset patrocinio fisci' (20. 30). The derivation of the one passage from the other is patent: 'auspicia honorum' (Victor is a stylist) giving 'honoris auspicium'. Likewise the manner of the impostor—total inadvertence, or rather a wilful perversion.[2]

In fact, he was not at the end of his tricks. A little later in erudite disquisition on the early career of Macrinus, he invents corroborative detail 'advocatum fisci factum sub Vero Antonino' (*Macr.* 4. 4). That is impossible. What then is to be done? Some scholars keep the post but change the identity of the emperor who appointed Macrinus.[3] Which is not legitimate. The item recalls, and perhaps derives from, the fable in the *Geta* that Severus held the office under Antoninus Pius (*Geta* 2. 4).

The author artfully casts doubt upon his own invention—'sed et haec dubia ponuntur, et alia dicuntur ab aliis.' He then goes on to turn out some scholarly variations about the pursuits of Macrinus (4. 5 f.). The post of *advocatus fisci* occurs again—but the context damns it, alleging that Macrinus had previously been a gladiator, a huntsman in Africa, and a courier.[4]

---

[1] *Sev.* 19. 2 f.
[2] For the not infrequent traces of Victor in the HA see now A. Chastagnol, *Rev. phil.* XLI (1967), 85 ff.   [3] Thus H. v. Petrikovits, P-W XVIII. 543.   [4] Above, p. 50.

Severus had been an *advocatus fisci*, according to the KG (as transmitted by Victor and by Eutropius). Barely possible.[1] The low-born Macrinus was a better candidate for this minor equestrian post. But the notice in the HA belongs to the category of things which might happen to be true but are not authentic.

To return to the *Vita Getae*. It carries some more elaborations on the Antonine name: an omen 'in villa cuiusdam Antonini, plebei hominis' (3. 5), and another, a village priest of the name conducting a sacrifice on Geta's birthday (3. 8). But the author characteristically slips in a note of dubitation about Geta as an Antoninus—'Antonini, ut quidam dicunt, nomen accepit' (5. 3).

Finally, the insertions in the *Vita Severi*. Two of them brief (10. 5; 16. 14). Then once again (19. 2), after the large piece incorporated from Aurelius Victor (17. 5–19. 1). It is followed by the allegation that Severus, from reverence towards Marcus, wanted all subsequent emperors to be called 'Antoninus' (cf. *Geta* 2. 3). Next, the notorious 'bad passage' introduced on the authority of 'Helius Maurus, Phlegontis Hadriani libertus' (20 f.), and containing an invocation of Diocletian. Severus (it is averred) felt happy when close to the end because, like Antoninus Pius, he was bequeathing the empire to a pair of Antonini. And, to conclude, the dying words of the old Emperor (with an echo of Sallust): 'firmum imperium Antoninis meis relinquens, si boni erunt, inbecillum, si mali' (23. 3).[2]

The *Caracalla* also betrays intrusions on this theme, but only two. It opens with the reference to the pair of Antonini, 'quorum unum Antoninum exercitus, alterum pater dixit' (1. 1). And, in an added passage, there is a reference to the 'concordia fratrum Antoninorum' (8. 3).

v. The *Vita Macrini* offers rich disquisition on the *nomen Antoninorum*. Why should his son have been given the name? As the author admits, 'mirum omnibus fortasse videatur' (2. 5). He can give a reason, namely a transaction which was related in 'annales'. When a proconsul under Antoninus Pius consulted the priestess of Caelestis at Carthage, she uttered the name of Antoninus eight times (3. 1).[3] The destined length in years of the ruler's reign, so the vulgar opined. The event disclosed that something different was portended, which the author expounds in his catalogue

---

[1] It has often been accepted, cf. M. Fluss, P–W II A. 1944. Dessau had uttered the proper warning, *PIR*[1], S 346: the item is in the *Geta*, not in the *Severus*. See now T. D. Barnes, *Historia* XVI (1967), 91 f.

[2] On this item cf. J. Straub, *Bonner Historia-Augusta-Colloquium 1963* (1964), 171 f.

[3] For other bogus 'vaticinationes' at this shrine cf. *Pert.* 4. 2.

of the eight Antonini. He subjoins annotation. The 'duo Gordiani' should not be reckoned in the total, on various grounds (3. 5). But he alleges that Severus called himself 'Antoninus', as did a number of other rulers such as Pertinax and Didius Julianus; also Macrinus.[1] The author winds up with emphasis on the 'desiderium' which the name evoked among the people and the soldiers after the murder of Antoninus Caracalla (3. 9).

A pair of contrasting devices reinforces the theme. First, the author reproduces the dispatch which Macrinus and his son sent to the Roman Senate. Second, he refers to the verses of an anonymous poet which showed that the 'Antonini nomen' took its origin from Pius, but suffered a sad degeneration, 'usque ad sordes ultimas' (7. 7). He registers the rulers who bore it (Verus is admitted, but not Geta) and he concludes,

postremo etiam quid de Heliogabalo, qui Antoninorum ultimus in summa impuritate vixisse memoratur?

Curiosity may be aroused. 'Versus extant cuiusdam poetae.' When the HA cites an anonymous author, suspicion is enjoined as much as when it names a source. And the word 'extant' is almost a guarantee of fraud. Compare the Greek epigram (a translation is given) in honour of Pescennius Niger, not obliterated by the victor (*Pesc.* 12. 5 ff.), or the literary productions, prose and verse, of the younger Gordian (*Gord.* 20. 6). None the less, the alert reader will recall that somebody existed who wrote poems about the Antonine rulers, ending with Elagabalus: that is, Ausonius.[2] His verse quatrains (such is the plausible conjecture) are indirect testimony to the *Twelve Caesars* of Marius Maximus.

Similar topics and fantasies continue in the *Vita* of Macrinus' son. At some length. The author had to fill up space. Macrinus, apprehensive because 'multi ex affinitatibus Antonini Pii erant inter duces' (1. 3), delivers a stirring 'contio' to the troops, with appeal to the *nomen*. They respond with suitable acclamations, and Diadumenianus addresses them —'scio enim me Pii, me Marci, me Veri suscepisse nomen' (2. 3). Other fabrications follow. It will be enough to cite the edict of Macrinus destined for the Roman populace: 'vellem, Quirites, iam praesentes essemus: Antoninus vester vobis congiarium sui nominis daret. incideret praeterea et pueros Antoninianos et puellas Antoninianas, quae tam grati nominis gloriam propagarent' (2. 10).

Further, the prediction of an astrologer, inspired by the horoscope of the prince which by the day and the hour coincided with that of

---

[1] *Macr.* 3. 6, cf. *Diad.* 6. 3.
[2] As pointed out by T. D. Barnes, *JRS* LVII (1967), 70.

Antoninus Pius (5. 4). Also on the same particular, a woman's prophecy, 'Antoninus vocetur' (5. 5).

The author states that he would not have contributed a separate biography of Diadumenianus but for the compulsion of the 'Antoninorum nomen' (6. 1). He goes on to exemplify its significance—'unde etiam quidam et Severum et Pertinacem et Iulianum Antoninorum praenominibus honorandos putant' (6. 3). He mentions an opinion about the two Gordians, and he promulgates a distinction between 'nomen' and 'praenomen'. There follow remarks about rulers who were genuinely 'Antonini', among them Verus and Geta, vindicating the latter, 'quem multi Antoninum negant dictum' (6. 9).

To conclude, the author subjoins a letter from Macrinus to his wife 'Nonia Celsa'. Macrinus is ecstatic. They have become parents of an Antoninus—'o nos beatos, o fortunatam domum, praeclaram laudem nunc demum felicis imperii' (7. 6).

Enough, and more than enough. The theme recurs in the *Elagabalus*, there is a long rigmarole in the *Alexander*, when the prince rejects the name which the Senate offers (*Alex.* 6–11). In epilogue, the Gordiani, who are mentioned several times in this connection.[1] The author now tries to make out that their family name was not 'Antonius' but 'Antoninus'.[2] It is a subsidiary element in his design (more ingenious devices contribute) of investing old Gordian with the paraphernalia of an ideal Antonine ruler, from ancestry and named relations down to personal and polite accomplishments. After that exhibition, the theme suffers total eclipse.[3]

VI. The author's extravagant play with 'Antonini' and the 'nomen Antoninorum' could not fail to engage the attention of scholars long since.[4] Various aspects invite study. For example, 'Antoninus' is only once described as a 'cognomen' (*Gord.* 17. 2). But it is also a 'signum' (4. 8). Furthermore two disquisitions about its function as a *praenomen*, the 'duo Gordiani' being dragged in (*Macr.* 3. 5; *Diad.* 6. 3 ff.). That notion reflects changes that Roman nomenclature had suffered through the ages.

---

[1] As 'duo Gordiani' in *Macr.* 3. 5; *Diad.* 6. 3. A little later the author styles them 'duos Gordianos . . . patrem et filium' (*Elag.* 34. 6). At this stage he had not realized that there were three of them, not two (cf. *Gord.* 2. 1). That is, he assumed Gordian III to be the son of Gordian I, as did Victor (27. 1) and Eutropius (IX. 2. 1 f.).

[2] As later in *Elag.* 18. 1; 34. 6; *Gord.* 4. 7 f.; 9. 5; 17. 2.

[3] Below, pp. 101; 168 f.

[4] First diagnosed by G. Tropea, *Rivista di storia antica* IV (1899), 233 ff. See further W. Hartke, *Römische Kinderkaiser* (1951), 123 ff.; 133 ff.

A passage in Ammianus is instructive, when he adverts on ostentatious *praenomina* in the aristocracy, with a most peculiar list of examples.[1]

The main question is this: why should the HA devote to the 'nomen' so much space and repetition. Baynes had an explanation.[2] It concorded with his theory that the figure of Severus Alexander stood for Julian. The Apostate had a notorious predilection for Marcus Aurelius. That explanation was far too narrow—and it was highly vulnerable. Marcus occurs three times in the *Vita Alexandri*, never by himself: merely as a name, not as a person.[3] The significant entries are Trajan and Alexander the Macedonian.[4] As so often, the attempt to discover a serious purpose of propaganda behind the HA leads to aberrance and obscures the understanding of the work as a whole.

The name of the Antonines (that is, Pius and Marcus in the first instance) had a general relevance, for it symbolized good emperors. Moreover, in a second sequence after the death of Commodus it remained a name of power down to Elagabalus. Which (it may be presumed) struck the author as he advanced in his historical reading—and soon incited him to embark on fictitious elaborations, in his fashion.

VII. It will be expedient to look for the genesis of his obsession. To that end, the distribution of references in the different portions of the biographies down to that of Severus Alexander must be kept in mind. The *Vitae* divide into several categories. The cut comes before the *Macrinus*. Up to that point the author had been compiling a sober biographical source, the *Ignotus*: it ran out with Caracalla. Hence the nine 'primary *Vitae*' of emperors.[5] Separate account must be taken of the five 'secondary *Vitae*': two princes (Aelius Caesar and Geta), and the three pretenders. Finally, the four *Vitae* from Macrinus to Alexander clearly belong together.

There is a proliferation of verbiage about the *nomen Antonini* in the *Macrinus* as in the *Geta*. The two products betray kinship.[6] But there is no need to pursue that topic. Precise enlightenment may emerge from one historical item: Macrinus' assigning of the name 'Antoninus' to his son. In several *Vitae* the reason is stated: the passionate yearning for the name among the soldiers after the murder of Antoninus Caracalla.

The phraseology is almost identical. The inspiration seems to come from a single source, Aurelius Victor or the KG. As Victor says 'eo quod ingens

---

[1] Ammianus XXVIII. 4, 7, on which cf. *Ammianus and the Historia Augusta* (1968), 150 f.
[2] N. H. Baynes, *The Historia Augusta. Its Date and Purpose* (1926), 93 f.
[3] *Alex.* 7. 3; 9. 1; 10. 5.   [4] Below, Ch. VI.   [5] Above, Ch. III.
[6] As in the two items about 'advocatus fisci' discussed above.

amissi principis desiderium erat, adolescentem Antoninum vocavere' (22. 2). There happens to be no trace of the phrase or the name in Eutropius and the *Epitome* (both extremely compressed at this point).

Observe the HA. First, in the *Caracalla*, 'idcirco quod a praetorianis multum Antoninus desideratus est' (8. 10). Then 'tantum desiderium nominis huius' (*Macr.* 3. 9); 'ingens maeror' (*Diad.* 1. 21); 'ingens desiderium' (*Diad.* 6. 10; *Elag.* 3. 1).[1]

The first of these passages stands a little apart. It occurs in one of the nine primary *Vitae*—but it does not belong to the original source. It comes at the end of what is patently an addition (7. 1–8. 10).[2]

The motive 'ingens desiderium' is of some interest. It indicates a source. More than that, it may have a bearing upon the order of composition in this section of the HA. A pair of related operations can be detected, viz. the writing of the five 'Nebenviten' and a revision of the nine *Vitae* (Hadrian to Caracalla). The revision brought in some items or devices from the 'Nebenviten'. Hence a theory was formulated. Both operations took place after the original compilation, before the author moved on to the series *Macrinus–Alexander*. It was recognized, however, that the two operations might fall later.[3]

One may now take a look at the treatment of the *nomen Antoninorum* in the nine *Vitae*. In compiling his basic source, the author found few references, or omitted what he found. In the year 195, Severus made a momentous change in his nomenclature, attaching himself to the dynasty as 'divi Marci filius, divi Commodi frater'. Of that the HA preserves no trace at this point. It has the conferring of the name on Caracalla in 196 at Viminacium (10. 3) followed by speculation about the reason, by the obtrusion of Geta as also an 'Antoninus', and by the vague notice, attributed to 'quidam', that 'Severus ipse in Marci familiam transire voluerit' (10. 6).

These observations are a patent insertion, interrupting a factual narration. Similarly, various other insertions (noted above) concerning Geta or the 'duo Antonini', and two in the *Caracalla*, viz. Geta as 'Antoninus' (1. 1), and the 'fratres Antonini' (8. 3). That *Vita*, it will be recalled, has the reference to Macrinus and his son at the end of the 'bad passage' (8. 10). On it follows a factual notice about the age of Caracalla and his funeral, concluding with the reference to his son Marcus Antoninus Heliogabalus—'ita enim nomen Antoninorum inoleverat ut velli ex

---

[1] The HA has the word 'desiderium' elsewhere only in *Avid.* 7. 3; *Maximin.* 11. 1.

[2] For the detail, W. Reusch, *Klio*, Beiheft xxiv (1931), 53 ff.

[3] Above, pp. 64; 71.

animis hominum non posset, quod omnium pectora velut Aug(usti) nomen obsederat' (9. 2).

So far Geta. The other 'Antoninus' devised by the HA is L. Verus. He is equipped with the *nomen* a number of times, but on bare mention without annotation (e.g. *Pius* 4. 5; 6. 10; 10. 3; *Marcus* 7. 7; *Verus* 1. 3). The first four of these items are patent additions.

Next, the 'Nebenviten'. L. Verus is duly 'Antoninus' twice in the *Aelius* (2. 9; 5. 12); and the theme was lavishly treated in the *Geta*. Nothing more need be said.

VIII. The *nomen Antoninorum* has left suspicious traces both in the primary *Vitae* and in two 'Nebenviten'. But not all of a piece. Sometimes there is a summary addition, elsewhere long and explicit divagations. A question of some interest arises. At what stage were the additions made? Do the traces represent a throw-back from the *Macrinus*, indeed from the whole series from Macrinus to Alexander?

The assassination of Caracalla evoked the 'ingens amissi principis desiderium', in the memorable phrase of Aurelius Victor (22. 2). And it operated again in the next year, against the usurper and his son. The intrigues of Julia Maesa brought up as a dynastic candidate her grandson, allegedly a son of Caracalla. The troops in Syria responded eagerly. According to the historian Dio, they at once hailed him as 'Marcus Aurelius Antoninus' (LXXVIII. 32. 2).

The potency of the dynastic name was thus dramatically disclosed by two events in rapid succession. Those transactions impressed the author of the HA. They encouraged him to come out with his list of eight Antonini in the *Macrinus*, with much verbiage in the sequel. Further, so it might be suggested, they impelled him to go backwards. He therefore imported his new preoccupation into the *Vitae* he had already compiled.

If that is so, a consequence of some interest for the stages of composition might emerge. The writing of the 'Nebenviten' and the revision of the nine primary *Vitae* might fall, not after the *Caracalla* (where there is a clear break, in sources, treatment, and validity), but somewhat later. That is to say, after the series which ends with Severus Alexander. The hypothesis could turn for support to other indications. The case deserves to be argued.[1]

However, it would be premature at this stage to dismiss the previous hypothesis. It can still be defended. The author, reading his Latin sources

---

[1] Above, pp. 64; 71; 75; 86. See now T. D. Barnes, *Historia-Augusta-Colloquium 1968/9* (1970), 30.

for Caracalla, would find at the end the 'ingens desiderium' in Victor or in the KG, if not elsewhere. Observe the phrase 'ita nomen Antoninorum inoleverat', etc. (*Carac.* 9. 2), which does not look like the author's invention. Thus Macrinus' son and Elagabalus, named as Antonini in the context of Caracalla's death, might operate as an adequate disclosure. He would not need to look further ahead, or write further ahead, before turning back and introducing the *nomen* into parts of the earlier *Vitae*.

VI · THE FAME OF TRAJAN

1. THE CANON of the good emperors (subsequent to Augustus) that obtained in late Antiquity is an obvious theme. The names are predictable. In short, the Antonine rulers, however defined. Nor is inquiry likely to yield much profit. Yet variants emerge; and there are surprises of emphasis and distribution.

First of all, a negative observation for preface, suggested by the *Panegyrici Latini*. No fewer than nine orations delivered between the years 289 and 321 are extant. Literature of this sort lives (in so far as it can be said to live at all) by tradition and convention. It appeals to *exempla* from the past. Why not then the Antonine names of ancient virtue and felicity? Inspection contradicts. The nine orations consecrated to the praise of the Tetrarchs and of Constantine carry only two references. Both are paradoxical. They evoke explicit parallels, not mere types.

First, the anonymous orator speaking before Constantius in 297 or 298. He mentions a speech of Fronto, 'cum belli in Britannia confecti laudem Antonino principi daret' (VIII. 14. 2), The allusion seems to be precise, the erudition unusual in that age. Who was familiar with the British War under Antoninus Pius (waged by Lollius Urbicus)?[1] Second, Nazarius to the Emperor Constantine at Rome in 321. He has been describing the formidable mailed cavalry which Constantine defeated near Turin in the year 312; and he is drawn to mention the fear which the sight of Parthian *cataphracti* had once inspired in a Roman emperor, inducing him to negotiate; the Parthian repulsed his overtures and was duly defeated (IV. 24. 6). The passage runs as follows:

Antoninus imperator in toga praestans et non iners nec futtilis bello, cum adversum Parthos armis experiretur, visis catafractis adeo totus in metum venit ut ultro ad regem conciliatrices pacis litteras daret.

The notice is enigmatic, but revealing. Since it opens with 'Antoninus imperator in toga praestans', one would expect Marcus to be meant. Yet it is clearly Verus, styled 'Antoninus', after the fashion of some late writers.[2]

---

[1] The occasion of Pius' imperatorial salutation in 142. The success might have been extolled the next year, in Fronto's consular oration. More likely, the panegyrist assumed that Marcus was the object of Fronto's laudation.

[2] Above, p. 80.

A passage in Fronto's eulogy of the prince confirms, mentioning overtures for peace made by Verus to Vologaeses.[1] There is something more. Fronto in fact describes the *cataphracti*; and he alludes to a victory won by Verus not long after the Parthian had spurned negotiation: 'barbarus male mulcatus est.'[2] Fronto goes on to draw a comparison between Verus and Trajan, detrimental to the latter ruler, who put his own glory above everything.

That is all. Where lies the explanation? The official orators (it appears) concentrate their efforts, whether for praise or for blame, on present transactions or on the exposition of timeless truths and consecrated platitudes. Even of Augustus there is scant mention: he occurs only four times in these orations.[3]

In fact, the age of the Antonines was remote from their vision and mostly forgotten. A vast chasm intervened: the epoch of tribulation in the middle of the third century. The phenomenon is confirmed by clear indications that emerge a little later. The Latin tradition had not preserved much of value about the emperors after Severus Alexander and before the accession of Diocletian: meagre facts along with strange misconceptions and positive errors of many types. That is patent when one inspects Aurelius Victor, Eutropius, and the *Epitome* or attempts some reconstruction of their basic source: that is, the 'Kaisergeschichte' postulated by Enmann. Hence the predicament which confronted the author of the HA. The Latin sources were brief and scrappy, there were some Greek writers—but in the main he used his own imagination, without restraint or reluctance.

There is another explanation, of a literary order, perhaps more to the point. It derives from the education of the orators: Cicero and the Republic. They were formed by the classics. The nine speeches adduce as *exempla* Marius, Cato, Pompeius (each twice), and Sulla (three times).

The next Panegyric conforms, forty years later. It was delivered on the first day of January, 362 at Constantinople by Claudius Mamertinus. The orator names the first consuls of the Republic (III. 30. 3); and he can expatiate on political events in its closing century, with an anecdote about the consular candidature of the orator Crassus (16. 2 ff.). He inserts a reference to 'Gabinios designatos et Catones repulsos' (19. 2), and he calls up the masters of jurisprudence—'Manilios Scaevolas Servios' (20. 1).

---

[1] P. Lambrechts, *Ant. class.* III (1934), 197 f.

[2] Fronto, *Princ. Hist.* 14 = Haines II. 212. Lambrechts neglected to adduce the *cataphracti* in Fronto—who is patently the source of Nazarius.

[3] *Pan. lat.* VI. 13. 4; VII. 11. 2; 13. 4; XII. 10. 1. None of any significance or adducing Caesar Augustus as a model in war or peace.

All very delightful. But no Roman emperor is adduced. Mamertinus enjoyed the favour of Julian and benefited from conspicuous promotion. He might have known that Julian held Marcus and Trajan in high estimation. Has Mamertinus missed an opportunity? No: the convention was still Republican.

Compensation arrives (though not much) with the last and the best of the *Panegyrici Latini*. Pacatus spoke his piece at Rome in the summer of 389, acclaiming the advent of Theodosius. The natal province of the Emperor evoked and imposed Trajan and Hadrian for predecessors in that distinction (II. 4. 5), whereas the archetype of the panegyrists three centuries earlier had discreetly avoided the theme of provincial origin. A little further on Pacatus furnishes the select catalogue of exemplary rulers. The 'res publica' herself is invoked to testify (11. 6):

quod cum me Nerva tranquillus, amor generis humani Titus, pietate memorabilis Antoninus teneret, cum moribus Augustus ornaret, legibus Hadrianus imbueret, finibus Traianus augeret, parum mihi videbar beata quia non eram tua.

11. Other writers of the period, covering a span of about thirty years, will repay brief inspection.[1] Symmachus, it is true, does not have much to offer. However, to exalt the martial energy and labours of Valentinian, he brings up for deleterious contrast four rulers whom he censures for addiction to leisure. First Augustus and Tiberius, then 'Pius otia Caietana persequitur, in Lycio et Academia remissior Marcus auditus' (*Rel.* I. 16). Elsewhere, writing to Ausonius in 376, he gives eager testimony to the pleasure he got from hearing the New Year oration of Gratian, whose virtues were all his own, whereas other good emperors benefited from the age in which they lived (*Epp.* I. 13. 3):

bonus Nerva, Traianus strenuus, Pius innocens, Marcus plenus offici temporibus adiuti sunt, quae tunc mores alios nesciebant.

The passage of three years brought a happy relevance to this epistle. Ausonius was elevated to the consulship of 379 and duly spoke his thanksgiving to the imperial patron. After gracefully touching on his own services, as a tutor, he comes out with a compliment—'non ego me contendo Frontoni, sed Antonino praefero Gratianum' (*Gratiarum Actio* 7). Then, in recounting the virtues of Gratian, notably benevolence and affability, he begins with Titus, citing his famous phrase 'perdidisse se diem quo nihil boni fecerat' (16). Remission of taxation evokes actions of

[1] For valuable indications see A. Lippold, *Historia* XVII (1968), 231 ff.

Trajan and of Antoninus; and the 'familiaris humanitas' of the Antonini towards their friends and towards the soldiers is commended. But, whereas Trajan merely visited his friends when they were sick, Gratian far surpassed the model in care for the troops—'in quot vias de una eius humanitate progrederis!' (17).

Ausonius in this season was paying some attention to Roman history.[1] He compiled an edition of the *Fasti consulares*, suitably terminating with the year 379.[2] Furthermore, verse quatrains to describe each of the Twelve Caesars whose biographies had been written by Suetonius. Then he produced a sequel of twelve, Nerva to Elagabalus inclusive. These mottoes bring no surprises. Emphasis is put where it might be expected to belong. With Nerva, 'imitatur adoptio prolem.' The theme of adoption continues with the next three rulers, to stop with Marcus, who bequeathed the power to his son—'hoc solo patriae, quod genuit, nocuit.'

In itself, this sequence of twelve Caesars is in no way peculiar. The total corresponds neatly with the facts. It suitably terminates with the last ruler to bear 'Antoninus' in his titulature,

> tunc etiam Augustae sedis penetralia foedas
> Antoninorum nomina falsa gerens?

None the less, it happens to permit deductions of some significance.[3]

Next, the historian Ammianus Marcellinus. From his wide reading he culled a selection of *exempla*, some of them highly original. As concerns emperors named as types of excellence, he is a conformist. In his panegyric of Julian, the names are Titus, Trajan, Antoninus, Marcus, with primacy accorded to Marcus, 'ad cuius aemulationem actus suos effingebat et mores' (XVI. 1. 4). In two other places, Marcus has a separate reference (XXI. 16. 11; XXXI. 10. 19), and there is one for Trajan (XXI. 16. 1). But, towards the end, the long character-sketch of Valentinian has 'ut Antoninus Pius erat serenus et clemens' (XXX. 8. 12); and, after a lacuna, 'si reliqua temperasset, vixerat ut Traianus et Marcus' (9. 1). Those two names epitomize the good ruler: the warrior and the sage.

The rubric ends with Claudian, whom fervour for the dynasty of Theodosius would not preclude from celebrating the blameless sequence of the adoptive emperors (*De VI cons. Honori* 417 ff.),

---

[1] The *Gratiarum Actio* mentions the seventeen consulships of Domitian (6) and the fact that Fronto was only consul suffect.

[2] The edition is referred to in four pieces of verse (ed. R. Peiper (1886), 190 f.).

[3] Above, pp. 79 f.; 83.

> quos mutua virtus
> legit et in nomen Romanis rebus adoptans
> iudicio pulchram seriem, non sanguine duxit:
> hic proles atavum deducens Aelia Nervam
> tranquillique Pii bellatoresque Severi.

The surprise is to have Septimius Severus linked to the series. However, he had got a good note from Ausonius who praised his plebeian energy, with no hint of the cruelty on emphasis in the standard tradition.[1]

Elsewhere, Claudian has five allusions to Trajan.[2] Some of them bring in Spain, the origin of Theodosius contributing thereto. The longest passage affords some instruction, for it matches Trajan with Marcus (*De VI cons. Honori* 335 ff.). The theme is warfare. It proceeds from the Dacian victories of Trajan to the campaigns of Marcus on the Danube, to conclude with the miracle of the thunderstorm, wrought by incantations of the Chaldaeans—or better, so the poet opines, vouchsafed by Jupiter as due indulgence to the virtues of the Emperor. He is addressed as 'Marce clemens'. Otherwise Marcus is absent, the name 'Antoninus' does not occur. In another passage the true glory of Trajan is reckoned to be clemency, not any of the triumphs in war—'patriae quod mitis erat' (*De IV cons. Honori* 319).

III. Sundry phenomena might arouse interest. Augustus, the founder of the Empire, was generally taken for granted. Or he seemed too remote, and some sources gave none too favourable an account. Titus secured admission. That was mainly through the Suetonian 'amor ac deliciae generis humani' or the aphorism 'amici, diem perdidi.' However meagre an epitomator may be, he can hardly refuse those items of benevolence.[3] But Titus tends to fade out, lacking stronger attachments, and Hadrian occurs sporadically as the link between Trajan and the Antonini. On short statement, the recognized paragons in late Antiquity are Trajan and Marcus (the latter sometimes blended with Pius): each for complementary excellence and together standing for the line of rulers chosen by merit, not a dynastic succession by blood inheritance.

Their fame had not suffered eclipse through the long ages of chaos or general indifference to the past history of the Empire. There is scant attestation. One must take into account the dearth of Latin literature since the age

---

[1] Ausonius, *XII Caesares* 87 f. The *Epitome* (20) has nothing but praise for Severus.

[2] Claudian, *De IV cons. Hon.* 18 ff.; 315 ff.; *De cons. Stil.* I. 193; *De VI cons. Hon.* 335 ff.; *Laus Serenae* 55 ff.

[3] Eutropius and the *Epitome* have both items, Victor the first only (10. 6).

of the Severi. Yet, for what it may be worth, the ritual acclamation in the Roman Senate cannot fail to be cited—'felicior Augusto, melior Traiano' (Eutropius VIII. 5. 3).

None the less, the preoccupation with exemplary rulers from the season of the Antonine prime is not fortuitous. It may be held to reflect the great renascence of Latin letters in the last thirty years of the fourth century. That revival was accompanied and inspired by a devotion to the Roman tradition, intensified as the perils gathered and doom threatened. Not merely the old Republic (as previously in the panegyrists), but the happy epoch of the imperial dispensation. The most mediocre of practitioners respond. History itself will revive, heralded by epitomators.[1]

Certain classic authors had kept their prestige all through, being school texts. That is, the *Quadriga*, as it was called: Cicero, Virgil, Sallust, Terence. What now ensued was the rediscovery of imperial authors.

Juvenal is the clear case.[2] Also and parallel, so it may be surmised, Marius Maximus. The significant witness is Ammianus, who censured the aristocracy for their deplorable choice of reading matter: the satirist and the biographer.[3]

The 'Twelve Caesars' as registered by Ausonius, in 379 or soon after, acquire sharp relevance: Nerva to Elagabalus, surely the theme of Marius Maximus. The list passes over Verus. That is a cardinal fact.[4] It permits and enforces the deduction that a different biographer was used by the Historia Augusta as basic source for the earlier *Vitae*. Hence another discovery of that age, though not perhaps known to many: the *Ignotus* who had written the lives of the emperors from Hadrian (or rather Nerva) down to Caracalla inclusive.

IV. How then does the HA fit in? It serves up lists of good emperors. Some are lengthy. They bring in rulers later than Marcus Aurelius, and, towards the end, they comprise military worthies such as Claudius and Probus. The items and the variants are more or less instructive (much depends on the author's whim at the moment), and might encourage a long disquisition. For present purposes, it will be enough to single out a pair of specimens that register the author's shortest statement of excellence, taken from different parts of the work. In the preface to the *Macrinus*,

---

[1] R. Syme, *Ammianus and the Historia Augusta* (1968), 104 ff.; 109 ff.

[2] G. Highet, *Juvenal the Satirist* (1954), 180 ff.; 296 ff.; A. D. E. Cameron, *Hermes* XCII (1964), 363 ff.

[3] Ammianus XXVIII. 4. 14, quoted above, p. 15.

[4] T. D. Barnes, *JRS* LVII (1967), 66, cf. above, p. 46.

a document of prime validity, the author deprecates the piling up of
trivial details about obscure emperors 'quasi vel de Traiano aut Pio aut
Marco' (*Macr.* 1. 4). The biography of Claudius ends with 'ut satis constet neque Traianum neque Antoninos neque quemquam alium principem
sic amatum' (*Claud.* 18. 4).[1] That is to say, previsible names and a close
concordance with the canon of Ammianus Marcellinus.

It is useful to tabulate by their incidence the references to earlier rulers in
different parts of the HA. That has been done by Hartke.[2] He comes to
several conclusions about Trajan.

First, there never was a *Vita Traiani*.[3] The HA began with Hadrian
abruptly, as now it stands. His argument is defective. The biographies in
the first series from Hadrian onwards carry few references backwards to
Trajan, it is true. The reason is obvious. The main *Vitae*, Hadrian to
Caracalla inclusive, go back to a sober factual source. The evocation of
Trajan tends to occur in contexts of fiction (for example, the *Alexander*
and the later biographies of military emperors) where the impostor is
not a compiler but an inventor.

A literary imposture, or a historical romance, normally opens with a
preface duly explaining how the manuscript came to light. All ages exemplify. There is no need to adduce the narrative of Dictys the Cretan.[4]
To be sure, a superior talent in mystification can make play with a document alleged to be fragmentary. The author of the HA is a clever rogue,
but there is no call to postulate that device in this instance. He enjoyed
prefaces and deceit, as witness the exordium of the *Vita Aureliani*.

Second, Hartke draws attention to the frequency of Trajan's name in the
series of biographies from Claudius to Carus. The phenomenon is in no
way abnormal. This was a sequence of military heroes, close to the author's
preoccupations.

Third, a concentration in the *Vita Alexandri*. That is what matters,
and it deserves to be examined in detail. It is not the bare mention of the
name, occurring in catalogues of good emperors, long or short. By contrast, this *Vita* discloses a number of special or significant evocations.
Trajan's name occurs no fewer than eight times. As follows:

I. 10. 2. In confrontation with the Senate at Rome, in the long rigmarole attending upon the alleged proposal of the name 'Antoninus'
(6–11), the young prince, refusing the honour, states 'si enim Antonini

---

[1] For Pius and Marcus subsumed as the 'Antonini', cf. *Tac.* 16. 6; *Prob.* 12. 2; 22. 4.
[2] W. Hartke, *Römische Kinderkaiser* (1951), 326.
[3] Hartke, o.c. 328.
[4] R. Syme, o.c. 124.

nomen accipio, possum et Traiani, possum et Titi, possum et Vespasiani.'
In its context, the item is not of much consequence.[1]

2. 13. 1 f. Among the 'omina imperii'. When the mother of Alexander
was giving birth to her son in a temple of Alexander the Macedonian
(and on the anniversary of his death), a picture of Trajan fell down on
the conjugal bed (in her house).

3. 25. 5. An enigmatic reference to a basin in some public baths:
'Oceani solium primus imperator appellavit, cum Traianus . . . non fecisset,
sed diebus solia deputasset.' There follows a reference to his completion
of the Baths of Caracalla: authentic, cf. *Elag.* 17. 9; Eutropius VII. 15. 2.

4. 26. 4. He set up statues in the Forum of Trajan, 'undique translatas'.

5. 26. 11: 'pontes quos Traianus fecerat instauravit paene in omnibus
locis, aliquos etiam novos fecit, sed instauratis nomen Traiani reservavit.'

6. 39. 1. Alexander would drink with the generals, honouring the
precedent of Trajan. But not 'usque quinque pocula'. The author alleges
'unum tantum poculum amicis exhibebat in honorem Alexandri Magni.'
The whole context is likewise fraudulent.

7. 48. 1–7. The anecdote about 'Ovinius Camillus'. This senator of
ancient family and luxurious habits aspired to the purple. Alexander sum-
moned him to the palace and commended his 'cura rei publicae'; and,
taking him before the Senate, 'participem imperii appellavit.' After which,
an 'expeditio barbarica' being announced, Alexander invited Ovinius to
share the hardships. Five miles on foot, then horseback, then a carriage
broke the pretender. Ovinius was allowed to go away to his country
estates, where he lived for many years, but Maximinus had him put to
death.

The author subjoins comment. The vulgar version, he says, attributes
the transaction to Trajan. But it is not to be found in Marius Maximus,
or in three other biographers of Trajan (whom he names).[2] But it is attested by three writers on Severus Alexander (likewise named).[3] Which
fact the author has properly registered as a warning, 'ne quis vulgi magis
famam sequeretur quam historiam'.

8. 65. 1. Addressing Constantine, the author asseverates that the Emperor is in the habit of asking what it was that made a 'Syrus et alienigena'
so exemplary a ruler. He directs due attention to something 'quod in
Mario Maximo legisti'. Namely that the commonwealth is in a better

---

[1] The documentation appealed to H. Peter, *Die Scriptores Historiae Augustae* (1892),
222: 'an dem Kern zu zweifeln zwingt uns nichts; es empfiehlt ihn uns vielmehr manches.'

[2] viz. 'Fabius Marcellinus', 'Aurelius Verus', 'Statius Valens'.

[3] viz. 'Septiminus', 'Acholius', 'Encolpius'.

posture when the ruler is evil than when his friends are. To corroborate the ostensible paradox, he goes on to cite what Homullus said to Trajan when they were discussing Domitian.

Eight items therefore: some plausible, others ridiculous, none entailing credence. The two anecdotes reveal habits of the impostor elsewhere on show.

First, 'Ovinius Camillus'. The documentation adduced in epilogue attests the sound methods and rigorous scruple of a good biographer. As for the name, 'Camillus' was an appropriate *cognomen* for a senator of ancient lineage. For 'Ovinius' no clue avails. The author, when creating fictitious characters, draws on names of prominence in his own time: he uses Ceionii, Faltonii, Maecii, Ragonii, and so on.[1] Hence a chance that descendants of Ovinius Gallicanus, the consul of 317, suggested the name.

Second, 'Homullus'. Some scholars have looked for the person in the annals of Trajan's reign; and M. Junius Homullus offers, consul suffect in 102.[2] That was an aberration. One should look in the HA. In the *Vita Pii*, shortly after a reference to Marius Maximus, comes an anecdote about Homullus (11. 8): and Valerius Homullus is the subject of a nasty story inserted in the next biography (*Marcus* 6. 9).[3] His identity is patent: M. Valerius Homullus (*cos.* 152).[4] And, since he was *ordinarius*, a person of some consequence: doubly so, for his ancestry is not on attestation.

The author has been operating one of his habitual tricks. He invents a Trajanic Homullus to convey an anecdote. For the reverse process, observe Lollius Urbicus, governor of Britain (*Pius* 5. 4), and later on the historian 'Lollius Urbicus' (*Diad.* 9. 2).[5]

v. The *Vita* of Severus Alexander brings in Trajan eight times. For what reason? No hesitation need delay an answer. The tradition, as represented in the epitomators and in Herodian, showed the reign of the prince in a favourable light—but without enough facts to support it. In any age the most superficial inspection would expose the incongruity.

It was expedient to build up and embellish the Syrian boy. Not only as a civilian ruler, well educated and delighting in the company of scholars, sagacious and clement, obeying wise counsellors and deferential towards the Roman Senate. He had to be a martial figure. Alexander is therefore

[1] R. Syme, o.c. 154 ff.; above, p. 11.
[2] Thus Groag, P–W x. 1040. And *PIR²*, J 760 has the note 'ut videtur'.
[3] Above, p. 38.
[4] Hohl in the Index to his edition of the HA included the Trajanic 'Homullus' in the entry '⟨M.⟩ (Valerius) Homullus'.   [5] Above, p. 4.

endowed with 'venustas et virilis decor', he impresses by his 'staturae militaris robur' (4. 4).

Further, a whole farrago of fabrications dispersed through the *Vita*.[1] Alexander keeps a precise military register, he is apprised of all that goes on, he knows many soldiers by name (21. 6 ff.). When on campaign, he makes exact dispositions in advance (45). There is unremitting care for commissariat, sick soldiers are visited in hospital or boarded out with 'patribus familias honestioribus et sanctioribus matronis' (47. 3). The army responded to his loving care with exemplary behaviour. On the march it resembled a procession of senators—'tribuni taciti, centuriones verecundi, milites amabiles erant' (50. 2). The prince also enforced strict discipline, which is duly documented by a harangue to the troops (53). Then, after victory celebrations (56 f.), Alexander enjoins various measures for the benefit of veterans, especially the 'limitanei' (58. 2 ff.).[2]

The author has been at some pains. In several passages he had Trajan in mind, though the name is absent. It is Alexander the Macedonian with whom the troops equate their 'imperator' (50. 4). He is the other component in this fancy picture. Tradition and rhetoric linked the two.[3] An identity of name did the rest. 'Alexander' was created for the Syrian on his accession: he had originally been called 'Alexianus'.[4] Hence many developments in the HA. It will suffice to mention the various *omina* (5. 1 ff.).[5]

So far so good. A deeper design has been surmised, relevant to Julian the Apostate. Alexander the Macedonian and Marcus Aurelius were the objects of his especial veneration. The Roman paragon duly wins the competition which Julian staged in his *Caesares*. Trajan outdistanced Caesar and Caesar Augustus.[6] It was not so much for military renown as for clemency. But Trajan at the end must yield the palm to Marcus.[7]

---

[1] Some of the military details or fantasies recall the *Vitae* of Avidius Cassius and Pescennius Niger, on which cf. above, p. 64. As for technical terms, observe the distribution in the HA of 'stellatura' (*Pesc.* 3. 8; *Alex.* 15. 5) and of 'papilio' (*Pesc.* 11. 1; *Alex.* 51. 5; 61. 2; *Tyr. trig.* 16. 1).

[2] For these measures, R. Syme, o.c. 46 f. Alexander's care for military discipline, however, was not an invention of the HA. The source used by the epitomators alleged that he cashiered whole legions (Victor 24. 3; Eutropius VIII. 23). Victor added the refinement that Alexander's *cognomen* took its origin from his 'severitas'.

[3] For this familiar theme cf. *Tacitus* (1958), 770 f., with the bibliography there cited.

[4] Herodian v. 3. 3; 7. 3.

[5] On which, J. Straub, *Heidnische Geschichtsapologetik in der christlichen Spätantike* (1963), 125 ff. Further, on Alexander in late Antiquity, L. Cracco Ruggini, *Bonner Historia-Augusta-Colloquium 1964/5* (1966), 79 ff.

[6] *Caesares* 328 b.

[7] ib. 356 c.

Those symbols of enduring fame could not fail to call up for confrontation their treatment in a romantic biography. Julian, as reflected in the
portrayal of Severus Alexander, such was the ingenious thesis of Baynes.[1]
Not a mere reflection, however. Baynes argued that the *Vita* was covert
propaganda, in favour of Julian and the cause of the old faith. Further,
composed precisely in the reign of Julian.

The authority of Baynes carried great weight and force. The impact
was redoubled when Hohl, after brief initial hesitations, announced his
agreement, decisively.[2] Others concurred.[3] There was not much open
dissent.[4] None the less, the thesis has lapsed.

Propaganda for Julian during his reign (when there was no need for
subtle and indirect methods), that does not seem plausible. There were
other vulnerable points, and central. Given the predilections of the
Apostate, Marcus Aurelius ought to stand in prominence in the *Vita*,
by name or by significant allusion. The contrary happens. His name occurs
three times near the beginning, in the long rigmarole of the accession
scene, where the author makes so much play with the 'nomen Antoninorum' (7. 3; 9. 1; 10. 5). The references are purely nominal. Marcus is
named in the company of other rulers—nothing about any action of his,
or any attitude. Then the philosopher emperor fades out entirely. That
phenomenon deserved emphasis, as did by contrast the repeated evocations of Trajan.

Furthermore, Julian would not have cared to see himself foreshadowed
in the son of Mamaea. His own verdict stands. The Syrian gets short
shrift in his *Caesares*.[5] For good reasons. Baynes (it was unfortunate)
did not face that objection or even mention the passage.[6]

Not that some relevance to Julian need be doubted or contested—
especially in the Trajanic aspects. But a posthumous relevance. Julian
was not forgotten by friends or enemies. Delineating a pagan saint, some
thirty years after the death of Julian, a writer of fiction whose theme

---

[1] N. H. Baynes, *The Historia Augusta. Its Date and Purpose* (1926).

[2] In his review, *CR* XLI (1927), 82: 'This book . . . has convinced me.' He had shaken his
head, so he avowed, after reading the preliminary paper of Baynes, published in *CR*
XXXVIII (1924), 165 ff.

[3] Thus Ensslin, Lambrechts, Seston, Palanque, according to A. Chastagnol, *Historia* IV
(1955), 180.

[4] The notable exception was the review by De Sanctis, *Riv. fil.* LV (1927), 402.

[5] Alexander the Syrian, seated in the lowest ranks, bewails his fate. Silenus addresses him
as μῶρε καὶ μέγα νήπιε (*Caesares* 313 a).

[6] There was another telling objection. The long address to Constantine in the *Vita*
(65 ff.) would not have been to the liking of the Apostate. In his panegyric on Julian,
Claudius Mamertinus carefully eschewed any hint of Julian's ancestry.

was emperors good and bad might be expected to reproduce features inherent in the historical Julian.[1]

VI. To proceed with Trajan. Other signs of the impostor's interests (literary rather than political) ought not to be neglected. Trajan registered among the good emperors, either in catalogue or in bare reference, that need not matter much. One turns to the deliberate pieces of fiction elsewhere on show, in the mature manner of the ingenious contriver. He creates several descendants of Trajan.

First, the Emperor Gordian. Trajan was the ancestor on the maternal side, and the Emperor's mother was called 'Ulpia Gordiana' (Gord. 2. 2). The author, however, turns aside and refrains from developing this seductive theme. The Vita carries no further reference to the names 'Ulpius' or 'Traianus'.

Second, two minor characters. When the Senate, after the destruction of Gordian and his son in Africa, is convoked to hold debate on the emergency, a good man comes out with firm resolution and a speech inciting to action. He is 'Vectius Sabinus, ex familia Ulpiorum' (Max. et Balb. 2. 1). The other is also an orator of forceful persuasion. When Aurelian requests (and the pontifices enjoin) a consultation of the Sibylline Books, it is 'Ulpius Silanus' who argues the case (Aur. 19. 3).

Third 'Ulpius Crinitus'. A splendid military character, 'qui se de Traiani genere referebat': there is a picture showing him and Aurelian in the Templum Solis (Aur. 10. 2). An earlier emperor, Valerian, signalized him—'Caesaris loco habere instituerat' (Aur. 10. 2). When 'Crinitus' fell ill on service, Valerian needed a substitute and appointed Aurelian to take his place: the letter of instruction is cited (11. 1 ff.). Recompense ensues for the services of Aurelian. The scene is an imperial council, held in the Thermae at Byzantium. Nine dignitaries are present, all named, among them 'Ulpius Crinitus'. He rises to his feet, holds discourse on the subject of adoption, and requests permission to take Aurelian as a son. As he states, 'quod et familiae meae amicum ac proprium fuit' (14. 5).

This descendant of Trajan cannot fail to afford instruction and delight. Whence the cognomen? Eutropius introduces the Emperor Trajan as 'Ulpius Traianus Crinitus' (VIII. 2).[2] That epitomator (or perhaps his source) provided the HA with the inspiration, it may be assumed.

The invention conveys a broader connotation, illustrating one of the

---

[1] Yet those features might merely be the conventional apanage of a heroic ruler. Thus, pertinently, Momigliano, Secondo Contributo (1960), 123 f.

[2] The explanation of the cognomen happens to be furnished by Lydus, De mensibus IV. 18: διὰ τὴν περὶ τὰς τῆς κεφαλῆς αὐτοῦ τρίχας σπουδήν.

favourite themes of the HA. As 'Ulpius Crinitus' asseverates, 'hoc igitur quod Cocceius Nerva in Traiano adoptando, quod Ulpius Traianus in Hadriano, quod Hadrianus in Antonino et ceteri deinceps' (14. 6).

The note is simple: adoption and military merit. Old Gordian had been more remunerative. The Trajanic ancestry, once mentioned there, is lost to mind. Instead, the author forges links with the Antonini. Thus Gordian acquired a wife, 'Fabia Orestilla', in the descent from Marcus, a daughter of 'Annius Severus' (*Gord.* 17. 4, cf. 6. 4); and his own daughter is 'Maecia Faustina' (4. 2).[1] Again, the author tries to make out that Gordian bore the name 'Antoninus' (4. 7; 5. 3). Further, Gordian in relation to his father-in-law (6. 4) patently alludes to Marcus and Pius (cf. *Marcus* 7. 2 f.).

Gordian is also a devotee of classical literature and philosophy, passing his days in communion with Plato, Aristotle, Cicero, Virgil (7. 1). In his youth he wrote poetry, emulating Ciceronian *parerga* (3. 2). Even as a boy, he composed an epic poem on Pius and Marcus in thirty books (3. 3). One recalls Severus Alexander: not only Plato for his reading, but Cicero, *De officiis* and *De re publica* (*Alex.* 30. 2). For confirmation, if needed, observe Alexander's choice of a poetical theme: 'vitas principum bonorum versibus scripsit' (27. 8).

Getting better as he goes on, the author expands and corroborates his fabrications. What he conveys in his portrayal of Gordian should be clear enough. An idealized Antonine ruler. But also, blended therewith, an aristocrat of his own time, bland, opulent, and cultivated.[2] The presentation is amicable. It also carries mild parody of literary pretensions and noble lineage.

VII. Antonine fancies, with or without Trajan, have now been illustrated. Other reasons, it is true, have been adduced to explain the prominence of Trajan in the HA, and notably in the *Vita Alexandri*. Hönn in his study of that biography came out with a bold statement.[3] The author was composing a kind of panegyric. He therefore had recourse to the classic performance of the younger Pliny. Hönn was not content to adduce the general resemblance of theme and emphasis. He brought up a large number of parallels of phraseology. Inspection shows them illusory.

Next, a contemporary relevance. That is, Theodosius, like Trajan an emperor from Spain. Pacatus in 389 was happy to draw the parallel.

---

[1] For the name 'Maecius', above, pp. 4; 12.   [2] For that notion, R. Syme, o.c. 161.
[3] K. Hönn, *Quellenuntersuchungen zu den Viten des Heliogabalus und des Severus Alexander im Corpus der S.H.A.* (1911), 179.

He had been anticipated by a Greek orator, Themistius.[1] The thing was obvious. Some acclaimed it joyously, others kept silent. Ammianus is lavish in praise of Theodosius' parent for his military exploits. In the last section of his work, Books XXVI–XXXI (written between 392 and 396 or 397), the historian compares him to heroes of the old Republic, such as Camillus and Papirius Cursor (XXVIII. 3. 9). There is also a reference to Scribonius Curio, who broke the 'Dardanorum ferocia' (XXIX. 5. 22); and Fabius Cunctator comes in (5. 32), also Pompeius Magnus (5. 33). Ammianus even has recourse to generals of the Empire, viz. Domitius Corbulo and Lusius Quietus (XXIX. 5. 4).[2] The latter, the notorious Moor, should have evoked the emperor under whom he served. But Trajan is conspicuous by his absence from the Theodosian context. Hardly by inadvertence. Rather, a historian's distaste for the 'species adulationis'. And he may have had no small doubts about the military performance of Theodosius himself.

From a close or enhanced parallel between two emperors, it was a short step to assert their kinship. It is implied in the language with which Claudian in 398 salutes the son of Theodosius,

> haud indigna coli nec nuper cognita Marti
> Ulpia progenies et quae diademata mundo
> sparsit Hibera domus.[3]

The relationship is stated as a fact in the *Epitome* of Pseudo-Victor composed in the near aftermath of Theodosius' decease. This production drew upon a source which had already been used by Aurelius Victor and by Eutropius, bringing the sequence of imperial biographies up to date. The opening sentence declares 'originem a Traiano principe trahens' (48. 1). The opuscule goes on to establish their resemblance both in physique and in character. It can be doubly documented—'fuit autem Theodosius moribus et corpore Traiano similis, quantum scripta veterum et picturae docent' (48. 8). So close is the likeness in character that each and any feature reported of Trajan can be applied to Theodosius—'mens vero prorsus similis, adeo ut nihil dici queat quod non ex libris in istum videatur transferri' (48. 9). Hence, 'clemens animus, misericors, communis', and so on. The catalogue of virtues is instructive. The panegyrist Pacatus had missed some opportunities.

---

[1] Themistius XVI, p. 205 Dindorf; XIX, p. 229.

[2] Several particulars about Lusius Quietus, it is noteworthy, are supplied by Themistius (XVI, p. 250).

[3] Claudian, *De IV cons. Hon.* 17 ff. Not, however, in *Laus Serenae* 55 ff., as stated by Ensslin, P–W V A. 1937.

A negative confrontation follows. Drink and glory, Theodosius was against. He loathed those things—'illa tamen quibus Traianus aspersus est, vinolentiam scilicet et cupidinem triumphandi' (48. 10). Instances of his high moral standards are adduced. And if, in polite studies, Theodosius might be rated 'mediocriter doctus', he had a mind of his own, and he liked history—'diligens ad noscenda maiorum gesta' (48. 11).[1]

This epitomator gives information about Trajan (and about Nerva) not to be found in his predecessors Victor and Eutropius. There is indeed a chance that he supplemented the common source from Marius Maximus.[2] His remarks on Nerva carry anecdotal particulars. For example, Arrius Antoninus commiserating with the new ruler (12. 3), and the story about the banquet at which Junius Mauricus made a famous remark (12. 5).[3] However that may be, this epitomator's presentation of Trajan is peculiar at first sight. No mention of Dacia or Parthia. He takes Trajan's military glory for granted. But a preoccupation with Trajan emerges indirectly. Alluding to the beneficial influence of empresses in his remarks on Constantine, he brings in an anecdote about Pompeia Plotina, 'incredibile dictu est quanto auxerit gloriam Traiani' (42. 21). This passage, by the way, conveys the solitary attestation of Plotina's gentilicium.[4] The same author, it will suitably be recalled, is the only source to register the ultimate and Italian origin of the Ulpii—'Ulpius Traianus ex urbe Tudertina' (13. 1). A late and isolated item of erudition, but not to be dismissed.[5]

VIII. The equation of Trajan and Theodosius has been adequately illustrated. It gives a starting-point for further deductions. Hartke, discussing at some length the treatment of Trajan in the HA, begins with the 'Vorliebe des Theodosius für Traian'.[6] Among other things, he puts emphasis on Theodosius' detestation of drink, as attested in the Epitome. Hence, so Hartke infers, the frequent references in the HA to excessive drinking, which he duly catalogues.[7] That is totally irrelevant. Only one of the recurrent fantasies of the author.

But Hartke takes one step further. Severus Alexander admired the Macedonian. But within limits: 'in eo condemnabat ebrietatem et

[1] Compare the interest in history exhibited by the Syrian prince (Alex. 16. 3).
[2] F. A. Lepper, JRS XLVII (1957), 97.
[3] viz. 'nobiscum cenaret', in reference to the deceased Catullus Messallinus. The ultimate source was Pliny, Epp. IV. 22. 6.
[4] She was the daughter of a L. Pompeius, as is proved by the nomenclature of freedmen (ILS 1912; AE 1958, 184).
[5] On the contrary, to be exploited, cf. Tacitus (1958), 796.
[6] W. Hartke, Römische Kinderkaiser (1951), 324.   [7] Hartke, o.c. 335 f.

crudelitatem in amicos' (*Alex.* 30. 3). That is significant. The author is not alluding to Julian. He means Theodosius. Hartke describes his conclusion as 'absolut sicher'.[1]

On that showing, a result of some interest might emerge: the author of the HA is amicably disposed towards Theodosius.

Hartke examines some of the passages in the *Vita Alexandri* referring to Trajan. Not all of them, and not systematically. Warfare and foreign policy come in. The opinions of the HA are clear enough. Hartke therefore concludes that the author would have wished Theodosius to exhibit the military vigour of the Trajanic epoch.[2]

The observation is pertinent. It is inconsistent, however, with Hartke's previous notion that the HA in the *Alexander Severus* was conveying approbation of Theodosius, as in the matter of sobriety. That objection might perhaps be got round. The HA is not consistent, even in themes of high concern. For example, it is all for 'adoptive emperors'. Yet it does not refuse the claims of blood when it extolls Claudius as the ancestor of the line of Constantine.[3]

A question therefore abides: Theodosius in relation to the HA. As soon as a date in the vicinity of 395 became plausible, it was legitimate to look for allusions to his policy and behaviour, in various aspects.

Theodosius was not born in the purple, but chosen as an 'Augustus' to carry the burden of empire. As Pacatus affirmed in choice and appropriate language, 'tantam molem subire et nutantia Romanae rei fata suscipere' (3. 5).[4] The HA ought to have approved. But Theodosius had sons. In extreme youth Arcadius and Honorius were associated in the power. Now the HA is hostile not only to hereditary succession but notably to boy princes. That is the theme that gives Hartke's book its title. As the consular 'Maecius Faltonius Nicomachus' declares in his fervent oration 'dii avertant principes pueros!' (*Tac.* 6. 5).

Allusion to Theodosius will therefore tend to be detrimental. Thus in foreign policy, west and east. Instead of destroying the Goths, Theodosius made a treaty which conceded the existence of a Gothic state on Roman territory. Observe how the HA exults in the victories of Claudius and of Probus over Goths and Germans. Again, the highly favourable presentation of Carus. That emperor made war on the Persians and marched to Ctesiphon. Theodosius, however, made a pact with the Persians. An

---

[1] Hartke, o.c. 335.   [2] Hartke, o.c. 350.

[3] The inconsistency annoyed and perplexed those scholars who assumed the HA to be a work of deliberate propaganda. On this non-existent problem, cf. R. Syme, o.c. 116; 134.

[4] For 'tanta moles' cf. Tacitus, *Ann.* I. 4. 3; II. I.

author who parades zeal for the Roman tradition might well be struck by the contrast and moved to yearn for an emperor of martial stamp.

The attitude of the HA concords admirably with a contemporary situation. A word of caution is enjoined. The treatment of Claudius, Probus, and Carus does not, in itself and by itself, prove an allusion to Theodosius.[1]

None the less, the matter must be kept in mind. And there is a temptation to venture a little further. What about Aurelian? Is he not the kind of emperor Theodosius ought to have been—vigorously punishing the enemies of Rome and devout towards the old gods? He requests the Senate to consult the Sibylline Books, using a powerful understatement: 'neque enim indecorum est diis iuvantibus vincere' (*Aur.* 20. 7). And the senator 'Ulpius Silanus' duly contributes eloquence (19. 3 ff.). Now Aurelian himself exhibits Trajanic ancestry through the great 'Ulpius Crinitus', who adopted him.

Hence, it might seem, a parallel and a contrast, devised to the detriment of Theodosius. However, once again, caution must intervene. It is not in fact necessary to invoke Theodosius to explain these developments in the HA. They have a justification of their own. Still less does Theodosius explain the prominence of Trajan in the *Severus Alexander*. Shaping his ideal emperor with lineaments borrowed from Alexander and from Trajan, the author would have deprecated hard drinking, in any event. He did not need to know or care about the opinions of Theodosius.

The 'vinolentia' was a standard item in the tradition about Trajan. In the phrase of Fronto, 'potavit satis strenue'.[2] It is curious to observe how the panegyristic epitomators deal with that blemish. Eutropius left it out. The *Epitome* condones, briefly.[3] Victor brought in extenuation, by a double device: Trajan shared the failing with Nerva, but he sagaciously abated any deleterious effects of his potations, 'curari vetans iussa post longiores epulas' (13. 10).[4] It would be worth knowing what the *Vita Traiani* had to say. The HA reports the excuse made by Hadrian, presumably going back to the Autobiography—'indulsisse se vino dicit Traiani moribus obsequentem' (*Hadr.* 3. 3).

---

[1] R. Syme, o.c. 117; 212.

[2] Fronto, p. 226 N = Haines II, p. 8. Cf. Dio LXVIII. 7. 4; Julian, *Caesares* 327 c; HA, *Hadr.* 3. 3.

[3] *Epit.* 13. 4: 'nisi quod cibo vinoque paululum deditus erat'.

[4] The same traditional remedy is reported for Galerius (*Anon. Val.* 4. 11) and for Maximinus Daia (Eusebius, *Hist. Eccl.* VIII. 14. 11).

IX. The fame of Trajan was preserved to the last ages by visible memorials. Men could contemplate the great buildings at the capital, they could see his name inscribed on arches, on milestones, on bridges in Italy and throughout the world. When Constantius, visiting Rome in 357, passed on from one monument to the other, he approached Trajan's Forum as the climax of ancient glory, 'singularem sub omni caelo structuram, ut opinamur'.

Thus Ammianus (XVI. 10. 15). Elsewhere the historian contributes an observation of a different order. He adverts upon the vanity of the City Prefect Lampadius, who had a mania for inscribing his name on public buildings in the place of the names of their original founders; and he goes on to report a jest at the expense of Trajan: 'quo vitio laborasse Traianus dicitur princeps, unde eum herbam parietinam iocando cognominarunt' (XXVII. 3. 7). The Epitome also has the remark, naming its author as Constantine, but without the imputation conveyed by Ammianus—'Traianum herbam parietariam ob titulos multis aedibus inscriptos appellare solitus erat' (41. 13).[1] The replacement of names on buildings is relevant to a passage in the HA. When Severus Alexander repaired bridges of Trajan, he behaved with due propriety—'instauratis nomen Traiani reservavit' (Alex. 26. 11).

About Trajan's building activity at Rome, as about other matters, the divergent treatment in the three epitomators is of some interest. In the Epitome the Forum only comes in at the end, being mentioned because the ashes of Trajan were interred at the foot of the Column (13. 11). Similarly Eutropius, who contributes a detail—the Column is 144 feet high (VIII. 5. 2).

Victor, however, when noting the decease of Trajan, says nothing about his burial. He had registered the buildings previously—'Romae a Domitiano coepta forum atque alia multa plusquam magnifice coluit' (13. 5). The sentence goes on to a remark about the food-supply of the capital—'et annonae perpetuae mire consultum'. Buildings and the Annona in conjunction, that may furnish a useful hint.

Trajan's constructions come into a vexed question: his dictum about Nero, which Victor and the Epitome reported in their account of Nero. The simpler version is that of the Epitome (5. 2 f.):

iste quinquennio tolerabilis visus. unde quidam prodidere Traianum solitum dicere procul distare cunctos principes Neronis quinquennio. hic in urbe amphitheatrum et lavacra construxit.

---

[1] On these two passages see Hohl, Klio XI (1911), 228 f.

The passage should not baffle interpretation. At the outset Nero was not all bad, for a period of five years, but he degenerated. As the author states, a little lower down, 'eo namque dedecore reliquum vitae egit' (5. 5). In between occurs a notice about the annexation of Pontus Polemoniacus and the Alpes Cottiae (5. 4).

So far, therefore, no trouble. This epitomator is referring to Nero's character as shown in the opening years of the reign. Aurelius Victor imports a refinement, and perhaps a confusion. His version is as follows (5. 2):

quinquennium tamen tantus fuit, augenda urbe maxime, ut merito Traianus saepe testaretur procul differre cunctos principes Neronis quinquennio; quo etiam Pontum in ius provinciae, etc.

After mentioning Pontus Polemoniacus and the Alpes Cottiae Victor proceeds with a moralizing sentence, and concludes with the same comment as that in the *Epitome*, 'namque eo dedecore reliquum vitae egit' etc. (5. 4).

What then emerges from the confrontation? Each compiler has four items in the same order, viz. a period of five years, Trajan's dictum on it, the annexation of the two territories, Nero's subsequent degeneration. Victor, however, appends to the *quinquennium* the remark 'augenda urbe maxime' and links the end of Trajan's dictum about 'Neronis quinquennium', by the word 'quo', to what follows (i.e. the annexations).

This pair of passages has provoked much discussion and signal divergences of opinion. A thorough and careful investigation, made not long ago, comes to a firm conclusion.[1] It takes the proper point of departure, namely the way in which the two epitomators use their common source refining the style but adding personal comment.[2] In this instance the *Epitome* seems closer to the original. Therefore, one can at once dismiss the temporal link which Victor declares between 'Neronis quinquennio' and the annexation of Pontus Polemoniacus and the Alpes Cottiae. It is Victor's own creation, and not a good one. Those actions occurred (it happens to be known) in 64 and 65. That is, not in a period which Victor assumes to be praiseworthy. Therefore, as a corollary, the addition of 'augenda urbe maxime' also represents a notion of Victor not to be found in the source he shared with the *Epitome*. Hence the source referred to the first five years of Nero's reign.

[1] F. A. Lepper, *JRS* xlvii (1957), 95 ff.
[2] For the source (or rather sources) of the two epitomators, and for the interrelations at this stage, see F. A. Lepper, o.c. 97 ff.

Therefore, one should follow the plain and uncorrupted testimony of the *Epitome*. 'Quinquennio tolerabilis visus': that is, Nero in the early epoch of his reign.

It is a normal scheme in biographers, and in historians, for an emperor's reign to fall into two contrasted parts. A scheme, but often corresponding with what happened. Thus Seneca in *De clementia* could single out 'Tiberi Caesaris prima tempora' (I. I. 6). As concerns Nero, the first years were a period of exemplary government (policy being directed by able ministers, notably Seneca and Burrus), and the turn for the worse, at least as concerns Nero's character, could be put in 59, with the murder of Agrippina.[1]

A period of five years is thus produced. It is to this *quinquennium* precisely that Trajan refers in the anecdote, as something recognized and familiar at the time. Modest as ever, the good Emperor outwits his flatterers through deprecation.

The interpretation is attractive, but comes against some difficulties. There is no trace of anything as definite as 'the *Quinquennium Neronis*' in the historians of Nero or in other writers.[2] Nor is it certain that Trajan in fact made the remark.

There is a way out, however. The point is kept if it be supposed that the anecdote was created in a later age by some senator holding discourse on the Ideal Rulers (and aware of the good Neronian years). An apposite parallel is cited, namely what Trajan allegedly said to Homullus about the friends of emperors (*Alex.* 66. 5).[3]

There was a temptation to go further. A recent theory employs the history of the phrase 'quinquennium Neronis' to illuminate an obscure area of intellectual history: namely doctrines of Stoic philosophers about kingship.[4] Praise of Nero (it is argued) should antedate 'the standard picture of Nero's reign' which had already established itself before the accession of Trajan.[5] The dictum attributed to Trajan is only comprehensible on the hypothesis that the phrase 'quinquennium Neronis' was familiar to Trajan's audience. How might that be? Speculation intervenes. The phrase might have been coined by Junius Rusticus in his biography of

---

[1] That emerges from Tacitus, whose account deserves careful study. It shows good government as negative rather than positive in its comportment. And the historian is cautious. Observe 'species libertatis' (XIII. 24. 1), a trivial action and abortive; and 'manebat nihilominus quaedam imago rei publicae' (28. 1).

[2] As conceded by Lepper, o.c. 102.

[3] Lepper, o.c. 103. He duly adduces M. Junius Homullus (*suff.* 102), but is aware of the relevance of M. Valerius Homullus (*cos.* 152), and seems disposed to dismiss the anecdote as apocryphal. For 'Homullus', above, p. 97.

[4] O. Murray, *Historia* XIV (1965), 41 ff. He followed an indication of Lepper (o.c. 101).

[5] Murray, o.c. 51.

Thrasea Paetus. It was in 59 precisely that the unimpeachable Thrasea first advertised his disapprobation of Nero. The eulogistic biographer needed to find an excuse for the conduct of Thrasea, who had put up with Nero thus far.[1]

Perhaps the wrong question has been asked. Trajan is supposed to be praising Nero for good government. These deductions derive from a paradox.

It might be better to ask what Trajan and Nero had in common. Late Antiquity gives a partial but significant answer—spectacles for the delight of the Populus Romanus. Both rulers occur (despite the ostensible ill fame of Nero) on the tokens called 'Contorniates'. Scholars are not in agreement about the occasion and purpose of their issue.[2] However, the phenomenon has some relevance to the discussion.[3]

Like Nero, Trajan was alert to the desires of the plebs. 'Panem et circenses', that was the easy sneer of a satirist. The rulers of Rome acknowledged an economic and political necessity. A passage in Fronto is of sharp relevance. Trajan, he says, was well aware of the facts—'populum Romanum duabus praecipue rebus, annona et spectaculis, teneri'.[4]

The last words of Nero come in: 'qualis artifex pereo!' They have not always been properly interpreted. It is not the artist or the aesthete bidding farewell to the world, but the great showman.[5]

Trajan also had his exhibits. Along with pageantry goes the splendour of public buildings. Each ruler had been magnificent. If Trajan, in the original form of the anecdote, had been referring to the embellishment of Rome, it had a clear and personal meaning: no emperor could equal five years of Nero. Thus might Trajan modestly answer those who praised his constructions. He had himself quite a lot to show for the five years that had elapsed since the conquest of Dacia. On the first day of the year 112, precisely, Trajan dedicated that Forum to which Ammianus pays the splendid tribute. The *Fasti Ostienses* register the ensuing celebrations.[6]

---

[1] Murray, o.c. 56. He refrained from discussing the post-Trajanic transmission of the anecdote.

[2] A. Alföldi, *Die Kontorniaten* (1943), with the dissident review of J. M. C. Toynbee, *JRS* xxxv (1945), 115 ff.

[3] Lepper, o.c. 100 f. (mainly negative).

[4] Fronto, p. 210 N = Haines II, p. 216.

[5] For this conception cf. *Tacitus* (1958), 41. Fronto's verdict on Trajan is there adduced and quoted. The standard view is conveyed by the translation 'what an artist dies in me!' Thus, e.g., Momigliano in *CAH* x (1934), 741, citing for the meaning of 'artifex' R. Cantarella, *Il mondo classico* i (1931), 53 ff.

[6] *FO* xxii. The Forum and the Basilica Ulpia were dedicated on January 1, the Column on May 14 of the following year.

Such, it appears, is the setting that might suitably evoke a dictum from the Imperator, in mock or ironical humility putting himself and all the other rulers together ('cunctos principes') inferior to Nero.

If this interpretation be found acceptable, Trajan, when evoking 'Neronis quinquennium', meant 'a *quinquennium*' not 'the *quinquennium*'.[1] Furthermore, had Trajan been referring to a known and notorious period, language would surely demand 'isto quinquennio' or 'illo quinquennio'. Thus there is no need to look for any specific period of five years during the reign of Nero.

It is worth giving a thought to the ultimate origin of the anecdote. Presumably Marius Maximus.[2] It was transmitted to the two epitomators by their common source.[3] That source may itself have made an error, conflating and identifying 'a *quinquennium* of Nero' with the initial years of the reign. It will be noted that the very brief *Epitome* has a reference to buildings, to 'amphitheatrum et lavacra', immediately after Trajan's notable dictum.

That source was itself a compilation, prone to strange aberrations and confusions, caused by hasty abridgement, as is patent in a number of items reproduced by the epitomators.[4] It is hazardous to rely upon an epitome that derives from an epitome, and more so to invoke the lost original. Whatever be thought of the interpretation here suggested, the digression has a modest use. It illustrates elements that kept the fame of Trajan alive in the late age: buildings and pageantry, not merely conquest and clemency.[5]

x. No writer who descanted upon good emperors could avoid Trajan (bare mention or corroborative detail). As has been shown above, with more documentation than was needed, Trajan and Marcus stand as the models for war and peace on the shortest statement. Alternatively, Pius is joined to Marcus or blended and subsumed as the 'Antonini'.

---

[1] Thus F. Haverfield in his note on the paper of J. G. C. Anderson, *JRS* i (1911), 178 f. Anderson, with emphasis on Victor, had argued for a five-year period—but at the end of the reign of Nero. Haverfield's notion is dismissed by Murray as 'wholly impossible' (o.c. 47).

[2] Likewise the source (but perhaps immediate) of the anecdote about Nerva in the *Epitome* (above, p. 103).

[3] Probably, for this anecdote, Enmann's KG. It deserves to be emphasized that the subject is Trajan not Nero. That is, perhaps an item grafted on to a text that concerned Nero.

[4] For flagrant errors in the KG, cf. below, pp. 231 f.

[5] As for the anecdote about Trajan, it does not merit long disquisitions. It is a *curiosum*. It tells nothing about any period of five years in the reign of Nero. And, being of dubious authenticity, it can be adduced to illustrate Trajan only at the cost of speculation. For the understanding of history, where would we be without it? The answer is brief and easy.

In late Antiquity, as was natural, Trajan ends by prevailing over Marcus. Eutropius concedes to Trajan primacy on the double claim—'rem publicam ita administravit ut omnibus principibus merito praeferatur, inusitatae civilitatis et fortitudinis' (VIII. 2. 1). The author of the *Epitome* is more explicit. Trajan in his one person combined the two virtues postulated for exemplary rulers—'cumque duo sint quae ab egregiis principibus expectentur, sanctitas domi, in armis fortitudo' (13. 4). The notion was not novel. The *Epitome* enhances, under the impact of Theodosius. The historian Ammianus Marcellinus, though averse from Theodosius, would have concurred.

So too would the HA. Trajan is adduced no fewer than eight times in the *Vita Alexandri*. That biography discloses no notable interest in Marcus. That is important, since the especial relevance of that biography to Julian has so firmly been proclaimed. Julian preferred Marcus to Trajan.[1]

There is something else: documentary evidence. In an edict preserved on a papyrus, Severus Alexander appeals to the precedent of his ancestors, Trajan and Marcus.[2] The fact deserved to be registered. What then emerges? Not much. The conjoined names were inevitable. They convey no guarantee that any one item in the *Vita Alexandri* is genuine.

As in other biographies, the portrayal of a good emperor discloses certain preoccupations and fancies of the genial impostor. He was not of set purpose composing a work of propaganda, but he has his own notions about Senate and emperors, albeit derivative and in the main predictable.

The evocation of Trajan tells nothing about Severus Alexander. Nor does it provide much illumination about Trajan. There is no sign that the author bothered to go back and cull specific items from the *Vita Traiani* of Marius Maximus. The two references to that biography betray their fraudulence (48. 6; 65. 4).[3]

The *Vita Alexandri*, the longest in the HA, is almost total fiction. For Elagabalus, the author had been able to draw on Marius Maximus.[4] That source now ran out. Where was he to turn? In the *Vita Macrini* he had used the Greek historian Herodian, without naming him. The *Alexander* carries two express citations: the 'bloodless reign' (52. 2, cf. 25. 1),[5] and Herodian's verdict on the Persian War, which (so the author alleges) was 'contra multorum opinionem' (57. 3).[6] Dexippus now comes in for

---

[1] Above, p. 98.   [2] *P. Fayum* 20.
[3] None the less, some of the military items might derive from reminiscence of Maximus.
[4] As argued below, p. 121.   [5] Herodian VI. 1. 7; 9. 8.
[6] Herodian VI. 6. 3.

the first time. He furnishes a detail (very valuable) about the wife of Alexander and her father (49. 3 f.).[1] It is followed by the assertion that Dexippus held Elagabalus to be the uncle of Alexander.[2]

The untidy composition of this *Vita* has given rise to elaborate theories of strata and sources.[3] Against which a simple explanation avails: the factual framework, exiguous enough, was supplied by the KG.[4]

[1] Below, p. 157.
[2] Not necessarily veracious.
[3] A. Jardé, *Études critiques sur la vie et le règne de Sévère Alexandre* (1925), 98 ff.
[4] As argued by T. D. Barnes, *Bonner Historia-Augusta-Colloquium 1968/9* (1970), 30 f.

VII · MORE ABOUT MARIUS MAXIMUS

A BIOGRAPHER being on record who wrote the lives of twelve Caesars from Nerva to Elagabalus, there lay the basic source of the HA. The assumption was easy, and it enjoys a recrudescence of favour. Various reasons tell against.[1] Not Marius Maximus but *Ignotus*, at least for the 'Nine *Vitae*' from Hadrian to Caracalla. It may be recalled in this late season that Dessau, aware of an excellent source, was careful not to utter the name of Marius Maximus.[2]

That is not the end of the matter. The HA embodies a certain amount of Maximus. The citations yield twenty-six 'fragmenta' in the standard collection.[3] In addition, the *Vita Alexandri* offers two items not counted as 'fragmenta': it has a doublet (30. 6), and a negative reference to the *Vita Traiani* of Maximus (48. 6). Then, after a long interval, Maximus finds commendation in a list of six conscientious biographers—and is denounced almost at once.[4]

1. When Maximus is cited, a glance at the context often enables more to be surmised in the vicinity; and express citation in the secondary *Vitae* may certify an anonymous passage elsewhere. The frequency exhibits a wide variation.[5] For investigating the source problem of the earlier biographies the *Vita Pii*, by structure and content, is the clear point of departure. In the search for Marius Maximus, other *Vitae* are more promising. A short and selective survey may be of some use for guidance, restricted to five *Vitae*.

1. Hadrian. The *Vita* begins well: Hadrian's origin and family and his early career down to the third of his military tribunates. But the account is interrupted before it gets to his quaestorship by a 'bad passage', not

---

[1] Above, Ch. III. Also 'Not Marius Maximus', *Hermes* XCVI (1968), 494 ff. No complete or reasoned statement of a case for Maximus has been presented in the recent age.

[2] Dessau, *Hermes* XXVII (1892), 601 f.

[3] Peter, *HRR* II (1906), 121 ff. The only other fragment is the *scholium* on Juvenal IV. 53: patently from the *Vita Nervae*.

[4] *Prob.* 2. 7; *Quadr. tyr.* I. 1 f.

[5] None in the *Vitae* of Verus, Didius, Caracalla, Macrinus. But those of Avidius Cassius and Clodius Albinus have four each.

all of one piece (2. 6–10).[1] Other disturbing features soon emerge, as in the other *Vitae* down to Caracalla: small additions, doublets, contradictions.[2] There is something more. Large sections have been added and even interwoven; and at several points the shift to a second source can be detected. A few specimens may be presented.

(*a*) On the news of Trajan's decease, Hadrian went from Syria to Selinus (in Cilicia). Then, returning to Antioch, he is abruptly conveyed to Rome—'per Illyricum Romam venit' (5. 10). The notice is premature, for there follow summaries of the dispatch he had sent to the Senate, with comment on the studious moderation of his attitude (6. 1–5). Then, trouble with the Sarmatae and Rhoxolani being reported, he goes to Moesia (6. 6), and the special Danubian command of Marcius Turbo is registered (6. 6). Next, the conspiracy of the Four Consulars (7. 1 f.), and Hadrian comes to Rome—'Romam venit Dacia Turboni credita' (7. 3). Turbo's command is specified twice, in similar language.[3] Likewise Hadrian's anxiety to abate the odium consequent on the execution of the four marshals.[4]

Failure to attend to the structure of this passage has got several scholars into trouble. They assume that Hadrian, having reached the capital in the summer of 118, soon departed and went to the Danube.[5] The facts are clear. Hadrian visited Moesia in the spring of the year, on the way to Rome from the city he had chosen for winter quarters (presumably Nicomedia or Byzantium).

(*b*) Separating Hadrian's sojourn in Britain (11. 2) and his departure (12. 1), a long passage is inserted (11. 3–7). Beginning with the disgrace of two officials (Septicius Clarus and Suetonius Tranquillus), which is brought into relation with the Empress, it alleges that Hadrian, 'ut ipse

---

[1] The passage carries an anecdote about Hadrian and his brother-in-law Servianus; a reference to the page-boys of Trajan; a 'sors Vergiliana'; an oracle reported by 'Apollonius Syrus Platonicus'; statements about Licinius Sura and about Hadrian's marriage to Vibia Sabina (the latter with comment, Marius Maximus being cited).

[2] Ch. Lécrivain, *Études sur l'Histoire Auguste* (1904), 103 ff.

[3] *Hadr.* 6. 7: 'praefecturae infulis ornatum'; 7. 3: 'titulo Aegyptiacae praefecturae, quo plus auctoritatis haberet, ornato'. For the definition of Turbo's command see *JRS* xxxvi (1946), 162; lii (1962), 89. The term 'infulae' is late. For 'infulae potestatis', cf. *C.Th.* ix. 41. 1; for 'infulae proconsulares', Jerome *Epp.* lvi. 7.

[4] *Hadr.* 7. 3: 'ad refellendam tristissimam de se opinionem'; ib.: 'ad comprimendam de se famam'. The second phrase belongs to the basic source, which now continues as far as 8. 11. Some scholars, it is true, deny a conflation of two sources in 5–7. Thus O. Th. Schulz, *Leben des Kaisers Hadrian* (1904), 30. Others have failed to draw the consequence for Marius Maximus.

[5] Ch. Lécrivain, o.c. 107; B. W. Henderson, *The Life and Principate of the Emperor Hadrian* (1923), 45, cf. 282.

dicebat', would have discarded Sabina 'ut morosam et asperam', had he been a private citizen. Details follow (but no names) about espionage on friends and adultery with their wives.

A palpable insertion. The compiler may have shoved it in at the wrong place. Observe the next item. When Hadrian proceeds from Britain to Gaul, the discovery of the bull Apis in Egypt is reported (12. 1). That engaging manifestation should belong to the opening year of the reign.[1] Hence there is no guarantee that the dismissal of the two equestrian officials occurred either in Britain or as early as the year 122. Speculation becomes legitimate.[2]

(c) A ruthlessly abridged section takes Hadrian from Syria to Egypt (in 130). The decease of Antinous is mentioned 'quem muliebriter flevit' (14. 5). Further, after consecration, the dead favourite became a source of 'oracula', which Hadrian is said to have composed (14. 7).

The narration now passes at once to Hadrian's literary and artistic attainments—'fuit enim poematum et litterarum nimium studiosus' (14. 8). A neat transition. The compiler has turned to a new source, beginning at this point, or one item earlier, with the comment on the death of Antinous. It proceeds from Hadrian's tastes to a sketch of his personality (14. 11).[3] Next, Hadrian's relations with his friends. The first sentence is laudatory (15. 1). The rest is hostile and defamatory. It catalogues the names of twelve friends whom the suspicious Emperor came to detest— and two of whom he drove to suicide, apart from Servianus (the husband of his sister). Next the autocrat's behaviour towards all exponents of polite learning: 'semper ut doctior risit, contempsit, obtrivit' (15. 10). After the famous anecdote about the sophist Favorinus (15. 13), literature is picked up again, with Hadrian's Autobiography (16. 1), the verses written by Florus, along with Hadrian's parody of them, his skill in the art of astrology (16. 7).

Most of this tract in the *Vita* (14. 8–16. 7) might be assigned to Marius Maximus. The basic source now resumes in sharp contrast. Though Hadrian was prone to censure artists, writers, and speakers, he felt contrition, 'si quem tristem videret' (16. 9). He was a warm friend to a numerous company, Favorinus above all; and, if he dismissed teachers for incompetence, they went not empty of praise and subsidy (16. 11).

(d) In the catalogue of the twelve friends with whom Hadrian quarrelled

---

[1] Dio LXIX. 8. 1ᵃ, cf. Boissevain ad loc.

[2] R. Syme, *Tacitus* (1958), 779; J. A. Crook, *Proc. Camb. Phil. Soc.* IV, 1956/7 (1958), 18 ff.; G. B. Townend, *Historia* X (1961), 107 ff.

[3] On this passage cf. E. Hohl, *Bursians Jahresberichte* CCLVI (1937), 135.

Nepos occurs (15. 2): that is, A. Platorius Nepos (*suff.* 119). Furthermore,

> Umidium Quadratum et Catilium Severum et Turbonem graviter insecutus est, Servianum sororis virum nonagesimum iam annum agentem, ne sibi superviveret, mori coegit (13. 7 f.).

The theme recurs at a later stage in the *Vita*. Hadrian after the term of his peregrinations (he returned to Rome in 134), fell ill and had to provide for the succession. His first thoughts went to Servianus, 'quem postea, ut diximus, mori coegit' (23. 2). Next Fuscus, whom he disliked (23. 3 f.). Then, after an insertion, more detail about Servianus, ending again with 'mori coegit' (23. 8).[1]

In the insertion Platorius Nepos is named, also Terentius Gentianus: the latter an especial object of Hadrian's hatred, because the Senate regarded him with favour (23. 4–6). The notice is out of place. There is no means of knowing when Nepos gave offence.[2] Gentianus, however, was dead before 130. His sister, with Hadrian on the Egyptian tour, engraved commemorative verses on a pyramid.[3] Gentianus had benefited from rapid promotion in Trajan's Parthian War, becoming consul suffect in 116 before he was thirty.[4]

Gentianus was not mentioned in the earlier passage. But Ummidius Quadratus and Catilius Severus, who occur there (15. 7), belong in fact with Servianus to the intrigues and dissensions from 135 to 138, in the course of which Hadrian chose as successor L. Ceionius Commodus (*cos.* 136), and, on his decease, an older man from a different group, viz. T. Aurelius Fulvus (*cos.* 120). Catilius Severus (*cos. II* 120), who conceived high hopes through his relationship to the young Annius Verus, was compelled to vacate the prefecture of the City (24. 6). Ummidius Quadratus (*suff.* 118) was clearly an important factor: at some time in these years he managed to get his son betrothed to the sister of Annius Verus.[5]

Hadrian's friends and the cognate question of the succession must have excited the interest, and the malice, of Marius Maximus. The compiler mentions a Fuscus (23. 3), with no awareness of his identity. He is the youthful son of Cn. Pedanius Fuscus Salinator (*cos.* 118) and Julia, the

---

[1] The phrase also occurs in 15. 8 and 25. 8.

[2] This friend of Hadrian (also named in 4. 2) may be a citizen of Italica: his tribe is the 'Sergia' (*ILS* 1052).

[3] *ILS* 1046a.

[4] For Gentianus and his father D. Terentius Scaurianus (*suff.* 102 or 104), see *Tacitus* (1958), 242; 604; 622.

[5] Annia Cornificia Faustina (*PIR*², A 708). These transactions, along with the passages in the HA, are examined in *Historia* XVII (1968), 93 ff.

niece of Hadrian.[1] When Hadrian turned against the next of kin and chose Ceionius Commodus, Pedanius Fuscus shared the fate of his nonagenarian grandfather Julius Servianus.[2]

2. Commodus. The author subjoins in a long transcript the vengeful acclamations of the Senate after the assassination of the tyrant: 'de Mario Maximo indidi' (18. 2). It is therefore reasonable to look for other traces of that documentary activity. The *Vita* happens to register, in the dry style of a catalogue, the honours and titles assumed by Commodus from 166 to 188 (11. 8–12. 9). Further, the total of his performances in the arena (12. 11 f.). In another passage the *Vita* states, on the authority of Maximus, that Commodus had his gladiatorial and other exploits put on record in the 'acta urbis' (15. 4). These sections may therefore be claimed for Maximus.[3]

3. Pertinax. This *Vita* carries a pair of valuable notices illustrating the literary technique of Marius Maximus. That biographer had a speech of Marcus who extolled Pertinax when giving him the consulate (2. 8). Also a letter of Pertinax: 'horruisse autem illum imperium epistula docet' (15. 7).[4] Far too lengthy to be included, says the author of the HA.

The *Vita* asserts that Pertinax was the son of a freedman and names his parent (1. 1). The correct version, so it has been claimed. Hence from Maximus.[5] The passage retailing the possessions of Commodus which were put up for public sale (8. 2–7) is a patent insertion: it interrupts notices about imperial freedmen and slaves (8. 1; 8. 8). A list of curious details is furnished, for example carriages with movable wheels. Why not Marius Maximus? Yet a doubt may obtrude. The list mentions swords, 'maceras Herculaneas' (8. 4). Appropriate, to be sure, because of Commodus' passion for that deity.[6] But it recalls one of the author's notorious inventions later on—'lanceas Herculianas duas, aclydes duas'.[7]

The whole passage calls for exacting scrutiny. Likewise the rest of this *Vita*. Unlike the *Didius Julianus*, it exhibits a large number of additions,

---

[1] The parents, not mentioned by the HA or by Dio, probably faded out quickly. The husband of Julia had stood next in the succession to Hadrian.

[2] Dio LXIX. 17. 2. The HA, with no mention of the young Fuscus, puts the destruction of Julius Servianus before the adoption of Ceionius Commodus (23. 8, cf. 10).

[3] H. Nesselhauf, *Bonner Historia-Augusta-Colloquium 1964/5* (1966), 127 ff.

[4] For the phrase, cf. 13. 1: 'imperium et omnia imperialia sic horruit.'

[5] W. Seston, *Bonner Historia-Augusta-Colloquium 1964/5* (1966), 218. See further below, p. 180.

[6] G. Barbieri, *Stud. it. fil. class.* XIII (1936), 189.

[7] *Claud.* 14. 6. The 'aclys' is a weapon employed exclusively by poets, cf. R. Syme, *Ammianus and the Historia Augusta* (1968), 186 f.

some from Marius Maximus. Thus presumably the unfriendly notices about the scandalous enrichment of Pertinax, his speculations in real estate and so on. And the hand of the impostor himself might be suspected. For example, the origin of the *cognomen* 'Pertinax' (1. 1), and the term 'land cormorant'—'ex versu Luciliano agrarius mergus est appellatus' (9. 5).

4. Caracalla. Though brief, the report of his assassination is excellent in the main (6. 6 f.). It stands in contrast to what precedes, namely the account of the years 213–17, which, though likewise from a good source, is intolerably compressed—and contains sundry suspect features.[1] Apart from Macrinus, the Prefect of the Guard, five names are registered, among them (Aelius) Triccianus, described as commander of the legion II Parthica.

Hohl, in a detailed study devoted to this passage and to other versions, concluded that the basic text in this *Vita* is either Marius Maximus or an abridgement.[2]

5. Elagabalus. This biography is scandalous, in more ways than one. Also most peculiar. None of the bogus authorities and documents and other devices that occur before and after, in the linked *Vitae* of Macrinus and of Severus Alexander. And, by paradox, it discloses a coherent piece of clear and accurate narration. The passage begins with attempts made by Elagabalus late in 221 to get rid of his cousin Alexander, whom the imperial ladies Maesa and Mamea had imposed as Caesar in the previous July; and it terminates with the massacre of March 13, 222 (13. 1–17. 2).[3]

The merits of the extract stand out when it is brought into comparison with Dio and Herodian (though Dio, it will be recalled, is extant only in the abridgement by Xiphilinus). In fact, no comparison is needed.[4]

Two features may be noted. First, topography. Elagabalus had taken up his residence 'ad hortos Spei Veteris' (13. 5). These gardens are not elsewhere on record, but the site is certain: the temple of Spes Vetus on the Aventine.[5] Again, the account specifies the Pons Aemilius as the spot where the corpse was thrown into the Tiber (17. 2). Another item a little lower down may come from the same source. Among the building operations of Elagabalus it records the Baths which Caracalla had not completed, 'in vico Sulpicio' (17. 8).[6]

Second, names. In transactions previous to January 1, one of the two

---

[1] R. Syme, o.c. 34 ff.   [2] E. Hohl, *Misc. Ac. Berol.* II. 1 (1950), 291; 293.

[3] Parts of 17. 4–18. 3 may also be admitted.

[4] For the detail, O. F. Butler, *Studies in the Life of Heliogabalus*. Univ. of Michigan Stud. IV (1910), 140 ff.; K. Hönn, *Quellenuntersuchungen zu den Viten des Heliogabalus und des Severus Alexander* (1911), 30 f.

[5] Platner–Ashby, *A Topographical Dictionary of Ancient Rome* (1929), 494.

[6] Platner–Ashby, o.c. 578 f.

Guard Prefects finds a mention, viz. Antiochianus. Also a tribune, Aristomachus (14. 8). One would not expect to be able to verify the latter. The former might be a Flavius Antiochianus, hence putative grandfather of Flavius Antiochianus, consul for the second time in 270.[1] Further, under pressure from soldiers of the Guard, Elagabalus agreed to disown three of his favourites: Hierocles, Cordius, Myrismus (15. 2). The infamous Hierocles is on independent attestation (*PIR*², H 172); likewise Cordius, the charioteer who became *praefectus vigilum* (C 1289);[2] and 'Myrismus' exists as a *cognomen*.[3]

Next, victims of the various disorders at Rome. The HA proffers three names. When Elagabalus ordered senators to leave the city, the consular Sabinus stayed behind. Whereupon Elagabalus told a centurion to kill Sabinus, but the centurion did not grasp the order, for he was deaf (16. 2 f.). The jurist Ulpian was in peril, also the *rhetor* Silvinus, who had been appointed instructor to the young Alexander; and Silvinus was in fact put to death (16. 4).

All very peculiar. Two persons of some consequence are under menace, but only a *rhetor* gets killed. And, a little later, the *Vita* in fact registers no single person perishing along with Elagabalus. The fate of his mother Sohaemias is reported subsequently, in epilogue (18. 3).

The other accounts may now be allowed to speak. Herodian adds nothing. He eschews names, like other precision of detail. Cassius Dio states that both Prefects of the Guard were killed. That is to say, Antiochianus and his unknown colleague. And Dio names three victims, viz. Hierocles, Aurelius Eubulus (otherwise not attested), and Fulvius, the *praefectus urbi* (LXXIX. 21. 1). Fulvius baffles identification. Borghesi suggested Fulvius Diogenianus, described by Dio in an incident of the year 217 as a senator not in his right mind (LXXVIII. 36. 5; 37. 1). The aspersion is no bar.[4]

Apart from excising names, the compiler made few changes. By keeping Sabinus, Ulpian, and Silvinus he avows his idiosyncrasy. That seems valuable.[5] Moreover, the scholiastic habit of annotation and the

---

[1] *PIR*², F 203. For the conjecture, E. Birley, *Bonner Historia-Augusta-Colloquium 1966/7* (1968), 47 f.

[2] Better, however, 'Gordius', cf. H. Solin, *Eranos* LXI (1963), 65 ff.

[3] A. Stein, P–W XVI. 1104.

[4] Groag rejects him, *PIR*², C 536. Other Fulvii might occur, such as Fulvius Aemilianus (*cos*. 206) or the Fulvius Maximus now attested as governor of Pannonia Superior in 210 (*AE* 1944, 103).

[5] However, caution is here in place. The section 16. 1–4 might be impugned, cf. remarks in *Bonner Historia-Augusta-Colloquium 1968/9* (1970), 320. The name of Ulpian attracted fiction.

parade of knowledge gets him into trouble. On the consular Sabinus he observes 'ad quem libros Ulpianus scripsit' (16. 12): Ulpian had in truth written 'ad Sabinum'. It was a commentary on Masurius Sabinus, a jurist of the early imperial epoch.[1]

11. The admirable piece of narration constitutes a serious problem. Whence derived? It brings up once again the whole question of the sources employed by the HA as far as the *Vita Alexandri*. Various notions may be put up and canvassed.

1. Enmann's KG. That is, the summary drawn upon by the epitomators—and by the HA, in different parts of the work. There is no sign that the KG carried any narration so extensive.

2. *Ignotus*. He ended with Caracalla, so it has been firmly concluded. Could the extract in the *Vita Elagabali* be claimed for *Ignotus*? If so, the previous argument lapses. One of its main supports was the character and structure of the *Vita Macrini*, which shows no trace of *Ignotus*. The difficulty must be faced. It would follow that the HA discarded its main and excellent source before it ran out. Illogical behaviour. But logic or method may not with safety be invoked to explain the procedure of a wilful and capricious author who had his own reasons for changing no less than concealing the sources of his information.

There is a further point. Precision about Roman topography has been asserted a distinctive feature of *Ignotus*.[2] Observe in the *Elagabalus* the 'Horti Spei Veteris' (13. 5). Again, an interest in Roman law and the teaching profession.[3] Both aspects combine with Ulpian and Silvinus (16. 4).

3. Another source. The historical transactions are a unity from the assassination of Caracalla by way of Macrinus to the proclamation of Elagabalus; and Alexander comes into the story of Elagabalus. A basic source has therefore been sought for these three *Vitae*, with the further postulate that it used a Greek writer, i.e. Dexippus, hence subsequent to 270.[4] To state it is to dismiss it. Inspection will show that the three *Vitae* in question are diverse by their structure and by the ultimate source of each.

---

[1] The author's blunder was duly pointed out by Dessau, *Hermes* XXVII (1892), 578.
[2] Above, p. 43.
[3] Above, pp. 42 f.
[4] A. Jardé, *Études critiques sur la vie et le règne de Sévère Alexandre* (1925), 109, cf. 115. Jardé toyed with the name of 'Acholius' (*Alex.* 14. 6; 48. 7; 64. 5). His other views about the composition and sources of the *Vita Alexandri* were untenable, cf. E. Hohl, *Bursians Jahresberichte* CCLVI (1937), 149.

4. Marius Maximus. At first sight the unsavoury repute of the consular biographer might seem a deterrent. On proper reflection, nothing impedes. By source and content, his *Twelve Caesars* must have been a variegated product. Though cast in the form of imperial biographies, the work came to resemble a senator's personal memoirs when it reached his own time and knowledge. Cassius Dio took that turn when writing what was ostensibly imperial history.[1] Dio had seen and heard many things, but he was not (it appears) in Rome in the month of March 222. Maximus from a close point of vantage witnessed the last months of Elagabalus and the final catastrophe. He could furnish a full and explicit narration, as suitable crown and epilogue to his *Twelve Caesars*. Everything encouraged him to be accurate at this point. No need for orations and documents, or even for the scandal and the insinuations he elsewhere found so congenial.

The exemplary piece of historical narration may therefore be reclaimed for Marius Maximus.[2] With no discomfort; and (let it be said) not for defence, to protect the hypothesis that *Ignotus* went no further than Caracalla.

A further step has in fact been taken: Maximus as the main source of the *Elagabalus* as a whole.[3] Not to be discountenanced, though the champion of that theory also adduced Maximus for the *Vita Alexandri*—which cannot be.[4]

III. The use of Maximus in the HA is most inconsistent. The *Vita Hadriani* stands by itself—passages of some length built into the structure. Alternative explanations offer. First, the author began with the idea of fusing Maximus with *Ignotus*. Second, on the revision, he was impelled by the same idea. On either hypothesis, he quickly gave it up. Too much trouble. Similarly, he found *Ignotus* too long for his purposes. Hence the drastic abbreviation of Hadrian's journey from Syria to Egypt; and the sequel of his travels, which took up four years, is squeezed out, with only a brief introduction later of their termination (23. 1). There is another symptom, the recourse in two *Vitae* to a shorter source, Eutropius in the *Marcus*, Victor in the *Severus*.[5]

---

[1] F. Millar, *A Study of Cassius Dio* (1964), 121.

[2] As briefly indicated in *Hermes* xcvi (1968), 500.

[3] Lécrivain, o.c. 208 ff.; 231 ff.; 235 f.

[4] But Maximus both can and should be claimed as the basic source of the *Vita Elagabali*, cf. now T. D. Barnes, *Bonner Historia-Augusta-Colloquium 1968/9* (1970), 31.

[5] Above, p. 33. It need not matter if the KG rather than Eutropius be claimed as the source of *Marcus* 16. 3–18. 1.

Maximus is drawn on for documentation in the *Commodus*. Elsewhere, as far as the *Commodus*, this biographer seems represented in the main by the named citations introduced on the revision. More can often be surmised from inspection of the context. For example, the anecdote in the *Pius* about Homullus (11. 8). Again, Maximus, when cited in the secondary *Vitae*, can certify something in one of the main biographies. Thus Hadrian's expertise in astrology which enabled him to predict what would happen to him each day for a whole year (*Ael.* 3. 9, cf. *Hadr.* 16. 7).[1]

So far, summary indications. Next, a double surprise. For the reign of Macrinus, the source of unique value was the eminent senator who had been *praefectus urbi*.[2] The HA shows not a trace. By contrast, the author (as is argued above) had recourse to Marius Maximus for a long and important section of the *Elagabalus* (13. 1–17. 2).

According to Hohl, Maximus was the ultimate source of what is historically of value in the HA (down to the *Elagabalus*).[3] Hohl furnished no detailed exposition of that thesis. As concerns the excellent account of the death of Caracalla, he referred it either to Maximus or to a source deriving from him;[4] and he assumed Maximus to be the kernel of the *Vita Pertinacis*.[5]

Those sporadic observations were not enough to establish Maximus as the immediate source. To the arguments adduced above in favour of *Ignotus* may be added an inference from the *Didius Julianus*. That *Vita* is equitable towards the usurper. Senators would have no good word to say for him. Maximus, it may be conjectured, was even more odious than Cassius Dio.[6]

There remains indirect derivation from Marius Maximus. Enmann's KG, so Hohl held, was little more than an abridgement of Maximus.[7] A number of erroneous or scandalous items common to the HA and to one or more of the late epitomators that used the KG can be referred back to the consular biographer.

---

[1] Also Hadrian's game-pie (*Ael.* 5. 4 f.), certifying *Hadr.* 21. 4.   [2] Above, p. 47.

[3] E. Hohl, *Berliner S-B* 1953, Abh. 2, 17, quoted above, p. 45, n. 6.

[4] Hohl, *Misc. Ac. Berol.* II. 1 (1950), 291, cf. 293.

[5] Hohl, *Berliner S-B* 1956, Abh. 2, 6, cf. 25. Hohl's views about the basic source followed by the HA in the early *Vitae* were not formulated with sufficient clarity; and he nowhere put the full case for Marius Maximus. One should add, however, the statement, in reference to the *Vita Commodi*: 'dieser zeitgenössische Berichterstatter ist schwerlich ein anderer als der viel berufene Marius Maximus' (*Berliner S-B* 1954, Abh. 1, 3). I much regret that I missed this statement when summarizing Hohl's opinions (above, p. 45, and in *Hermes* XCVI (1968), 496).   [6] Above, p. 44.

[7] Hohl, *Klio* XXVII (1934), 156; *Bursians Jahresberichte* CCLVI (1937), 144.

These items generally occur in passages of the HA otherwise under suspicion of being additions to the basic source. A pair of specimens may suffice. First, Didius Julianus is alleged to have instigated the murder of Pertinax: in all three of the epitomators, and four times in the HA.[1] Second, Julia Domna as the stepmother of Caracalla: likewise in each epitomator and four times in the HA.[2]

A question that much exercised the efforts of scholars was this: is the KG or is Victor being drawn upon by the HA (Eutropius comes less into the account)? It was of decisive concern to those who disputed Dessau's dating of the HA. They could play the KG as a card (that is, assuming it written soon after 284). However, the KG cannot in any way save the 'traditional date' of the HA.[3]

The KG transmitted errors. Victor added some, all his own; and, given his clear idiosyncrasy as a writer (in contrast to the less pretentious Eutropius), his influence can be detected or surmised. Victor's identification of Didius Julianus with the jurist Salvius Julianus (cos. 148) provides the telling instance (19. 2 ff.; 20. 1 ff.). The HA knew that passage. It evaded Victor's error of identifying the two, but it retained the name 'Salvius Julianus' for the Emperor; and it reflects the comments of Victor in the phrase about Severus 'Salvii Iuliani decreta iussit aboleri: quod non obtinuit' (Sev. 17. 5). Hohl insisted on that point, with justice.[4]

Other traces of Victor can be detected elsewhere.[5] Not that it now matters any more for the controversy. A simple conclusion emerges. The author had on his desk the KG, Victor, and Eutropius. He consulted each of them from time to time as need or whim dictated.

A further question intervenes, not of any great relevance in this place. Enmann's KG transmitted recognizable items from Marius Maximus. Ignotus also comes into the reckoning as a source of the KG.

And finally, is it certain that each and every citation of Maximus in the HA should be held authentic?[6] An author who could evoke the Emperor Constantine and remind him of what he had read in Marius Maximus (Alex. 65. 4) was not above faking a reference.

---

[1] Victor 18. 2; Eutropius VIII. 16; 18. 3 f.; Epit. 18. 2; HA, Did. 3. 7; Clod. Alb. 1. 1; 14. 2 and 6.
[2] Victor 21. 3; Eutropius VIII. 20. 1; Epit. 21. 5; HA, Sev. 20. 2; 21. 7; Carac. 10. 1 ff.; Geta 7. 3.
[3] The KG should belong soon after 337, cf. below, p. 222.
[4] E. Hohl, Historia IV (1955), 220 ff.; Wiener Studien LXXI (1958), 149.
[5] Below, pp. 148; 238; 252; 285. See further A. Chastagnol, Rev. phil. XLI (1967), 85 ff.
[6] K. Hönn, o.c. 47.

iv. Some estimate may now be given of Marius Maximus as a writer. Suetonius piled up personal details of a kind disdained by the high style of the senatorial annalists. His books *De vita Caesarum* would serve as a useful supplement—and he may have chosen not to wait until the *Annales* of Cornelius Tacitus saw the light of day.

Suetonius was duly proud of his researches in the archives of the Palace. Maximus went one better, appending actual documents. He also produced whole orations or letters. That was an innovation in biography, taken over from formal history, and an excuse for exercises good or bad in the constructive imagination. In the pages of Tacitus, Sejanus and Tiberius exchange letters, and Nero and his minister compete with set speeches.[1] A skilful practitioner might have used the oration of Marcus (*Pert.* 2. 8) to display the sagacity of the Emperor and summarize the career of the plebeian general.

Another habit of historians was the digression, the picturesque or the exotic not being excluded. Thus Tacitus on the phoenix.[2] Maximus might have dilated upon the marvels of Egypt or the luxury of Antioch, themes attractive to the Roman reader. In any event, there was nothing to prevent this 'homo omnium verbosissimus' from inflating his volumes as he fancied.

These twelve biographies must have presented a peculiar mixture. Not only anecdotes and jokes, dreams and omens, food and drink and sex and all that the virtuous author of the HA dismisses as 'indigna memoratu'. Poems were quoted, catalogues (it may be supposed) were inserted, such as *curiosa* or the victims of a tyrant. Finally, speeches and documents. In short a 'satura', liberally spiced with obscenity (Suetonius showed the way).

Emperors and their consorts furnished ample scope for fun as well as malice. Tacitus had seen that.[3] Hence a social history of the blessed age of the Antonines in its less edifying aspects, suitably continuing Juvenal as well as Suetonius.

Maximus had recourse to a pair of imperial autobiographies. From the HA and from Dio six 'fragmenta' can be collected for Hadrian, and six for Severus.[4] In the *Vita Hadriani* a little more can be divined, for example the details of the Emperor's extraction and early career. Further, attention will go to traces of apologia (Hadrian had much to explain away). Perhaps therefore the anecdote illustrating the jealousy shown by his sister's husband Julius Servianus when legate of Germania Superior (2. 6),

[1] *Ann.* IV. 39–41; XIV. 53–6.
[3] *Tacitus* (1958), 539.
[2] *Ann.* VI. 28, cf. *Tacitus* (1958), 471 f.
[4] H. Peter, *HRR* II (1906), 117 ff.

or the notices implying friendship with Licinius Sura (2. 10; 3. 10).[1] However, the former, if not the latter, may be only an invention of Marius Maximus.

For economy of effort Maximus might have had a use for the sober and prosaic *Ignotus*. Otherwise the quest for written sources is baffled—and for a large part of the work superfluous.

The spoken word and traditions current in high society account for the general picture which Cassius Dio transmits of the second century—and also for many of the details.[2] The young profited from converse with venerable survivors; and by the time a senator reached the sixtieth year (which was regarded as the normal term of a career in public life) his own experiences had accumulated, to blend and cohere, giving a long perspective backwards.

What a man learned from his seniors might be dubious as well as unverifiable. Tacitus was on guard.[3] Dio, however, furnished without qualms the true relation concerning the decease of Trajan at Selinus in August of the year 117: he heard it from his father, who had been governor of Cilicia (c. 182).[4]

The equestrian parent of Marius Maximus had achieved the procuratorship of Lugdunensis and Aquitania.[5] No subsequent post is known. Plague or the wars may have carried him off. Maximus himself, to judge by his career, was born c. 160, consul suffect c. 199. He was about sixty-three when he assumed the *fasces* for the second time, in 223. Of his *Twelve Caesars*, the greater part, from Marcus onwards, is personal memories.

The main themes cannot evade conjecture: emperors good and bad, their attitude towards Senate and senators. The doctrines he conveyed (if deserving that name) would be obvious and predictable. They took shape with the establishment of the Principate, even though one has to look later for express (or ambiguous) formulations, for example in the pages of Tacitus. Elementary truths about government echo down the ages, transmitted by eloquent panegyrists to the last days—and enthusiastically declared by the HA.

It was not the purpose of Marius Maximus merely to extol the Senate and recall the traditions of the Republic, to pay homage to exemplary rulers and expose tyrants as public enemies. He was more subtle. The imperial system was built up at the expense of the Senate, and it went on

---

[1] As assumed in *Tacitus* (1958), 600 f.
[2] Thus, for Hadrian, cf. F. Millar, o.c. 60 ff.
[3] *Ann.* III. 16. 1: 'neque tamen occulere debui narratum ab iis qui nostram ad iuventam duraverunt.'   [4] Dio LXIX. 1. 3.
[5] *ILS* 1389, cf. below, p. 135.

encroaching everywhere. The high assembly forfeited dignity as well as power. Senators of old families (few survived) and the *novi homines* deferential to class and tradition refused to relent or condone. Hence malice and detraction everywhere, in their writings no less than in the talk of the salons.

Hadrian and Severus took up the pen in defence, not of the system itself, but of their own actions as imposed by the necessities of fate or empire. The biographer was alert to their design, eager to controvert the apologia.[1]

v. The *Vita Hadriani* offers the best clue to Marius Maximus. Four passages have been adduced where he may be surmised as the 'second source' of that biography. Of set purpose, nothing was said about the four brief citations of Maximus as an authority.

As follows. Hadrian was cruel by nature: therefore he was intent on behaving well, for he remembered what had happened to Domitian (20. 3). An incident in his last illness is put down to dissimulation (25. 4). Again, a meeting of deputies from the cities of Spain held at Tarraco: it shows Hadrian taking the opportunity to administer a rebuke to his fellow citizens, the men of Italica (12. 4).[2]

Finally, and most significant, the earliest citation of the biographer. It concerns Hadrian's marriage to Vibia Sabina, the grand-niece of Trajan. The match was made 'favente Plotina, Traiano leviter, ut Marius Maximus dicit, volente' (2. 10).

The motive 'favor Plotinae' recurs twice in the sequel (4. 1; 4. 4). And finally 'factione Plotinae', the adoption of Hadrian is contrived when the Imperator had already breathed his last (4. 10). That was the story that gained credence, no doubt at once, with support from sundry suspect features. It was not left for subsequent scandal to invent.

In fact, Trajan had not seen fit to associate Hadrian in the power. About his motives, speculation was, and is, legitimate. Suffice it to say that the proud Imperator was not expecting to die; and no autocrat likes to take the step that announces his own supersession. The situation was unfortunate, but not enigmatic.[3] For the rest, Hadrian was the next of kin, and he had been left in charge of a great army in Syria.

The HA has something further to disclose (4. 8 f.). Trajan wanted the power to go to Neratius Priscus, and he once said 'commendo tibi

---

[1] G. Barbieri, *Riv. fil.* XXXII (1954), 44 ff.; 59 ff.

[2] For this interpretation, see *JRS* LIV (1964), 145 f. It entails an emendation of the text.

[3] *Tacitus* (1958), 233 ff.; 240 f.

provincias si quid mihi fatale contigerit.' Further, so many affirm, Trajan would emulate the Macedonian, dying without a designated successor: he proposed to send a dispatch to the Senate, resigning the choice, but indicating some names for guidance.

The notion is fanciful, not to say deleterious.[1] The corroborative detail helps to discredit the whole story. The jurist Neratius Priscus (*suff.* 97) was a close coeval of Trajan: but not, so far as known, in any especial favour. He had not been signalized by a second tenure of the *fasces*. On the other hand, his son was patently too young for the portentous charge, being not yet consul.[2]

The passage may be assigned without impropriety to the fertile imagination of Marius Maximus. If so, there is no warrant that it is an echo of contemporary discussions about high politics. Hence no clue to Trajan or to Neratius Priscus, but an item for the rubric 'capax imperii'. The notion that somebody other than the natural or designated heir deserved the power, and might have acquired it, had a seductive appeal for the curious or the malignant. The prime document is the anecdote about Caesar Augustus who, when close to the end, assayed the quality and ambitions of three consulars. Tacitus found the item in a subsidiary source (or sources) and grafted it on to his narration, along with a variant for one of the three names and a comment of his own (*Ann.* I. 13. 2 f.). It might afford entertainment to speculate about the original source of the fable.[3]

The motive duly recurs. Trajan at a drinking party brought up the question and did not wait for a response: Julius Servianus was the man. Such is the account of Cassius Dio.[4] Maximus in a similar context employed Neratius Priscus.

Maximus could not fail to be stimulated by the theme of Hadrian's designs for the succession. A passage in the *Vita Hadriani* mentioning two names in the context of Julius Servianus and Pedanius Fuscus (23. 4 ff.) has been discussed above. It concludes with the remark 'omnes postremo de quorum imperio cogitavit quasi futuros imperatores detestatus est.' One might wonder whether Maximus was alive to the significance of Ummidius Quadratus, who in certain respects might well seem 'capax

[1] It has been accorded credence. Thus W. Weber, *Untersuchungen zur Geschichte des Kaisers Hadrianus* (1907), 30; W. Hartke, *Römische Kinderkaiser* (1951), 115.

[2] For the Neratii in relation to this story, see *Hermes* LXXXV (1957), 489 f. The son was still praetorian. His governorship of Pannonia Inferior (*ILS* 1034) falls about this time, cf. *Historia* XIV (1965), 350.

[3] The Memoirs of Agrippina would not have neglected the attractive and damaging notion.

[4] Dio in the version of Zonaras has Hadrian the speaker (LXIX. 17. 3). Xiphilinus, however, has Trajan, which is preferable.

imperii'. He had been governor of one of the armed provinces, viz. Moesia Inferior.[1]

The close of the reign was clouded by discord and crime, like the inception. The destruction of Servianus and the young Fuscus came as a suitable pendant to the suspicious adoption and the execution of the Four Consulars. Alert to intrigue and dissension in the Palace, Marius Maximus made play with the 'favor Plotinae' as determining the fortunes of Hadrian, her stratagem ('factio') as managing the scene at Selinus.

Vibia Sabina could also be exploited to the detriment of Hadrian. The *Vita* in a passage added to the main source cites his verdict on her character (11. 3, cf. above). Further, the chapter about Servianus and Fuscus concludes with her death—'non sine fabula veneni dati ab Hadriano' (23. 9). The *Epitome* of Pseudo-Victor has a variant—Hadrian drove her to commit suicide (14. 8). It adds a refinement. Knowing the 'immane ingenium' of her husband, Sabina took precautions not to conceive a son 'ad perniciem generis humani'. The consular biographer might be the ultimate source, here as elsewhere.[2]

VI. There was much more to be made of another imperial lady, the consort of Marcus. The *Vita* has a general reference to her 'impudicitia' (26. 5), supported in the appendage with the names of three of her lovers, and an anecdote alluding to one of them, Tertullus, viz. the buffoon in the mime who exclaimed 'iam tibi dixi ter, *Tullus* dicitur' (29. 2). Further, Faustina committed adultery with Verus, who told Lucilla about it, whereupon Faustina contrived the death of Verus through poisoned oysters (*Verus* 10. 1).

Finally, to account for the propensities of Commodus, there is the fable that he was the son of a gladiator, the occasion of the amour being indicated—'si quidem Faustinam satis constet apud Caietam condiciones sibi et nauticas et gladiatorias elegisse' (*Marcus* 19. 7). Marcus, being informed, refused to repudiate Faustina, saying 'si uxorem dimittimus, reddamus et dotem' (19. 8). The misconduct of Faustina in Campania recurs in Aurelius Victor, who, however, omits gladiators and has only the fishermen, with the helpful comment 'quia plerumque nudi agunt, flagitiis aptiores' (16. 3).

A more serious charge may now intervene, complicity in the rebellion of Avidius Cassius (24. 6). The HA is impelled to defend Faustina. The

---

[1] As argued in *Historia* XVII (1968), 88 f.

[2] The *Epitome*, written shortly after 395, may itself have drawn on Maximus. Observe the anecdotes about Nerva (12. 3 and 5), cf. above, p. 103.

source of the allegation is Marius Maximus, 'infamari eam cupiens' (*Avid.* 9. 9). Faustina, on the contrary, exhorted Marcus to take swift action against the usurper and punish his adherents without mercy. Such is the gist of two of her letters, which the HA cites.

The proclamation of Avidius stood in need of explanation. The testimony of Dio is of some value.[1] The Empress, he says, was alarmed by the precarious health of Marcus. In apprehension of his death, which might annul the succession of Commodus (and her own position), she wrote secretly to Avidius, urging him to make due preparation and offering her hand. Hence, when a premature report reached Syria that Marcus had perished, Avidius made his proclamation.

The allegation was not implausible. The pretender was not only governor of Syria. He had been invested with special authority over the eastern parts of the Empire several years previously. According to Dio, he was all that could be desired in a ruler, but for his parentage. The parent was equestrian, rising from the post of secretary *ab epistulis* to be Prefect of Egypt in the last years of Hadrian's reign.[2] Avidius was therefore not inferior to that other Syrian, Ti. Claudius Pompeianus, to whom Marcus consigned Lucilla in 169 after the decease of Verus (with a second consulate in 173). Pompeianus was elderly: also 'genere Antiochensi nec satis nobili' (*Marcus* 20. 6).[3]

Avidius was a great general, the hero of the Parthian War. He may well have been a cultivated person like his father, hence a figure at Court in the fifties and known to Faustina, his coeval (she was born *c.* 130).[4] If Marcus was close to death in the spring of 175, the question of the regency became acute, Commodus being only thirteen years old. Faustina may have looked to the great marshal in the East for curb or counterpoise against the ambitions of Pompeianus and Lucilla—or the prospects of some other group.

The transactions of the year 175 could not fail to engender both rumour and rational conjecture. Dio's account bears witness. Whatever the truth, a malicious writer would be tempted to use the women of the dynasty for impairing the repute of blameless rulers. The philosophical emperor

---

[1] Dio LXXI. 22. 3 f.; 23. 1.   [2] *PIR²*, A 1405.

[3] By contrast, the extraction of Avidius Cassius may have been illustrious. An Avidius Antiochus claimed descent from the royal line of Commagene (*OGIS* 766, cf. *PIR²*, A 1401). Further, well-connected Cassii in Syria. Julia T. f. Berenice, of Seleucid stock, was the daughter of a Cassia Lepida (*OGIS* 263, of the year 116).

[4] Neither the age nor the consular year of Avidius is on attestation. Perhaps a youthful consul, still a legionary legate early in the Parthian War. He is named in the context of the Third Legion (III Gallica, or perhaps III Cyrenaica) by Lucian, *Quomodo historia* 31. Cf. E. Ritterling, P–W XII. 1524.

therefore comes under censure because he ignored or covered up the misbehaviour of Faustina (26. 5). The miscellaneous appendage to the *Vita* goes further. It opens with the names of the lovers, to whom Marcus gave advancement (29. 1); and it moves on to record an imputation of hypocrisy—'quod et fictus fuisset nec tam simplex quam videretur' (29. 6).

Elsewhere an atrocious allegation is served up. Marcus brought death to Verus by offering him a piece of meat which had been cut with a knife poisoned on one side (15. 5); and a variant version is added, with the corroborative detail of a doctor's name (15. 6). The fable of the poisoned knife has its use. Not so much as a specimen of the childish enormities that might be retailed, but as guidance in the study of sources and composition. First, it is registered and refuted with indignation by Aurelius Victor (16. 5 ff.). Second, it is repeated in the appendage to the *Vita Veri* (11. 2), where the invocation of Diocletian follows. That is to say, both items were added to that *Vita* when the author of the HA turned back and revised the earlier biographies.[1]

The scandalous stories to the discredit of Marcus or of Faustina in the HA betray their character and origin. They are without exception accretions on the basic source. To take the clearest instances. First, the appendages to the biographies of Marcus and of Verus. Second, the poisoning of Verus by Marcus (*Marcus* 15. 5). Third, Faustina's frolics with gladiators and fishermen (19. 7). That story is embedded in a notoriously 'bad passage' (19. 1–12), which terminates on the invocation of Diocletian, with appeal to the especial veneration which that ruler showed to Marcus —'qui eum inter numina vestra non ut ceteros sed specialiter veneramini'.

Much detrimental matter therefore to the credit of Marius Maximus.[2] But far from being all his own invention. He reproduces the verbal tradition current in high society. For Faustina's culpability in the proclamation of Avidius Cassius one may compare the account in Dio. That historian happens not to preserve any precise details about adulteries of Faustina. In epilogue on Marcus he merely notes and approves the indulgence he showed towards mistakes made by Faustina and by others (LXXI. 34. 3). There is a faint hint in a later place. Cornificia, driven to death by Caracalla, asserts that she is the true daughter of Marcus, though some deny it (LXXVII. 16. 6a). Further, the sinister version about the end of Verus. Dio mentioned an abortive conspiracy of Verus and his death by poison (LXXI. 3. 1[1]). In confirmation (if that is the word) Marcus

---

[1] Above, p. 71.

[2] Hence the clear appeal to the author of the HA, to enliven the basic source.

suspected that Herodes Atticus had been a guilty accomplice of Verus, according to Philostratus.[1]

VII. It may be instructive to adduce for comparison insidious features in the portrayal of another good ruler, P. Helvius Pertinax. By the estimation of senators and in the tradition they propagated, this old general was an admirable character. He did his best to curb the Guard and restrict state expenditure, he was moderate in demeanour and deferential towards the high assembly. How then would a senatorial biographer depict his personality and assess the brief interval after Commodus between tyranny and the military proclamations?

Pertinax paraded an old-fashioned parsimony. That virtue could degenerate into avarice—or be represented as such. One passage in the *Vita* registers his agricultural operations at Vada Sabatia in Liguria, to show that he was 'parcus et lucri cupidus' (13. 4). But there is a doublet about Vada Sabatia, mentioning extortionate rentals and expropriations (9. 4).[2] There follows the term applied to him, 'ex versu Luciliano agrarius mergus' (9. 5). Appended are remarks, 'multi autem . . . rettulere', about his money-getting practices when a consular legate (9. 6). And finally, 'subito dives est factus' (9. 7). The whole passage interrupts the sequence of the exposition. It separates the Emperor's economies about the *Alimenta* (9. 3) and his restoration to their owners of property that had been confiscated by Commodus (9. 8).

Nor were his morals above reproach. His wife had an affair with a harp-player. Pertinax seemed not to mind. Indeed, he was possessed by a passion for a lady of high birth—'Cornificiam infamissime dicitur dilexisse' (13. 8). That is, not Annia Cornificia Faustina, the sister of Marcus, but his daughter: very much the junior of her alleged paramour, who was born in 126.[3]

Finally, a noteworthy verdict on his personality—'magis blandus quam benignus nec unquam creditus simplex' (12. 1). The *Epitome* reproduces the phrase as 'blandus magis quam beneficus, unde eum Graeco nomine χρηστολόγον appellavere' (18. 4). The Greek term also occurs in the HA,

---

[1] Philostratus, *Vit. soph.* 560. To conclude with an item significant of what might be said or believed. It was not disease but the doctors that killed Marcus, to gratify Commodus, ὡς ἐγὼ σαφῶς ἤκουσα (Dio LXXI. 33. 4[2]). Not in the HA.

[2] By contrast the item about 'multis agris coemptis' in Liguria (3. 4) seems neutral.

[3] Cornificia (*PIR*[2], C 1505) was, it appears, the widow of M. Petronius Sura Mamertinus, who was killed *c.* 190. Compare, discussing the family and descendants of Marcus, H.-G. Pflaum, *Journal des Savants* 1961, 36 f. She was put to death by Caracalla (Dio LXXVII. 16. 6[a]).

but separately, a little later—'male Pertinacem loquebantur, chrestologum eum appellantes, qui bene loqueretur et male faceret' (13. 5). Marius Maximus once again, it is to be presumed. Compare the designation of Marcus as a 'faux bonhomme' (*Marcus* 29. 6, quoted above).

Rome in past ages had been familiar with the plain blunt man who was not so simple as he seemed. He might be discovered among the military no less than among the political managers. The type recurred, with an enhancement of duplicity, in the subtler society of the Empire. Generals would advertise the frugality of ancient days or enforce discipline with cruel rigour. Their attitudes often covered incompetence, or subservience to power. The historian Tacitus was not loath to show up such characters.[1]

His unfriendly portrayal of the Emperor Galba is a telling instance. It may have encouraged Maximus to subvert the conventional estimate that favoured and embellished P. Helvius Pertinax. To any who reflected upon history, the two names evoked one theme and a similar catastrophe. In the HA they happen to be adduced together, in two places.[2]

Galba, the descendant of the patrician Sulpicii, was a failure—'omnium consensu capax imperii nisi imperasset'. Also a fraud. Nor was the *novus homo* Pertinax to be conceded immunity. Inspection of his career might have shown him an intriguer and a time-server.

In the Roman historians from Sallust onwards a steady habit of detraction obtains. Suspicious of received truths, they go beneath the surface and bring up the discordant and detrimental. Insight into the political process (and sometimes a personal disappointment) sharpens the edge of their subversive criticism.

A large part of imperial history was secret history. The interpreter had to guess and combine, to transmit rumour and conjecture in default of ascertained facts. He covered himself by evading or disclaiming a verdict for or against. The biographer Maximus abounded in evil reports. Some no doubt of his own construction. It may be supposed that, like the historians, he put in a caveat, from time to time.

VIII. The history of Rome presented Maximus with a potent and seductive theme: the decline and fall of a dynasty, or rather of two, the one ending with Commodus, the second (and fraudulent) with Elagabalus. Suetonius closed his last sequence of rulers with a pair of predictions.

---

[1] *Tacitus* (1958), 544.

[2] *Avid.* 8. 5; *Claud.* 12. 5. Editors expunge the name of Pertinax in the first passage (an alleged verdict of Marcus) because it would be a patent anachronism. Not a valid reason: the item is fictitious.

A raven on the Capitol, speaking Greek, foretold happier times, and a dream of Domitian indicated the same outcome—'beatiorem post se laetioremque portendi rei p. statum'.[1] The *Twelve Caesars* of Marius Maximus no doubt conveyed testimony to the present felicity and radiant prospects for the new regime, himself its first *consul ordinarius*.

Cassius Dio had paid a double tribute to a new emperor. He wrote a pamphlet chronicling the dreams and the portents that vouchsafed the destiny of Septimius Severus. Also a monograph on the wars.[2] The latter work may have terminated with the defeat of Clodius Albinus at Lugdunum in February of 197.[3] Otherwise, perhaps, the invasion of Mesopotamia and the fall of Ctesiphon early in 198: the official date (it appears) was arranged to reproduce that of Trajan's victory.[4]

Dio spent those years at Rome. Maximus had been in the thick of events. Legate of I Italica in Moesia Inferior, he led the legion to Perinthus and commanded the force charged with the long and arduous siege of Byzantium. He took his force through Illyricum to Gaul, fighting at Lugdunum. Then, governor of Belgica for a short spell (and perhaps occupied with rounding up partisans of the deceased pretender), he had the consulship as his reward, in 198 or in 199.[5]

This was the man (it should seem) destined to write military memoirs or a monograph. Or, better, because of his subsequent occupations, civilian as well as military, an annalistic narration of his own times in the grand manner, comparable in scope to the *Historiae* of Cornelius Tacitus. There was a given subject, from the death of Marcus down to 217 or 222.

The period had witnessed developments in government and society, decisive and irreversible. It would not have been either easy or congenial to trace those changes in a broad survey. The precedents in Latin historiography, though not contemptible, were imperfect. Dio in his last books on the Severan dynasty did not make the attempt. He has no eye for themes of imperial policy (military, administrative, or fiscal), or for the processes of social change. Instead, comments on the rulers as individuals, or sporadic indications about favourites or upstarts: brutal, immoral, or uneducated.

Similarly Marius Maximus. He dealt in gossip and scandal. But it is premature and unjust to decry him as a 'historicorum dehonestamentum'

---

[1] Suetonius, *Dom.* 23. 2.   [2] Dio LXXII. 23. 1.   [3] F. Millar, o.c. 29.
[4] Observe the item on the *Feriale Duranum* (January 28), with the comments in *Yale Classical Studies* VII (1940), 77 ff.
[5] For his career, see below, Ch. VIII.

in the picturesque and Sallustian phrase with which the HA labelled a fictitious author.[1] On a friendlier estimate, Maximus portrayed life and manners. He supplied facts (the items gleaned from the HA cannot count as a fair selection), and also documents. On the other side, sporadic documentation is never enough to guarantee a conscientious historian.[2]

Maximus, who had known provinces and armies, chose the easy path: to be the new Suetonius, but embellished, not a dull and pedestrian imitator. He had recourse to bold innovation—and he inspired the author of the HA. That serves to damn him, unless one discovers talent in that impostor and is moved to meditate upon the lost model.

[1] *Claud.* 5. 4, namely 'Gallus Antipater'.

[2] Maximus, the documentary historian, was acclaimed in an eloquent discourse on Faustina by J. Toutain, *Mélanges Bidez–Cumont.* Coll. Latomus II (1949), 331 ff. For Toutain, Faustina was 'une de ces souveraines au tempérament ardent et voluptueux, qu'aucun frein moral ne retenait, qu'aucun excès de luxure n'effrayait' (ib. 338). Truth or falsehood in allegations about the Antonine dynasty, as retailed by Maximus (or by Dio), was not the main concern of the present brief and modest inquiry.

I. BY RARE GOOD FORTUNE, two senators bear witness to the Age of the Antonines, in the wide extension of that term. In double measure, by their lives as well as by their writings. Their testimony converges, though they used different idioms and ostensibly contrasted media. And, diverse by origin, career, and attainments, each endured through many hazards to earn recognition at the end through the most conspicuous of public honours: consuls for the second time, in 223 and 229.

Like Cornelius Tacitus a century earlier, the author of the imperial biographies, by his full style L. Marius L. f. Quir. Maximus Perpetuus Aurelianus, had for parent (birth or adoption) one of the high equestrian procurators. Destined therefore, if all went well, to enter the Senate and reach the consulship. Such is the pattern.

In the families that rose and prospered through the service of the Caesars, the antecedent generations, whether reputable or not (and they belong for the most part to the local aristocracies, the 'boni viri et locupletes'), seldom find commemoration. An inscription reveals the grandfather L. Marius Perpetuus, as a minor official. He was a *scriba quaestorius* in the *consilium* of a proconsul of Africa called Marcellus.[1] The date would be worth having. The proconsul, so it happens, can be identified without effort and assigned to the year 136/7.[2]

Next his son, the homonymous procurator of Lugdunensis and Aquitania.[3] His career had not started with the *militia equestris*. Instead, civilian employments: five of them, all held at the capital. On which followed a procuratorship in Gaul, which always carried firm prospects.[4] Thus recently under Pius a certain C. Junius Flavianus went on to the financial secretariat as *a rationibus* and became *praefectus annonae*.[5] Indeed, Egypt and the Guard were not out of reach.[6]

---

[1] *I. l. Afr.* 592. Hence comparable to the ignoble Curtius Rufus, who began as 'sector quaestoris, cui Africa obtigerat' (*Ann.* XI. 21. 1).

[2] viz. Q. Pomponius Marcellus (*suff.* 121). For identity and date, *Rev. ét. anc.* LXI (1959), 314; LXVII (1965), 343.

[3] *ILS* 1389 (Lugdunum).

[4] For his career, H.-G. Pflaum, *Les Carrières équestres sous le Haut-Empire romain* (1960), no. 168. Hereinafter cited as *Carrières*.   [5] *ILS* 1342.

[6] Thus M. Petronius Honoratus, Prefect of Egypt (in 147), after the procuratorship in Belgica, the post *a rationibus*, and the charge of the *Annona* (*ILS* 1340).

K

A useful parallel, and variously instructive, is furnished by L. Alfenus Senecio, who held the other Gallic procuratorship, Belgica, *c.* 170.[1] His son turns up as consul early in the reign of Septimius Severus (*c.* 197) and proceeds to govern consular provinces.[2] His earlier occupations are a blank.

Alfenus was a close coeval of the consular biographer, about whose *cursus* inscriptions afford full detail.[3] No serious problems, but grounds more than once for rational conjecture. When military tribune, Maximus was transferred from Germania Superior to Raetia. Service in two armies was unusual, and permits various explanations (the identity of the commander is often a clue).[4] Under Commodus the young senator benefited from an abnormal advancement. After holding the tribunate of the plebs he was promoted to the rank of ex-praetor.

The armed proclamation of the legate of Pannonia Superior in April of 193 found Maximus in a position of advantage and of action, legate of I Italica at Novae on the lower Danube. His was the first exploit in the campaign against Pescennius Niger—to occupy Perinthus, to fight in battle there, and to lay siege to Byzantium.

Maximus was later present with his corps at the battle of Lugdunum (in February of 197). He then acceded to the governorship of Gallia Belgica, one of the provinces normally held for three years. Maximus no doubt had a brief tenure, as occurred in earlier periods of warfare or crisis. Fact or surmise about the year 97 is relevant, when Trajan was imposed on Nerva by a veiled *coup d'état*.[5] Similarly, consulates held in absence by men whom a new ruler needed to keep with the armies.[6] Marius Maximus passed from Belgica to Germania Inferior. His consulship may be assigned to 198 or 199. A close parallel offers: Statilius Barbarus, after service in Mesopotamia in 194, becomes governor of Thrace and is promoted to Germania Superior.[7]

---

[1] *ILS* 9489, cf. *PIR*², A 520.   [2] *PIR*², A 521, cf. below, p. 139.

[3] They are conveniently reproduced by B. E. Thomasson, *Die Statthalter der römischen Provinzen Nordafrikas von Augustus bis Diocletianus* II (1960), 114 f. The vital text is *ILS* 2935, which alone furnishes the posts before the consulship.

[4] The three tribunates of P. Aelius Hadrianus (*ILS* 308; HA, *Hadr.* 2. 2 ff.) naturally excite speculation, cf. *Tacitus* (1958), 34; *JRS* LIV (1964) 143 f. Likewise the three of L. Minicius Natalis (*suff.* 139), recorded by *ILS* 1029; 1061. On which, *Arheološki Vestnik* XIX (1968), 104 f.

[5] One would wish to know the successor in Belgica of Q. Glitius Agricola (*ILS* 1021), who became consul suffect in 97, or the posts held by Q. Sosius Senecio and A. Cornelius Palma, the *ordinarii* of 99. For the occupations of L. Fabius Justus (*suff.* 102), cf. *JRS* XLVII (1957), 131 f.

[6] For example, *JRS* XLVIII (1958), 6 ff.   [7] *ILS* 1144.

The alert consular is next heard of in 208 in charge of Syria Coele (Septimius Severus had split the province of Syria in 194 or 195). Papyri found at Dura illustrate two aspects of the governor's activities. He signs warrants for horses to be supplied to an auxiliary regiment; and he makes provision for the reception and travel of an envoy sent by the Parthian monarch.[1]

Under the practice of the previous age, a senator became eligible for Asia or Africa about fifteen years after his consulship. Various perturbations in the appointments to Asia were caused by Caracalla.[2] By anomaly (and no precedent whatsoever), Marius Maximus held both proconsulates —and his tenure of Asia was prolonged to a second year.

The standard catalogue for Africa puts his proconsulate in 220/1 or 221/2.[3] Much too late, it can be contended. Various reasons counsel an earlier dating.

In 212/13 the proconsul of Africa was Scapula: i.e. P. Julius Scapula Tertullus Priscus, the *consul ordinarius* of 195.[4] Therefore Marius Maximus might be assumed to succeed Scapula. Yet he could just as well have the subsequent tenure, in 214/15. If that be so, Maximus was transferred from Africa to Asia by Caracalla, who was in the eastern lands at this time— he spent the winter of 214/15 at Nicomedia. Further, his predecessor in Asia might be conjectured: Julius Avitus, the consular husband of Julia Maesa.[5]

Maximus, it follows, was still in enjoyment of his biennial tenure of Asia when Caracalla was murdered in April of 217. His *biennium* may not have terminated when Macrinus appointed him *praefectus urbi*, to replace the first choice, soon seen to be ridiculous: namely Oclatinius Adventus, the usurper's former colleague in the command of the Praetorian Guard.[6]

II. The *novus homo* at Rome tends to be an isolated figure in any age— ambition and talent, but no support of family. Patronage compensates,

---

[1] *P. Dura* 56, A–C; 60.

[2] Towards the end of the reign. For the imbroglio at that time and under Macrinus see Dio LXXVIII. 22. 2 ff. It concerns C. Julius Asper (*cos. II* 212), M. Aufidius Fronto (*cos.* 199), Q. Anicius Faustus (*suff.* ? 198).

[3] Thomasson, o.c. 116; 'mit großer Wahrscheinlichkeit'. Further, a date subsequent to 217 is implied in the statement, unduly compressed and misleading, in *Ammianus and the Historia Augusta* (1968), 89.

[4] The dedicant of Tertullian's notable piece *Ad Scapulam*.

[5] His tenure of Asia seems to be implied by Dio LXXVIII. 30. 4. Doubted in *PIR*², J 190. But see now C. Habicht, *Die Inschriften des Asklepieions* (1969), 12 (an erased proconsul's name, of 214). [6] Dio LXXVIII. 14. 3.

or marriage, or luck. In 193 the legate of I Italica had been serving under P. Septimius Geta, the brother of Severus, governor of Moesia Inferior.[1] At Perinthus the supreme command was taken over by L. Fabius Cilo (*suff*. 193), later consul for the second time (in 204) and *praefectus urbi*.[2]

There might be a younger brother to profit from success. A certain L. Marius Perpetuus is on record, who, after commanding a Syrian legion in 200 under Alfenus Senecio, went on to be governor of Arabia and duly became consul *c*. 202. He later held two consular provinces, namely Moesia Superior and Dacia.[3]

Furthermore, a kinsman may be detected, perhaps a cousin. He is the consular Q. Venidius Rufus Marius Maximus L. Calvinianus.[4] After commanding I Minervia (in Germania Inferior), Venidius is governor of Cilicia, and also of Syria Phoenice (where he is attested in 198).[5] His consulship falls in the vicinity of 200; and he becomes legate of Germania Inferior *c*. 201.

In the campaigns of Septimius Severus (from 193 to 198) the senior and conspicuous generals were P. Cornelius Anullinus (*suff*. *c*. 176), proconsul of Africa in 193, and L. Fabius Cilo (*suff*. 193).[6] Both, so it happens, from Spain.[7] That country had not made such showing in the annals of war or peace since the days of Trajan and Hadrian. Next comes Ti. Claudius Candidus, 'dux exercitus Illyrici expeditione Asiana item Parthica item Gallica'.[8] Probably eastern by origin, he had been promoted from equestrian rank under Commodus.[9]

These three marshals find admittance to the meagre and fragmentary chronicle of the wars. Epigraphy contributes abundant detail about the other senators of the time: legionary legates in 193 or soon after, and praetorian governors enjoying rapid promotion. From this group come the consular legates in charge of the armed provinces of Caesar, eleven in number.[10]

---

[1] For his *cursus*, *IRT* 541. He passed from Moesia Inferior to Dacia.

[2] *ILS* 1141 f.

[3] *ILS* 1165.

[4] *CIL* xiii. 7994. This person is absent from P–W.

[5] *AE* 1933, 206. The successor of Ti. Manilius Fuscus (*suff*. *c*. 196).

[6] *ILS* 1139; 1141 f. The African proconsulate of Anullinus is generally assigned to 193/4. Thus *PIR*², C 1322; Thomasson, o.c. 99. Better, 192/3.

[7] The *patria* of Anullinus is Iliberri in Baetica. The tribe 'Galeria' and other indications suggest a Spanish origin for Cilo, cf. *PIR*², F 27.

[8] *ILS* 1140.

[9] Candidus probably became consul *c*. 194.

[10] For this standard type of promotion cf. *Tacitus* (1958), 53; 649 ff.; *Historia* xiv (1965), 342 ff.

A dozen names will serve to illustrate that notable company, the coevals of Marius Maximus; and several of them will reappear in this chapter, for various purposes. Not all, it is true, carry the full detail of a *cursus* either before or after the consulate. But their consular commands, so far as known, will be summarily registered.[1]

C. Valerius Pudens (*suff.* ? 194). *PIR*[1], V 122. Germania Inferior ? 197–9. Britannia in 205 (*AE* 1962, 260).

Ti. Manilius Fuscus (*c.* 196, *cos. II* 225). *PIR*[1], M 106.

Alfenus Senecio (*c.* 197). *PIR*[2], A 521. Britannia ? 202–5.

Q. Anicius Faustus (? 198). *PIR*[2], A 595. Moesia Superior ? 202–5.

T. Statilius Barbarus (*c.* 198). *PIR*[1], S 591. Germania Superior *c.* 198–200.

Q. Venidius Rufus Marius Maximus L. Calventianus (*c.* 199). *PIR*[1], V 245. Germania Inferior *c.* 201–4.

Ti. Claudius Claudianus (*c.* 199). *PIR*[2], C 834. Pannonia Superior *c.* 202.

C. Caesonius Macer Rufinianus (*c.* 200). *PIR*[2], C 210. Germania Superior *c.* 203–6.

L. Marius Perpetuus (*c.* 202). *PIR*[1], M 237. Moesia Superior *c.* 205, Dacia in 214.

Claudius Gallus (*c.* 204). *PIR*[2], C 878, with *AE* 1957, 123. Dacia *c.* 208.

Q. Aiacius Modestus Crescentianus (*c.* 206, *cos. II* 228). *PIR*[2], A 470. Germania Superior *c.* 208.

The list would repay a proper inquiry. For present purposes it may suffice to point out that none of these men had consular parentage (which conforms to the normal pattern), that most of them look provincial rather than Italian. The ascertainment of origins brings a powerful reinforcement to the study of social and political history. Local ties and alliances had been much in evidence earlier, especially in Spain and Narbonensis, and they can be adduced with advantage.[2] But the assessment of regional groups and influences calls for discretion everywhere. Trajan, it is clear, showed favour to senators from Spain. He did not create them. They were already there. Trajan is a symptom rather than a cause.

---

[1] For the details, see G. Barbieri, *L'albo senatorio da Settimio Severo a Carino* (193–285): published in 1952. Hereinafter cited as *Albo*. Also, the standard catalogues of consular legates: for the two Germanies, Ritterling–Stein (1932); Moesia and Dacia, A. Stein (1940; 1944); Pannonia Superior, W. Reidinger (1956); Syria Coele, J. F. Gilliam, *AJP* LXXIX (1958), 225 ff.; Britain, A. R. Birley, *Epigraphische Studien* IV (1967), 63 ff. Finally, the list of legates both consular and praetorian under Septimius Severus established by G. Alföldy, *Bonner Jahrbücher* CLXVIII (1968), 256 ff.

[2] *Tacitus* (1958), 601 ff.

Similarly the Africans in high office under Septimius Severus. Their prominence is liable to be misunderstood; and the pretender who was born at Lepcis should not be regarded as the leader or candidate of an African faction.[1] In seizing the power he employed the ready aid of ambitious persons—and of small groups, so it may be conjectured. Africans are no surprise (they were moving in a steady ascension), but Lepcis lies apart, a long way from the rest of Africa Proconsularis and from Numidia. None the less, the first emperor from Africa may have felt and acknowledged regional as well as local affinities.

Alfenus Senecio came from Cuicul, Claudius Claudianus from Rusi-cade.[2] The name of Caesonius Macer and his tribe, the 'Quirina', would fit an African origin, if there were other evidence. It is not enough that Africa should present a dozen Caesonii.[3] As for Aiacius Modestus, the *nomen* is so rare and remarkable that, by paradox, it seems to baffle localiza-tion.[4] An imperfect clue might be discovered in the fact that his presumed daughter, Junia Aiacia Modesta, married a Q. Aradius Rufinus.[5] The Aradii, destined for long duration, derive from Bulla Regia in procon-sular Africa.[6] They show their first senator in the Severan age.[7]

There is something more. The wife of Aiacius Modestus, governor of Arabia, now emerges at Petra; viz. Danacia Quartilla Aureliana.[8] The *nomen* 'Danacius' is most peculiar. Also unique, for the only other instance is precisely 'Danacia Quartilla Aureliana c. f.': at Horrea Caelia to the north-west of Hadrumetum.[9]

[1] On that notion, T. D. Barnes, *Historia* XVI (1967), 97 ff.; A. R. Birley, *Bonner Jahrbücher* CLXIX (1969), 274 ff.

[2] *ILS* 9485 (Senecio); 1146 f. (Claudianus).

[3] A fragment at Uchi Maius (*CIL* VIII. 26262) records the name of his son, Caesonius Lucillus—who, however, was legate in proconsular Africa *c.* 230 (*ILS* 1186). Barbieri proclaimed Caesonius Macer 'senza dubbio italico' (*Albo*, no. 99).

[4] W. Schulze (*LE* 116) cites *CIL* v. 1983 *add.* (Opitergium); *Supp. It.* (ed. Pais) 1166 (Aquileia); XIV. 2964 (Praeneste).   [5] *CIL* XV. 8088, cf. *PIR²*, A 471; 1016.

[6] Groag in *PIR²*, A 1013. All the Aradii in *CIL* VI as in *CIL* VIII happen to be senatorial. For parallel to this *nomen*, Schulze (*LE* 113) cites 'Sidonius', 'Tyrius', etc. For 'Sidonius' in Africa, *CIL* VIII. 14106; 24425²; *I. l. Alg.* II. 809. Relevant to 'Aradius' is not only Phoenician Aradus but the Biblical Arad. It is indeed a rarity when persons of the upper order in the western provinces bear *gentilicia* that are not Latin or Italian in form. Given the African origin of the Aradii, it was not necessary to assume that the 'Aradio' whom Probus killed (*Prob.* 9. 2) is a perverted form of 'Arabio': see above, p. 9.

[7] viz. Q. Aradius Rufinus, attested in 219 (*PIR²*, A 1016, perhaps identical with 1017, a homonymous consul). Add Aradius Paternus, legate of Cappadocia in 231 on the inscription published by R. P. Harper, *An. Stud.* XIV (1964), 164. He there comments (ib. 166) on the inscription at Bulla Regia of the consular Q. Aradius Rufinus Optatus Aelianus, now re-produced by A. R. Birley in *Epigraphische Studien* IV (1967), 83.

[8] Published by J. Starcky and C. M. Bennett in *Syria* XLV (1968), 45 f. It is on an altar, dedicated by Aiacius, his wife, and two sons.   [9] *CIL* VIII. 11152.

By its nomenclature Africa attests ancient immigration. *Nomina* crop up that are of rare enough occurrence in the Italian regions or towns of their ultimate origin.[1] Palmary specimens can be adduced in this period. Thus at Rusicade the Austurnius who married the sister of Ti. Claudius Claudianus;[2] and a Coculnius of Cirta was admitted to the senatorial career in the early years of Septimius Severus.[3]

Venidius Rufus also offers substance. The *nomen* 'Venidius', at first sight unobtrusive, turns out to be very uncommon. The signs point to Africa.[4] What then may be inferred about his kinsfolk?

The Marii Maximi, it has been asserted, are 'Romains de Rome'.[5] Rather from Africa or Spain, as their tribe suggests, which is the 'Quirina'. And Africa by preference. Not only because of Venidius Rufus. There is the grandfather, a humble official in attendance on the proconsul Marcellus.

III. The anomalous proconsulate of Asia shows Maximus in esteem with Caracalla. Appointed to the city prefecture by Macrinus, he had no long tenure. In the summer of the next year the Syrian princesses Julia Maesa and Julia Sohaemias raised rebellion against Macrinus. They worked upon the soldiers, loyal to the memory of Caracalla, and they brought forward the boy-priest of Emesa, passing him off as the son of Caracalla. The principal agent was a certain P. Valerius Comazon, at the time equestrian commander of the legion II Parthica.[6]

Comazon duly became the first *praefectus praetorio* of the new reign. Not only that. He went on to acquire the rank of a senator, becoming *praefectus urbi* and consul in 220. And, after an intermission, he held the urban prefecture for a second time. Being providentially out of office in March of 222, Comazon missed the massacre in which perished not only the ignominious favourites of Elagabalus, but the two Prefects of the Guard and Fulvius, the *praefectus urbi*.[7] He was therefore available for a third tenure of the illustrious office in the first days of the new dispensation.

In any age artful agents at court emerge again to places of honour or influence, and the loyal official serves as a bridge between reign and

---

[1] For instances, *Historia* IV (1955), 56 (on 'Aufustius').

[2] *ILS* 1147. For the *nomen*, Schulze, *LE* 131. Elsewhere perhaps only in *CIL* VI (four instances).

[3] viz. M. Coculnius Quintillianus (*ILS* 6587). This Etruscan *nomen* has so far not turned up outside Cirta.

[4] As argued in *Historia* V (1956), 210 f.

[5] Thus Pflaum in *Carrières*, no. 168.

[6] For the details of his career, Pflaum, *Carrières*, no. 290.   [7] Above, p. 119.

reign. Senators, knights, or imperial freedmen, it had happened often enough. But nothing had yet been seen (not even Cleander under Commodus) to match P. Valerius Comazon, who combined humble extraction with an office normally the prerogative of senior consulars. In his earlier existence, Comazon had been an actor, also a soldier in Thrace in the days of Commodus when Claudius Attalus was governor of that province.

Dio furnishes the main and vivid particulars about Comazon.[1] The HA eschews his name. He is lumped together anonymously with two ignoble creatures promoted to official posts by Elagabalus:

ad praefecturam praetorii saltatorem qui histrionicam Romae fecerat adscivit, praefectum vigilum Cordium aurigam fecit, praefectum annonae Claudium tonsorem (*Elag.* 12. 1).

Like the narration of the destruction of Elagabalus a little further on (13–17), this passage may have been taken from the consular biographer.

The name of Comazon is suppressed—and no hint that he became *praefectus urbi* in 218 or 219, supplanting Marius Maximus. The fact justifies a suspicion.

The impulsion to write the imperial biographies and the inception of the task evade conjecture. Maximus may thus have occupied the empty years under Elagabalus, or again, have sought (or proclaimed) encouragement from the accession of Severus Alexander. However it be, a distasteful manifestation such as Comazon must have sharpened his anger and his style.

Consul for the second time in 223, Maximus had waited long for the honour. Standing and merit made him eligible in earlier reigns. Severus, it is true, was grudging—four men only apart from the Guard Prefect Fulvius Plautianus in 203, whose *ornamenta consularia* were reckoned, by an innovation that soon became standard, the equivalent of a first consulate.[2] Caracalla was more generous, no fewer than five in his brief reign, viz.

212 C. Julius Asper
213 D. Caelius Calvinus Balbinus
215 Q. Maecius Laetus
216 P. Catius Sabinus
217 T. Messius Extricatus

Several of the names are baffling, notably T. Messius Extricatus,

[1] Dio LXXVIII. 39. 4.; LXXIX. 3. 5; 4. 1 f.; 21. 2.
[2] The iterations are C. Domitius Dexter (196), P. Cornelius Anullinus (199), P. Septimius Geta (203), L. Fabius Cilo (204). The cessation is noteworthy.

about whom nothing can be established.[1] Later history was to bring the second of them into brief and anomalous fame.[2]

In Rome of the Caesars, as before under the old order, one of the high priesthoods was the visible sign of political success no less than of social eminence. Yet there are surprises which disconcert the normal assumptions.[3] Three inscriptions set up after 223 show that Maximus was only a *fetialis*.[4] Yet his coevals Venidius Rufus and Aiacius Modestus, with no apparent benefit of superior birth, were *quindecimviri sacris faciundis*, high on parade when Severus celebrated the *Ludi Saeculares* in 204.[5] Maximus seems to have enjoyed the favour of Caracalla, but he comes off badly in comparison with a younger man, C. Octavius Appius Suetrius Sabinus, the consul of 214, who was both *pontifex* and *augur*.[6] That cumulation, two of the four major sacerdotal honours, had few precedents.[7]

However that may be, Maximus was able to perpetuate the *nobilitas* of a new family. His son became *consul ordinarius* in 232, his nephew in 237.

IV. To the vigorous opportunist, who in a long career had come to know all the chief military zones of the Empire (apart from Britain and Cappadocia), there stands no sharper contrast than Cassius Dio, a product of the urban aristocracies in the eastern lands, and born to high estate. His *patria* was Nicaea in Bithynia. The father, Cassius Apronianus, came to his consulate *c.* 182 from the governorship of Cilicia and went on to hold Dalmatia.[8]

Dio was praetor in 194.[9] Hence born in 162 or 163, junior by about three years to Marius Maximus. Consular parentage apart, his consulship should fall not later than 205. Without overt misdemeanour or discontent, a senator might miss his due advancement. There are examples, in any age. For Dio, however, no evidence avails to support that

---

[1] For the *nomen* 'Messius', below, p. 196. Africa has over thirty instances, notably a knight at Gigthis (*ILS* 9394) and a senator there (*CIL* VIII. 22720). The high official P. Messius Saturninus came from Pheradi Maius (*AE* 1932, 34 = *I. l. Tun.* 250). On whom, Pflaum, *Carrières*, no. 613. He is identified as the jurist in *Dig.* XLIX. 14. 50: 'Papinianus et Messius novam sententiam induxerunt.' As for the *cognomen* 'Extricatus', 161 out of 178 are African according to I. Kajanto, *The Latin Cognomina* (1965), 352.

[2] Below, Ch. X.

[3] *ILS* 1034 (Saepinum) registers the illustrious L. Neratius Priscus (*suff.* 97) and his consular son: the latter, however, is *septemvir epulonum*.

[4] *CIL* X. 6567; 6764; *AE* 1955, 188.   [5] *ILS* 5050.   [6] *ILS* 1159.

[7] In fact, only one so far, viz. P. Cluvius Maximus Paullinus (*AE* 1940, 99), consul suffect *c.* 141. Add perhaps the *Ignotus* of *AE* 1904, 109 (Praeneste).

[8] *PIR*², C 485.

[9] For his life and career, Stein in *PIR*², C 492; F. Millar, *A Study of Cassius Dio* (1964), 13 ff.; 204 ff.

assumption; and Dio had been quick to publish homage to Septimius Severus by his earliest writings. However, some doubt and contestation subsists about the date of his consulship (see below).

The historical work discloses no sign of any employment abroad before the year 218. Macrinus appointed him to be curator of two cities in Asia, viz. Pergamum and Smyrna. He was occupying that post in the winter of 218/19 while Elagabalus sojourned at Nicomedia on his progress from Syria to Rome (LXXIX. 7. 4).

It was not clear how long that post lasted. Dio was still in Asia, he states, when the false Alexander turned up in Moesia Superior, promenaded through Thrace, and disappeared at Chalcedon (LXXIX. 18. 3). That episode occurred 'not long before' Elagabalus associated his cousin in the power (18. 1). That is, the summer of 221. The false Alexander is generally assigned to 221.[1] Better, perhaps, the previous year.

The date is relevant to the subsequent employments of Cassius Dio: governorships in Africa, Dalmatia, and Pannonia. His own statement, while clear about the order, betrays an inconsequence in the argument. Recounting the end of Elagabalus (March 13, 222), he states that he had narrated the events, with proper accuracy, as best he could. From that point onwards, however, he was precluded from furnishing an adequate account, not having been at Rome for any time. From Asia he went to Bithynia, where he fell ill. From Bithynia he departed in all haste to take up the governorship in Africa. After his return to Italy, he proceeded almost at once to Dalmatia, thence to Pannonia Superior (LXXX. 1. 2 f.).

The inconsequence is patent. The historian, so he professes, could not furnish full detail about the first years of Severus Alexander, for he was away from Rome. Yet, on his own showing, he had also been absent during the reign of Elagabalus (218–22). Africa, Dalmatia, and Pannonia were not out of reach for news from Rome.

That being so, a doubt may arise about the impression Dio wishes to convey: no high office before the exemplary rule of Severus Alexander. The phenomenon is normal enough. Senators who benefit from what turns out to be the late epoch of an evil dispensation tend to be vague in the sequel, or silent. The transition from Domitian to Nerva and Trajan furnishes classic examples.[2]

Before this notion can be entertained it is necessary to fix the date of Dio's consulship. Estimates diverge, widely. Dio was curator of two cities in Asia. Such posts are normally praetorian in rank. Next, Dio mentions his 'governorship in Africa'. That also, it has been argued, might

---

[1] Millar, o.c. 214.   [2] Tacitus (1958), 82.

be praetorian. That is to say, not the proconsulate but Numidia.[1] Therefore Dio did not accede to the consulate until 222 or 223.[2]

On that showing, Cassius Dio suffered a long retardation. Anything could happen to a senator. M. Antonius Gordianus, born c. 158, was still of praetorian rank in the year 216, when he was legate of Britannia Inferior.[3]

A case can therefore be made. On the other side, the 'governorship in Africa' is prima facie the proconsulate. It is to be preferred.[4] No known fact precludes Cassius Dio from his consulship in the normal expectation, about 205.

To proceed to the proconsulate. It is generally put in 223/4.[5] In this season there is an unfortunate dearth of names for Africa as for Asia, and the system had recently undergone perturbations.[6] Hence alternatives avail. Dio might have been assigned his province (by the ballot, or rather perhaps through influence of the government), in the early months of 221 or of 222, before the suppression of Elagabalus.

Not that it matters much. Persons of station and repute performed the normal functions whoever the ruler might be. Dio in his late emergence to consular offices went on to be governor first of Dalmatia then of Pannonia Superior. The legionaries on the Danube did not relish his efforts to impose discipline. Honoured with a second consulship in 229, Dio had reason to apprehend the animosity of their congeners in the Guard: and Severus Alexander, though benevolent, was in no posture to protect. After assuming the *fasces* in absence, Dio went away to his native Bithynia, out of the turmoil (he quotes Homer) and preserved by divine providence, as a dream had foretold (LXXX. 4. 2–5. 3).

---

[1] Thus E. Gabba, *Rev. stor. it.* LVII (1955), 289.

[2] The advantages in this view are brought out by G. W. Bowersock, *Gnomon* XXXVII (1965), 473. Furthermore, in this period Numidia forfeited its function as a province for military men predestined to hold the consular commands. This was pointed out by E. Birley, who put the change 'after the accession of Severus Alexander' (*JRS* XL (1950), 67).

[3] Below, p. 166.

[4] A. Stein, *PIR*², C 492. The case is fully argued by Millar, o.c. 205 ff.

[5] Thomasson, o.c. 119.

[6] Above, p. 137. Two known proconsuls probably belong in the period 219–23, viz. C. Caesonius Macer Rufinianus (*ILS* 1182), *suffectus c.* 202, and Ap. Claudius Julianus (*CIL* VIII. 4845) who held the *fasces* for the second time in 224.

IX · THE REIGN OF SEVERUS ALEXANDER

I. THE PREDICAMENT of Cassius Dio illustrates the deplorable condition of affairs at Rome in the seventh year of the new dispensation. Instructive as an episode, but large questions subsist and annoy. It is not easy to reach, or even approach, an adequate estimate of the reigns of the two boy princes (from 218 to 235). Still less, to reconstruct them as an intelligible piece of history.

It is not only the paucity and perversity of the sources. A problem of diagnosis is involved. As the imperial system developed, it disclosed its various *arcana* one by one. How much does the personality of the ruler matter? Less and less, it should seem. Be he boy, buffoon, or philosopher, his conduct may not have much effect on the administration. Habit and routine took over, with groups and grades of bureaucrats at hand to fill the posts. For the senator, the career of public honours, as previously; and in any age a man can take credit for serving the State whoever the Emperor may be.

The scandalous behaviour of Elagabalus engrosses the attention of historians no less than of biographers, to the neglect of Julia Maesa— and of other factors of continuity and stability. A doubt obtrudes whether his follies had much repercussion outside the capital or impaired the administration of the provinces. However, the continuation of his antics (many of them due to the fact that this deluded priest took his religion seriously) threatened to subvert the dynasty. Julia Maesa had a long and deep experience of court and government. Promoting the cousin, she exploited their rivalry to its murderous conclusion with the aid of the city troops.

The reign of Severus Alexander presents graver problems, notably because of its duration: thirteen years. About the first nine, before the prince went out on the Persian expedition in 231, next to nothing is known. Herodian, after a brief account, with no name of a Roman senator or knight (VI. 1. 1–10), passes at once to the Persian War—after Alexander had been reigning for thirteen years, so he states (2. 1). That is an error. Herodian's chronology is four years out; and he conflates the period 231–5 to the limits of a single year (cf. 9. 8).

On his accession, Alexander was only twelve or thirteen.[1] How then

---

[1] For the data, *PIR²*, A 1610. His 'dies imperii' now emerges as March 13, cf. *Dura, Final Report* v. 1 (1959), 198.

was the government conducted? According to Herodian, the princesses Maesa and Mamaea had the arbitrament. Which is no doubt correct. Herodian also mentions a council comprising sixteen senators of age, rank, and repute (VI. 1. 4); and he duly commends an exemplary choice of officials and army commanders (1. 4). Thus the Empire was managed, for a long time (1. 5). Then old Maesa ends her days; and Herodian adds comment about the guidance now exercised by Mamaea (1. 6). It may be observed that, contrary to the impression here conveyed, Maesa died at no long interval, perhaps as early as 223.[1]

II. Search must therefore be made for agents of power and framers of policy. In the first place, the Prefects of the Guard. Inevitably the names occur of the masters of jurisprudence Domitius Ulpianus and Julius Paulus —and with them trouble, induced by errors and misconceptions in the various Latin sources.

At the outset a warning is enjoined. Paul is never there named save in the company of Ulpian. The one name seems to evoke the other, by inevitable association. Moreover, no unimpeachable evidence confirms for Paul any official equestrian post. For Ulpian, two are on clear record. Rescripts of Alexander furnish the dates. On the last day of March 222, Ulpian was *praefectus annonae*, on the first of December, *praefectus praetorio*.[2]

Allegations about the careers of the two jurists must now be put under sharp scrutiny. The HA has two parallel passages. First, in the *Vita Pescennii*. Paul and Ulpian, it is stated, had both served as advisers on the *consilium* of the Guard Prefect Papinian (7. 4). That is, in the period 205–11. Which might well be true—without being authentic.[3] The author then proceeds to a bolder assertion—'postea cum unus ad memoriam alter ad libellos paruisset, statim praefecti facti sunt.'[4] Fortunately, the fraudulent character of the whole context evokes instant distrust. The author has just been furnishing the gist of letters written by Pescennius to Marcus and to Commodus, suggesting reforms in provincial government and ending with remarks about *assessores* (7. 2 f.); and he winds up the chapter by retailing anecdotes about Pescennius in the land of Egypt (7. 7 f.), where he never was.

Second, in the *Vita Alexandri*. Opening with Paul and Ulpian, the author states: 'quos praefectos ab Heliogabalo alii dicunt factos, alii ab

---

[1] H. W. Benario, *Historia* XI (1962), 192. See however J. F. Gilliam, *Hommages* II (1969), 285.

[2] *C. Just.* VIII. 37. 4; IV. 65. 4. He is 'amicus meus' in the first, 'parens meus' in the second.

[3] Attested in fact for Paul (*Dig.* XII. 1. 40).

[4] As for the post *a memoria*, in 215 it was held by Caracalla's freedman Marcius Festus (Herodian IV. 8. 4; *CIL* XIV. 3638). Not plausible therefore for Paul.

ipso—nam et consiliarius et magister scrinii perhibetur—qui tamen ambo assessores Papiniani fuisse dicuntur' (26. 5 f.). A complicated sentence. For the moment, let the parenthesis about a post of Ulpian in the imperial secretariat be postponed. The prime point of issue is the prefectures of Ulpian and Paul. The HA reports (but deserts) the opinion, 'alii dicunt', that the pair had been appointed by Elagabalus.

Where did the HA light upon that opinion? Aurelius Victor might seem the answer.[1] Writing about Alexander he says:

Domitium Ulpianum, quem Heliogabalus praetorianis praefecerat eodem honore retinens Paulloque inter exordia patriae reddito, iuris auctoribus . . . (24. 6).

The passage is doubly instructive—for Paul and for Ulpian. Victor alleges that Ulpian held the prefecture under both rulers. He may, or may not, have found in the source which he abbreviated (i.e. the KG), the statement that Paul as well as Ulpian was made *praefectus praetorio* by the new emperor. Let that pass. However, a point deserves attention: a cursory glance at the passage in Victor might have left in a reader's mind the idea that Paul as well as Ulpian was Prefect of the Guard under Severus Alexander.

Therefore Victor might well be responsible for the further notion in the HA that the two jurists were colleagues in office under Alexander (26. 6).[2] It recurs a little later in the *Vita Alexandri*, which mentions a project of the Emperor—'sed hoc Ulpiano Pauloque displicuit' (27. 2).

What follows? In any event the joint prefecture goes. It is most unlikely, it clashes with the other evidence about Ulpian. Not but that some scholars, in imperfect assessment of the HA, are still disposed to accept a prefecture of the Guard for Paul.[3] That can go likewise.[4] In fact, nothing shows Paul still among the living in the year 222—apart from Aurelius Victor and the HA.

In epilogue, a brief note on the alleged secretarial posts of Paul and Ulpian. In the *Pescennius* the pair are stated to have been holding them

---

[1] A. Chastagnol, *Rev. phil.* XLI (1967), 90 f.

[2] In the other passage (*Pesc.* 7. 4) the emperor who made the appointment is not named.

[3] i.e. after the death of Ulpian. Thus A. Passerini, *Le coorti pretorie* (1939), 327; W. Kunkel, *Herkunft und soziale Stellung der römischen Juristen* (1952), 244; A. M. Honoré, however, in his study of the Severan jurists, *SDHI* XXVIII (1962), 225, has him prefect '*c.* 222'. In *PIR*², J 453 Paul is prefect 'certe post mortem Ulpiani'.

[4] The brief comment of Dessau in *PIR*¹, J 303 was not encouraging. A stray doubt was voiced by A. Jardé, *Études critiques sur la vie et le règne de Sévère Alexandre* (1925), 39; and a firm negation was pronounced by L. L. Howe, *The Pretorian Prefect from Commodus to Diocletian* (1942), 105 f.

when promoted to the Guard (7. 4): no emperor is there named. In the *Alexander*, Ulpian (on one report) is the 'magister scrinii' of Alexander (26. 6): i.e. the secretary *a libellis*. Similarly Eutropius on that emperor— 'adsessorem habuit vel scrinii magistrum Ulpianum' (IX. 23). The notion has been dismissed as totally erroneous: Ulpian, who is in charge of the *Annona* three weeks after the accession of Alexander, cannot have been demoted to the post *a libellis*.

What then subsists? Some have argued that Ulpian may in truth have held that secretarial post—but in an earlier reign, perhaps under Caracalla or even under Severus.[1] It might be so.[2] But these speculations need not detain, since they juggle with the evidence. What emerges from the garbled testimony (fiction may be suspected as well as error) concerns the sources of the HA. Aurelius Victor had Ulpian Guard Prefect in office already under Elagabalus and kept by his successor. The remarks of the epitomator, as was suggested above, may have induced the author of the HA to assume that Paul also held the office, under Severus Alexander, as colleague of Ulpian.

But the source of Victor comes into the reckoning, with superior co-gency. The HA carries the detail that Ulpian was *magister scrinii* under Alexander (*Alex.* 26. 6). The office and the phrase stand in Eutropius. Likewise in the *Breviarium* of Festus.[3] But not in Victor. Hence from the KG, beyond a doubt.

Each of the three great jurists of the Severan prime attracted fiction at an early stage in the transmission. Victor reports a scandalous story. Caracalla urged Papinian to compose a memorandum in defence of the murder of Geta, the jurist being at the time a state secretary—'quippe quem ferunt illo temporis Bassiani scrinia curavisse' (20. 33). Victor in strong language rejects the whole fable—'sed haec improbe absurda sunt' (20. 34).[4]

The item is instructive. It declares a fabricated post for one of the jurists in the source of Victor. It therefore becomes hazardous to keep anything that the KG may have had to say about Ulpian. A welcome issue. Sound method and the easy way alike discountenance the post *a libellis*, in any reign.[5]

---

[1] Thus, with a doubt about authenticity, W. Kunkel, o.c. 246. A. M. Honoré, with no doubts, argued for the reign of Septimius Severus (o.c. 188 f.; 207).

[2] Papinian had held this post (*Dig.* XX. 5. 12 praef.).

[3] Festus 22: 'hic Alexander scriniorum magistrum habuit Ulpianum, iuris consultorem.'

[4] Likewise the HA, *Carac.* 8. 5 ff. Presumably following Victor.

[5] It was in fact discarded by Pflaum, *Carrières*, no. 294. He appealed to the fraudulence of the *Vita Pescennii*, but failed to discuss the other passages.

Nevertheless, a path opens whereby to explain Ulpian as *a libellis* to Severus Alexander. The first weeks, it was generally assumed, left no room available: Ulpian is *praefectus annonae* by March 31. Brief reflection shows that the objection was not valid. In a disturbed season or under a new reign court favourites advance with celerity; and in the immediate sequel this agile performer may not have held the *Annona* for more than a month or two before he acceded to the Guard.

A further hypothesis intervenes.[1] The prince had held the rank and title of Caesar since July of the previous year. As such, he was entitled to secretaries of his own.[2] On that showing, Ulpian was *a libellis* to the Caesar Alexander. And, if so, why not also continuing for a few days after March 13, 222?

The hypothesis is tenable, since it comports no strain or distortion of the notice as transmitted. Caution is to be enjoined—and no encouragement to redeem any of the more suspect allegations adherent to Ulpian and Paul. The sources present an imbroglio. It has to be recognized and brought into some kind of order.[3]

So far so good, on brief statement. It might seem sheer torture to insist at this point on another episode in the story or legend of the jurists. Victor (and he alone) suggests that Paul had been exiled by Elagabalus—'Paulloque inter exordia patriae reddito' (24. 6). A doubt might arise.[4] As for Ulpian, it appears that he encountered peril in the last days of Elagabalus— 'removit et Ulpianum ut bonum virum' (*Elag.* 16. 4). The main body of the narration stated that senators had been ordered to leave the city.[5] The item might (it is true) be taken to imply Ulpian's dismissal from some office.[6] Banishment would be too strong a term.[7]

III. Much being discredited or discarded, as is proper, the inquiry can now be brought to bear upon the theme of central import: Ulpian the Guard Prefect in the early years of Severus Alexander. A sentence from Cassius Dio (extant only in epitome) states that Alexander on his accession

---

[1] I owe the suggestion to W. Seston (orally, on February 21, 1969).

[2] Thus the knight L. Domitius Rogatus, 'ab epistul. Lucii Aelii Caesaris' (*ILS* 1450).

[3] For a systematic exposition, see the paper 'Three Jurists' in *Bonner Historia-Augusta-Colloquium 1968/9* (1970), 309 ff.

[4] Exile is generally accepted. Thus W. Kunkel, o.c. 244; *PIR*[2], J 453. A. M. Honoré puts it *c.* 219 and indulges in speculation about writings of Paul during that period (o.c. 205, cf. 217 f.).

[5] For the context, above, p. 119. It is here assumed that the anecdote about Ulpian and the *rhetor* Silvinus goes back to the basic source. Doubts might be conceived.

[6] But the inference lacks cogency.

[7] The term is employed, however: Kunkel, o.c. 246 ('Verbannung'); Honoré, o.c. 208.

at once appointed Ulpian to the Guard and put the government in his charge (LXXX. I. I).

That is not accurate. Ulpian was not the first prefect of the new regime. The account in Zosimus, when combined with further statements in Dio, reveals something of the true story.[1] The first prefects appointed were Flavianus and Chrestus.[2] The mother of Alexander, however, installed Ulpian as their superior; and Ulpian, after carrying out some reforms, killed the pair in order to take their place. Then Ulpian, not long after, himself fell victim to the violence of the soldiers (Dio LXXX. I. 2). The passage implies that, after the suppression of Flavianus and Chrestus, Ulpian was sole prefect in the sequel until he met his end; and no other prefect is named as his colleague in that transaction, the date of which is of vital importance.

As has already been indicated, the first epoch of Severus Alexander is obscure and mysterious (but Ulpian seemed to help). About Prefects of the Guard, illumination (and no little perplexity) comes from the Album of Canusium which records the *patroni* of that city.[3]

Ap. Claudius Julianus heads the list. Hence the date, toward the end of 223. This man was to iterate the *fasces* in 224, and was perhaps already *praefectus urbi*. The next four of the 'c(larissimi) v(iri)' are as follows:

T. Lorenius Celsus
M. Aedinius Julianus
L. Didius Marinus
L. Domitius Honoratus

These names stand above a number of ex-consuls, the second of whom is M. Statius Longinus, who had been governor of Moesia Inferior in 216.[4] The four 'clarissimi viri', it is generally held, owe their position on the list to their tenure of the Guard, the award of the *ornamenta consularia* having become not merely frequent but normal. Actual membership of the Senate for high equestrian dignitaries also occurs, but that question

---

[1] Zosimus I. II. 2 f. (not in complete accordance with Dio).

[2] The former now emerges as Julius Flavianus, previously holding the Guard as the colleague of Valerius Comazon in 218 (*AE* 1961, 86: Histria). Chrestus is Geminius Chrestus (*PIR*², G 144), attested as Prefect of Egypt from August of 219 into 221. His successor was L. Domitius Honoratus, on record in January of the next year, cf. A. Stein, *Die Präfekten von Ägypten* (1950), 124 ff.

[3] *CIL* IX. 338. The text as reproduced in *ILS* 6121 is defective and misleading. It stops after the fourth name, omitting L. Domitius Honoratus (who is highly significant); and, of the twenty-three senators, only three are registered.

[4] A. Stein, *Die Legaten von Moesien* (1940), 90 f.

(likewise the mixed careers, equestrian and senatorial) can be waived in this place, otherwise there would be no end to discussion.[1]

T. Lorenius Celsus, the first of the four, is a total enigma, the *nomen* 'Lorenius' a rarity.[2] Yet it is borne by a senator and consul of the period.[3] M. Aedinius Julianus, however, is a known character, familiar from the inscriptions set up in the year 238 at the chief city of the Vidiocasses in the province Gallia Lugdunensis. In short, the famous 'Marbre de Thorigny'.[4]

The inscription on the right-hand side of the monument reproduces a letter from Aedinius Julianus, styled 'praefectus praetorio'. It mentions his own governorship of Lugdunensis, and it refers to certain transactions under his predecessor in office there, Claudius Paullinus.

To cut short a long story. Paullinus went on to hold the governorship of Britannia Inferior (Caracalla had divided the province). He is attested there in 220.[5] Aedinius, it follows, was in Lugdunensis in the period 217–20: an equestrian occupying the place of the imperial legate.[6]

There is further evidence about Aedinius. He became Prefect of Egypt. He is attested there on November 3, 222, and his tenure extended into the next year.[7] Hence an obvious candidate for the Guard not long after.

Next, L. Didius Marinus. His career is registered as far as a procuratorship in Asia.[8] That post belongs about the year 215, when Caracalla was in the province: at Pergamum Marinus dedicated statues to the Emperor and to Julia Domna.[9] A lead pipe found at Ostia discloses the remarkable fact that he had acquired for wife the elderly Cornificia, a daughter of Marcus Aurelius.[10] She was put to death by Caracalla.[11] Not a necessary reason to impede the ulterior ascent of the survivor.

Last of the four, L. Domitius Honoratus.[12] This man held the prefecture

---

[1] For the vexed and confused passage in the *Vita Alexandri* (21. 3 ff.) see A. Chastagnol, *Recherches sur l'Histoire Auguste* (Bonn, 1970), 39 ff.

[2] For the *nomen*, Schulze, *LE* 151 f.

[3] L. Lorenius Crispinus is on attestation as a *frater arvalis* in 231 and further as a consul (*PIR*[1], L 254).

[4] *CIL* XIII. 3162, with the full and excellent commentary of Pflaum, *Le Marbre de Thorigny* (1948).

[5] *CIL* VII. 1045 = *RIB* 1280. Cf. A. R. Birley, *Epigraphische Studien* IV (1967), 88.

[6] Thus Pflaum, o.c. 35; *Carrières*, no. 297.

[7] *PIR*[2], A 113; A. Stein, *Die Präfekten von Ägypten* (1950), 127 f.

[8] *ILS* 1396, cf. *PIR*[2], D 71.

[9] See now C. Habicht, *Die Inschriften des Asklepieions* (1969), 14 f.

[10] *AE* 1954, 171, cf. Pflaum, *Journal des Savants* 1961, 37.

[11] For Cornificia, above, p. 131.

[12] *PIR*[2], D 151.

of Egypt under Elagabalus, attested in January of 222.[1] His successor
in that post was Aedinius Julianus. Once again, normal prospects of the
Guard.

The conclusion is ineluctable: four prefects of the Guard, before the end
of 223. They look like two pairs. If that is so, what of the great Ulpian? An
explanation is propounded. Though prefects, they were his subordinates
only, like Flavianus and Chrestus in the early months of the new regime.[2]

Ulpian finds mention in no fewer than nine passages of the *Vita
Alexandri*.[3] Which need not impress. On the contrary. The biography
offers no hint that he came to a violent end.[4] The *Vita* is intent to convey
the impression that the jurist in his predominance was not only notable
but of long duration. Most scholars conform. The accepted date for his
murder stands as 228.[5] Yet it occurred not so long after the suppression
of Flavianus and Chrestus, according to Cassius Dio (LXXX. 2. 2).[6] A careless assumption has been propagated.

The album of Canusium might have suggested a doubt. The alert
town council chose other 'viri clarissimi', not Ulpian.

The best investigation into the Guard Prefects (and commendable
for its firm principles about the HA) assigned the fate of Ulpian to the
year 223.[7] Confirmation is now to hand. The prime agent in the deed
was a certain Epagathus, according to Dio; and he was discreetly sent
away to be Prefect of Egypt (LXXX. 2. 4). A papyrus shows M. Aurelius
Epagathus in office in May or June of 224.[8]

IV. The consequences are momentous. The good jurist, upright and
sagacious, not only bringing to affairs of state the resources of a trained

---

[1] A. Stein, o.c. 125 f.   [2] Pflaum, o.c. 42: 'une sorte de superpréfet'.

[3] *Alex.* 15. 6; 26. 5; 26. 6; 27. 2; 31. 2; 34. 6; 51. 4; 67. 2; 68. 1.

[4] The HA asserts 'Ulpianum pro tutore habuit, primum repugnante matre, deinde gratias
agente, quem saepe a militum ira obiectu purpurae suae defendit' (51. 4). The allegation
about Mamaea is surely false (cf., though not precise proof, Zosimus I. 11. 2); and Alexanders'
protecting Ulpian from the Guard represents a deliberate concealment of the truth.

[5] e.g. M. Durry, *Les Cohortes prétoriennes* (1938), 183; A. Passerini, o.c. 326; W. Ensslin
in *CAH* XII (1939), 64; W. Kunkel, o.c. 246; M. Hammond, *The Antonine Monarchy* (1959),
387; A. M. Honoré, o.c. 207; A. Piganiol, *Histoire de Rome*[5] (1962), 406. Even Stein in *PIR*[2],
D 169 had 'paulo ante a. 229'.

[6] Dio has οὐ πολλῷ ὕστερον. Emphasized by A. Jardé, o.c. 39. A rare and welcome
exception.

[7] L. L. Howe, o.c. 100 ff. (published in 1942). Little heed was paid.

[8] *P. Oxy.* 2565 (published in 1966). See the exhaustive discussion by J. Modrzejewski
and T. Zawadzki, *Rev. hist. de droit français et étranger* XLV (1967), 565 ff. As they demonstrate,
the dating to 228 goes back to Lenain de Tillemont, who, however, came to express stray
doubts (ib. 570). Long lists are appended of the guilty men, both historians and jurists
(570 f.).

mind, but directing policy for six years, that was an explanation of no small comfort. A piece of papyrus subverts it. The beneficent influences of Ulpian suffer drastic curtailment. Nor, for that matter, is it clear that men who had the advantage of knowing Ulpian were disposed to regard him with approbation. A master of jurisprudence, but also a subtle intriguer who exploited court favour to further a ruthless ambition—and who destroyed the two prefects who blocked his path.

Quoting from an earlier jurist the definition of law as the 'ars boni et aequi', Ulpian affirmed that its practitioners might with propriety be designated priests. And indeed, he opines, votaries of a philosophy not feigned but genuine.[1]

This sage had amassed potent influence in the last months of Elagabalus, if not earlier. A stray notice states that he had been ordered to leave the city (*Elag.* 16. 4). Significant, if the notice be held authentic. In any event, Ulpian was deep in the confidence of Julia Maesa and Julia Mamaea, as is demonstrated by his rapid rise to high office in the sequel.

Under Severus Alexander, the first *praefectus urbi* was Valerius Comazon; and as the new prefects of the Guard emerge Julius Flavianus and Geminius Chrestus. Flavianus had already held the Guard as colleague of Comazon in 218.[2] That fact proclaims court favour (and its alternations), continuing through the reigns of the boy princes.

Ulpian himself might have held some governmental post under Elagabalus. Hardly the prefecture of the Guard—that was a notion of Aurelius Victor, discarded by the author of the HA.[3] Better, he was *a libellis*—but the evidence is suspect.[4] However it be, absence from the city saved him from the fate that destroyed certain court favourites, along with the two Guard prefects and the *praefectus urbi*.

Ulpian (or some other sage) was a desirable ingredient in the romance of the virtuous prince. There is something else. The jurist is a tragic or deleterious figure—the scholar who abandons erudition (albeit for the most part compilatory), succumbing to the seductions of management and politics.

Pure fiction has enhanced his fame, to the obscuration of historical fact and significant parallels. Ulpian by his appointment, set over the two prefects Flavianus and Chrestus, recalled the abnormal post that Commodus had created for his favourite, the freedman M. Aurelius

---

[1] *Dig.* 1. 1. 1: 'cuius merito quis nos sacerdotes appellet', etc.
[2] *AE* 1961, 86 (Histria).
[3] But kept by A. M. Honoré, o.c. 208.
[4] Yet admitting a new interpretation, cf. above, p. 150.

Cleander.[1] And, by the sole predominance Ulpian soon achieved, Fulvius Plautianus might occur as a precedent. Seen in perspective (not distant) Ulpian also takes on the features of a precursor. When in 225 a wife was found for Severus Alexander, namely Seia Sallustia, her father acquired exorbitant power.[2] Next, the Guard Prefect Furius Timesitheus, a man of some education as well as an equestrian official of long experience, who imposed his daughter on the boy Gordian.[3] All of them save Timesitheus came to a violent end.[4] Ulpian succumbed quickly—before Alexander became marriageable.[5]

Another item of favourable testimony to the reign has recently faded out. In the oration he put into the mouth of Maecenas, the historian Dio portrays the institutions and policy of a benevolent autocracy, not omitting some ideas of his own. A pervasive assumption suggests that Dio wrote his piece in the time of Severus Alexander—and with an eye to the situation. It was an easy step to enrol the historian among the chief advisers of the prince.[6]

The career of Dio on his own showing declares him absent from Rome almost all the time from 222 to 229. Moreover, an argument from the rhythm and economy of the work renders an earlier date more plausible for the writing of Book LII: namely 214/15, when Dio was in the company of Caracalla at Nicomedia.[7]

Good counsellors or bad, the theme occupies a large place in the annals of the Empire. It is on abundant display in the HA, and most lavishly in the *Vita Alexandri*. The purpose of the author was to delineate an ideal ruler, with features borrowed from Alexander the Macedonian and from Trajan. To that end, it was necessary to suppress awkward facts, such as the murder of Ulpian; and (inadvertence or design) there is no mention of Julia Maesa or of Valerius Comazon.

Given the youth of the prince it was natural to lay emphasis on his education and training. The HA duly responds, inventing a catalogue of

---

[1] Pflaum, *Carrières*, no. 180 *bis*, cf. *Add.*

[2] Below, p. 157.

[3] *PIR*², F 581; Pflaum, *Carrières*, no. 317.

[4] Timesitheus died a natural death during the campaign (Zosimus I. 18. 2). The HA has that version—and the alternative, poisoning by Philip (*Gord.* 28. 1), to which it adds corroborative detail (28. 5 f.).

[5] The wife (perhaps illustrious) of Ulpian is not on record, or any offspring. Cn. Domitius Annius Ulpianus, known from a lead pipe (*CIL* XI. 3587 = XV. 7773), might be a son by adoption—or the jurist himself. A suitable parent for Ulpian is discovered in the pedantic grammarian Ulpianus the Tyrian, mentioned in the preface of Athenaeus, *Deipnosophistae*.

[6] J. Crook, *Consilium Principis* (1955), 91.

[7] F. Millar, *A Study of Cassius Dio* (1964), 102 ff.

ten teachers (*Alex*. 3. 2 f.). Further, the imperial counsellors. The biography rises to its climax on this topic, which takes up four chapters.

The section opens with appeal to the Emperor Constantine,

soles quaerere, Constantine maxime, quid sit quod hominem Syrum et
alienigenam talem principem fecerit (65. 1).

The author proceeds to satisfy the well-grounded curiosity of Constantine,
by various devices. For example, he evokes a maxim which the Emperor
knows from having read Marius Maximus, namely that bad advisers do
more harm to the State than bad emperors (65. 4); and he quotes what
'Homullus' said to Trajan on the subject of rulers and their friends (65. 5).[1]
Again, he deprecates the influence of eunuchs, at some length (66. 3–
67. 1); and the name of Ulpian is slipped in (67. 2). Finally, to exemplify
the counsellors, those sterling characters 'qui bonum principem Syrum
fecerunt', the author brings corroborative testimony: eight members of
the imperial *consilium* (68. 1). Among them Ulpian and Paul, inevitably.
The rest are fictitious.[2]

Even without this impudent fabrication, extreme distrust would invest
anything that the HA had to say about Alexander's *consilium*. The prime
exhibit alleges a body of twenty jurists, with the adjunction of at least
fifty persons endowed with wisdom and eloquence (16. 1).

The passage (it was to be expected) has been the subject of long and
earnest debate, both for itself and in relation to a different piece of testimony. That is, the group of sixteen senior senators which Herodian
registers at the beginning of the reign (VI. 1. 2).[3] Some kind of council
of regency, it is presumed. How long it subsisted might be a question.
When the reign ended these counsellors recur: Maximinus dismissed them,
without exception. Herodian adds the implausible refinement that they
had all been selected by the Senate (VII. 1. 3).

The written sources being feeble and fraudulent, it is expedient to
look for facts and names. Guard Prefects in 222 and 223 have already
been indicated, along with sundry complex problems. Curiosity will still
linger upon the four names registered on the Album of Canusium. If
they represent two pairs, there had been a rapid mutation before the end
of the year that witnessed the fall of Ulpian. Which does not pass belief.[4]

---

[1] Above, p. 97.   [2] Below, p. 248.

[3] For a careful discussion, J. Crook, o.c. 89 f. He concludes, however, that the 'council
of seventy cannot be rejected outright' (ib. 90). Ensslin did not bother even to mention it
(*CAH* XII. 58 f.).

[4] This differs from Pflaum's theory. He assumed that the two pairs functioned in succession, under Ulpian the 'superpréfet' (o.c. 42). Then, after the death of Ulpian (for which
Pflaum nowhere indicated a date), Paul became 'superpréfet' (ib. 44). A prefecture of

In 227 or 228 supervened a mysterious catastrophe. They had found a wife for the young emperor: Seia Sallustia, whose name is not preserved in any written source.[1] The HA, citing Dexippus, calls her father Macrianus and states that he acquired the title of Caesar but came to grief, having conspired against Alexander (49. 3 f.).[2] In the version of Herodian (no names) his ruin is put down to the jealousy and contriving of Julia Mamaea. In the last emergency he fled for refuge to the camp of the Praetorian Guard (VI. 1. 9 f.). Hence a conjecture might be permitted: the ephemeral Caesar was, or had been, a prefect. Herodian, it is true, states that the daughter belonged to a noble family. That would not be enough to rule out the conjecture; and high equestrian dignitaries tend to annex aristocratic brides.

Otherwise the rest of the reign is a blank, except for the prefecture of M. Attius Cornelianus c. 230.[3] Nor can anything of significance be gleaned from the Prefects of Egypt.

v. Despite the encroachments of equestrian officials, in provincial governorships as well as at the capital, the senator retains utility. The government has to find men to hold the consular provinces, now fourteen in number, of which twelve had legionary garrisons.[4] Unfortunately the record is very thin. Likewise for Asia and Africa. They exhibit a singular dearth. For Asia only two proconsuls;[5] and not many more for Africa.[6]

Paul is likewise assumed by Modrzejewski and Zawadzki: 'nous pouvons admettre que Paul succède à Ulpien comme superpréfet' (o.c. 607). They go on, however, to present a complicated schema (ib. 608):

223, spring. Ulpian appoints Didius Marinus and Domitius Honoratus as subordinate prefects.

223, summer. After the murder of Ulpian, Lorenius Celsus and Aedinius Julianus are appointed prefects.

224, May–June. A new pair of prefects—'avec Paul comme superpréfet (s'il a jamais exercé cette fonction)'.

[1] PIR¹, S 252. By her full style 'Gnaea Seia Herennia Sallustia Barbia Orbiana Augusta' (coins and inscriptions).

[2] Some scholars have adopted the conjecture 'Macrinus'. Thus Dessau in PIR¹, M 22; A. Stein, P-W I A. 1910 f. For the further problems touching this person, who ought to have both 'Seius' and 'Sallustius' in his nomenclature, see R. O. Fink, AJP LX (1939), 326 ff., adducing an item in the Feriale Duranum (cf. YCS VII (1940), 74 ff.); Barbieri, Albo, no. 463, with p. 399 (the usurper Sallustius). Fink suspects the authenticity of the 'Macrinus' or 'Macrianus' in the HA (o.c. 329). [3] ILS 1334 (Uchi Maius).

[4] Caracalla made Pannonia Inferior consular. Of the fourteen provinces, two lacked legions, viz. Dalmatia and Bithynia–Pontus.

[5] Between C. Aufidius Marcellus in 220 or 221 (CIL III. 7195 = IGR IV. 1206) and M. Asinius Sabinianus in 239 or 240 (IGR IV. 1315), only two proconsuls are registered on the list of D. Magie, Roman Rule in Asia Minor (1950), 1585. Namely, M. Clodius Pupienus Maximus and Q. Vibius Egnatius Sulpicius Priscus.

[6] For proconsuls under Alexander, Thomasson, o.c. 116 ff. He includes Cassius Dio.

The advice of ex-consuls might be worth having; and one of their functions was to serve as a link between the Palace and the high assembly, should the government care to have its policy expounded there. Respect for tradition could be advertised, harmlessly, or superficial contrasts emphasized with advantage by honours conferred on senior statesmen or venerable relics.

As in earlier ages, the City Prefecture offered, or iteration in the *fasces*. As *praefectus urbi* after P. Valerius Comazon at the outset, and Ap. Claudius Julianus soon after, there is only M. Clodius Pupienus Maximus who (it is reasonable to suppose) took up office about the time of his second consulship (in 234).[1] Altogether, seven senators enjoyed the latter distinction. As follows:

223 L. Marius Maximus (*suff.* ? 198)
224 Ap. Claudius Julianus (?)
225 Ti. Manilius Fuscus (*c.* 197)
226 C. Aufidius Marcellus (*c.* 203).
228 Q. Aiacius Modestus Crescentianus (*c.* 205)
229 Cassius Dio Cocceianus (*c.* 205)
234 M. Clodius Pupienus Maximus (?)

Not much is on record about the consular employments of these men, apart from Maximus and Dio. Manilius Fuscus is a blank;[2] but Claudius Julianus, *praefectus urbi* before the end of 223, had held the proconsulate of Africa, probably under Elagabalus;[3] and Aufidius Marcellus was proconsul of Asia in 220 or 221.[4] Aiacius Modestus governed Germania Superior *c.* 208.[5] Finally, Pupienus Maximus, governor of one of the Germanies and proconsul of Asia. There is much more to be said about this remarkable character.[6]

The other six present certain features in common. Their consulates fell in the early years of Septimius Severus; and, except for the anomalous Dio, their imperial governorships, where ascertainable, also belonged to a distant past. No consul of Caracalla or of Elagabalus is on the list. Some were no doubt eligible. But C. Octavius Appius Suetrius Sabinus (*cos.*

Another, Caesonius Macer (*suff. c.* 202), may fall under Elagabalus. And D. Caelius Calvinus Balbinus (*cos. II* 213) cannot stand, cf. below, p. 172. The sudden deficiency in the epigraphical evidence from both opulent provinces might excite surmise.

[1] Herodian notes and emphasizes the prefecture (VII. 10. 4, cf. 6; VIII. 8. 4).

[2] He was not governor of Dacia, cf. A. Stein, *Die Reichsbeamten von Dazien* (1944), 52 ff. Stein (ib. 54) inclined to believe that he rather than Anicius Faustus (*suff.* ? 198) is the proconsul of Asia whose truncated name is preserved on *MAMA* IV. 27.

[3] *CIL* VIII. 4845.   [4] *CIL* III. 7195 = *IGR* IV. 1206.

[5] *ILS* 433; 5909.   [6] Below, Ch. X.

214), who became proconsul of Africa *c.* 230, was passed over.[1] Nor, supposing him to survive, was there a thought for C. Julius Avitus Alexianus (*suff. c.* 208), legate of Dalmatia in 219 and proconsul of either Asia or Africa soon after: from Emesa, and close kin to Julius Avitus, the husband of Julia Maesa.[2] The surprising absentee is C. Caesonius Macer Rufinianus (*suff. c.* 202), who was with Alexander as his *comes* either in the East or on the Rhine: his long career had begun with a military tribunate (and decorations) in the last campaigns of Marcus Aurelius.[3]

So far the indications, positive or negative, furnished by second consulates. The honouring of eminent survivors does not perhaps take one very far or very deep. A reaction was published against what had gone before—Caracalla as well as Elagabalus—despite the dynastic continuity and the alleged parentage of Alexander. Beneath the surface the autocratic tendencies which Septimius Severus had encouraged (or rather could not stem) keep their course unimpeded: court and bureaucracy, the Guard and the legions.

VI. Much must remain enigmatic about the reign of the Syrian prince. The answer vouchsafed to the curiosity of Constantine will not appease other inquiries: thirteen years, with perils to surmount both abroad and at Rome. The eastern lands were the scene of military tumults. At least one pretender arose in Syria: it is not clear how many persons lurk under the names Taurinus, Antoninus, and Seleucus transmitted by late and brief and garbled sources.[4] Seleucus might be a Roman senator. Observe Julius Antonius Seleucus, legate of Moesia Inferior under Elagabalus.[5] And also M. Flavius Vitellius Seleucus (*cos.* 221).[6]

The greater danger lay in a proclamation issuing from the armies of the northern frontier. There is no clear sign of any trouble from their commanders. Nor did the abortive expedition against the Persians impair the government. It was anger among the Danubian troops congregated at Moguntiacum in March of 235 that brought an equestrian officer to the purple.

---

[1] For his proconsulate, *CIL* VI. 1476; his *cursus*, *ILS* 1159.   [2] *PIR²*, J 192.

[3] *ILS* 1182.

[4] For the evidence about these usurpers, Barbieri, *Albo*, pp. 400 f. Antoninus, or Uranius Antoninus, must be distinguished from the Uranius Antoninus who rose against Philip, and who is attested by coins (*PIR²*, J 195).

[5] *PIR²*, J 154. He is there held identical with the Antonius Seleucus who was consular legate of Syria Coele in 231, cf. J. F. Gilliam, *AJP* LXXIX (1958), 231 f.

[6] The bare names carry useful evidence about the reign of Elagabalus. These persons may have asserted an illustrious ascendance. Compare remarks about the lineage of Avidius Cassius (above, p. 129).

When Maximinus had been three years in the power with none to oppose, a local disturbance in Africa set in motion a whole train of events. The proconsul, M. Antonius Gordianus, was induced or compelled to make a proclamation. The Senate responded with alacrity; and, though the African rebellion was quickly suppressed, they prosecuted the war against the Balkan usurper with decision and energy, producing a pair of emperors from their own ranks.

The comportment of the Senate excites surprise and admiration. An easy explanation of their conduct offers. The Senate had recovered prestige under the enlightened rule of Alexander and his counsellors, it drew sustenance from sound principles and public spirit. The tyranny of Maximinus added fear and resentment. Hence the call to action and glory. On this showing, the events of 238 can be used as favourable testimony to the reign of Severus Alexander.

The topic requires brief inspection in a separate study; and it will also be necessary to examine with some care the evidence about Gordianus and that strange pair of emperors, Pupienus and Balbinus.[1]

VII. Old men emerge and capture attention in that momentous year. More names therefore to be enrolled among the coevals of Marius Maximus and Cassius Dio. That company has found abundant illustration in these pages, notably a dozen *consules suffecti* from the early years of Septimius Severus.[2] Their extraction was heterogeneous, and their vicissitudes might entertain a philosophical mind—if more were known. Along with Maximus and Dio, four of them enjoyed late distinction, to adorn the *Fasti* as consuls for the second time under Alexander. To the most elderly of all the survivors of that generation was granted sudden action to compensate for dormant or thwarted ambitions.

Those who came to manhood in the last years of Marcus Aurelius looked back upon a vast and variegated panorama of history, the memory of Marcus enhanced and their own thoughts darkened by the sequence of calamities: Commodus, civil war, military despotism. The senator saw the authority and the prestige of his own order decline steadily. The essential distinctions of rank and honour had been set at naught, with knights taking the place of senators in provincial commands; and Guard Prefects, in virtue of being 'viri clarissimi', can stand in front of ex-consuls.

More odious, the deterioration in quality and culture. The Danubian wars of Marcus brought officers of humble extraction to high commands, and some to senatorial rank and the consulate. The rough and uneducated

[1] Ch. X.   [2] Above, p. 139.

issuing from Italy or the western provinces aroused distaste, not least in a cultivated senator from the Greek East, such as Cassius Dio. The process went on, the civil wars of Severus accelerating. Then Caracalla and a low-born knight from Mauretania as emperor in the person of Macrinus, and worse to follow: the regiment of women and favourites, and the boy priest from Emesa.

Relief came, after four years, with happy prospects advertised, as at the inception of any new reign. Governmental proclamations will not deceive—and they often betray their own weakness as well as dishonesty.[1] Men of understanding, who reflected upon the past and remembered Commodus, had their doubts and forebodings. Respect was paid to the Senate, with public honours for the illustrious, while age and wisdom were enlisted in councils of state. Confidence may (or may not) have been inspired by the authority of Ulpian. But Ulpian soon fell a victim to his own ambition and the ferocity of the Guard.

The Guard, which now drew its recruitment from the Danubian lands, presented a more difficult problem than did the armies and the generals on that frontier. Rome suffered an early tumult, and a three days' battle in the streets.[2] Then the murder of Ulpian, and later the peril incurred by Cassius Dio. No less disturbing, the odd fact that a sexagenarian historian devoid of military experience had been deemed a proper governor for Pannonia Superior. No good symptom in a government—which, however, had a long duration.

VIII. The year 235 appears to mark the end of an epoch. The reign of Severus Alexander has been regarded as an after-glow, not lacking brightness or even hope, of the blessed Antonine prime of the Empire. That season saw the best elements in Greek and Roman life associated, and even blended. The governing class was in fact an alliance between the city aristocracies, west and east: education and large estates on both sides. Their harmony in the world empire was advertised by Hadrian—or, for that matter, by Aelius Aristides.

Maximus and Dio illustrate that theme. They also conclude an epoch. There are no more consular historians—and few writers of consequence in the Latin language until a long interval has elapsed. The classic age of jurisprudence also verges to its end, after Ulpian and Paul.[3] The

---

[1] As in Alexander's edict preserved in *P. Fayum* 20. On which, sharp comments by C. Préaux, *Chronique d'Égypte* XXXI (1941), 123 ff.; J. Moreau, *Scripta Minora* (1964), 34 f.

[2] Dio LXXX. 2. 3.

[3] Both were commentators, and compilers of enormous volume. Their senior, Papinian, seems the better name.

last name that matters is that of Herennius Modestinus, a disciple of Ulpian.[1]

A sharp line of division is drawn at 235. According to Aurelius Victor, Alexander left the state in a condition of great strength. By virtue and signal merit he arrested Rome's decline from a high peak,

rem publicam reliquit fundatam undique. quae iam tum a Romulo ad Septimium certatim evolans Bassiani consiliis tamquam in summo constitit. quo ne confestim laberetur, Alexandri fuit (24. 7 ff.).

After this solemn pronouncement Victor vouchsafes the fruits of his own reflections on the abrupt declension into the age of tribulation, at some length (24. 9 ff.). In short, power went to anybody, including barbarians and the illiterate. He attributes the blame to Fortuna, who in her violence 'etiam infimis genere institutoque publica permisit' (24. 11).

On that note Victor effects his transition to the repellent figure of Maximinus. This emperor deserves a better estimation. The Danubian soldier grasped the true and urgent needs of the Empire. The court and counsellors of Alexander had embarked upon a great war against the Persians. The new power which supplanted the feeble Arsacids (who had so often proved an accommodating rival or reluctant enemy to the Romans) adopted a provocative attitude, claiming as its heritage all the lands that Achaemenid Persia had ruled in ancient days.[2] The same claim had been put up earlier by the Parthians,[3] to be eluded or repelled by means other than open war.[4] The Sassanids constituted a menace. How great, it evades ascertainment. Diplomacy and patience might have availed. Such was the sober lesson inculcated by past history, more than once. The mirage of the Macedonian conqueror and the fame of Trajan were more potent incentives.[5]

Victor's verdict and point of division raises a doubt. It also has a bearing on questions of periodization and terminology. The 'Age of the Antonines' has been employed with differing connotations, some of them deriving from the nomenclature of rulers rather than their policy. A cognate theme is the emergence of the emperors from Illyricum. On the standard showing, Claudius opens the roll in 268. Some thought should go to the forerunners, namely Maximinus and Decius.

[1] *PIR²*, H 112; W. Kunkel, o.c. 259 ff.; A. M. Honoré, o.c. 213 ff.
[2] Dio LXXX. 3. 4.
[3] Tacitus, *Ann.* VI. 31. 1.
[4] For the policy of Tiberius Caesar, enacted by L. Vitellius, cf. *Tacitus* (1958), 494.
[5] As later with Julian.

X · GORDIANUS, PUPIENUS, BALBINUS

I. THE ACTIONS of the year 238 start from a small riot in Africa in the month of March. At variance with the fiscal agent of Maximinus, young men of the propertied class formed a plot and armed their serfs. Killing the procurator, they made approaches to the proconsul Antonius Gordianus, then at the city of Thysdrus. One of them delivered an oration, blending menace with exhortation.

Diffidence and reluctance was the normal comportment of usurpers anywhere, and it serves as a standard device in fictional history. After due protestation, the old man gave way: he rated his present peril worse than that to come, and, if he must perish let it be in the purple.

Thus Herodian.[1] On a rational calculation the thing seemed hopeless. Victorious already against the enemies of Rome beyond Rhine and Danube, the energetic Maximinus stood at Sirmium, in the strategic centre of the Empire, with the armies under firm control (it should seem), the soldiers loyal and eager, resentful against interference from any sort of civilian usurpation. And the Senate, in due timidity or recognizing the military urgencies of the northern frontier, might have chosen to ignore the proconsul of Africa, leaving him to a brief tenure of the purple and an ignominious fate.

It turned out otherwise. The news impelled the Senate to act. They recognized Gordian as emperor, with his son as partner in the power. More than that, to direct public policy and conduct war against the Danubian armies, twenty consulars were nominated.[2] The full list would be worth having. Six names can be recovered.[3] Four are mentioned in the literary sources, viz. Pupienus and Balbinus, that notable pair, and the two generals who defended Aquileia against the usurper, Crispinus and Menophilus. Inscriptions fill out the nomenclature of the last two and add two more. As follows:

M. Clodius Pupienus Maximus (*cos. II* 234). *PIR*², C 1179.
D. Caelius Calvinus Balbinus (*cos. II* 213). *PIR*², C 126.

[1] Herodian VII. 4 f., whence *Gord.* 7 f. (with distortion and fictional embellishments).
[2] Absent from Herodian, but in Zosimus I. 14. 2; *Gord.* 10. 1 f.; 21. 1 (cf. 14. 3 f., the speech of Maximinus). In *Maximin.* 32. 8 the author states that Dexippus put their appointment after the death of the Gordiani.
[3] Barbieri, *Albo*, nos. 1106; 99; 1147; 1071; 978; 1173.

Rutilius Pudens Crispinus (*suff. c.* 235). *PIR*[1], C 1295.
Tullius Menophilus (*c.* 235). *PIR*[1], T 231.
L. Caesonius Lucillus Macer Rufinianus (*c.* 234). *PIR*[2], C 209.
[V]alerius Claud[. . . .] Acilius Priscillianus (*cos.* 233). *ILS* 8979.

It is a miscellaneous collection, Balbinus by far the senior. For Crispinus inscriptions reveal an unusual career.[1] This man, a *praefectus cohortis* before he acceded to the higher order, reached his consulship after no fewer than three praetorian provinces (Lusitania, Thrace, and Syria Phoenice) and the proconsulate of Achaia. Menophilus is on subsequent record as governor of Moesia Inferior (238–41). As for his *gentilicium*, opinions have been divided between 'Tullius' and 'Julius'. The former is correct.[2]

Caesonius Lucillus is the son of C. Caesonius Macer Rufinianus (*suff. c.* 202), who had recently been *comes* of Severus Alexander. The full career of each has been preserved.[3]

Finally, the polyonymous patrician disclosed by an inscription at Lavinium.[4] After his consulship he had been curator of the Tiber. Since the document describes him as 'consul ordinarius', no choice subsists but to identify him with the consul of 233, L. Valerius Maximus.[5] That person, it is true, has been supposed *cos. II*, but without reason.[6]

Various problems infest the Valerii Maximi of this age.[7] One of them is the *consul ordinarius* L. Valerius Poplicola Balbinus Maximus.[8] He should be held identical with a Valerius Maximus who is attested as the consul of 253.[9] He bears for tribe the 'Claudia'. On the inscription from Lavinium stands 'Claud['. A conjecture can be ventured: it is the tribe abbreviated. Not a normal practice, between *nomen* and *cognomen* without the filiation. But not without parallel.[10]

As concerns social distinction, Balbinus was also a patrician. The Caesonii are a new consular family, perhaps from Africa.[11] Crispinus was

---

[1] For the list, Barbieri, no. 1147. Notably *AE* 1929, 158, on which A. Stein, *Hermes* LXV (1930), 228 ff.

[2] As demonstrated by G. Mihailov, *Klio* XXXVII (1959), 227 ff. 'Julius' had been awarded the preference by A. Stein, *Die Legaten von Moesien* (1940), 98 f.

[3] *ILS* 1182; 1186.   [4] *ILS* 8979.

[5] Barbieri, *Albo*, no. 1176 regards this as the probable solution.

[6] Thus Barbieri and Degrassi, *I fasti consolari* (1952). But the sign of iteration is not certain on *CIL* III. 3427 = 10380 (Aquincum).

[7] See the remarks in *Albo*, nos. 1176, 1741, 1742, 1656.

[8] *ILS* 1190 f.

[9] And both with the Valerius Maximus who was *praefectus urbi* in 255 (*Albo*, no. 1741).

[10] *ILS* 1042.

[11] Above, p. 140. Caesonius Lucillus was made a patrician before his quaestorship.

equestrian; and Tullius Menophilus may be supposed to derive from the eastern lands.

The last two names on the list are due to fortuitous knowledge. Surmise might bring in other persons. For example, M. Flavius Latronianus, consul before 231: the next *praefectus urbi* on certain record after the Sabinus who was killed at the end of March, 238.[1] And there is the Sabinus who became consul for the second time in 240 (the only iteration in the six years of Gordian III).[2] Finally, two notices assign a role of prominence to the consular P. Licinius Valerianus, who was destined to have the purple fifteen years later.[3]

11. In the event, the rebellion in Africa collapsed quickly, the legate of Numidia intervening. The son of Gordian was killed in a battle near Carthage, and the old man hanged himself. They had three weeks in the purple.[4] Not deterred, the Senate elected from the *XXviri* a pair of emperors, viz. Pupienus (whom the Greek sources preferred to call Maximus) and Balbinus. But, an ominous sign, a riot at Rome compelled them to associate in the power the third Gordianus, the grandson through a daughter: he was a boy, aged thirteen.[5]

An invasion of Italy had now to be faced. Emona opened her gates, the citizens fleeing, but Aquileia put up a firm resistance. In the siege Maximinus came against difficulties he had not reckoned with. His troops grew impatient and restive, a prey to rumours. The loyalty of that élite body, the legion II Parthica, was overborne by personal motives: they feared for their women and children in the camp at Albanum near Rome. The soldiers killed Maximinus and his young son.

Hence a paradoxical victory for the cause of the Senate. No long enjoyment resulted for Pupienus and Balbinus. Discord arose between the partners. Balbinus (it is said) suspected that Pupienus wished to supplant him; and he may have been moved by envy as well as pride. While Pupienus at Ravenna superintended the campaign, Balbinus had not been

---

[1] *PIR²*, F 297. Presumably earlier than Caesonius Lucillus (*ILS* 1186).

[2] *PIR¹*, S 22. On whom below, p. 177.

[3] Zosimus I. 14. 1 (garbled); *Gord.* 9. 7 (where Dexippus is cited for the previous item, viz. Gordian's son as legate in Africa).

[4] For the chronology of 238, R. A. G. Carson, *Am. Num. Soc.*, Centennial Volume (1958), 181 ff.

[5] *PIR²*, A 835. That he was the son of old Gordian's daughter is stated by Herodian VII. 10. 7; *Epit.* 27. 1. Likewise the HA, noting the variant, 'ut unus et alter, nam amplius invenire non potui', that he was the son of Gordian II (*Gord.* 22. 4), cf. 'ut plerique dicunt' (*Max. et Balb.* 3. 4). That version is elsewhere attributed to Dexippus (*Gord.* 19. 9; 23. 1); and it is in Zosimus I. 14. 1. For a figment about Gordian III, see below, p. 233.

able to keep order at the capital. Finally, in a confused mutiny the pair fell victims to the soldiers.

The Senate had elected Pupienus and Balbinus. That fact needs to be interpreted as well as registered. In the version of Herodian, the Senate is convoked to meet in the temple of Capitoline Jupiter, there to hold debate behind closed doors; persons of age or repute are nominated; and from the voting emerge the two names.[1]

How far can the Senate be said to have chosen the two emperors? It would be needful to know the number of candidates put forward—and allow for discreet operations behind the scenes. Rival groups may be surmised, and the hand of seasoned intriguers: it was expedient to dissuade or compensate other competitors.

A pair of emperors, that was perhaps the solution emerging from a compromise between rival interests. Yet there was something to be said for an experiment which not only recalled the supreme executive of the Republic or the joint rule of Marcus and L. Verus, but also enlisted diverse and complementary talents at the head of the government. Some may have hoped for a healthy emulation, to the benefit of the Commonwealth. Others set their calculation on discord.

When by some happy chance the Senate gets a voice in the election of an emperor, age has a heavy premium. As precedents stand Nerva and Pertinax, contrasted by birth and career, but parallel in their exit. Faced after a year by an insurrection of the Guard, Nerva could only save himself by a virtual abdication, surrendering before the legate of Germania Superior.[2] Pertinax was killed after three months of rule. Such was also the tenure which fate and the Guard conceded to Pupienus and Balbinus.

III. Gordian was in his eightieth year, according to Herodian.[3] The ages of the other two are a problem—only one among many. Family, rank, and public offices must be scrutinized in all three.

M. Antonius Gordianus the proconsul of Africa had no success or celerity to vaunt in his earlier career. In 216 he was still of praetorian rank. The welcome aid of inscriptions now reveals him as governor of Britannia Inferior, which by paradox was a tranquil region in this period.[4]

---

[1] Herodian VII. 10. 3. The HA has a delightful account, with plethora of detail, beginning with a session in the temple of Concord and a faked date (*Max. et Balb.* 1. 1).

[2] For this interpretation, *Tacitus* (1958), 10 ff.; 35.   [3] Herodian VII. 5. 2.

[4] *CIL* VII 1043 = *RIB* 216 (the name erased); *RIB* 1049 (with ']diani' surviving); 509 (where R. P. Wright reads the beginning of the *cognomen* 'Sempronianus'). On which see now A. R. Birley, *Epigraphische Studien* IV (1967), 87. The conjecture, based on the first two inscriptions, goes back to E. Birley.

Since Gordian was born in 159 (or perhaps a year or two later), a consulship should have been within his reach long since. Some lapse from favour may be surmised in the days of Septimius Severus.

Gordian got the honour at last from Elagabalus or from Alexander. To determine the date, the year of his proconsulate in Africa (237/8) does not help as much as would normally be expected: the period shows hardly any names for comparison. Gordian may have become consul before 222. The reign of Elagabalus was propitious for senators from the East (such, it will be shown, was Gordian's origin). It opened with Q. Tineius Sacerdos (*suff.* 192) as colleague of the Emperor. The senatorial Tineii may belong to one of the oriental provinces,[1] though their *gentilicium* is notoriously Etruscan, deriving from the name of the supreme god in that language. Nor will M. Flavius Vitellius Seleucus (*cos.* 221) be omitted: presumably from Syria.[2]

Herodian states that Gordian came of a good family and had governed many provinces,[3] but no details are specified on either count. About the extraction of Gordian, faith in the HA has propagated error. A common persuasion holds that he belonged to an old Italian stock.[4]

By full nomenclature he is M. Antonius Gordianus Sempronianus Romanus.[5] Senatorial Antonii of the Empire tend to be provincial; and the *cognomen* 'Gordianus' points to Asia Minor.[6]

Next, the item 'Sempronianus Romanus'. It evokes Sempronia Romana, wife of a senator and daughter of a secretary *ab epistulis Graecis* called Sempronius Aquila.[7] There also may come into the reckoning somewhere the *rhetor* Antoninus Aquila, commended by Fronto; the *rhetor* Aquila Romanus: and Aquila, a sophist from Galatia.[8]

More solid evidence avails. Philostratus dedicated his *Vitae Sophistarum* to an Antonius Gordianus, whom the superscription designates as 'consul' (that is, probably short for 'consular'). The opening sentence makes

---

[1] H. v. Petrikovits, P–W VI A. 1374, cf. 1382, where Volusia Laodice is noted (*IGR* III. 829: Syedra): she is the wife of a Sacerdos, presumably Q. Tineius Sacerdos Clemens (*cos.* 158).   [2] Above, p. 159.

[3] Herodian VII. 5. 2, whence *Gord.* 9. 1, with the remark 'ut diximus'—which is false.

[4] 'Senza dubbio di antica famiglia italica, forse romana' (Barbieri, *Albo*, no. 944).

[5] PIR², A 833, where it is implied that he took the *cognomen* 'Romanus' on his proclamation—'neque prius ut videtur Romanus'. For the notion that it was meant to advertise a contrast to Maximinus, W. Ensslin, *CAH* XII (1939), 77; Barbieri, *Albo*, no. 944.

[6] A. R. Birley in *Essays Presented to E. Birley* (1966), 56, adducing Ti. Claudius Gordianus, legate of Numidia in 188 (*AE* 1954, 138: Tyana). For two Gordii and a Gordianus at Comana, R. P. Harper, *An. Stud.* XVIII (1968), nos. 5. 18; 26; 6. 27. Further, L. Robert, *Les Noms indigènes dans l'Asie-Mineure gréco-romaine* (1963), 526 f.; 548 f.

[7] *IGR* III. 188 (Ancyra), cf. Birley o.c. 58. Add T. Flavius Sempronius Aquila (*AE* 1937, 257: Isaura).   [8] PIR², A 792; 983; 981.

appeal to his descent from the great Athenian sophist Herodes Atticus. Further, he is addressed as 'the most excellent of proconsuls'.

The standard assumption identifies this Gordianus with the proconsul of Africa.[1] Only sporadic doubts have been expressed. The matter called for rigorous inquiry. How can Gordianus, born *c.* 159, be a descendant of Herodes (*cos.* 143)? Factors unknown as well as implausible would have to be evoked.[2]

It is easier on all counts to suppose that the son of the proconsul received the dedication of the *Vitae Sophistarum*.[3] That is, the son who was his father's legate in Africa, but previously (before his consulship) may be assumed a proconsul: a proconsul of Achaia.[4]

The problem of descent from Herodes Atticus subsists, with differe n possibilities and surmises.[5] The consular son of the great sophist was M. Appius Atilius Bradua Regillus Atticus, the consul of 185. His daughter, it will be supposed, was the Claudia Regilla who married M. Antonius Antius Lupus, a senator who was killed by Commodus.[6] Claudia Regilla, however, can hardly come into the reckoning as a wife for the elder Gordian. She predeceased Antonius Lupus.[7]

What then follows? In the present condition of knowledge (and ignorance) another bride must be found. Not a daughter of Herodes Atticus. None seems available, and there is no hint of any such alliance in the evidence about Herodes and his family. Rather a grand-daughter. That is, provisionally, an unattested sister of Claudia Regilla, the wife of Antonius Lupus.[8] The hypothesis need occasion no disquiet.

So far the facts about the extraction and career of Gordian, supported by rational conjecture. Lacking facts, the HA invented, with no reluctance. It was the author's design to portray an ideal Antonine emperor. Like some other characters in the HA, Gordian is endowed with descent from

---

[1] *PIR*², A 833, cf. C 802; Barbieri, *Albo*, no. 944.

[2] For recent discussion see A. R. Birley, o.c. 58 f. (inconclusive); T. D. Barnes, *Latomus* XXVII (1968), 581 ff. (the full case for Gordian II); G. W. Bowersock, *Greek Sophists in the Roman Empire* (1969), 6 ff. Bowersock, however, states that Gordian I 'has a slightly superior claim as the honorand of Philostratus' (ib. 8).

[3] As firmly argued by Barnes.

[4] Barnes, o.c. 588. The son was a consular legate under his father (*Gord.* 4. 2; 7. 2). Not in Herodian. Further, the HA cites Dexippus in the near context (9. 6). Some doubts are expressed about the authenticity of that citation by Barnes, o.c. 592.

[5] For the stemma of the family, *PIR*², C, facing p. 182; for the children of Herodes, Barnes, o.c. 582 ff.

[6] *PIR*², C 812.

[7] As emerges from *ILS* 1127. Not therefore his widow, as stated by Birley, o.c. 59.

[8] Barnes, o.c. 587.

Trajan;[1] and he duly takes to wife 'Fabia Orestilla, Antonini proneptis' (*Gord.* 17. 4).

In his choice of names (common, rare, or significant) and in the combinations of *nomen* and *cognomen* the author had habits and predilections that can be classified to advantage. He liked 'Maecius': five instances, and three of 'Maecianus', all figments.[2] Now 'Maecius Marullus' is the father of Gordian, 'Maecia Faustina' the daughter (2. 2; 4. 2). The paternal line, it is alleged, goes back to the Gracchi—but the HA nowhere, so it happens, invokes the 'Sempronianus' in the proconsul's nomenclature.[3] A clue to the name and the notion can be discovered in the existence of Furius Maecius Gracchus, *praefectus urbi* in 379.[4]

The author's purpose being patent, and the resources of his technique, no good is likely to come from taking an item in isolation and arguing for authenticity. A Junius Balbus exists, an equestrian official attested in 203.[5] No warrant, however, for supposing that he might be the parent of the consular 'Junius Balbus' who marries 'Maecia Faustina' (4. 2).[6] The nomenclature is indistinctive, homonyms abound. It is a wonder that no senatorial Annius Severus is on record—the label which the HA devised for the father of 'Fabia Orestilla'.

More plausible at first sight is the rhetor Maecius Faustinus who crops up on an inscription at Corinth.[7] Attention has recently been drawn to this person. He is none other, it is claimed, than the paternal grandfather of Gordian I; and that emperor was adopted by a M. Antonius. Hence a stemma can be supplied.[8]

It is permissible and safer to admit a mere coincidence of name between Maecius Faustinus and the Emperor's daughter 'Maecia Faustina'. The *nomen* is not so rare: in old days Maecii abounded in the trading community at Delos.[9] Something stronger is needed to vindicate 'Maecia Faustina', whose *cognomen* is significant of the author's purpose, just as

[1] Above, pp. 4; 10.   [2] Above, p. 4.

[3] *PIR²*, A 833 suggests 'quod fictum videtur ex cognomine Semproniani'. That item is not preserved in any of the written sources.

[4] Above, p. 12; R. Syme, *Ammianus and the Historia Augusta* (1968), 162 f. (along with kindred genealogical fantasies).

[5] *ILS* 2163.

[6] 'Junius Balbus' is, however, admitted as a 'possibly genuine character' by E. Birley, *Bonner Historia-Augusta-Colloquium 1966/7* (1968), 50.

[7] *Corinth* VIII. 3. 264.

[8] J. H. Oliver, *AJP* LXXXIX (1968), 345 ff. That entails discarding the Herodian ancestry of a Gordian (whom Oliver assumes to be Gordian I). So far nobody else seems to have disallowed the testimony of Philostratus, a contemporary of the Gordiani.

[9] F. Münzer, P–W XIV. 232. Note also Maecianus, a son of Avidius Cassius (*PIR²*, A 1406).

'Orestilla' bears witness to his literary tastes.[1] Nor would the Emperor's mother at once become a historical character, if some inscription of Asia Minor disclosed an Ulpia Gordiana. Tyana in Cappadocia is the home of the senator Ti. Claudius Gordianus.[2] Similarly, a Flavius Gordianus or an Aelius Gordianus may well emerge.[3]

'Maecia Faustina' is not again named in the HA. The boy Gordian, it is true, refers to his mother in a letter he addressed to Timesitheus, the Prefect of the Guard (i.e. not before 241), blaming her for unwise decisions taken under the influence of her counsellors: 'Gaudianus', 'Reverendus', 'Montanus' (25. 3).[4] No coin or inscription certifies the mother of the boy-emperor, no evidence shows that she was among the living as late as 238. For the reign of Gordian III, the HA drew upon the historian Dexippus for some facts. For example, the items reported under three years, with the consuls registered (for 240, 242, and 243).[5] Segregation is easy, the fictitious flagrant. Dexippus therefore should not be invoked to support any of the fantasies about the family and relatives of the old proconsul.[6]

That person is the product of a cultivated and literary milieu. Furthermore, by his great age and by his relationship to the family of the illustrious Athenian sophist, he is a genuine link with the Antonine prime. Gordian was the friend and kinsman of the leading senators, according to Herodian.[7] Which may be assumed true, but cannot be established by any names on high prominence in the year 238. In his long survival another marriage (or marriages) into opulent families may have supervened. Nor need the consular son of Gordian be fancied a pertinacious bachelor.[8]

iv. About the two Augusti, Pupienus and Balbinus, Herodian furnishes a copious narration, but not much in the way of detail about their persons and careers. The HA, allocating a separate *Vita* (that was hardly necessary), displays not only a wealth of fiction but an unexpected command of literary skill.

---

[1] From Aurelia Orestilla (Sallust, *Cat.* 15. 2). She owes the 'Fabia' to the sister of L. Verus (*PIR*², C 612), previously mentioned in *Marcus* 29. 10; *Verus* 10. 4; *Pert.* 10. 2.

[2] *AE* 1954, 138.

[3] No homonym is likely to redeem 'Aelius Gordianus', a relative of the Emperor and one of the counsellors of Severus Alexander (*Alex.* 68. 1).

[4] For the names, designed to indicate Christians, R. Syme, o.c. 173 f.

[5] For Dexippus, see further below, pp. 235 f.

[6] He is invoked by Oliver, o.c. 34.   [7] Herodian VII. 6. 3.

[8] As in *Gord.* 19. 8—on the authority of 'Cordus'.

The HA asserted that the second Gordian was forty-six.[1] It neglected to invent ages for the pair of Augusti. A late authority, Zonaras, has Pupienus seventy-four, Balbinus sixty.[2]

The matter needs to be looked into. For Balbinus, the figure is incorrect, demonstrably. Becoming consul for the second time in 213, Balbinus cannot have been born as late as 178. Perhaps c. 165, with his first consulship c. 203. Yet he might be younger by as much as five years.[3]

Is there a remedy? Perhaps the figures in Zonaras should be reversed. That would give a plausible result, at least as showing Pupienus aged sixty. However, the procedure is not legitimate. It presupposes both precise information to begin with, in the source of Zonaras, and accurate transmission. Which is uncertain.

In any event, though on papyri and inscriptions his name invariably precedes that of Balbinus, Pupienus (cos. II 234) should be the younger man. He, not Balbinus, has charge of the war in northern Italy. Pupienus may be supposed not much over sixty. But not under, for his putative son M. Pupienius Africanus was consul ordinarius in 236.[4]

Their portraits on the coinage might be invoked, but not to a complete satisfaction. Pupienus can pass for sixty or so. The contrast in features is striking: Pupienus with a long nose, thin face, and vertical beard, whereas Balbinus is smooth, plump, and heavy-jowled. Balbinus looks nowhere near seventy-four—if that figure were to be admitted, based on a mere conjecture about Zonaras.

To proceed. As emerges from Herodian, Pupienus had been governor of either Germania Superior or Germania Inferior.[5] An inscription at Ephesus shows him proconsul of Asia;[6] and his city prefecture may be put in the vicinity of the second consulate (234). If Pupienus came direct to that honour from Asia, his first consulate might belong c. 217; but perhaps a little earlier.

So far an approximate estimate for the ages of the two Augusti. Balbinus by his full style is D. Caelius Calvinus Balbinus.[7] He may be identified as a son (birth or adoption) of Caelius Calvinus, attested as

---

[1] Gord. 15. 2. Perhaps close to the truth, cf. Barnes, o.c. 593.

[2] Zonaras XII. 17. In PIR², C 1179 the figure for Pupienus is not impugned; in C 126 that for Balbinus is deemed 'vix credibile'.

[3] There is a chance that Balbinus, as a loyal adherent in emergency of Caracalla, was abruptly shoved into the consulate of 213. I owe this suggestion to T. D. Barnes, who argues that Geta was murdered on December 26, 211 (JTS, N.S. XIX (1968), 523 f.).

[4] PIR², P 804, cf. below, p. 174.

[5] Herodian VIII. 6. 6; 7. 8.

[6] ILS 8839.

[7] PIR², C 126.

legate of Cappadocia in 184.[1] He was a patrician, being admitted into the *Salii Palatini* in a year not later than 191.[2]

Given his eminence, Balbinus might have been supposed a proconsul of Asia or Africa. The second consulate in 213, however, may have precluded it. That sequence of honours was not normal.[3]

To be sure, the HA alleges that Balbinus held both proconsulates. They head a list of seven implausible governorships.[4] The anomaly in itself is not inconceivable (as witness Marius Maximus) but it is not to be conceded on the authority of the HA.

A double rectification is in place. The standard catalogue of the African proconsulates admits his name, as not deserving summary rejection.[5] As for Asia, Balbinus was discovered on an inscription in Phrygia.[6] Drastic revision soon expunged his name.[7] That is to say, no consular occupation of this person is on record. Such there may have been, while seniority and second consulate might have recommended him for the post of *praefectus urbi* under Elagabalus or Alexander. No surmise is of profit—save that this old man, commanding potent influence in 238, was opulent and well connected. His allies and relatives evade ascertainment.

So far the uncontroverted facts, which are few enough. To turn to Herodian, as he introduces the pair. Pupienus had held many military commands, he was a firm Prefect of the City, acquiring a popular repute for sagacity and honesty; Balbinus, a nobleman by birth, reached a second consulship, with provincial governorships to his credit, and an open nature (VII. 10. 4).

A contrast in social status seems here to be conveyed. Yet Pupienus and Balbinus are both styled aristocrats and worthy of empire (VIII. 8. 1). In the sequel, when their dissidence is put on record, both are aristocrats; but, whereas Pupienus put the emphasis on his prefecture of the city,

---

[1] *ILS* 394. Barbieri (*Albo*, no. 99) conjectured descent from the *ordinarius* of 137, P. Coelius Balbinus Vibullius Pius (*PIR*[2], C 121).   [2] *CIL* VI. 1981.

[3] The Asian proconsulate of P. Juventius Celsus (*cos. II* 129) is the notable exception, assigned to 130/1 by R. Syme, *Historia* XIV (1965), 130; to 129/30, however, in *PIR*[2], J 129. For the proof of the latter date, see now C. Habicht, *Die Inschriften des Asklepieions* (1969), pp. 56 ff. (discussing another proconsul, no. 22). In any event, the interval after the first consulate (to be presumed in 117) is also a striking anomaly, due to special favour from Hadrian.

[4] *Max. et Balb.* 7. 2: 'nam et Asiam et Africam et Bithyniam et Galatiam et Pontum et Thracias et Gallias civilibus administrationibus rexerat, ducto nonnumquam exercitu.'

[5] Thomasson, o.c. 118.   [6] *CR* XXII (1908), 214 = *AE* 1909, 175.

[7] W. M. Calder, *CR* XXVII (1913), 11. Missed by *PIR*[2], C 126 and by Barbieri, *Albo*, no. 99. Registered, however, by D. Magie, *Roman Rule in Asia Minor* (1950), 1561; but he kept Balbinus on his list, with a mark of interrogation (ib. 1585). An undeserved compliment to the HA.

Balbinus appealed to superior birth and a second consulate (vii. 8. 5). In epilogue, their noble status and eligibility for empire is again affirmed (viii. 8. 8, cf. previously 8. 1).

The contrast drawn by Herodian lacks clarity of definition; and his testimony is impaired by a grave omission. As he states the matter, Balbinus was fortified by a second consulate. Herodian is not aware that Pupienus had become consul for the second time, and recently (in 234).[1] And, as touches birth, both Augusti, he states, were aristocrats.

The Latin sources import perplexity. In the brief assessment of Eutropius, both Pupienus and Balbinus were 'obscurissimo genere' in contrast to the boy Gordian who is a 'nobilis' (ix. 2. 1).[2] This is plain folly. Eutropius and his source (each or both) committed hasty error, or errors. The thing cannot be unravelled.

The HA is relevant. From the KG or from the first passage in Herodian (vii. 10. 4), noted above, the author caught the notion that Pupienus was a *novus homo*. It excited at once his fertile fancy. He spreads himself on an elaborate exposition, setting up for parallel the two Augusti, sharply contrasted in birth and public career, in demeanour, character, and habits. All clear and vivid—and fraudulent.[3]

v. It was high time to make some investigation into the rank and extraction of M. Clodius Pupienus Maximus. In the first place, there is a presumed son Ti. Clodius M. f. Pupienus Pulcher Maximus, whose *cursus* is revealed by an inscription at Tibur, of which city he was *patronus*.[4] It carries a consular post. This man, it is assumed, had been consul before 238, i.e. *c.* 235. That would dissuade putting the birth of the parent subsequent to 175. The document has a further value. The son began his career as *triumvir monetalis*; and he passed directly from quaestorship to praetorship. Hence a patrician. Not necessarily born such. But the item might show the family acquiring high distinction in the period 210–20. Any social advantage of Balbinus over Pupienus diminishes.

Next, the daughter. She is on record as Pupienia Sextia Paulina Cethegilla.[5] The forms 'Pupienus' and 'Pupienius', it will be observed, are interchangeable, compare 'Alfenus' and 'Alfenius'. The items 'Sextia' and 'Cethegilla' suggest the highest ranks in the Roman aristocracy; and, on the lowest estimate, they permit the assumption that Pupienus had

---

[1] The HA happens to register this pertinent fact (*Max. et Balb.* 15. 2). Dexippus is named or cited five times in this *Vita* (1. 2; 15. 5; 16. 3, 4, 6).   [2] Eutropius ix. 2. 1.
[3] Ch. XVI.   [4] *ILS* 1185, cf. *PIR*², C 1180.
[5] Known from five inscriptions (*PIR*¹, P 805).

made an advantageous marriage. Female descendants of two illustrious houses come into the reckoning, Sextii and Cornelii Cethegi. Their last consuls, so far as known, were T. Sextius Lateranus (*cos.* 197) and M. Gavius Cornelius Cethegus (*cos.* 170).[1]

The signs are promising. Three items can be added to the rubric.

First, M. Pupienius Africanus, who inaugurates the year 236, sharing the *fasces* with the Emperor Maximinus. Not otherwise known, but perhaps another son of Pupienus Maximus. The conjecture deserves to be resuscitated.[2] Further, the *cognomen* 'Africanus' had in fact been borne by the illustrious Sextii.[3]

Second, documents from Athens, to be dated to 229–31.[4] They disclose the sons of the consular M. Ulpius Eubiotus Leurus, viz. Ulpius Tisamenus and Pupenius Maximus (the latter being also named 'M. Ulpius Pupienius Maximus'). Some kind of link between the Athenian worthy, consul and son of a consul, and M. Clodius Pupienus Maximus cannot be denied. To investigate its nature and pursue the implications would exceed the scope of the present inquiry. It may, however, be of use to put on record the latest known of the senatorial Pupieni, viz. 'M. Ulpius Pupienius Silvanus, *signo* Gennadius', described as an orator.[5]

Third, a youth of senatorial family called L. Clodius Tineius Pupienus Bassus.[6] The inscription was set up by Tineius Eubulus, the freedman of his mother. It follows that a Clodius Pupienus had married a Tineia. The Tineii exhibit as their first consul Q. Tineius Rufus (*suff.* 128), as the last Q. Tineius Sacerdos (*cos. II* 219).[7]

Whatever the provenance of M. Clodius Pupienus Maximus and the paths that conveyed him to public honours, he may be deemed to benefit from potent influences in high society, notably a resplendent marriage, as witness the nomenclature of his daughter Sextia Cethegilla. Apart from persons belonging to the upper order, the *nomen* 'Pupienus' is portentously rare. At Rome only the gravestone of Pupiena Rufina, daughter of P. Pupenius Maximus.[8] As for the cities of Italy, the *libertus*

---

[1] The *Epitome* registers Lateranus as one among four friends of Septimius Severus, notably enriched by him (20. 6).

[2] Not noted by Stein in *PIR*[2], C 1179: the conjecture goes back to his article on the Emperor, P–W IV. 91.

[3] viz. the consul of 112, and perhaps a later member of the family (*CIL* VI. 1518, on whom Groag, P–W II A. 2052 f.).   [4] *SEG* XXI. 505 f.

[5] *CIL* X. 682.   [6] *AE* 1945, 22, cf. Barbieri, *Albo*, no. 1832.

[7] Above, p. 167. It is not easy to place M. Tineius L. f. Ovinius Castus Pulcher, a consul suffect bearing the tribe 'Arnensis' (*CIL* XIV. 3614). The Ovinii have the 'Quirina,' cf. *CIL* II. 4216.

[8] *CIL* VI. 25233 f.

of a 'L. Clodius Pup(? ienus)' is discovered at Ricina in Picenum.[1] Otherwise only Volaterrae, where Sextia Cethegilla is honoured by her 'nutritores', two freedmen Pupieni.[2] That ancient city of the Etruscans may therefore be designated the *patria* of the *gens Pupiena*.

VI. Pupienus and Balbinus have suffered sore neglect. The above comments, however, are not a mere digression. The events of 238 stand in close relation to the last years of Alexander, and may be used to illuminate the whole of that reign, the evidence about persons supplying connection and continuity no less than when it links the four years' interlude of Elagabalus to the regime of the cousin who supplanted him.

In the war against Maximinus, the Senate displayed an energy that confounded all prediction. Was their comportment due to concord established under Alexander between Senate and Court, with a genuine participation in government? Hence a resurgence, when occasion offered, of good men and sound principles that had suffered a momentary eclipse under the tyranny of a military usurper.

A proper and sceptical inspection of that reign discountenances the facile assumption. The administration was feeble, not invigorating—and discredited towards the end by the failure of the war against Persia.

Other paths should therefore be explored. One explanation comes out with a precise cause. In anger and resentment against the fiscal policy of Maximinus, which bore heavily on the propertied class throughout the Empire, the leaders of the Senate planned an insurrection.[3] As the event showed, they were alert and ready when the news arrived from Africa. Those who managed the plot had selected Antonius Gordianus as their agent—and as their candidate for the purple.[4]

This reconstruction has no warrant in the sources, which represent the rising as an African affair, with local and trivial causes. The objection is faced, or rather eluded, by the author of the theory. Those sources, it is contended, were deceived by official propaganda; and they lacked the means of ascertaining the truth about secret politics.[5]

Ignorance and credulity (and worse) will cheerfully be conceded in Herodian, the primary source for these transactions. None the less, a general dubitation impinges. Design is invoked where the facts proclaim pure accident.

A parallel offers, a hundred and seventy years in the past. The rising of Julius Vindex, legate in Gallia Lugdunensis, touched off the train of

[1] *CIL* IX. 5765.   [2] *CIL* XI. 1740.   [3] P. W. Townsend, *YCS* XIV (1955), 50.
[4] Townsend, o.c. 55.   [5] Townsend, o.c. 50 f.; 64.

events that demolished Nero. No conspirators would have chosen as initial agent the governor of a province without an army, liable to be suppressed at once by the consular commanders on the Rhine. And the ensuing proclamation of Galba in Spain seemed folly and error—until Fortuna took a hand.

If in the spring of 238 a plot was contrived against Maximinus, its authors were not well advised should they propose to start with Africa (an isolated region) and an octogenarian proconsul. It was accident—and accident again that first baffled Maximinus at Aquileia and then destroyed him.

VII. Other factors in the general situation since the year 231 invite brief inspection. The absence of the ruler may weaken a government, allowing discontent to gather. Alexander, his mother, and the Court were far from Rome for the greater part of the years 231–5.

Policy and its agents in those years elude conjecture. Next Maximinus, whose elevation provoked no repercussions in the other armies. Intent on the wars, Maximinus neglected the capital, not even according it the useful solemnity of a brief visit. His origin and career kept him aloof from the senatorial politics and alliances that engaged and commended Pupienus or Balbinus. Therefore no close group of interests already acquired in his favour, or any coalition other than opportunistic and impermanent.

Normal prudence dictated a careful selection of consular legates.[1] It would also enjoin public honours for influential senators. The eponymous consuls of 236–8 deserve attention, notably Pupienius Africanus.[2] His presumed parent, consul for the second time in 234, held the post of *praefectus urbi*. He may well have continued in office, being not at once superseded by Maximinus.

In the spring of 238 the Prefect of the City was Sabinus, assassinated in the tumult provoked by the glad tidings from Africa.[3] That *cognomen*, among the most common, precludes any certain identification. Herodian, reporting the incident, states that Sabinus acceded to the post after many consular occupations. The generalization need not be supposed to derive from precise information, or have much meaning. A thought might go to C. Octavius Appius Suetrius Sabinus, the eponymous consul of 214.[4]

[1] Below, p. 191.
[2] For the others, below, p. 191.
[3] Herodian VII. 7. 4, whence *Maximin*. 15. 1; *Gord*. 13. 9.
[4] *ILS* 1159. On whom, above, p. 158. Or, for that matter, since Balbinus survived, P. Catius Sabinus is possible (*cos. II* 216).

But there might be other candidates, given the dearth of information in this period. However, the fate of Maximinus' *praefectus urbi* rules out the Sabinus who held the *fasces* for the second time in 240.[1] This consul might be the C. Appius Sabinus known to have been 'consul bis'.[2]

No conclusion, therefore. But the facts ought to be put on record somewhere, since confusion has been imported by two items in the HA.

The proposal to elect a pair of emperors, and precisely Pupienus and Balbinus, was brought forward by 'Vectius Sabinus, ex familia Ulpiorum' (*Max. et Balb.* 2. 1). Which being accepted, and another piece of business dispatched, they appointed as Prefect of the City Sabinus, a 'vir gravis' well matched with the character of Pupienus (4. 4). There has been a temptation to accept and combine the two notices;[3] and a Vettius Sabinus would not pass credence in this age (or for that matter in any other).

Inspection of the context deters. In the previous sentence the author had made appeal to the biographer 'Junius Cordus'. And, next after the City Prefect, is appointed a commander of the Guard, viz. 'Pinarius Valens'.

After brief remarks about biography, with censure directed against 'Junius Cordus', the author elaborates a delightful sketch of the parentage and upbringing of Pupienus. It includes the particular that 'Pinarius' was his uncle (5. 5). Pupienus being himself 'natu grandior' (2. 1), the age of the Guard Prefect might arouse curiosity or disquiet, if he ever existed. Some scholars accept 'Pinarius Valens' without a question. Indeed, one searching and sceptical inquiry declines to relegate him to the rubric of the bogus.[4]

Hence, it follows, no warrant for a second Sabinus as *praefectus urbi* in 238;[5] and no evidence about the identity of the Sabinus who was consul for the second time in 240.

Preoccupation with names and persons needs no defence—and, when the HA is in cause, many items have to be scrutinized and discarded. In

[1] *PIR*[1], S 22. Registered as the colleague of Venustus in *Gord.* 23. 4, but without sign of iteration. [2] *PIR*[2], A 952.

[3] Thus *PIR*[1], V 340. And further, to conjecture a possible identity with Sabinus, *cos. II* 240. Thus Barbieri, *Albo*, no. 1753. By inadvertence Degrassi on the *cos. II* stated that he was probably identical with either C. Appius Sabinus or with the (Vettius) Sabinus *praefectus urbi* in 238 of Herodian VII. 7. 4. The Herodian reference concerns the Sabinus killed in March of 238. For the same error, R. Hanslik, P-W VIII A. 1867 f.

[4] L. L. Howe, o.c. 78. No doubts were felt by Passerini, o.c. 334.

[5] Since he, like 'Vectius Sabinus,' has no existence outside dubious tracts of the HA. Patently a figment is 'Fabius Sabinus, Sabini insignis viri filius, Cato temporis sui', one of the imperial counsellors (*Alex.* 68. 1); and a doubt might attach to the consular Sabinus of the anecdote in *Elag.* 16. 2 (above, p. 119).

general it is expedient to turn aside from the rulers and look for signs that suggest a normal continuity. For the urban prefecture Maximinus may not have felt or imposed any strong personal preference. Nor was it perhaps urgent to interfere in the ballot which selected the proconsuls of Asia and Africa.

Antonius Gordianus had Africa for the tenure 237/8. That is clear. The HA asserts that he held the consulate as colleague of Alexander, then proceeded to Africa by decree of the Senate (*Gord.* 2. 4; 5. 1);[1] and a letter of the Emperor is subjoined, expressing gratification at the Senate's choice (5. 3). All false. Gordian may, or may not, have benefited from an extended tenure. That cannot be ruled out. Not, however, a proconsulate extending from 234 or 235 to 238.[2] Gordian went to Africa under the regime of Maximinus: a matter of indifference to this Danubian usurper, even perhaps of mild approbation.

A paradox begins to take shape. The weak regiment of Alexander enhanced the pretensions of the leading senators; and, towards the end, not only liberation from the presence of the ruler but frustration resurgent, or conceit. Maximinus they detested. The Senate forfeited power, but Maximinus attacked security and property. More the latter—there is no record of any named senator put to death. Herodian is the evidence, eschewing names and facts all the time.[3] The Greek sophist conveys a generalized impression—exactions felt and resented in all classes throughout the Empire. His portrayal reflects the prejudices of the upper order in society, and he may have had a patron among them.

Taxation provoked discontent. Another reason was the Emperor's absence from the capital, his neglect to explain and enforce his policy before the Senate at Rome.

---

[1] The immediate passage to the proconsulate reflects the norm of a much later age.

[2] That is assumed by Ensslin, *CAH* XII (1939), 77, and regarded as plausible by Barbieri, *Albo*, no. 944. Against, Thomasson, o.c. 121.

[3] Herodian VII. 3. 3 f., whence *Maximin.* 13. 5.

XI · THE EMPEROR MAXIMINUS

THE EMPIRE, as Gibbon observes, 'was saved by a series of great princes who derived their obscure origin from the martial provinces of Illyricum'. The formula was obvious. It corresponds with plain facts. Superfluous therefore to look for the source of the historian's inspiration, though it happens to reside in Aurelius Victor. In comment on Diocletian and the Tetrarchs, the epitomator affirms

his sane omnibus Illyricum patria fuit: qui quamquam humanitatis parum, ruris tamen ac militiae miseriis imbuti satis optimi rei publicae fuere (39. 26).

Further, Victor proceeds to salubrious reflections. Praising the exemplary concord of those rulers, he takes their military excellence back to the training they received from Aurelian and from Probus.

It is worth asking where the series ought to start. Gibbon put the inception with Claudius in 268. Others may prefer to begin in 235 with the catastrophe of Severus Alexander and the proclamation of Maximinus. Various benefits accrue. Maximinus leads off, inaugurating half a century down to the accession of Diocletian.

In an earlier sequence issuing from families of Baetica and Narbonensis the rulers are products of a long historical process, with recognizable stages: knights in the service of the Caesars, senators, consuls, and commanders of the armed provinces. By the same token, to understand the emergence of the Danubian emperors it would seem expedient to cast about for premonitions, and for precursors.

1. Warfare foreign or civil brings up new men and groups, even new classes. The Danubian wars under Marcus enforced a notable acceleration. Soldiers and centurions rise to the high equestrian posts; and officers acquire the rank of senator and the consulship. Of the low-born Italians, the paragon is P. Helvius Pertinax, consul suffect in 175, *praefectus urbi* in 192. According to Cassius Dio, his birth was obscure and he had just enough education to make a living from it.[1] The HA confidently reports some further particulars. Pertinax was the son of a freedman. After some

---

[1] Dio LXXIII. 3. 1, cf. Herodian II. 3. 1.

time as a schoolmaster, with scant profit, he put in for a centurionate (in vain, it appears), but the patronage of an eminent consular got him a post in the *equestris militia*.[1]

A discrepancy in the testimony affords instruction and entertainment. Pertinax may have covered up the shame of his libertine origin, deceiving Dio—but not the author drawn upon by the HA. That explanation has been put out.[2] An alternative offers. The senatorial historian, though it was his congenial habit to show up defects of birth and education, and enhance them at need, must have known the facts. He is here extenuating; for Pertinax was a 'good emperor', whom the Senate soon had cause to regret.

That epoch also exhibits the first senator from Pannonia, M. Valerius Maximianus. A long inscription furnishes the detail of his manifold occupations. Maximianus began as an equestrian officer *c.* 162, was adlected into the Senate *c.* 177, commanded several legions in succession, and, after the governorship of Numidia, reached the consulship *c.* 186. One of the exploits of this military hero was to kill a chieftain of the Naristae with his own hand.[3]

Maximianus was the son of a magistrate at Poetovio, a veteran colony established by Trajan at the beginning of his reign. Therefore socially superior to Pertinax. None the less, though his *patria* is a *colonia*, he may well be of native extraction ultimately. The phenomenon can be verified in colonies of an earlier time, for example in Narbonensis.[4]

Analogy and the evidence about senators who emerged from other provinces might suggest that the Pannonian Maximianus would soon have emulators in his ascent. It is not so. In the course of the next sixty years Danubian senators are far to seek. To explain the dearth, various reasons contribute. The Senate of the Antonine prime represents the educated and wealthy class in the cities of the empire, west and east. The Danubian lands by contrast came late to civilization: few cities (and

---

[1] HA, *Pert.* 1. 1 ff. The patron was Lollianus Avitus (1. 5), that is, the consul of 144. The item is valuable. According to the *Epitome* (18. 4), Pertinax later avowed himself a client of Lollius Gentianus, the son of that consul, himself suffect consul under Commodus (*PIR*², H 42). For the equestrian career of Pertinax, see the observations in *PIR*², H 73: now to be supplemented by the inscription found near Köln, *AE* 1963, 62.

[2] W. Seston, *Bonner Historia-Augusta-Colloquium 1964/5* (1966), 218. He argues firmly for Marius Maximus as the source of the notice about the libertine origin of Pertinax. That does not entail the consequence that Maximus is the basic and immediate source of the *Vita Pertinacis* as a whole.

[3] *AE* 1956, 124 (Diana Veteranorum). For a commentary, H.-G. Pflaum, *Libyca* III (1955), 123 ff.; *Carrières*, no. 181 *bis*.

[4] *Tacitus* (1958), 620.

they not large), also few owners of great estates. Illyricum produces soldiers and officers, not urban magnates. And those officers have a career and an ambition of their own—not to sit beside senators in decorative ease but to compete in real power, and in the end to extrude them from the positions of command. Hence a sharp cleavage between the Danubian military and the traditional senatorial class. The divergence is not so much racial as social: it derived from differences of wealth, education, and occupations.

The wars of Domitian and Trajan's conquest of Dacia confirmed the military primacy of the Danubian frontier zone. Henceforth its army comprises ten legions, and their recruitment is local or regional. When the purple came into competition in 193, Pannonia proclaimed Septimius Severus. One of his first actions on reaching Rome was to purge the Praetorian Guard. Expelling the Italians, he brought in legionaries and ordained that system for the future. Inscriptions furnish clear testimony. The Guard draws in heavy preponderance on Pannonia, Moesia, and Thrace.

Severus filled the city with a horde of savages, hideous to eye or ear, so Cassius Dio affirms (LXXIV. 2. 6). Dio himself, governing Pannonia Superior under Severus Alexander, had incurred the dislike of the troops. Therefore, because of the Guard, the Emperor, when conferring his second consulship, helpfully intimated that Dio had better spend his term of office somewhere else (LXXX. 5. 1).[1]

II. The epoch turned black for senators, and highly distasteful to the pretentious exponents of the renascent and now dominant Hellenic culture. To the military, all ranks, the new regime held out bright prospects. In this auspicious season, at some time in the first decade of the reign of Septimius Severus, the young Maximinus entered upon the career of arms.

Precision is baffled. The sole evidence for his age comes from Zonaras, who has him perish at sixty-five: that is, born in 172/3.[2] Zonaras is not good. In the same sentence he doubles the reign of Maximinus, according him six years. And in this context he has the Emperor Balbinus born in 178. That cannot be believed.[3] His figure for Maximinus might even be a decade in error. The coins do not present the emperor proclaimed in 235 as anything like a sexagenarian.[4] Against which, to be sure, some might

---

[1] Above, p. 145.   [2] Zonaras XII. 17.   [3] Above, p. 171.
[4] R. A. G. Carson, *BMC, R. Emp.* VI (1962), 95 f., with Plates 38–40 (the earliest issues were hopelessly idealized).

urge that a sound stock and healthy habits made Maximinus younger to outward view than the decadent aristocracy of the metropolis.[1]

The paucity of precise information about Maximinus is compensated by the rich fantasy of the HA. A glance, however cursory, at the *Vita* devoted to the emperor and his son should be enough; and brief study of the impostor's general procedures will confirm disbelief.[2] Nevertheless, the temptation persists to accord credence to isolated assertions of the biographer. It is not always easy to confute fiction—nor should it be necessary in this late season. However, four items may be put on exhibit.

First, the origin of Maximinus. He was born in a Thracian village, which lay in the close vicinity of 'barbari', and such were his parents. The father, 'e Gothia', the mother from the people of the Alani: the one is called Micca, the other Hababa (1. 5 f.). In his later life Maximinus gave up service after the death of Caracalla, returned to his native village, and entered into relations of trade with the Goths; and he was on friendly terms with the Alani who came to the bank of the river (4. 4 f.).

The anachronism is patent, likewise the age to which it belongs.[3] The word 'Gothia' should have sufficed for condemnation.[4] Not but that some accept the fable and exploit it. Maximinus, a Goth by his male parent, is hailed as the first German on the imperial throne, with suitable elaborations. And, with appeal to linguistic science, 'Micca' and 'Hababa' are put up for authenticity.[5]

Second, Maximinus and Septimius Severus. The robust youth came to the notice of the Emperor when he was in Thrace, celebrating the birthday of his younger son with martial exercises (2. 4). An engaging problem for scholarly inquiry. When might Severus have been passing through Thrace, on the march to the East, or back again? Now the birthday of

---

[1] Thus E. Hohl, P-W x. 854.

[2] Hohl's rigorous demonstration (P-W x. 852 ff.) retains validity. See also his commentary on *Maximini Duo* (*Kleine Texte*, 1949). A regression, on all fronts, is patent in the lengthy and erudite book of A. Bellezza, *Massimino il Trace* (1964).

[3] As shown by Dessau, *Hermes* xxiv (1889), 359 f. Indeed, the HA, so it appears, is thinking of transplanted barbarians. Compare Maximinus of Sopianae, with ancestry 'a posteritate Carporum quos antiquis excitos sedibus Diocletianus transtulit in Pannoniam' (Ammianus xxviii. 1. 5).

[4] Surely post-Constantinian. It occurs once only in Ammianus—'quia rem Romanam alius circumsteterat metus totius Gothiae' (xxx. 2. 8).

[5] F. Altheim, *Die Soldatenkaiser* (1939), 246 ff.; *Die Krise der alten Welt* iii (1943), 118. Against, W. Ensslin, *Rh. Mus.* xc (1941), 1 ff.; E. Hohl, *Klio* xxxiv (1942), 264; *Rh. Mus.* xci (1942), 164 ff. After long disquisition A. Bellezza concludes that 'l'autenticità dei nomi è un fatto positivo' (o.c. 35). Hohl had argued that 'Micca' and 'Hababa' in the HA derive from μιξοβαρβάρων in Herodian vi. 8. 1 (*Neue Jahrbücher* xxxiii (1914), 708). The notion is commended in *PIR*[2], H 1.

Geta is stated to be May 27 (*Geta* 3. 1). Hence Severus can be certified in Thrace in 196.[1] Or better perhaps in 194.[2] The month of May in either year, so it is argued, might do. Credulity has overreached itself. Geta's birthday, supported in the HA by the invention of a pair of suffect consuls, is a fabrication.[3]

Third, Maximinus and Macrinus. The loyal client of the house of Severus left the army in detestation after the murder of Caracalla (4. 1). Though the motive might be dismissed as an embellishment, the chronology fits for the 'honesta missio' of an auxiliary soldier, and there should be no reason to doubt the fact.[4]

Fourth, the five educators of Maximinus' son (27. 3 ff.). One of them, the jurist Modestinus, is a historical character; and one might concede the *grammaticus* Philemon.[5] Why not others, such as the younger Titianus, his instructor in rhetoric? Indeed the HA may have been drawing on a source which registered the careful attention Maximinus had devoted to the education of his son. The upstart no doubt saw the urgent need to palliate his own deficiencies.[6]

The ingenious author (it may be noted in passing) did not miss another of the devices for acquiring social recognition: an aristocratic bride for the youth. He invents 'Junia Fadilla', a great-granddaughter of the Emperor Marcus—who subsequently married 'Toxotius, eiusdem familiae senator' (27. 6).[7]

The aspirations of Maximinus are credible, but not verifiable. The author, however, did not know the true name of the son, which was Maximus, let alone the identity of his mother.[8] As ever, his habits of fabrication must be borne in mind. For Severus Alexander are produced

---

[1] S. N. Miller, *CAH* XII (1939), 11. [2] A. Bellezza, o.c. 44.

[3] Likewise Mediolanum for the place of his birth: it was Rome (*Sev.* 4. 2). All three items are fraudulent, cf. R. Syme, *Ammianus and the Historia Augusta* (1968), 123. The primary *Vitae* have some consular dates (above, p. 42), but none by *suffecti*. The effort is therefore idle to retrieve the 'Severo et Vitellio coss.' of the *Vita Getae*. An attempt is made by A. R. Birley, *Historia* xv (1966), 251 ff. That scholar assumed May 27 as the birthday of the prince. The true date, March 7, is provided by the Passion of S. Perpetua, cf. now T. D. Barnes, *JTS* N.S. XIX (1968), 522 f. The rubric of *Geta* 3. 1 may now be regarded as closed.

[4] A. Bellezza, o.c. 45. [5] Above, p. 10.

[6] A. Lippold, *Bonner Historia-Augusta-Colloquium 1966/7* (1968), 85.

[7] For 'Toxotius', one of the primary exhibits in the HA, duly brought out by Dessau, cf. above, p. 12. Whether the girl be 'Junia Fadilla' or 'Julia Fadilla' (on MSS. authority the latter now acquires the preference in *PIR*², J 668) is immaterial to her existence. No point therefore in casting about (as in *PIR*²) for a putative descendant of the half-sister of Antoninus Pius, viz. Julia Fadilla (*Pius* 1. 5).

[8] He is 'Maximinus' in HA: elsewhere only in Victor 25. 1. No literary source has the mother's name, cf. below, p. 192.

ten teachers (*Alex*. 3. 2 f.). All bogus. Elsewhere he blends genuine characters with the fictitious, as in the list of the six sterling biographers (*Prob*. 2. 7), or the eleven generals formed in the school of a military emperor (22. 3). The younger Titianus may stand unquestioned in modern books of reference.[1] But no source other than the HA distinguishes two Julii Titiani. Ausonius, who mentions the writer of fables and the orator, gives no sign that they are separate persons.[2] Julius Titianus, the teacher of young Maximus, belongs to the class of the second Scaurinus and the second Serenus Sammonicus.[3]

Indeed, if all five were demonstrably characters in history, there is no warrant that any of them imparted instruction to Maximus.[4] The curious or the frivolous might be disposed to ask about the boy's age in relation to the employment of a jurist, or wonder why it is that Severus Alexander and the son of Maximinus, each deemed to enjoy the best education the epoch could offer, none the less managed to avoid having the same instructors.[5]

III. About this *Vita* a principle was promulgated long ago: 'entweder herodianisch oder apocryph'.[6] It stands, with three modest exceptions, viz. an item from the KG (8. 1) and two from Dexippus (32. 3; 33. 1).[7]

Otherwise, all that does not derive from Herodian is to be discarded. This is negative benefit. But it does not mean that Herodian be supposed to convey the literal truth. Herodian was a rhetorician, fluent, dishonest, and inventive. His delinquencies have been put on ample show.[8] Moreover, he detested precise detail. This fellow mentions no Guard Prefect

---

[1] P–W x. 842 f.; *PIR*², J 604 f.

[2] Ausonius, *Epp*. XVI, *praef*., and in l. 81 and l. 102; *Grat. actio* 7. None the less, A. Lippold retains the two Julii Titiani (o.c. 85). For Titianus and other writers seldom or never occurring save in the HA and in late sources (especially scholiasts), see *Ammianus and the Historia Augusta* (1968), 185.   [3] Above, p. 10.

[4] As concerns (Herennius) Modestinus, the fact has been assumed without hesitation and used for deductions about that jurist. Thus S. Brassloff, P–W VIII. 669; W. Kunkel, *Herkunft u. soziale Stellung der r. Juristen* (1952), 260; A. M. Honoré, *SDHI* XXVIII (1962), 214. Nor is the fact questioned in *PIR*², H 112.

[5] For the age of Maximus the coins furnish no clear guidance, cf. *BMC, R. Emp*. VI (1962), p. 93 with Plates 37 and 40. The figures in the HA, twenty-one at death, or, 'ut aliqui autem dicunt', eighteen (27. 3), have no substance. Compare the fraudulent variants about the next boy-prince (*Gord*. 22. 2).

[6] Mommsen, *Hermes* XXV (1890), 259 = *Ges. Schr*. VII (1909), 240.

[7] The items from Dexippus (for the second, cf. *Max. et Balb*. 16. 5) occur in the appendage to *Maximini Duo*. There is no sign that Dexippus had previously been drawn on in this *Vita*. To be sure, he will be invoked to bolster up allegations about the origin of Maximinus. Thus F. Altheim, *Literatur und Gegenwart im ausgehenden Altertum* I (1948), 187 ff.

[8] E. Hohl, *Berliner S-B* 1954, Nr. 1; 1956, Nr. 2. Hohl styled him 'der windige Levantiner'.

of Severus Alexander, or any of his counsellors; and he can narrate the Persian War (an elaborate operation which employed three armies of invasion) without needing to name a general or a regiment or a city.

What Herodian asserts about the origin and career of Maximinus should therefore be put under sharp scrutiny (to predictable and scanty results). Maximinus, he states, came from the semi-savage Thracians of the furthest interior, from some village, so it was said; as a boy he was a shepherd.[1]

Suspicion is aroused. A country boy tending his flocks, but destined for great things, the notion may well be schematic and traditional. There are precedents. Thus one of the military who came up in the wars of Caesar and the Triumvirs, viz. Salvidienus Rufus, out of the back country: consul designate for 39 B.C. although not yet a senator.[2]

Defamation operates with regional as well as social prejudice, and distortion is easy. Caesar the Dictator, it is alleged, brought aliens into the Senate, trousered natives of Gaul.[3] These new senators, so it may plausibly be contended, derive not from the tribes of Gallia Comata but from civilized communities in Narbonensis. Again, there is Decidius Saxa whom Cicero derides: 'ex ultima Celtiberia'.[4] He belonged to a Samnite refugee family that had settled somewhere in Spain.[5]

Language of this sort is relevant to the local origin of Maximinus: from the 'innermost Thracians'. In the conceptions of a Greek author (and especially one writing in Asia or Syria) what does that term convey? Presumably furthest from the coast of the Aegaean. Therefore not the Roman province of Thrace, but Thracian country extending beyond Mount Haemus northwards to the Danube, and included in Moesia. Herodian lacks interest in the Roman provincial system, and exact knowledge about it. Compare the misleading way in which he designates Capellianus, the legate of Numidia in 238.[6] Therefore Moesia. In its earliest period the Roman province did not extend eastwards much below Oescus. At Dimum (a dozen miles short of Novae), began the 'ripa Thracia' or

---

[1] Herodian VI. 8. 1: τὸ μὲν γένος τῶν ἐνδοτάτω Θρᾳκῶν καὶ μιξοβαρβάρων, ἀπό τινος κώμης, ὡς ἐλέγετο, πρότερον μὲν ἐν παιδὶ ποιμαίνων, etc.

[2] Dio XLVIII. 33. 2. Salvidienus probably came from the land of the Vestini, cf. R. Syme, Sallust (1964), 229.

[3] Suetonius, Divus Julius 80. 2.

[4] Cicero, Phil. XI. 12, etc.

[5] JRS XXVII (1937), 127 ff.; Rom. Rev. (1939), 80.

[6] Herodian VII. 9. 1: ἡγεῖτο δὲ Μαυρουσίων τῶν ὑπὸ ʽΡωμαίοις, Νομάδων δὲ καλουμένων. Which deceived the HA—'Mauros regenti' (Maximin. 19. 1). No one of the Danubian provinces finds an explicit mention in Herodian. A. Bellezza, however, describes Thrace as 'provincia ben nota ad Erodiano nella sua estensione e nei suoi confini' (o.c. 34).

'ripa Thraciae', which belonged to the vassal kingdom of Thrace until it was annexed in the year 44.[1] A welcome fact, it might seem—and a suitable country for the family of Maximinus.[2]

However, a large piece of Thracian tribal territory further west comes into the account and may deserve preference: the land of the Treballi in the region of Oescus. The old name had survived: in the time of Tiberius an equestrian prefect had charge of the peoples of 'Moesia et Treballia'.[3] When Domitian divided the province in 86, Oescus and the Treballian land went to Moesia Inferior, the rest (with Ratiaria) to Moesia Superior: the river Ciabrus formed the frontier.

The military occupation (*auxilia* as well as legions) brought prosperity, civilization, and the use of the Latin language.[4] In due course Trajan after the Dacian Wars established military colonies at Ratiaria and at Oescus.[5] In this zone (the former 'Moesia et Treballia') the home of Maximinus may plausibly be sought. For what it is worth, the Byzantine writer Syncellus styles him a Moesian.[6]

Moesia, not Thrace: the conclusion is not novel. But it should be kept free from any influence of the stories about Maximinus consorting with his kinsmen the Goths and the Alani on the bank of the river. Rational conjecture is different from sheer fable. There is no point in mixing them.

'Maximin the Thracian', such is the standard designation among the moderns. The ethnic label occurs only once in the Latin sources, in the *Epitome*: 'Iulius Maximinus Thrax' (25. 1). The term is improper when applied to a Roman citizen, even if he came from a part of Moesia that was originally Thracian.

IV. Next, the career of Maximinus. After indicating his origin, Herodian goes on to state that because of his size and strength he was enrolled 'among the cavalry soldiers' (VI. 8. 1). What should be made of this vague phrase?

---

[1] For the 'ripa Thracia' (that seems the correct term), see C. Patsch, *Wiener S-B* CCXIV (1932), Nr. 1, 94 f.; 146; 151; H. Nesselhauf, *Epigraphica* I (1939), 333; *Laureae Aquincenses* II (1941), 44.

[2] F. Altheim, *Die Krise der alten Welt* III (1943), 117.

[3] *ILS* 1349. The extent of the territory is indicated by the terms in Ptolemy: ῾Ρατιαρία Μυσῶν and Οἶσκος Τριβαλλῶν (VI. 9. 4; 10. 10).

[4] C. Patsch, *Wiener S-B* CCXVII (1937), Nr. 1, 219 ff.; B. Gerov, *Studi Urbinati*, N.S. (1959), 173 ff. For the earliest military posts, B. Gerov, *Act. Ant. Ac. Sc. Hung.* XV (1967), 85 ff.

[5] It has often been supposed that Ratiaria, like Oescus, had been a legionary camp. No evidence has yet emerged. For the high civilization attained by the colony see V. Velkov, *Eirene* V (1966), 155 ff.   [6] Syncellus 674; 681 Bonn.

First, enlistment in an *ala*. That would not entail the belief that Maximinus was rustic or a savage. As the *civitas* spread in the frontier zone, the proportion of Roman citizens in cavalry regiments showed a steady increase. Some figures are to hand.[1] Further, the *decurio* who commands a *turma* of cavalry can earn promotion to the centurionate in a legion.[2]

Second, *equites singulares*. The guards of a provincial governor were selected from the élite of the cavalry regiments.

Third, the *equites singulares Augusti*. This body of about 1,000 strong was probably created by Trajan at the outset of his reign, while he was still on the Rhine.[3] It was recruited almost exclusively from the regiments on Rhine and Danube; and the troopers, if not already in possession of the citizenship, received it at once (so it appears).[4] Nearly a thousand of them happen to be on record. About ninety per cent carry imperial *gentilicia* (not all of which, however, reflect the rulers under whom they entered the corps). Despite their origin from the lands along the frontier the *equites singulares* are not a barbarian bodyguard. They are picked troops, parallel to the Guard, and under the command of the *praefectus praetorio*.[5] Further, the *decurio* can become centurion in a legion. Hadrian awarded that promotion, into I Minervia, to a *decurio* called M. Ulpius Marcellus.[6]

Fourth, the cavalry corps of the Praetorian Guard. Direct enlistment is not inconceivable in a season of perturbation.

So far, therefore, cavalrymen of various types have been put on exhibit, with some indication of the promotion offering. In normal times distinctions obtained: *auxilia*, legionaries, soldiers of the Guard. Septimius Severus overrode them. Anything might have happened in the early years of his reign. At the outset, the twelve cohorts of the Guard to be replenished. Not only perhaps from legionaries but from *alae*. That had occurred in 69 when Vitellius enrolled new cohorts.[7] Herodian, asserting that Maximinus was a native Thracian, 'from a village, so it was said', conveys the imputation that he was not a 'civis Romanus' by birth. No source ventures the explicit denial of that status.

His name is 'C. Iulius Verus Maximinus'. At first sight, not the nomenclature of a new citizen. The *gentilicium* 'Iulius' deserves attention. In this age as in others, argument from *gentilicia*, whether imperial or not, should be conducted with extreme discretion. Rank and province and period have to be allowed for. Among the notables of Tres Galliae,

[1] K. Kraft, *Zur Rekrutierung der Alen und Kohorten an Rhein und Donau* (1951), 80.
[2] *ILS* 305 (Trajanic).   [3] M. Speidel, *Die Equites singulares Augusti* (1965), 92.
[4] M. Speidel, o.c. 66.   [5] M. Speidel, o.c. 66 f.; 91.
[6] *ILS* 2213.   [7] Tacitus, *Hist.* II. 94. 1.

'Iulius' indicates the citizenship acquired from Caesar or his successors in the Julian line. But elsewhere, and in general, 'Iulius' does not avail to take the status of a provincial family back to that dynasty: like 'Valerius' and other *nomina*, it was in permanent fashion and commended by tradition. Observe, for example, the eleven non-commissioned officers in a *turma* of the *equites singulares* in the year 200: three of them are Julii.[1]

This factor must be taken into account. Further, there subsists the chance that if Maximinus acquired the *civitas* when enlisted under Septimius Severus (in whatever branch of the armed forces) he would bear the *nomen* of that emperor.[2] Therefore nothing forbids the assumption that he was the son or grandson of a soldier from the region later known as Dacia Ripensis.[3]

Neither the year of his entry into the army can be ascertained, nor the corps in which he served. No matter. He acquired equestrian status. Herodian, in language as vague as might be expected, alludes to his passage through all sorts of military occupations to independent commands, as fortune conducted him forward.[4] Which may be accepted without discomfort or enlightenment. The next piece of testimony occurs in the oration which Maximinus delivered before the troops at Sirmium (not the Emperor's composition, so Herodian avers). Maximinus makes appeal to their exploits in the Persian War, and to his own command beside the rivers of Mesopotamia.[5] At last, so at least it has seemed, the glimmering of a fact. Maximinus may have held an important governorship, being *praefectus Mesopotamiae*, with two legions under his command.[6] Or perhaps not, only a 'dux ripae'.[7] It would not be wise to insist.

Finally, Herodian furnishes a fact. When troops were concentrated at Moguntiacum in the spring of 235 for a campaign against the Germans, Severus Alexander put Maximinus in command of the new levies (VI. 8.2). Most of them were Pannonians (8. 3).

That is all. Brief statement must suffice. To repeat the obvious, nothing

[1] *ILS* 2186.

[2] At first 'Septimius'—but soon deemed 'Aurelius', because of the usurper's entry into the previous dynasty.

[3] Hence by legal status a citizen of Ratiaria or of Oescus, with the tribe 'Papiria'.

[4] Herodian VI. 8. 1: εἶτα κατ' ὀλίγον αὐτὸν χειραγωγούσης τῆς τύχης ἐλθὼν διὰ πάσης τάξεως στρατιωτικῆς ὡς στρατοπέδων τε ἐπιμέλειαν τῶν ἐθνῶν τε ἀρχὰς πιστευθῆναι.

[5] Herodian VII. 8. 4: πείρᾳ τῶν ἐμῶν πράξεων ἃς ἔγνωσαν ὅτε τῶν ἐπὶ ταῖς ὄχθαις στρατοπέδων ἡγούμην.   [6] E. Hohl, P-W x. 857; *Klio* xxxiv (1942), 273 f.

[7] J. F. Gilliam, *TAPA* lxxii (1941), 162. A previous command, that of the legion II Traiana in Egypt in 232, was deduced by Wilcken from *P. Par.* 69. Against, A. Stein, *Charisteria Rzach* (1930), 179.

apart from Herodian has validity; and Herodian is flimsy and deceptive. Maximinus, it is true, might have come to the notice of Severus in Thrace (or somewhere else), he might have served as a centurion under Caracalla, or have left the service in 217, and so on. Why not? He might also have been vigilant for his son's education. To accept items of this nature and complete them with vague indications in Herodian or optimistic conjecture about times and dates is sheer aberration.

v. It remains to assess the career of Maximinus and the significance of his elevation. Aurelius Victor, summing up the reign of Severus Alexander (which he and others saw in too favourable a light), proclaims that the immediate sequel was ruin and chaos. The spirit of domination was now let loose, and it wrecked the Commonwealth—'Romanum statum quasi abrupto praecipitavere.' Hence all kinds of emperors emerging, 'promiscue boni malique, nobiles atque ignobiles, ac barbariae multi' (24. 9).

The declension began with the barbarous usurper. As Victor says, 'primus e militaribus, litterarum fere rudis, potentiam cepit suffragiis legionum' (25. 1). Maximinus was the first soldier to seize the power. That point was emphasized in the KG. Thus Eutropius, 'ex corpore militari primus' (IX. 1. 1), and the *Epitome*, 'ex militaribus' (25. 1).[2]

In the cruder version, that of Eutropius, Maximinus came to the power 'sola militum voluntate, cum nulla senatus intercessisset auctoritas'. That is false. Victor concedes that Maximinus was duly recognized by the Senate, though they did not like it—'dum periculosum existimant inermes armato resistere' (25. 2).

Such were the facts.[3] No alert inquirer will be deceived. For comparison stand the transactions of the year 217. Macrinus, when proclaimed emperor after the murder of Caracalla, secured unquestioned recognition from the Senate, at once. Where lies the difference? Not in the manner whereby the power was seized and legitimized.

Macrinus was a knight. Therein lay the defect of a usurper not unresponsive to the demands of empire. All would have been well if he had consigned the imperial authority to a senator, so Cassius Dio implies—or rather declares.[4]

[1] The HA was incautiously used for reconstructing the career of Maximinus by M. Bang, *Hermes* XLI (1906), 300 ff. More recently by A. Bellezza, o.c. 46 ff.

[2] cf. *Maximin*. 8. 1: 'primum e corpore militari'.

[3] Observe the firm statement of G. M. Bersanetti, *Studi sull'imperatore Massimino il Trace* (1940), 9 ff.

[4] Dio LXXVIII. 41. 2 f. For balanced views of Macrinus, see H. v. Petrikovits, P–W XVIII. 543; H. Mattingly, *BMC, R. Emp.* v (1950), ccxxv ff.; *Studies Presented to D. M. Robinson* (1953), 962 ff.

To see Maximinus in the proper perspective, sundry developments of the previous generation need to be estimated. Notably high rank in the government acquired by persons of humble extraction. Macrinus came from Caesarea in Mauretania, of obscure origin. He had risen from civilian occupations of no great prestige to the command of the Guard in the last years of Caracalla.[1] His colleague was Oclatinius Adventus, who had begun as a soldier in the Praetorian Guard. Macrinus on his accession appointed him *praefectus urbi* and consul for 218: an elderly man, barely literate or even vocal, according to Dio.[2]

Another new senator though not so conspicuous was Aelius Triccianus. He had once been a soldier in the army of Pannonia, a door-keeper of the governor. In 217 he commanded the legion II Parthica, and was an accomplice in the murder of Caracalla. Macrinus enhanced his station and made him governor of Pannonia Inferior.[3]

By those examples or precedents, Maximinus is no scandalous anomaly. Rather a product (and not the worst) of the wars and tumults in the age of Severus: a symptom of social transformation, a manifestation of the potency now gathering among the Danubian military.

vi. Macrinus, to save his own life, engineered the conspiracy against Caracalla. Accident and the anger of the soldiers against an unmilitary emperor brought about the elevation of Maximinus. He at once undertook that invasion of Germany which Alexander prepared but evaded through the offer of peace and subsidies. The next year saw the indefatigable Maximinus active in the Danubian lands and victory advertised by the titles 'Sarmaticus' and 'Dacicus' (the latter indicates the Carpi). He remained there in 237. In the spring of 238 he was at Sirmium, on the eve of a fresh campaign (the Gothic menace was looming), when the news came that M. Antonius Gordianus had been proclaimed emperor in Africa and recognized by the Senate. Further, the Senate showed energy and initiative as never before under the Caesars.[4]

All for the military needs of the Empire, Maximinus had not bothered to visit the capital and enlist civilian or ceremonial support for his regiment. There was a double miscalculation. He underestimated both the resentment of the upper order (which his exaction of money for the wars had sharpened) and the resources at their disposal.

[1] For his career, Pflaum, *Carrières*, no. 248. Also above, p. 50.
[2] Dio LXXVIII. 14. 1. Cf. Pflaum, *Carrières*, no. 247.
[3] Dio LXXVIII. 13. 2 f., cf. *PIR²*, A 271. By a change of boundary, to take in Brigetio with the legion I Adiutrix, Caracalla had converted Pannonia Inferior into a consular province.
[4] Above, p. 175.

The usurper, it should seem, had not omitted some measures or gestures to reassure the high assembly.[1] Normal prudence would show the way— an attitude of deference and no abrupt innovations to alarm them. If he had any notions about domestic policy, there is no sign that he declared them anywhere. The types and legends on the coinage are conventional and indistinctive.[2]

It would be worth asking what friends Maximinus had among senators, what eminent patrons he had acquired in the long service with the armies. Further, a new ruler, whatever his other preoccupations, at least gave some thought to the choice of the *consules ordinarii*.

Assuming the consulate in 236, Maximinus had for partner in the *fasces* M. Pupienius Africanus. The *nomen* at once evokes M. Clodius Pupienus Maximus, one of the chief men of the Senate, consul for the second time in 234 and *praefectus urbi*—and perhaps retained in office by Maximinus.[3]

The consuls of 237 were L. Mummius Felix Cornelianus and L. Marius Perpetuus. Of the former, who seems a nonentity, nothing is known apart from his official career as far as the praetorship.[4] The latter is the son of a consul. His homonymous father, brother of the illustrious Marius Maximus, had been governor of Moesia and of Dacia.[5]

Fulvius Pius and Pontius Proculus Pontianus inaugurated the year 238. Fulvius Pius, it has been conjectured, goes back to the man of the same name who was the maternal grandfather of Septimius Severus.[6] As for his colleague, a consular parent can be discovered: Pontius Pontianus, governor of Pannonia Inferior under Elagabalus.[7]

What then emerges? Not much, it will be confessed. The distinction of the eponymate went, as was proper, to rank and prestige in the Senate. But it may also reflect some personal gratitude of the ruler. The parents of two of those consuls had commanded armies in the Danubian lands.

More important, the governors of the armed provinces in that triennium. The subject calls for a thorough investigation.[8] On first inspection, the evidence fails to indicate startling promotions or the intrusion of military upstarts. Rather perhaps a continuity of the administration. Which need not surprise.

---

[1] A. Lippold, o.c. 73 ff.   [2] R. A. G. Carson, *BMC, R. Emp.* VI (1952), 90.

[3] Above, p. 176.

[4] *CIL* VI. 1464. Cf. L. Mummius Maximus Faustianus (31740)—who, however, is a patrician.   [5] Above, p. 138.

[6] Thus Groag, *PIR*[2], F 553, drawing attention to *Sev.* 1. 2.

[7] *PIR*[1], P 608, cf. now J. Fitz, *Act. Ant. Ac. Sc. Hung.* XI (1963), 291 f. According to Fitz, the successor of Aelius Triccianus. The family may derive from Philippi, cf. Barbieri, *Albo*, no. 1137.

[8] For the complete list of the known provincial governors, G. M. Bersanetti, o.c. 37 ff.

One name stands out, that of Q. Decius Valerinus. He is attested as legate of Tarraconensis in 238 by some seventeen milestones.[1] It is inferred that Decius stood loyal to Maximinus when various other governors went over to the cause of the Senate. This man, as now appears certain, is none other than the emperor proclaimed in 249.[2]

Any indication, however slight, that brings together Maximinus and Decius is attractive and advantageous. The untutored soldier, savage by nature and by race, as Herodian styled him (vii. 1. 2), suffered manifold detraction from both Greek and Latin writers eager to defend culture and education, and conventionally deferential to the ideals of the senatorial class. And not all in the recent age have shown equity or understanding. Maximinus can still be called the son of a Thracian peasant, or even 'der Barbar'.[3]

To the defamation of Maximinus, time in its course provided a fresh impulsion. As was suitable, the cruel barbarian ordained a general persecution of Christians. That was an invention of Eusebius: Lactantius was not aware of this welcome supplement to a catalogue of miscreants.[4]

Piety and ignorance duly issued in fiction: Maximinus murdered his wife (not named).[5] The lady was commended by Ammianus for the gentle and moderating influence she exerted on the truculent husband.[6] Coins and inscriptions disclose her as Caecilia Paulina.[7]

Maximinus as a persecutor constitutes a link with Decius that 'exsecrabile animal'.[8] It is flimsy and fraudulent. The facts declare something better. Not merely in that Decius, the governor of Tarraconensis, stood loyal to the soldier who had rid the world of Severus Alexander (and his mother). Maximinus, cut short in his work on the Danube and subverted by the Senate, baffled before Aquileia and assassinated by his own

---

[1] *PIR*², D 28.

[2] Below, p. 196. The identity was not accepted by Bersanetti. The decisive document accrued later (*AE* 1951, 9).

[3] An anthology of epithets and verdicts is provided by Hohl, *Klio* xxxiv (1942), 286 ff. Hohl and Bersanetti have made the signal contributions to a revaluation of Maximinus. Rostovtzeff was obdurate—'I do not doubt that Maximin was an honest man and an able general. But his aim was to destroy the fabric of the Roman state, as based on the cities' (*SEHRE*² (1957), 734).

[4] Eusebius, *Hist. eccl.* vi. 28. See now G. W. Clarke, *Historia* xv (1966), 445 ff. There was sporadic activity in Cappadocia, instigated by the governor Licinianus, as attested by the letter to Cyprian from the bishop Firmilian (*Epp.* lxxv. 10).

[5] Zonaras xii. 16.   [6] Ammianus xiv. 1. 8.

[7] *PIR*², C 91. Add *AE* 1964, 220; 236.

[8] The label of Lactantius, *De mort. persec.* 4. 1.

troops, may none the less be matched with Decius as a martyr to public duty and a manifestation of the valour of Illyricum.[1]

From modesty or inadvertence Maximinus neglected to use the coinage for advertisement. Decius comes out with the legends 'Dacia Felix', 'Pannoniae', 'Genius exercitus Illyriciani', and even 'Genius Illyrici'. Each for the first time in history.[2]

[1] G. M. Bersanetti, o.c. 35 f.; 94 f.
[2] *RIC* IV (1949), 111; 114.

XII · EMPERORS FROM ILLYRICUM

I. DECIUS CAME from Sirmium, beside the left bank of the river Savus, on the high road from Italy which by Singidunum, Naissus, and Serdica linked Aquileia to Byzantium. To gain control of that route, binding East to West through the conquest of the land mass of Illyricum, such had been the clear design and prime achievement of Caesar Augustus.

In the sequel, warfare on the frontier and a shift in the balance of power declared the primacy of the Danubian lands all through, until the backbone of the Empire was broken. Emperors elected the cities for their residence, anticipating the central role which fell later to Nicomedia and then to Byzantium; and Constantine, it is reported, had Serdica first in mind for his new capital.[1]

The native pride of the Danubian legions proclaimed many usurpers either transient or successful: the latter often isolated (on surface show) yet forming a link, and some even founded a dynasty. In the competition for the purple, the cities faced siege or sack, and great battles were fought along the highway or near it: Margus, Cibalae, Mursa.

The military rulers issuing from the Danubian and Balkan countries acknowledged the potent spell of 'urbs aeterna'. They were inspired by fervent patriotism and iron duty in the evil days.[2] Their heroic efforts to save the sum of things were not always accorded recognition. The new Romans, Illyrian and Pannonian, who appealed to an old Roman tradition of valour and energy, came against the barriers of class and education. Humble for the most part in their extraction, they enjoyed scant commendation for polite and civil studies. 'Humanitatis parum', that is the defect which Aurelius Victor deplores when paying a generous tribute to the 'virtus' and the 'concordia' of Diocletian and his colleagues in the Tetrarchy (39. 26).

Despite the parade of 'genius Illyrici', emperors who had come up from below lacked any impulsion to publish the facts about their origin.[3] Nor would the official panegyrists be explicit. They prefer to observe a discreet silence. When emboldened to break it, they promulgate a

---

[1] *FHG* IV, p. 199 (the anonymous continuator of Dio).

[2] See the eloquent tribute of Alföldi, *CAH* XII (1939), 200.

[3] O. Seeck, *Geschichte des Untergangs der alten Welt* I⁴ (1922), 444 ff. He cites Libanius, who avows the difficulties confronting a panegyrist (*Or.* XVIII. 7).

fiction, as when the ancestry of Constantine is extolled.[1] The exception is Pannonia and its 'virtus', with a hint of Sirmium, in the laudation delivered before Maximianus.[2]

Even when an emperor died or suffered discredit, it was not easy to ascertain his origin and parentage. Of Diocletian nothing could be known save that he came from Dalmatia. Of Constantius, so it appears, even less. Hence an open field for fable or for deliberate fraud. Obscurity enveloped the middle years of the third century. In the next generation, no Latin writers of imperial biographies can be certified, still less a historian.

The extant sources for the period are in consonance. They betray positive ignorance about emperors (age, parentage, relatives) or grave discrepancies. Of necessity the common source drawn up by Victor, Eutropius, and the *Epitome* of pseudo-Victor acquires importance: that is, Enmann's 'Kaisergeschichte'. The KG was not a work of any great compass; and it transmitted error, misconception, fiction. In the search for certain elementary facts and dates, recourse must be had to Greek writers: Dexippus, a contemporary, but surviving only in fragments; Zosimus; or the tardy echoes of other historians to be found in chronographers of the Byzantine period. For all of which reasons the lost books of Ammianus Marcellinus inspire regret, and a curiosity that can seldom be of much profit.[3]

II. Sirmium first enters history in A.D. 6 when Bato, the leader of the insurgent Pannonians, tried at the outset to capture the place: he showed a true instinct for strategy and communications. The legate of Moesia came up in time, rescuing Sirmium and the Roman garrison.[4] Later, under the Flavian emperors, Sirmium became a citizen colony.[5]

The *patria* of Decius was registered in the KG, which (by a notable exception) added the actual place of birth, the village of Budalia.[6] The emperor's extraction may be presumed native, as often in the veteran colonies. He bears the *gentilicia* 'Decius' and 'Messius'. Both are old Oscan

---

[1] *Pan. lat.* VI. 2. 2, cf. V. 2. 5; 4. 2. Below, p. 204.
[2] *Pan. lat.* X. 2. 2: 'quis enim dubitat quin multis iam saeculis . . . Italia sit quidem domina gloriae vetustate, sed Pannonia virtute?' The orator proceeds with 'in illo limite, illa fortissimarum sede legionum'.
[3] For the sources both Latin and Greek, see further, Ch. XIV.
[4] Dio LV. 29. 3.
[5] Presumably under Domitian. Pliny has 'civitas Sirmiensium et Amantinorum' (*NH* III. 148).
[6] Eutropius IX. 4; *Epit.* 29. 1, cf. below, p. 222.

names from Italy. But the latter is also Illyrian.[1] Or rather, both Celtic and Illyrian.[2]

Victor implies that Decius was a military upstart—'militari gradu ad imperium conspiraverat' (29. 1). Quite untrue: Victor was misled by what he knew about other pretenders. Decius is that rare and almost unique specimen, a Danubian senator and consul. On the analogy of other provinces one might look for a parent or relative who had acquired rank in the service of the Caesars. Q. Decius Vindex, procurator of Dacia, deserves a passing mention.[3] Nor will Messii be neglected.[4]

The consular Q. Decius governed Moesia Inferior in 234, and Q. Decius Valerinus held Tarraconensis under Maximinus in 238. One man, not two, such is the general presumption.[5] Further, none other than the Emperor Decius. That was the opinion of Borghesi and of Mommsen.[6]

Dissent intervened. On various grounds, and especially because no document exhibited the *cognomen* 'Valerinus' in the nomenclature of the ruler.[7] Some doubt subsisted. Standard histories refrained from registering the notion.[8] Nor was the emperor assimilated with the provincial governor Q. Decius Valerinus in *PIR*[2], D 28. However, all is now in order. An inscription found at Nicopolis ad Istrum supplies for the governor of Moesia Inferior the nomenclature 'C. Messius Q. Decius Valerianus'.[9] Some hesitate, it is true. And the argument has been put out that this provincial governor is not the emperor but a brother.[10]

III. To proceed. Introducing Decius in 249, in the reign of Philip, Zosimus states that he was among the foremost by birth and repute.[11] There is further testimony. Johannes Antiochenus asserts that Decius was of consular descent, that he had been Prefect of the City.[12]

---

[1] H. Krahe, *Lexikon altillyrischer Personennamen* (1929), 73 f. He also cites 'Messor' 'Messorius', 'Messus', etc. Add, as peculiarly significant, M. Messius Messor, procurator under two Augusti (*AE* 1920, 64: Poetovio).

[2] Since *CIL* XIII can show a dozen specimens.

[3] *CIL* III. 1404 (Aquae, near Apulum). Not closely datable.

[4] Above, p. 143 (on T. Messius Extricatus, *cos. II* 217). Some of them originate from Gigthis, in Africa.

[5] *PIR*[2], D 28; A. Stein, *Die Legaten von Moesien* (1940), 97.

[6] Also maintained by K. Wittig, P–W xv. 1251.

[7] Thus A. Stein, o.c. 57 f.; G. M. Bersanetti, *Studi sull'imperatore Massimino il Trace* (1940), 43; G. Barbieri, *Albo*, no. 1662   [8] *CAH* XII (1939), 225.

[9] *AE* 1951, 9. Cf. B. Gerov, *Klio* XXXIX (1961), 222 ff. The new inscription is not noted in the article of K. Gross, *RAC* III (1957), 611 ff. Nor is the legate of Tarraconensis.

[10] G. Barbieri, *Omagiu lui Constantin Daicoviciu* (1960), 11 ff.

[11] Zosimus I. 21. 1.   [12] *FHG* IV, pp. 597 f.

Some scout the idea.[1] Others are disposed to entertain it.[2] To defend small scraps of ostensible evidence from late and bad authorities is a hazardous operation, and sometimes superfluous. None the less, to deny outright needs more knowledge than is available about the social history of a period that witnessed rapid changes and unexpected elevations—for example Macrinus or Maximinus invested with the purple.

Decius was born about the year 190. The evidence is late and unreliable —but it accords with his consular commands.[3] A few years earlier Poetovio had produced a consul, viz. M. Valerius Maximianus.[4] He appears to be exceptional. But exceptions are not always unique, and they have a tendency to create precedents. Another colony in Pannonia might not have had to wait too long for its consul.

So far so good. Prefect of the City, that might seem hard to swallow. A brief pause for meditation makes it comestible. Both social change and political continuity are declared in the splendid career which another partisan of Maximinus achieved. In 238 D. Simonius Proculus Julianus was governor of Arabia and consul designate. The events of that year did not disturb his advancement. He went on to govern Dacia and Coele Syria; and he ended as *praefectus urbi*.[5] No man can divine the origin of this new senator. The strange *nomen* 'Simonius' appears to be unique.[6]

Decius occupied a high eminence under the Emperor Philip, so Zosimus affirms. The nomenclature of his wife shows that he had made a good marriage. Coins and inscriptions disclose her as Herennia Cupressenia Etruscilla.[7] The *nomen* 'Cupressenus' is patently Etruscan, and extremely rare: elsewhere on attestation only for Cupressenus Gallus, consul suffect in 147.[8] Further, the second son of Decius (i.e. Hostilianus) has 'Perperna' among his names, as a casual notice in the *Epitome* reveals (30. 2). Marriages of this order in the new aristocracy of the Empire (like others before them) excite no surprise. One would wish to know the identity of Caecilia Paulina, the spouse of Maximinus. Not so much later comes Regalianus, who rose against Gallienus in the Danubian lands in the year

---

[1] A. Stein, P–W x. 754.

[2] K. Wittig, P–W xv. 1250.

[3] *Chron. Pasch.* 1. 503 Bonn. The figure in the *Epitome*, fifty at his death (29. 1), is too low.

[4] *AE* 1956, 124. Above, p. 180.

[5] *PIR*[1], S 529; A. Stein, *Die Reichsbeamten von Dazien* (1944), 72 ff.; Barbieri, *Albo*, no. 1159.

[6] Not registered by Schulze, *LE*. But 'Siminius' exists (*CIL* x. 2960: Neapolis), cf. 'Simnius' (ix. 5772: Ricina; xi. 6449: Pisaurum).

[7] *PIR*[2], H 136.

[8] Revealed by *FO* xxviii. Otherwise the nearest is Cypressenia Servanda (*CIL* vi. 22199).

259. His wife was Sulpicia Dryantilla. She belonged to an influential nexus of families from Lycia, long since intermarried with the best names in the Antonine nobility: Q. Pompeius Sosius Falco (*cos.* 193) had for wife Sulpicia Agrippina.[1] There is a perpetual coalescence between birth and power in high society.[2]

IV. Maximinus who seized the power (or had it thrust upon him) had risen from the ranks. That was an outrage. Decius was a senator. He is also a palmary specimen of the 'reluctant usurper'. That figure (and apologia) was a normal phenomenon in the annals of the Empire. Even Zonaras happens to specify several instances.[3] And the notion carried a strong appeal to a writer of fictional history.[4]

Zosimus and Zonaras tell how Decius came to the power.[5] Confronted by various emergencies (pretenders in different parts of the Empire) Philip in 249 appointed Decius to a special command in Pannonia and Moesia. The sagacious Decius, well aware of what might be the sequel, warned Philip, but to no purpose. The troops invested him with the purple. Thus Zosimus. The account in Zonaras elaborates. Decius, after his proclamation, wrote a letter to Philip. He urged him not to be perturbed, he promised that he would surrender the imperial power.

Decius, propelled into a war he detested, could not avoid defeating Philip. The manner of his acquiring the power was noble and blameless, and he departed from it in a blaze of glory. In the summer of 251 Decius and his elder son, fighting the Goths, met their end at Abrittus in the Dobrogea (near Tropaeum Traiani). Decius was the first of the Roman emperors to fall in battle.

That event would find ample repercussion in the Latin sources, however meagre or compressed. Eutropius is very curt. Registering the death of the two Decii he states 'senior meruit inter divos referri' (IX. 4). The *Epitome* does not provide much more (29. 2 f.). Victor, however, reports what the parent said when the soldiers tried to console him for the loss of his son: 'detrimentum unius militis parum videri sibi' (29. 5). A noble pronouncement, and worthy of the old Republic.

'Such was the fate of Decius . . . who, together with his son, has deserved to be compared, both in life and death, with the brightest examples

---

[1] For the *stemma*, PIR², C, facing p. 166.

[2] For the cosmopolitan aspects, cf. relatives of Pupienus (above, p. 174); and M. Valerius Maximianus had for wife an Ulpia Aristonice (*AE* 1933, 70).

[3] Zonaras XII. 15 (Maximinus); 19 (Decius); 29 (Carus).

[4] *Ammianus and the Historia Augusta* (1968), 56.

[5] Zosimus I. 21 f., Zonaras XII. 19.

of ancient virtue.' Thus Gibbon. Their end, it should seem, inevitably called up the 'duo Decii' who at the interval of a generation each immolated himself to secure victory for the Republic.[1] Each practised the ceremony of a 'devotio'. The notion of a 'devotio' comes into the KG (Victor and the *Epitome*), but it is in reference to Claudius (see further below). Victor states that Claudius repeated for Rome the 'Deciorum morem' (34. 2). Which Decii, the recent or the remote? Victor is generally taken to indicate the emperor and his son.[2] But Victor says 'longo intervallo'. Nineteen years only had elapsed. Victor must have had in mind the old schoolroom *exemplum*, which Ammianus and Claudian duly bring up.[3]

That *exemplum* would not have been missed by the author of the HA. To the heroic death of the two Decii he would respond with zeal and zest. Resources of traditional rhetoric were at his call, as he demonstrates when exalting the victories of Claudius and Probus over the German and the Goth. The Decii occurred in that part of the *Aeneid* he knew best and often exploited for inventions, the end of Book VI.[4] And in this instance a writer familiar with Juvenal might have slipped in a hint of 'plebeiae Deciorum animae' (Juvenal VIII. 254).

v. The *Vita* of the two Decii is not extant. A cause for regret. From 244 to 260 a gap intervenes in these imperial biographies. After the *Gordiani Tres* and its supplement, the book devoted to Maximus and Balbinus, the text breaks off, to resume with the appendage to *Valeriani Duo*, reproducing the letters sent by the vassal princes to the Persian monarch after he had captured Valerian. The reigns of Philip, Trebonianus Gallus, Decius, and Valerian are missing.

The gap is also a cause of speculation. Decius and Valerian persecuted Christians. Some ingenious scholar may (or may not) have indulged the pleasing fancy that a devout scribe, angered by what he came upon in the HA, censored the manuscript by tearing off a large portion. A similar notion has been brought into play to explain why the greater part of Tacitus, *Annales* V, is no longer extant: the profane historian gave an unsatisfactory account of certain transactions in 33 (if that was the year).[5]

---

[1] For the formula 'duo Decii', Cicero, *De off.* III. 16; *Cato Maior* 75.

[2] Thus *TLL*, *Onom.* III. 79.

[3] Three times in Ammianus, twice in Claudian.

[4] *Aen.* VI. 824. For the restricted range of the author's quotations, cf. Dessau, *Hermes* XXVII (1892), 582 ff.

[5] E. Koestermann in his commentary, II (1965), 28; S. Borzsák, P-W, Supp. XI. 446; 473.

That notion is refuted by the way in which Tacitus introduces Christians in the famous chapter 44 of Book xv. Clearly for the first time. Tacitus knows how to save up his effects. Some, but not all, of the Palestinian vicissitudes of the procurator Pontius Pilatus were no doubt narrated in Book vii.[1]

Casaubon opined that the *Vita* of the Decii had never figured in the collection. It was never written. The author, inspired by pious zeal and by detestation of the Decii, decided to leave them out—and also some other rulers who came into the story.[2]

Casaubon's idea has recently been taken up, with a necessary modification. The author was a pagan, and he came against a difficulty: how was he to narrate the lives of two flagrant persecutors of the Church?[3] An unscrupulous performer (and such he was) might imply that the manuscript was damaged. A mutilated document, that is in fact one of the devices on abundant show in exponents of historical fiction in later ages. And indeed, extreme sophistication was not beyond the reach of the impostor who passes himself off as a collection of six biographers.

To cope with the HA demands a measure of ingenuity. A pity to waste it. Strong doubts must intervene, on five counts.

1. The investigator in the modern world, be he cleric or layman, when he comes to deal with Decius is mesmerized by the Persecution. Whatever his own persuasions, he tends to devote inordinate space to that theme—and perhaps far too much significance. In the reign of Decius the Empire had more urgent preoccupations.

2. A historian or a serious biographer must have mentioned the policy of Decius and of Valerian, so some would fancy. Not Zosimus, however. The Latin epitomators, writing under Christian princes, betray no sign anywhere that Christianity exists, except for an isolated remark in Eutropius towards the end. Of Julian he says, 'religionis Christianae nimius insectator, perinde tamen ut cruore abstineret' (x. 16. 3). These were epitomators, it is true, whereas the impostor was composing fluently, to fill up space and for the fun of the thing. Yet nothing constrained him to expatiate on the punishment of Christians by Decius, or even allude to it.

---

[1] *Tacitus* (1958), 449. The historian would there recount certain actions of L. Vitellius, the legate of Syria. Vitellius met the Parthian monarch at the Euphrates; he also ordered the procurator of Judaea to depart and render account before Tiberius.

[2] Casaubon said 'compositorem huius corporis pietatis Christianae fervore impulsum, in Deciorum odium praeoptasse principes aliquot . . . silentio transmittere'. In the *Variorum Editio* of 1674, ii. 166.

[3] A. R. Birley, in *Latin Biography* (ed. T. A. Dorey, 1967), 125 f.

3. Despite a dozen references elsewhere to Christians (which call for careful assessment), the new faith was not among the author's main preoccupations.[1] He is a frivolous writer, enamoured of literature and scholarship, a collector of 'curiosa'. Not a devout believer, still less the deliberate and dedicated (or at least subsidized) advocate of some cause in religion and politics.

4. The author was not under forbidding constraint to dissemble his opinions. Neither were other adherents of the old ways in the vicinity of 400 after Christianity had won the mastery.[2] In the *Vita Aureliani* the attitude is frankly pagan. Observe the insistence on the Sibylline Books, or confidence in the gods of Rome as a requisite for victory, or the Emperor's rebuke (mild enough) to a sluggish Senate—'proinde quasi in Christianorum ecclesia non in templo deorum omnium tractaretis' (20. 5).

5. The author's own statements. As 'Julius Capitolinus' he wrote the books from Maximinus down to the year 244. Introducing Gallienus (he had meanwhile become 'Trebellius Pollio') the author takes his inception with the year 260, implying that he has furnished in full the reign of his father: 'capto Valeriano (enimvero unde incipienda est Gallieni vita nisi ab eo praecipue malo quo eius vita depressa est?), nutante re p.', etc. (*Gall.* 1. 1). Next, the author leads off *Tyranni triginta* with the words 'scriptis iam pluribus libris' (1. 1). And, touching those usurpers, he states that much had already been put on record 'vel in Valeriani vel in Gallieni vita' (1. 2). Furthermore, in the exordium of the *Vita Aureliani* 'Vopiscus' holds converse with the Prefect of the City 'de Trebellio Pollione qui a duobus Philippis usque ad divum Claudium et eius fratrem Quintillum imperatores tam claros quam obscuros memoriae prodidit' (2. 1).[3]

Elementary prudence counsels distrust of the HA in each and all of its professions. The impostor takes delight in deceit, sometimes pointless; and he does not care if he contradicts himself. This time the author has a clear purpose, to authenticate one of his earlier selves; and he uses the device again, for 'Pollio' (*Quadr. tyr.* 1. 3) and for two others (*Prob.* 2. 7). Again, few scholars are so rigorous as to reject the avowal that he writes

---

[1] A. Momigliano, *Journal of the Warburg and Courtauld Institutes* XVII (1954), 40 f. = *Secondo Contributo alla storia degli studi classici* (1960), 129 f.

[2] P. R. L. Brown, *JRS* LI (1961), 1 ff.; A. D. E. Cameron, *JRS* LV (1965), 241 f.

[3] In the preface to *Philippi Duo* the author, it may be supposed, named the friend and dedicant whose existence is assumed later—'Herennium Celsum, vestrum parentem' (*Tyr. trig.* 22. 12).

at breathless speed: 'non scribo sed dicto, et dicto ea festinatione . . .
ut respirandi non habeam facultatem' (*Tyr. trig.* 33. 8).

VI. Nothing is gained or explained by the adventitious notion that the
author omitted all the biographies from 244 to 260. The later 'volumina'
happen to carry few references backwards to that period. Philip along
with his son is mentioned only twice (*Aur.* 2. 1; 42. 6); and there is no
vestige anywhere of Trebonianus Gallus and Aemilius Aemilianus, the
rulers intervening before the accession of Valerian. The author may have
elected to say very little about them. As Eutropius reports of the latter,
'obscurissime natus obscurius imperavit ac tertio mense extinctus est'
(IX. 6).

Again, the three pretenders of some consequence who rose against
Philip, each properly attested by coins. First Uranius, plainly asserting
descent from the sacerdotal dynasty of Emesa and styling himself an
Antoninus.[1] Second, Iotapianus, 'Alexandri tumens stirpe' (Victor 29. 2):[2]
the name may show a claim to ancestry from the rulers of Commagene,
two princesses of that family being called Iotape.[3] Third, Marinus, who
was proclaimed in the Danubian lands: by his full style 'Ti. Claudius
Marinus Pacatianus'.[4]

None of these authentic usurpers gets a mention in the HA. To fill
up his catalogue of 'Thirty Tyrants' the author was reduced to strange
shifts as well as pure invention. Ostensibly they rose against Gallienus,
that is the argument. For one of them the author goes back, avowedly
to the beginning of the reign of Maximinus. He employs 'Titus' (32),
who derives from the 'Quartinus' in Herodian.[5] Again, after Valens, he
produces 'Valens superior' his great-uncle, or 'as some say', his uncle in
the time of 'earlier emperors' (20. 2). This is the ephemeral Julius Valens
Licinianus, insurgent against Decius.[6] Victor has him (29. 3), and the
Epitome (29. 5), but there are no coins.

The HA exhibits no knowledge of notorious transactions in the reign
of Philip: it was to establish order in Pannonia and Moesia after the usurpation of Marinus that Philip sent Decius there.[7] And no sign of interest

---

[1] *PIR*[2], J 195. By his full style 'L. Julius Aurelius Sulpicius Uranius Antoninus'.

[2] *PIR*[2], J 49.   [3] *PIR*[2], C 47 f.   [4] *PIR*[2], C 390.

[5] From Herodian VII. 1. 9, cf. *Maximin.* 11. 2. Introducing 'Titus', the author makes the
fraudulent assertion 'docet Dexippus nec Herodianus tacet omnesque qui talia legenda
posteris tradiderunt' (*Tyr. trig.* 32. 1). The lie about Herodian is patent. It cannot therefore
be taken as certain that the author is either honest or correct in all of his other citations.

[6] *PIR*[2], J 610.

[7] Zosimus I. 20. 2; 21. 2.

either. Worse is to follow. The *Vita Aureliani* presents a catalogue of good emperors, from Augustus down to Aurelian and Claudius. Valerian, so the author explains, must be segregated—'cum optimus fuerit, ab omnibus infelicitas separavit' (42. 4). He then proceeds to deleterious rulers: 'quis ferat Maximinos et Filippos?' After which, at the end he has the notice 'tametsi Decios excerpere debeam quorum et vita et mors veteribus comparanda est' (42. 6).

Most peculiar. The notice looks like an afterthought. The *Vita Deciorum* could not fail to be a panegyric of rulers who died as they had lived, in devotion to Rome. If the author had written that *Vita* he could not have denied to the Decii their due place on the roll of honour.

VII. There may be a different, and a modest, explanation: incompetence or sheer inadvertence. The HA must be judged by standards all of its own. Its failure to exploit an item about Claudius in the KG is revealing on several counts. In the emergency of the Gothic War recourse was had to the Sibylline Books. The sacred scrolls declared that for victory the foremost among the senators should be offered up. The personage indicated duly came forward, but the Emperor interposed his own supreme claim to death and glory. And so the enemy were defeated, 'postquam imperator vitam rei publicae dono dedit'. Thus Victor (34. 1 ff.), with edifying commentary (and a reference at the end to the virtues of Constantius and Constantine). The *Epitome* has the same story, adding the name of the eminent senator, Pomponius Bassus (34. 3).[1]

The behaviour of the HA is paradoxical. It soberly states that after the termination of the Gothic War the Emperor perished from the plague (*Claud.* 12. 2). Which is correct.[2]

The HA is lavish in laudation of Claudius. Death in the field would be just the thing, even without a ritual 'devotio'. Yet the HA turns aside from the edifying fable that consecrates a pagan hero worthy of the old Republic—and it also neglects an opportunity to exploit the Sibylline Books.[3]

---

[1] Ti. Pomponius Bassus, twice consul and *praefectus urbi* (*CIL* VI. 31747 = *IG* XIV. 1076) is presumably to be identified with Bassus (*cos.* 259) and Pomponius Bassus (*cos. II* 271). For the problem, Barbieri, *Albo*, no. 1698. That this prefect should be absent from the Chronographer of the Year 354 is not a valid objection.

[2] P. Damerau, *Klio*, Beiheft XXXIII (1934), 61. It will be noted that Ammianus has the 'devotio' story (XXXI. 5. 7, cf. XVI. 10. 3). For source problems, see E. Hohl, *Klio* XI (1911), 210 f.

[3] Therefore the HA at this point neglected the Latin tradition and followed a Greek source (i.e. probably Dexippus).

The HA goes on to describe the brief reign and decease of Quintillus, the brother of Claudius. There follows an exercise in the technique of genealogy devoted to the pedigree of Constantius in relation to Claudius (13. 1 ff.). That subject furnishes manifold instruction and entertainment.

VIII. Addressing the son of Constantius in the summer of the year 310, a panegyrist disclosed a great truth that had lain hidden: 'quod plerique adhuc forte nesciunt, sed qui te amant plurimum sciunt. ab illo enim divo Claudio manat in te avita cognatio' (*Pan. lat.* VI. 2. 1 f.).

Constantine as grandson of Claudius, the invention falls into place in the political setting. Three years previously he had celebrated 'felices nuptiae' with Fausta, the daughter of old Maximianus.[1] Constantine now had to rid himself of that awkward and perfidious ally, who in the sequel of confused transactions was permitted or compelled to commit suicide.[2] Discarding Maximianus Herculius, the husband of Fausta stood in need of a new legitimation.[3]

Political fraud was duly accompanied by supernatural sanction. The panegyrist describes the vision vouchsafed to Constantine in a temple somewhere in Gaul—'vidisti enim, credo, Constantine, Apollinem tuum comitante Victoria coronas tibi laureas offerentem' (21. 4). That was not all. The young Augustus recognized, embodied in himself, the world ruler announced in prophecy (and in Virgil's poem)—'vidisti teque in illius specie recognovisti cui totius mundi regna deberi vatum carmina divina cecinerunt' (21. 5).[4]

Apollo and Divus Claudius thus conspire to reinforce the claims of Constantine to the supreme power. Apollo had to recede under the effects of a second and more potent vision in due course; but Claudius maintained his role as an ancestor.[5] Inscriptions declare Constantine as 'divi Claudi nepos'.[6] The corollary that Constantius might be a bastard son of Claudius does not appear to have been insisted upon. And there were variants. In Eutropius Constantius is 'per filiam nepos Claudi'.[7] A later writer assumed him not a son or grandson but a grandnephew—'nepos ex fratre'.[8]

---

[1] *Pan. lat.* VII. 1.

[2] For the variants, W. Ensslin, P–W xv. 2514 f.

[3] The situation is firmly expounded by Baynes, *CAH* XII (1939), 680.

[4] If the scene be an amiable fiction of the orator, the fiction does not forfeit significance.

[5] For the suspicious variants. H. Dessau, *Hermes* XXIV (1889), 343 f.; J. Moreau, *JAC* II (1959), 159.

[6] *ILS* 699; 702. In 723 Constans the son of Constantine is duly styled 'divi Claudi abnepos'; in 725, however, he becomes 'pronepos'.

[7] Eutropius IX. 22. 1.

[8] *Anon. Val.* I. 1.

Disdaining brief or vague statements about the pedigree, the HA imports authentication through named persons. Claudius left no children. But he had a third brother, 'Crispus'. Now 'Claudia', the daughter of 'Crispus' married 'Eutropius', of noble Dardanian stock. Constantius was the fruit of this match, and he had sisters: one of them, 'Constantina', married a 'tribunus Assyriorum', but did not live long (13. 1 ff.).[1]

Eutropius also has the Claudian ancestry of Constantius. It probably occurred in the KG; and the 'devotio' of Claudius is reproduced both by Victor and by the *Epitome*. Fiction or governmental fraud in the age of Constantine coloured or distorted the earlier history in various ways.[2]

Decius was a usurper. The fact is extenuated: edifying stories showed him an exemplary friend of Philip, and reluctant to assume the power. Decius fell in battle. He may (or may not) have been a good general:[3] his end was embellished, and the Roman defeat was put down to the treachery of Trebonianus Gallus.[4] Again, Gallienus was saddled with the disasters of the sixties, and defamed. As Victor says 'cum neque Gallieni flagitia, dum urbes erunt, occultari queant' (33. 29). Finally, it was Claudius who by his victory over the Goths redressed the Empire.[5]

As with Decius, the end of Claudius was embellished. And his accession was expurgated.[6] According to the common source of Zosimus and Zonaras, when the marshals in camp outside Mediolanum formed the plot against Gallienus, the Prefect of the Guard, Herculianus, brought Claudius into it.[7] In contradiction stands the KG. In the version of Aurelius Victor, Gallienus in his dying breath designated Claudius as his successor. The *Epitome* is in accord, adding a name for corroboration: Gallonius Basilius conveyed to Ticinum the 'indumenta regia' (34. 32).[8] Claudius was absent at the time, in command at Ticinum; and Gallienus sent to

---

[1] Constantius is here explicitly a grandnephew of Claudius—a better device than the official version of *ILS* 699. In the earlier passage of the *Vita Claudii*, which introduced the string of prophecies (9. 9), Constantius was only a 'nepos'—which indeed might cover a 'grandnephew'.   [2] The theme deserves a full investigation.

[3] Previously a legate of Moesia Inferior (above, p. 196) Decius ought to have known the terrain.

[4] Zosimus I. 23. 2; Zonaras XII. 20. Compare the word 'fraude' in an obscure sentence of Victor (29. 2).

[5] Of the ancient sources only Zosimus has Claudius win a great victory at Naissus (I. 45. 1). That it should be transferred to Gallienus is argued very plausibly by Alföldi, *CAH* XII (1939), 149; 189; 723.

[6] P. Damerau, o.c. 44 ff.

[7] Zosimus I. 40. 2; Zonaras XII. 25. See further below, p. 210.

[8] The name does not seem to have been impugned by scholars. Yet the whole incident is fictitious. 'Basilius' (*PIR*², G 49 adds '? Basileus') is singularly appropriate for one who bore the 'indumenta regia'.

him the 'insignia imperii' (33. 28). The HA conforms to the expurgation. It states briefly and without detail that Claudius had no share in the plot.[1]

Several of the items adduced above offer clues to the KG. Enmann put its terminal year at 284. Nothing precludes 337, and much speaks for it.[2] As concerns the HA, for present purposes it is irrelevant whether it drew on KG, on Victor, or on Eutropius. The matter belongs to source criticism rather than to the dating of the HA.

IX. In that controversy the Claudian ancestry of Constantius occupied from the outset a place of predilection—and kept it for longer than was necessary or useful. The old ways die hard. Dessau detected the date as well as the purpose of the fabrication, which demolished the pretence of 'Trebellius Pollio' that he was writing when Constantius was Caesar, that is between 293 and 305.[3]

Mommsen refused to follow. He put up a variety of pleas. The *Vita Claudii*, he suggested, was composed precisely to demonstrate the ancestry; possibly the author himself was responsible for the fiction; not improbably the fiction helped to acquire authority for the HA.[4] Not content with which, he was impelled to deny that the removal of Maximianus Herculius in 310 had anything to do with the novel claim now published by the son of Constantius. Mommsen's obdurate stand (or evasive argumentation) was great comfort to conservative critics in the melancholy sequel. Indeed, it accorded well with Peter's inference that the 'six biographers' were alert and artful courtiers.[5] In recent years it has been held not beyond credence that 'Pollio' circulated some years in advance the disclosure made by the panegyrist in 310; and that, in general, the use of Claudius in the HA smacks of the age of Constantine.[6]

Taken by itself, the *Vita Claudii* has encouraged misconceptions. If, as was so lightly assumed, the HA was composed with some serious political purpose, the praise of Claudius baffled comprehension if not published under Constantine, his ostensible descendant. Thus Mommsen, enouncing

---

[1] *Gall.* 14. 2, cf. 15. 3. The *Vita Claudii* has 'etiamsi non auctor consilii fuit' (1. 3).

[2] See further below, p. 222.

[3] *Hermes* XXIV (1889), 342 ff. Dessau also demonstrated that the prophecies (*Claud.* 10) disprove the ostensible date of the *Vita*. Writing at the same time, Klebs showed up the faked pedigree of Constantine (*Hist. Zeitschr.* LXI (1889), 229 ff.)—but failed to see the necessary consequences. Further, he put the composition of the *Vitae* in 300 to 303.

[4] Mommsen, *Ges. Schr.* VII (1909), 326.

[5] H. Peter, *Die Scriptores Historiae Augustae* (1892), 7 ff.

[6] A. Momigliano, *Secondo Contributo* (1960), 119 f. He affirms that 'Mommsen's remarks . . . remain decisive' (ib. 119, n. 24). For E. Manni it was 'fuori di dubbio' that the *Vita Claudii* was written precisely in the lifetime of Constantine (*L'impero di Gallieno* (1949), 98).

his 'cui bono?'.[1] There was a way out, which followed the same kind of assumption. Why not Julian, who was a grandson of Constantius?[2]

As brief inspection shows, the exploitation of Claudius has its own easy explanation when it is contemplated, not in isolation, but in close conjunction with the *Vita* of another military hero, viz. Probus. The same themes dominate. And indeed, Probus can be held superior even to Claudius (*Tac.* 16. 6).[3]

For convenience of annotation, a subsidiary point may be added, though there is no need for any further showing-up of 'Pollio's' pretence to be writing under Constantius. As elsewhere, fictitious names furnish instruction. The author produced 'Eutropius' for parent to Constantius, 'Crispus' for grandfather. Not bad.[4] Both names occur in the dynasty. Theodora, daughter of Eutropia and stepdaughter of Maximianus, married Constantius (who then discarded Helena): whence six children, among them Eutropia, the half-sister of Constantine, a lady of some historical consequence, at least in the year 350.[5] Crispus was the eldest of Constantine's sons, made a Caesar in 317: the son of Minervina, a concubine.[6] In 326 he was put to death by his father, himself the issue of the connection (not certainly legal) between Constantius and Helena.[7]

[1] Mommsen, o.c. 303. According to Momigliano, 'Mommsen's simple question "cui bono?" has never been answered in a really satisfactory way' (o.c. 129).

[2] N. H. Baynes, *The Historia Augusta* (1926), 58 ff.

[3] For this explanation, cf. *Ammianus and the Historia Augusta* (1968), 116 f.

[4] And not refutable. What source would have revealed to the HA the parent of Constantius? He might have been a Flavius Dalmatius, as conjectured by A. Piganiol, *L'Empereur Constantin* (1932), 32. One of Constantius' sons by Theodora bore the name Dalmatius; and his son was Dalmatius Caesar, killed soon after the decease of Constantine.

[5] O. Seeck, P–W VI. 1519.

[6] Id. P–W IV. 1722 f. Minervina is noted in language almost identical in *Epit.* 41. 4; Zosimus II. 20. 2.

[7] For Helena see *PIR*², F 426a. In the same year (326) Constantine promulgated a law forbidding concubinage, at least to married men (*Cod. Just.* v. 26).

XIII · FROM DECIUS TO DIOCLETIAN

I. THE HA OFFERS a strange blend: artifice or ineptitude, cleverness and inadvertence. Estimated as biographies most of the *Vitae* are bad compositions. The author lacks a sense of structure. None the less, the fabrications exhibit an unexpected talent for linking themes and persons. It comes out already in the first section of the work, in some of the 'secondary *Vitae*'. A dozen letters of commendation, reproduced or cited, extol the virtues of the three pretenders Avidius Cassius, Pescennius Niger, Clodius Albinus.[1] Another device brings a ruler into significant connection with others through blood or marriage. The prime specimen is old Gordian, paraded as an Antonine emperor. The whole thing is artfully elaborated.[2]

The later *Vitae* show a startling development in technique. The ingenious impostor forges concatenations, not only direct, but at several removes, imbricated in a long sequence of good emperors from Decius to Carus—and leading on to the Tetrarchy.

Many such links existed. They are declared by facts of history—or, more often, suggested by notices in other writers, though not always to be taken for authentic. Zonaras happens to come in useful. A vague phrase indicates that Valerian held a high post in government under Decius (XII. 20). Claudius, as has been shown above, participated in the plot against Gallienus: so did Aurelian (XII. 25, cf. Victor 33. 21). Further, Claudius intended that Aurelian should be his successor (XII. 26). Probus, when proclaimed in the East, was holding an important military command (XII. 29, cf. Zosimus I. 64. 1): he had perhaps received it already from Aurelian, not during the brief intermission of Tacitus.[3] Carus was brave and skilled in war (XII. 30). He had been appointed *praefectus praetorio* by Probus (Victor 38. 1). And Diocletian was with Carus on the campaign against the Persians (XII. 31, cf. Victor 39. 1).

II. Several of the emperors in the series acknowledged a common origin from the Danubian lands. Decius came from Sirmium, likewise Probus (Victor 37. 4). For the rest, precision was not easily had. Few facts survived. The evidence presented gaps and discrepancies, it encouraged speculation or fiction.

---

[1] Above, p. 65.   [2] Above, p. 101.   [3] Below, p. 244.

The obscure extraction of Claudius was further darkened by fraud as well as fiction. The HA in a bogus letter describes him as 'Illyricianae gentis vir' (*Claud.* 14. 2). Elsewhere it suggests that he was from Dalmatia, though some held him Dardanian—and indeed descended from Dardanus the Trojan (11. 9). The notion accords with the detail that his niece 'Claudia' married the noble Dardanian 'Eutropius', the father of Constantius (13. 2).[1]

Dardania is the region between Scupi and Naissus, allocated by Aurelian to his Dacia Mediterranea when he gave up Trajan's Dacia.[2] Constantine, it happens to be stated, was born at Naissus.[3] Not in itself any proof of the *patria*. Further, meditating a new imperial capital, that emperor consigned his first thoughts to Serdica, in Dacia Mediterranea.[4] That is no proof either. The strategic situation explains. One must fall back on a statement of Julian in the *Misopogon*, who was a grandson of Constantius. He says that the family derived from the Moesians who dwell on the bank of the Danube between the Pannonians and the Thracians.[5] That should indicate the other province, Dacia Ripensis.

If so, no sign for Claudius. The discovery that Claudius was an ancestor in some way or other of Constantine owed its inspiration to reasons of high politics. It cannot be taken to imply identity of local provenance. Claudius reverts to his appropriate obscurity.

Next, Aurelian, the associate and ally of Claudius. The KG is the only safe evidence. Eutropius has Dacia Ripensis (IX. 13. 1). The *Epitome*, however, introduces perplexity. It comes out with a double piece of information, the first part vague, the second suspiciously precise (35. 1). Aurelian was born 'inter Daciam et Macedoniam'; his father had been the 'colonus' of a distinguished senator called Aurelius.

That notice evokes in a disturbing fashion sundry fancies of the HA. And in this instance the artful author once again indulges in his habit of

---

[1] Above, p. 205. A tendency persists to regard Dardania as the most plausible. Thus P. Damerau, *Klio*, Beiheft XXXIII (1934), 41. He argues 'wie hätte man sonst Constantius mit ihm genealogisch verbinden können?' Not valid. There is no evidence that Constantius came from Dardania; and, as concerns Claudius, there is only the HA, with its typical variants that conceal ignorance and simulate research.

[2] For the extent of the two new provinces, H. Vetters, *Dacia Ripensis* (1950), 6 ff. Further, below, p. 233.

[3] *Anon. Val.* 2. 2: 'natus Helena matre vilissima in oppido Naisso atque eductus, quod oppidum postea magnifice ornavit'. Helena was the daughter of a tavern girl according to Ambrose, *De obitu Theod.* 42.

[4] Above, p. 194.

[5] Julian, *Misopogon* 348 d: καὶ τοῖς ἐν μέσῳ κειμένοις Θρᾳκῶν καὶ Παιόνων, ἐπ' αὐταῖς Ἴστρου ταῖς ᾖόσι Μυσοῖς, ὅθεν δὴ καὶ τὸ γένος ἐστί μοι πᾶν ἄγροικον, αὐστηρόν, ἀδέξιον, ἀναφρόδιτον, ἐμμένον τοῖς κριθεῖσιν ἀμετακινήτως.

scholarly dubitation. As follows. Most say that Aurelian came from Sirmium, some from Dacia Ripensis; but, so the author affirms, he had read a source that declared for Moesia (*Aur.* 3. 1 f.). Elsewhere he styles the emperor a 'homo Pannonius' (24. 3). All of which will be dismissed. There is no remedy save to accept Eutropius and opt for Dacia Ripensis.[1]

The predominance of the Danubian or Balkan military comes out in the events at Mediolanum in 268.[2] The prime mover in the plot to which Gallienus succumbed was the *praefectus praetorio* Heraclianus, otherwise Herculianus. His full name, Aurelius Herculianus now emerges on the inscription which was set up in his honour by the military man Traianus Mucianus.[3] Beside Heraclianus stood Marcianus, according to the HA (*Gall.* 14. 1, cf. 7) which is here following a good source.[4] Marcianus was an experienced general.[5] His origin is not on attestation. Further, 'Ceronius sive Cecropius, dux Dalmatarum qui eos urbanissime et prudentissime adiuvit' (14. 4). He was the assassin who dealt the blow (14. 9).[6] Aurelian was one of the conspirators.[7] Likewise Claudius, whom the favourable tradition exculpates, with, in one version, the helpful detail that he was absent on duty at Ticinum.[8]

Several of these men had held command over the independent cavalry corps which Gallienus created, a notable and necessary innovation in warfare.[9] Claudius, towards the end, had become the right-hand man of Gallienus. Victor, no admirer of Gallienus, condemns the conspiracy in

---

[1] Thus E. Groag, P-W v. 1350. Many, however, are prepared to accept Sirmium, e.g. L. Homo, *Essai sur le règne de l'empereur Aurélien* (1904), 27; J. Maurice, *Rev. arch.*[4] xvii (1911), 391. And H. Mattingly has 'perhaps a native of Sirmium' (*CAH* xii (1939), 296). The influence of the HA appears to linger.

[2] On which, P. Damerau, o.c. 44 ff.; A. Alföldi, *CAH* xii (1939), 189 ff. Indispensable items accrue from Zosimus I. 40 and Zonaras xii. 25. On comparison with which, the HA becomes utilizable: it was patently following a Greek source.

[3] *AE* 1948, 55 = *IGBR* (ed. G. Mihailov) iii. 1568 (Augusta Traiana, i.e. Stara Zagora). Augusta Traiana is the *patria* of Traianus Mucianus (ib. 1570 = *ILS* 9479). It also furnishes a dedication in honour of M. Aurelius Apollinarius, governor of Thrace and brother of the *praefectus praetorio* (ib. 1569).

[4] That is, Dexippus, as suggested by items of phrase or nomenclature, as certified by the consular dates for 261, 262, 264, 265. Note also 270 (*Claud.* 11. 3), the termination of his History. Compare previously the four years 240–3 thus labelled in *Gordiani Tres*.

[5] *PIR*[1], M 153. See the inscription from Philippopolis (*AE* 1965, 114), and the discussion of his career by B. Gerov, *Athenaeum* xliii (1965), 333 ff.

[6] The act and the person (without the name) are certified by Zosimus: the commander of the Dalmatian cavalry (I. 40. 2). Given a good source for the HA at this point, there is no call to question 'Cecropius' ('Ceronius' remains baffling). A 'vir clarissimus' called 'Cecropius' is on attestation (*CIL* vi. 836), but not datable.

[7] Victor 33. 21; Zonaras xii. 25.

[8] Above, p. 205. Zosimus has him (I. 40. 2), but not Zonaras.

[9] E. Ritterling, *Festschrift Hirschfeld* (1903), 345 ff.; A. Alföldi, *CAH* xii (1939), 216 f.

violent terms, adverting on the lust for power and denouncing (after the manner of Sallust) the perversions of political language—'hinc quoque rerum vis ac nomina corrupta' (33. 24). None of which, however, touches the sanctified Claudius.[1]

A whole group of marshals emerges and takes shape. The evidence is adequate, and convincing. Brothers in arms are here, some perhaps from the same locality and related by ties of blood or marriage. Claudius and Aurelian may be assumed close coevals. The birth year for the former is given as 214; and likewise for the latter.[2] The figures are perhaps the result of artifice or guesswork. Probus, not named in this formidable company, was a little younger. The precise date of his birth is on record, August 19, 232.[3] The year may derive from an estimate of fifty as his age at death.[4]

To round off the list may be cited three generals holding high commands in Illyricum who rose against Gallienus. First, Aureolus, who was a cavalry commander.[5] He came from Dacia Ripensis, as the language of Zonaras implies.[6] Next, two other usurpers, Ingenuus and Regalianus.[7] There is nothing, it is true, to certify the local origins of either. For the latter, a fancy of the HA may be cited as a curiosity—'gentis Daciae, Decibali ipsius, ut fertur, adfinis' (*Tyr. trig.* 10. 8). There is no point or value in citing the fact that the historic name of Trajan's adversary is attested for natives of the Danubian lands.[8]

III. A school of generals in any age, the concept was obvious enough. It was grasped and promulgated by Aurelius Victor. In comment on Diocletian and his loyal colleagues in the Tetrarchy, Victor commends the 'ingenium usumque bonae militiae, quanta his Aureliani Probique instituto fuit' (39. 28). They all came from Illyricum, he says. The facts confirm, so far as they can be ascertained.

Diocletian was Dalmatian: Salonae as his *patria* is merely a deduction

---

[1] Exemplary conduct is registered by Victor 33. 27, 33; 34. 1.

[2] For the data, *PIR*², A 1526; D 135.　　　　　　　　　　[3] *PIR*², A 1583.

[4] It will be instructive to note the uncertainty about the age of Constantine, cf. A. Piganiol, *Historia* I (1950), 86. Similarly for Diocletian, W. Ensslin, P–W VII A. 2421; W. Seston, *Dioclétien et la Tétrarchie* I (1946), 44 f. Of Maximianus the *Epitome* alleges 'aetate interiit sexagenarius' (40. 11). No source offers a figure for Constantius or for Galerius.

[5] *PIR*², A 1672. Zosimus certifies him in command of the cavalry (I. 40. 1). Also twice in Zonaras (XII. 24 f.).

[6] Zonaras XII. 24: ἐκ χώρας ὢν Γετικῆς τῆς ὕστερον Δακίας ἐπικληθείσης.

[7] For the former, *PIR*², J 23. For the latter, whose *gentilicium* is missing, *PIR*¹, C 2; A. Stein, P–W I A. 462 ff. For their vicissitudes, J. Fitz, *Ingenuus et Régalien*. Coll. Latomus LXXXI (1966). The central field of their activities seems to be in the region of Sirmium.

[8] Three specimens are cited in *TLL, Onom.* III.

from the residence he elected when abdicating the power in 305.[1] According to the *Epitome*, Maximianus was born near Sirmium (40. 10). As for Constantius, the question has been blurred by the fictions about Claudius: the testimony of Julian indicates Dacia Ripensis. About Galerius there is an awkward and enigmatic conflict of evidence. Eutropius says 'in Dacia haud longe a Serdica natus': that is, in Mediterranea. But the *Epitome* supplies Ripensis, and names the small place where Galerius was both born and buried, viz. Romulianum (40. 16).[2]

The same holds for the new rulers coming up after the departure of Diocletian and Maximianus. Victor has the phrase 'Severus Maximinusque Illyricorum indigenae Caesares' (40. 1). Severus, it is alleged, was a lowborn drinking friend of Galerius;[3] and Maximinus Daia was the nephew of Galerius. Finally, Licinius, whom Galerius produced as 'Augustus' in 308. As Eutropius states, 'Dacia oriundus, notus ei antiqua consuetudine et in bello' (x. 4. 1).[4]

Conclusions of some interest emerge when the evidence about the Tetrarchs and their predecessors is summed up. Though some sources state only 'Dacia', not specifying whether they mean Ripensis or Mediterranea, the former region is high on show. 'Ripensis' may be employed as a convenient term, though the territory was still Moesian when those emperors saw the light of day. It will further be recalled that, well before then, Maximinus derived his origin from that martial zone.[5] Next to Dacia stands Sirmium, the *patria* of Decius, Probus, Maximianus.[6]

iv. Taking a hint from Aurelius Victor, or inspired by facts and names in his sources (Greek as well as Latin), the author of the HA boldly carries the idea of a school of generals backwards in history, to the reign of Valerian. In remarks upon the usurper Regalianus, he adduces four other names: Claudius, Macrianus, Postumus, Aureolus. All of them were worthy to bear the purple—'cum mererentur imperium' (*Tyr. trig.* 10. 14).

---

[1] *Epit.* 39. 1, cf. below, p. 233. The earliest witness, Lactantius, describing the abdication, says 'reda per civitatem veteranus rex foras exportatur in patriamque dimittitur' (*De mort. persec.* 19. 6). Next, Eutropius who has him 'Dalmatia oriundum, virum obscurissime natum' (ix. 19. 2). For the problem, W. Seston, o.c. 38 ff.

[2] Below, p. 226.

[3] *Anon. Val.* 4. 9: 'Severus Caesar ignobilis et moribus et natalibus, ebriosus et hoc Galerio amicus'.

[4] *Anon. Val.* 5. 13: 'Licinius itaque ex Nova Dacia vilioris originis, a Galerio factus imperator'.

[5] Above, p. 188.

[6] This evidence about regional groups and alliances has a general relevance for the emergence of new dynasties in the Roman Empire. Notably for Trajan and for Severus.

It was sheer genius in Valerian that the men whom he picked as generals each and all won the suffrages of the soldiers—'postea militum testimonio ad imperium venerunt' (10. 15). This emperor, though aged, responded by his sagacity to the clamorous requirements of 'Romana felicitas'.

Next, passing over Claudius and Aurelian, the author praises Probus for having trained a whole school of famous generals, 'whom our fathers admired, and several of them emerged as good emperors':

nam ex eius disciplina Carus, Diocletianus, Constantius, Asclepiodotus, Annibalianus, Leonides, Cecropius, Pisonianus, Herennianus, Gaudiosus, Ursinianus, et ceteri (22. 3).

Eleven names. The first five are historical characters—but no warrant that they were in fact disciples of Probus. To have Asclepiodotus named together with Annibalianus is a singular felicity. An inscription shows Afranius Hannibalianus and Julianus Asclepiodotus as colleagues in the Praetorian Prefecture about the year 288.[1] They also held the consulate together in 292. Hannibalianus was *praefectus urbi* in 297.[2] In that same year Asclepiodotus, serving as *praefectus praetorio* under Constantius, defeated Allectus the usurper in Britain. Both Victor (39. 42) and Eutropius (IX. 22. 2) have his name and rank. Rational curiosity asks where the author of the HA found both Hannibalianus and Asclepiodotus, together.[3]

He had already employed an 'Asclepiodotus' in a Diocletianic context. After reporting what that emperor after his abdication told his own father (*Aur.* 43. 2), he subjoins some more testimony. Diocletian, when censuring the harshness of Maximianus, often added the remark that Aurelian should have been a general, not an emperor. 'Asclepiodotus' had heard this more than once from Diocletian's *praefectus praetorio*, namely 'Verconnius Herennianus' (44. 2).

There is no sign that this prefect existed.[4] Therefore he may suitably be held identical with the ninth name in the catalogue of Probus' generals —or, for that matter, with the 'Herennianus' in a letter of Gallienus (*Claud.* 17. 3).

The next item also concerns 'Asclepiodotus'. Diocletian ascertained the fact that Aurelian had once consulted 'Gallicanas Dryadas' about the destiny of emperors, so 'Asclepiodotus' is held to have told a third party— 'Asclepiodotus Celsino consiliario suo dixisse perhibetur' (44. 3). Here,

---

[1] *ILS* 8929 (Oescus).　　　　　[2] For their careers, *PIR*², A 444; J 179.
[3] Perhaps in the KG.
[4] Like many others, this prefect is properly discarded by L. L. Howe, *The Pretorian Prefect from Commodus to Diocletian* (1942), 118. For the *nomen*, and for 'Verconius Turinus' (*Alex.* 35 f.; 67. 2), see *Historia* v (1956), 211.

if not also in the former passage, the author appears to introduce 'Asclepiodotus' as a person in the narration, not as a writer.

'Asclepiodotus' in the list of generals may, or may not, be regarded as a 'historical character': it depends on definitions. Nothing can vindicate his confidant 'Celsinus' in the second anecdote about Diocletian. The others to present that name in the HA are 'Clodius Celsinus', an alleged relative of the pretender Clodius Albinus (*Sev.* 11. 3), and the 'Celsinus' to whom 'Flavius Vopiscus' dedicates his Life of Próbus (*Prob.* 1. 3).[1]

The *cognomen* 'Celsus' falls into place. Ten of the twelve Celsi in the HA incur suspicion.[2] One of them is 'Herennius Celsus' a relative of the person to whom 'Trebellius Pollio' dedicated his section of the HA (*Tyr. trig.* 22. 12). The name of the dedicant presumably stood in the exordium of the missing *Vita* of Philip: before that the author had still been 'Julius Capitolinus'.[3]

Certain names, it is clear, were associated in the mind of the author. The first anecdote about Diocletian carries 'Verconnius Herennianus', the second, 'Celsinus'. Further, 'Herennius Celsus' and another 'Celsinus' come into play (in the ostensible entourage of the author himself).

The nexus discredits 'Herennianus', the ninth name on the list of the generals.[4] A dark cloud hangs over the remaining five. Three of them baffle scrutiny, the other two are revealing. 'Cecropius' derives from the man who murdered Gallienus (*Gall.* 14. 4).[5] 'Gaudiosus' is one of the happiest exhibits in the whole HA. His bare name declares a Christian.[6]

v. The HA thus produced two rulers with talent for choosing generals and potential emperors. These devices show the author alert to continuity in warfare and government. They are amplified in a plethora of corroborative detail. The author forges close links between the good emperors occurring in a series that ends with Carus.

Several of those rulers were Danubian. The author registers that provenance for Claudius, Aurelian, and Probus. But he fails to put emphasis on any community of origin or proclaim the 'virtus Illyrici'.

The term is absent, and the theme. It might have had some advertisement at a dramatic juncture, in the biography of Decius. For the rest, the Danubian and Balkan lands appear to excite little interest. Sirmium and Emona, it is true, come into the history of Maximinus: they could hardly

---

[1] For those characters, R. Syme, *Ammianus and the Historia Augusta* (1968), 155; 193; 199.
[2] R. Syme, o.c. 58.   [3] Above, p. 201.
[4] The name is later in employ for a son of Proculus and 'Vituriga' (*Quadr. tyr.* 12. 4).
[5] Above, p. 210. This doublet is strangely not impugned in *PIR*², C 596.
[6] R. Syme, o.c. 173 f.

have been left out. Sirmium occurs further three times in relation to Probus (it was in the KG); and it is wilfully brought into a scholarly and superfluous discussion about the origin of Aurelian—'ortus, ut plures loquuntur, Sirmii' (*Aur.* 3. 1). By contrast other cities of high fame on or beside the highway of empire are omitted: Mursa, Singidunum, Naissus, Serdica.

The KG carried a number of precise details about places in the Danubian lands or geographical features. The HA tends to drop them. For example, the Mons Aureus in the account of Probus' activities as a planter of vineyards;[1] or the city of Mursa in relation to Ingenuus and Regalianus.[2]

Nor is it under temptation to employ such names to support fiction. The exception comes in the letter by which Claudius (in the reign of Gallienus) commends Regalianus for his valour. 'Bonitus et Celsus' have told him 'qualis apud Scupos in pugnando fueris' (*Tyr. trig.* 10. 11).[3] The reader observes with regret that 'Ulpius Crinitus', that great military man, fights no battle.

vi. In the conception of the HA, the series begins with Decius. The devices are elaborate and interlocking. Especial use is made of the 'iudicia principum' which testify to excellence and designate a future ruler, sometimes well in advance. The catalogue will repay inspection.

First, Valerian (*Val.* 5. 4–6. 9). The Decii intimated to the Senate that it might elect a censor. On October 27 (of the year 251) the praetor brought up the matter, duly calling on the senator 'qui erat princeps tunc senatus' (Valerian was absent in the field with Decius).[4] The Senate's response was eager and unanimous—who but Valerian? On receipt of the *senatus consultum*, Decius convoked his counsellors and incited Valerian to assume the office (he enumerated its high prerogatives). Valerian modestly declined an honour which appertained to the Emperor himself.

Second, Claudius. When he was 'adulescens in militia', he received military decorations from Decius after an incident which illustrated his 'virtus et verecundia' (*Claud.* 13. 8). Again, Claudius being tribune, Decius indited a missive to 'Messala', the governor of Achaia, instructing him to furnish a mixed body of troops 'ex regione Dardanica': Claudius was on a mission to Thermopylae (16. 1 ff.).

Next, Claudius is tribune in command of the legion V Martia. Valerian

---

[1] Below, p. 224.
[2] Certified by Victor 33. 2; Eutropius IX. 8. 1.
[3] Like these two characters (R. Syme, o.c. 58), the Battle of Scupi had no existence.
[4] Decius, so it happens, was no longer among the living in the autumn of 251.

writes a letter to 'Zosimio', the procurator of Syria (14. 1 ff.). He is to furnish Claudius with all manner of supplies and equipment. It is a long list. It includes 'lanceas Herculianas duo, aclydes duas' (14. 6).[1] At a later date, Valerian reassures 'Ablavius Murena' his *praefectus praetorio*, who complained that Claudius for all his merits was only a tribune, not general in command of an army.[2] Valerian announces that he has appointed Claudius 'dux totius Illyrici' (15. 1 ff.).

Third, Aurelian. Valerian commends him to the consul 'Antoninus Gallus'. The letter is quoted—the author found it 'in Ulpia Bibliotheca inter linteos libros' (*Aur.* 8. 1). He proceeds to reproduce another document, 'ex scriniis praefecturae urbanae' (9. 1). It carries the praises of Aurelian to the Prefect, 'Ceionius Albinus', requesting him to furnish supplies and sustenance (9. 2 ff.).[3] Similarly, when Aurelian has been made consul, a letter to the *praefectus annonae*, called 'Aelius Xiphidius' (12. 1 f.).[4]

Valerian also wrote a personal letter: he needed Aurelian in an emergency for an employment in the Balkans, the great general 'Ulpius Crinitus' having fallen sick: 'fac, quidquid potes' (11. 2). Aurelian will have charge of a mixed force (the details are specified), also the legion III Felix and eight hundred 'cataphractarii'. And also staff officers—'tecum erit Hariomundus, Haldgates, Hildomundus, Carioviscus' (11. 4).[5] In the sequel, in the council held at Byzantium (eight military commanders are present), it is Valerian who enjoins the adoption of Aurelian by 'Ulpius Crinitus' (13 ff.).

Nor would Claudius be blind to the merits of Aurelian. He put him in command of the whole cavalry corps (18. 1). Further, he writes to Aurelian putting the Gothic campaign in his hands, with extensive powers, to embrace 'omnes exercitus Thracicos, omnes Illyricianos totumque limitem' (17. 3).

When the news of Aurelian's murder along with the 'missive of the

---

[1] The term 'aclys' is conclusive and significant, cf. R. Syme, o.c. 186 f. From Virgil, *Aen.* VII. 730 (or from a scholiast), and not a weapon in real warfare (Servius, ad loc.). The 'document' was held genuine and Constantinian by C. E. Van Sickle, *Ant. class.* XXIII (1954), 45 ff.

[2] 'Ablavius Murena' is instructive. The rare *cognomen* would be familiar to an adept of the classics: the oration *Pro Murena*. The *nomen* may reflect Ablabius, the notorious *praefectus praetorio* of Constantine (P–W I. 103).

[3] A Nummius Albinus had in fact been *praefectus urbi* in 256 and in 261–3, presumably the Albinus consul in 263 (P–W XVII. 1409 ff.). But there is no warrant that he had 'Ceionius' in his nomenclature. Cf. R. Syme, o.c. 154 f.

[4] The name 'Xiphidius' is not a free invention of the author, as was suggested above, p. 8. The uncle of a pupil of Libanius bore it (*Epp.* 766). Cf. R. Syme, o.c. 167.

[5] A group of Germans. For fun about foreign names, R. Syme, o.c. 173 f.

army' reached Rome, the consul 'Aurelius Gordianus' introduced business in the 'Curia Pompiliana' (41. 3). A long panegyric on the glorious conqueror was then delivered by 'Aurelius Tacitus, primae sententiae senator' (41. 4 ff.).

Tacitus, becoming emperor himself, proposes a variety of honours, down to the injunction that everybody should acquire a portrait of the dead ruler (*Tac.* 9. 5). Further, the notion of continuity is stated in a later place: Tacitus and Florianus were 'quasi quidam interreges inter Aurelianum et Probum' (14. 5).

Fourth, Probus. Many say that Probus was related to Claudius (*Prob.* 3. 3); and the author remembers reading in an 'ephemeris' that Probus had a sister, 'Claudia', who saw to his obsequies (3. 4). Next, letters are cited. Valerian, writing to Gallienus, informs him that he has given the young Probus a tribunate and the command of a mixed force (4. 1 f.); and he instructs the *praefectus praetorio*, 'Mulvius Gallicanus', to accord supplies and equipment (4. 3 ff.).[1]

Probus earned a mass of military decorations in a Bellum Sarmaticum (5. 1). In that campaign Probus rescued from captivity among the Quadi a relative of the Emperor, 'Valerium Flaccinum, adulescentem nobilem' (5. 2). The grateful Valerian awarded him the 'corona civica', also the command of the legion III Felix. That legion he had never before confided to anybody lacking seniority—he received it himself when his hair was already white (5. 6).[2]

From Aurelian, Probus got another legion, the famous Tenth, with which he had achieved great exploits. Aurelian writes to Probus— 'decimanos meos sume, quos Claudius mihi credidit' (6. 6).[3]

Probus exercised a good influence on Aurelian: he often dissuaded him from cruelty (8. 1). Indeed, Aurelian intended that Probus should be his successor (6. 7).[4] It would be tedious, the author adds, to retail the 'iudicia' of Claudius and of Tacitus concerning Probus; but Tacitus, so it was held, when he was being offered the power, said that Probus ought to be the emperor. The author, ever the scrupulous researcher, concludes

---

[1] The *nomen* is familiar to the moderns because of the Pons Mulvius outside Rome (the Ponte Molle). In fact, it happens to be rather uncommon, and is borne by only one person of class under the Empire, viz. Mulvia C. f. Placida, the wife of a senator (*PIR*[1], M 510). For nomenclature deriving from a building at Rome, cf., 'Caesonius Vectilianus', (*Avid.* 5. 5), above, p. 68.

[2] That is to say, from Decius.

[3] The author has in mind Caesar's famous Tenth Legion. For bogus legions in the HA, H. U. Instinsky, *Klio* xxxiv (1942), 118 ff.

[4] Similarly, Claudius wanted Aurelian to succeed him (Zonaras xii. 26).

'sed ego senatus consultum ipsum non inveni' (7. 1).[1] However, Tacitus on his accession at once wrote to Probus in warm tones, inciting him to share in the tasks of empire and consigning to him the 'totius Orientis ducatus' (7. 4).

Fifth, Carus. The exordium of the *Vita*, deploring the death of Probus, embarks on a rhetorical survey of Rome's history from Romulus onwards. After the calamities under Gallienus, the malice of Fortune denied length of rule to Claudius; Aurelian was killed, Tacitus carried off, and Probus slain (*Car*. 3. 6 f.). Let us now come to Carus, to be estimated among the good rulers rather than the bad—and a better ruler had he not bequeathed the Empire to Carinus (3. 8, cf. *Prob*. 24. 4).

Probus appointed Carus *praefectus praetorio*, and after the murder of Probus, Carus was clearly the only one worthy of empire (5. 4). Some suspected (the author is aware) that Probus perished through a plot of Carus.[2] Which is contradicted by the attested conduct and virtues of them both. And a letter to the Senate can be cited. To honour the 'integritas' of Carus, an equestrian statue should be set up and a marble palace built at public expense—Probus will provide the marble (6. 3).

VII. A whole system of contrivances emerges, ingenious and elaborate, with a plethora of corroborative detail designed to exemplify the careers and actions of military men: generals and officers, legions and field armies. And with convincing documentation, the fruit of erudite inquiry, various archives being cited in support. Most notable are the long lists of equipment and supplies: food, drink, clothing, weapons, money.

All bogus. Or at least, in what has here been retailed, there stands perhaps only one authentic fact: Carus appointed *praefectus praetorio* by Probus.[3]

The effort is vain and pointless to segregate plausible items in this mass of homogeneous fiction, to essay a defence of what cannot be disproved. Many modern accounts of those rulers, admitting or condoning suspect information, could be abbreviated with advantage for history. The

---

[1] Despite which, the author a little earlier was able to cite the document, asserting a precise reference—'ac ne quis me temere Graecorum alicui Latinorumve aestimet credidisse, habet in bibliotheca Ulpia in armario sexto librum elephantinum, in quo hoc senatus consultum perscriptum est' (*Tac*. 8. 1). The author's interest in documents and in the Bibliotheca Ulpia excites suspicion and surmise, cf. R. Syme, o.c. 98 f.; 183.

[2] *Car*. 6. 1: 'non me praeteriit suspicatos esse plerosque et eos in fastos rettulisse Cari factione interemptum Probum.' Zonaras brings up Carus as a reluctant usurper (XII. 29). Nothing in Zosimus.

[3] Victor 38. 1.

inventions have their own utility. They illuminate the education and tastes of the author; and the manner of their employment discloses not a little about his character, and even about his true purpose.

Such are the manifold fabrications designed to connect and interlock certain emperors from Decius to Carus inclusive. There are also links forward to the Tetrarchy. Claudius is paraded as an ancestor of Constantius; while Carus, Diocletian, and Constantius are generals formed for empire in the military school of Probus.

Despite the prediction made by a 'Dryas' in Gaul about the killing of a boar, Diocletian had to wait a long time for Aper, whom he struck down at Nicomedia. Aurelian acquired the power, then Probus, Tacitus, Carus. Diocletian had gone on hunting. As he observed, others got the meat (Car. 15. 3).

The author slips in various devices. Carus, shocked by the luxurious habits of his son Carinus, had once decided to kill him, to adopt Constantius in his place (Car. 17. 6); and the campaign of Carus against the Persians evokes a flattering reference to Galerius (9. 4). Finally, a generous tribute to the Tetrarchs, 'quattuor principes mundi fortes, sapientes, benigni et admodum liberales', etc. (18. 4).

The sequence of military emperors from Decius to Carus was interrupted by three gaps. In the first two, deleterious rulers occupied the intervals, viz. Trebonianus Gallus, Aemilius Aemilianus, Gallienus. The third gap was of a different order. Probus seemed the destined successor to Aurelian, but Tacitus came between, a mild and civilian ruler, created by the Senate, adored by the Senate. The interval could be regarded as an 'interregni species' (cf. Victor 35. 12; Epit. 35. 10)—which original notion was misunderstood by the KG, with dire consequences.[1] And there is a chance that Tacitus himself issued from the Danubian military.[2]

VIII. Inspection has revealed a master in the technique of forging links between the emperors of his predilection. He is bold, resourceful, unremitting. For all that, he missed some opportunities. Valerian musters eight generals as his counsellors in the Thermae at Byzantium when he pays honour to Aurelian (Aur. 13. 1). Their commands are specified (most of them implausible). Yet only one of them is exploited in the transaction or subsequently, viz. 'Ulpius Crinitus, dux Illyriciani limitis et Thracici'.[3]

---

[1] Below, p. 237.   [2] Below, p. 247.
[3] 'Ulpius Crinitus' was brought on previously (Aur. 10. 2; 11. 1); and he recurs in the sequel as recipient of an epistle, 'Aurelianus Augustus Ulpio patri' etc. (38. 3).

Nor has he bothered in these pages to employ the motive of alliances by marriage. Of all the Roman emperors from Claudius to Carinus inclusive, none is equipped with a named wife. Here was abundant scope for his rich fantasy, more attractive than the bogus parents or the children (generally anonymous) with which he credits some of the rulers. The best he can offer is a fable about Carinus; he married nine wives, most of whom were discarded when pregnant (*Car.* 16. 7).

The written sources (it is an easy presumption) did not, or could not, supply the names and identity of many empresses. To this day only the wives of Aurelian and Carinus are on attestation. Coins and inscriptions certify Ulpia Severina, the consort of Aurelian.[1] Her family and relatives evade ascertainment. Carinus married a certain Magnia Urbica.[2]

Zealous for Trajan and for tradition, the impostor invented 'Ulpius Crinitus', with orations and pageantry to celebrate the occasion when he adopted Aurelian (*Aur.* 13 ff.). A pity that he was not aware of Aurelian's wife, Ulpia Severina. Modern scholarship steps into the breach: the lady might be the daughter of 'Ulpius Crinitus'.[3] Further, that general might even have held an important command in Pannonia *c.* 256, just before Ingenuus.[4]

The memory of Trajan was a potent force in the provinces of Danube and Balkans. Cities carried his name, and individuals annexed it, such as Traianus Mucianus of Augusta Traiana in Thrace.[5]

Decius, arriving at Rome from Pannonia, at once added 'Traianus' to his nomenclature.[6] The HA could not know it. In fact, no extant author has the significant item.[7] What this ingenious performer would have done with it baffles the imagination.

---

[1] *PIR*[1], V 586.   [2] *ILS* 610.

[3] E. Groag, P–W v. 1353. Approved by Barbieri, *Albo*, no. 1766.

[4] J. Fitz, *Act. Ant. Ac. Sc. Hung.* XI (1963), 301.

[5] *ILS* 9479 (above, p. 210).   [6] K. Wittig, P–W xv. 1247.

[7] But it happens to stand in the *Passio Pionii* in the consular date of 250 (23). On which document cf. T. D. Barnes, *JTS*, N.S. XIX (1968), 529 ff.

XIV · ILLYRICUM IN THE EPITOMATORS

To EXPLAIN ITEMS common to the *Caesares* of Aurelius Victor, the *Breviarium* of Eutropius, and the Historia Augusta, Enmann produced the necessary hypothesis: a common source.[1] It stands to this day, with the slight modification that the HA drew also on the two epitomators. And it has been corroborated. Enmann could have brought in the *Epitome* of pseudo-Victor.[2] Also, though of less consequence, the *Breviarium* of Festus (*c.* 370) and the Chronicle of Jerome.[3]

For Enmann, the 'Kaisergeschichte' had to be composed not long after 284: the HA gave the *terminus ante quem*. Enmann, following the consensus of scholarship, had no doubts that the HA belonged to the time of Diocletian and Constantine. Therefore, to account for the resemblances which he detected between Victor and Eutropius after 284, he postulated a 'continuator' of his KG. However, another scholar at once pointed out that the original KG could be carried further, as far as the abdication of Diocletian in 305.[4]

A few years elapsed after Enmann, and Dessau demolished the 'traditional date' of the HA. The corollary for the KG should have been perceived and exploited.[5] None the less, habit or inadvertence preserved Enmann's terminal date for the KG.[6] There was something else. The KG conveyed a strong appeal to conservative or retrograde scholars. Without it, they would have to admit the distasteful and irreparable consequence that the HA drew on Victor and even on Eutropius.[7] Their confidence in the date of the KG was premature. A victory of Septimius Severus at the Pons Mulvius registered in error both by Victor and by Eutropius clearly indicated a date subsequent to 312.[8] Nothing forbids (and everything

---

[1] A. Enmann, *Philol.*, Supp. IV (1884), 337 ff. For a careful exposition (and development) of the thesis, see E. Hohl, *Klio* XI (1911), 187 ff.

[2] E. Hohl, o.c. 206 ff.

[3] For Festus, C. Wagener, *Philol.* XLV (1886), 534 ff. It is admitted as a possibility by J. W. Eadie in his edition (1967), 95, cf. 98. For Jerome, R. Helm, *Rh. Mus.* LXXVI (1927), 304 f.   [4] C. Wagener, o.c. 545.

[5] The corollary was at once pounced upon by Seeck, *Jahrbücher für cl. Phil.* XXXVI (1890), 638. He decreed that the KG was subsequent to 337—'wie jeder sich leicht überzeugen kann'.

[6] For an exception, note W. H. Fisher, *JRS* XIX (1929), 126.

[7] To be sure, attempts were made to evade that consequence through elaborate hypotheses about 'interpolations' or late 'editors'.   [8] Below, p. 232.

commends) the postulate that the KG was written not long after the death of Constantine.[1] Source criticism and its problems in the HA kept the KG on the boards, though not all the time.[2] Another aspect suffered neglect. Nobody has observed the accurate and special knowledge which it exhibits of the Danubian lands. Fourteen items can be adduced (varying in value).

1. The birthplace of Decius. He came from Sirmium, a Roman *colonia*. Aurelius Victor has 'Sirmiensium vico ortus' (29. 1). But Eutropius (IX. 4) and the *Epitome* (29. 1) in identical words supply the name of the village where he was born—'e Pannonia inferiore, Budaliae natus'. They use the old name of the province, the southern part of which since the ordering of Diocletian was called 'Pannonia Secunda'. Budalia lay on the high road west of Sirmium towards Cibalae (the junction of the roads from Siscia and from Mursa). It was situated about eight miles west of Sirmium.[3]

The precision is abnormal. In law and history and for official record the *patria* matters. The actual place of birth might be anywhere. Thus Hadrian was a citizen of Italica, but he saw the light of day at Rome.[4] And, though Constantine was born at Naissus, that city might not be his *patria*.[5] The distinction is often blurred by the incompetence of writers ancient and modern. Biographers, however, followed the practice of registering the actual place of birth, if it could be ascertained. Thus Suetonius on Vespasian: 'natus est in Sabinis ultra Reate vico modico cui nomen est Falacrinae.'[6] Suetonius was happy to advertise careful research, though Vespasian and a village in the Sabine country were not far from reach. The author of the KG, writing a century and a half after the birth of Decius, registers the *vicus* of Budalia in the *territorium* of Sirmium. He deserves earnest commendation—and excites curiosity.[7]

2. The origin of Aurelian. Eutropius merely furnishes Dacia Ripensis (IX. 13. 1). The *Epitome* offers an elaboration and a variant—'genitus patre mediocri et, ut quidam ferunt, Aurelii clarissimi senatoris colono

---

[1] See now T. D. Barnes, *JRS* LVIII (1968), 265; *Bonner Historia-Augusta-Colloquium 1968/9* (1970), 20.

[2] Some, it is true, are impelled to deny that the HA used the KG. Thus T. Damsholt, *Class. et Med.* XXV (1964), 147 f.

[3] Registered in the *It. Ant.* and the *It. Hieros.*, Budalia is attested as the *vicus* of a soldier in the Guard (*ILS* 2044).   [4] For the distinction, *JRS* LIV (1964), 142 f.

[5] Above, p. 209.

[6] Suetonius, *Divus Vesp.* 2. 1.

[7] Persons from villages have the *civitas* for *patria* (*Dig.* L. 1. 1. 30). Thus on official documents. The gravestones of Danubian and Balkan soldiers sometimes give the *vicus* (e.g. *ILS* 2043 f.; 2670).

inter Daciam et Macedoniam' (35. 1). The variant is perplexing. The only region lying between Dacia (i.e. Ripensis) and Macedonia is Dacia Mediterranea which comprised the old Dardanian land along with two districts taken from Thrace (see the next item).

3. Aurelian and Dacia. Eutropius, after mentioning the 'templum Solis' which the Emperor constructed, goes on to tell how he abandoned Trajan's Dacia, 'desperans eam posse retineri', withdrew the population to the right bank of the Danube, and established 'eam Daciam quae nunc duas Moesias dividit' (IX. 15. 1). The passage takes up nearly the half of what he has to say about the reign of Aurelian. It is precise and valuable, with a small exception: it does not indicate that Aurelian's new Dacia comprised two provinces: Dacia Ripensis and Dacia Mediterranea. These provinces came into existence at once, or at no long interval. Gaianus, the *praeses* of one or other of the two, is attested for a boundary regulation under Carus and Carinus.[1]

The limits of the two Daciae were in fact drawn with careful regard to the facts of geography and civilization.[2] Ripensis, from a point opposite Dierna, below the Iron Gates of the Danube, went as far as the old boundary against the Ripa Thraciae, just short of Novae: its chief cities were Oescus and Ratiaria, now stations of the two legions removed from Transdanubian Dacia (V Macedonica and XIII Gemina). Dacia Mediterranea took in five inland basins. Moesia Superior surrendered Scupi, Ulpianum, and Naissus; while Pautalia and Serdica were taken from the province of Thrace. The innovation was admirably conceived, not to be denied to an emperor who was born in the territory now to be designated Dacia Ripensis.

The comportment of the different sources deriving from the KG is not devoid of instruction. Eutropius has been cited. Victor mentions the 'templum Solis', but nothing about Dacia. The *Epitome* omits even that small item. The HA, however, beginning with the 'templum Solis', shows in its remarks about Aurelian's Dacia a resemblance so close and verbal to Eutropius (*Aur.* 39. 6 f.) that the epitomator can be claimed as the source.[3] At first sight plausible. Yet the passage might be a piece of KG, lifted by each with little change.

4. The nomenclature of (M. Aurelius) Probus. The *Epitome* styles him 'Equitius Probus' (36. 2). The name is suitable. It is borne by two

[1] *AE* 1912, 200.

[2] For the detail, H. Vetters, *Dacia Ripensis* (1950), 6 ff.

[3] H. Dessau, *Hermes* XXIV (1889), 371 f. Cf. now A. Chastagnol, *Rev. phil.* XLI (1967), 93 f.

Pannonians in the pages of Ammianus.[1] The one Equitius, 'asper et sub-agrestis' (XXVI. 1. 4), rose to high rank under Valentinian and held the consulship as colleague of Gratian in 374.[2] The other, an officer and a relative of Valens (XXXI. 12. 15), comes into the list of the notable casualties at the Battle of Adrianople (13. 18). However that may be, there is no call to suspect fiction in the *Epitome* and a retrojection, after the fashion of the HA. The name 'Aequit.' or 'Equit.' happens to occur on coins of Probus.[3] It may be regarded as a 'signum'.

5. The parentage of Probus (who came from Sirmium, cf. Victor 37. 4). The *Epitome* vouchsafes curious particulars—'genitus patre agresti hortorum studioso, Dalmatio nomine' (37. 1). Whatever be thought of the rustic gardener, the name 'Dalmatius' excites the suspicion of an invention—and might contribute to corroborating the date of the KG.[4]

6. Probus the promoter of vineyards. According to Eutropius, 'vineas Gallos et Pannonios habere permisit, opere militari Almam montem apud Sirmium et Aureum apud Moesiam superiorem vineis conseruit' (IX. 17. 2). The sentence is reproduced word for word in the *Epitome* (37. 3).[5] Victor, however, goes his own way. This African, matching Probus with Hannibal for valour and discipline, states that Hannibal used soldiers to plant olives, and continues in a generalized fashion 'eodem modo hic Galliam Pannoniosque et Moesorum colles vinetis replevit' (37. 3). Victor suppresses the local detail which the KG furnished, viz. Mons Alma and Mons Aureus. The HA drops the latter. Its version of the KG is 'ipse Almam montem in Illyrico circa Sirmium militari manu fossum lecta vite conseruit' (*Prob.* 18. 8). But, like Victor, it has a generalized statement. It brings in several provinces. Victor mentioned Gaul. The HA introduces its notice with 'Gallis omnibus et Hispanis ac Britannis hinc permisit ut vites haberent vinumque conficerent.' A wilful elaboration, as elsewhere in the HA.

To turn instead to topography. The Mons Alma is the conspicuous range of hills along the Danube to the north-east of Sirmium (the fertile Fruška Gora). It came into the story of the insurrection of A.D. 6. Bato the Pannonian, after his failure to take Sirmium, occupied this strategic position on the flank of the road, commanding the Roman line of

---

[1] O. Seeck, P-W VI. 321 f.

[2] His action in concert with Merobaudes in 375 is mentioned, in closely similar language, by the *Epitome* (45. 10) and by Zosimus (IV. 19. 1).

[3] *PIR*[2], A 1583, cf. G. Vitucci, *L'imperatore Probo* (1952), 3.   [4] Below, p. 232.

[5] And Jerome in his Chronicle (under the year 280) is very close: 'Gallos et Pannonios vineas habere permisit Almamque et Aureum montem militari manu consitos provincialibus dedit.'

communications between Singidunum and Siscia.[1] The Mons Aureus is the bank of the Danube below Singidunum a dozen miles beyond Tricornium. No other author names it except Eutropius (on the battle of Margus, IX. 20. 2).

7. The death of Probus. He was killed by soldiers at Sirmium. Eutropius is brief—'interfectus tamen est Sirmi tumultu militari in turri ferrata' (IX. 17. 3). The *Epitome* is even curter—'hic Sirmi in turri ferrata occiditur' (37. 4). Illumination comes from Victor, though he omits the iron tower: Probus was employing the troops to drain the marshes and make a canal near Sirmium, his native city (37. 4). The HA, mentioning the iron tower which Probus had constructed to superintend operations, is also explicit (*Prob.* 21. 2 f.). It has both the marshes and the canal—but also the river Savus. Clearly therefore drawing on the KG. As in the matter of the vineyards, the various ways in which these writers use the basic source are highly instructive.

8. The defeat of Carinus by Diocletian at Margus (in 285). Eutropius describes the site as 'inter Viminacium atque Aureum Montem' (IX. 20. 2).

9. Maximianus. He came from Pannonia, as the oration delivered in the year 289 declares. Italy is 'gentium domina gloriae vetustate, sed Pannonia virtute' (*Pan. lat.* x. 2. 2). He was brought up on the frontiers, 'in illo limite, illa fortissimarum sede legionum'. That is, Sirmium. The *Epitome* confirms. It adds detail, implying authentic knowledge: 'ortu agresti Pannonioque. nam etiam nunc haud longe Sirmio eminet locus palatio ibidem constructo ubi parentes eius exercebant opera mercennaria' (40. 10).

10. The origin of Galerius. There is a discrepancy. For Eutropius, he was born 'in Dacia haud longe a Serdica' (IX. 22. 1). Serdica, at the time when Galerius was born, belonged to Thrace: Aurelian allocated it to his Dacia Mediterranea. The *Epitome* has the other province: 'ortus Dacia Ripensi ibique sepultus est; quem locum Romulianum ex vocabulo Romulae matris appellarat' (40. 16).

As with Maximianus (40. 10, cf. above), the precise detail surprises. And, abnormal in the documentation on these Danubian emperors, the mother is named. She happens to be very much a historical character, thanks to Lactantius, who puts her on parade in terms of no amenity. Galerius was a savage, foreign to Roman blood. No wonder, given his mother. She was a refugee from beyond the river: 'mater enim Transdanuviana infestantibus Carpis in Daciam Novam transvecto amne

[1] Dio LV. 30. 3.

transfugerat.'[1] Romula, he avers, was an adept of native worships, 'deorum montium cultrix', and she transferred her fanaticism to her son.[2]

On the showing of Lactantius (if he cared for exact chronology), Romula should be an earlier refugee, some twenty years before Aurelian's evacuation of Dacia: since the birth of Galerius (no facts are on record) should fall about the year 250.[3] Otherwise, however, the term 'Dacia Nova' in Lactantius would imply the later date.

That need not matter. The *Epitome* states that Galerius was both born and buried at the place to which he gave the name 'Romulianum'. That place is on record, registered along with Florentianum in the territory of Aquae by Procopius in his account of the forts constructed by Justinian.[4] It should be sought on the Danube somewhere above Bononia (Vidin) towards the mouth of the river Timacus.[5] According to a reputable source, Galerius died at Serdica.[6] To take the corpse or the ashes to Romulianum beside the river entailed no long journey.

11. A nickname of Galerius. Victor calls him 'Armentarius', without proffering any explanation of the term (37. 4; 40. 1, 6). Likewise the *Epitome* (39. 2; 40. 1). Later on, the *Epitome* itself furnishes the requisite annotation: 'ortus parentibus agrariis, pastor armentorum, unde ei cognomen Armentarius fuit' (40. 15). No other source reveals this name.

12. An operation of Galerius. He invaded Italy, but went away after a fruitless siege of Rome. Shortly after, he died from the effects of a wound: 'pauloque post vulnere pestilenti consumptus est, cum agrum satis reipublicae commodantem caesis immanibus silvis atque emisso in Danubium lacu Pelsone apud Pannonios fecisset. cuius gratia provinciam uxoris nomine Valeriam appellavit.' That is the account of Victor (40. 9 f.).

The precise details invite inspection. Which was the lake the waters of which Galerius conveyed into the Danube? Perhaps the Neuseedlersee.[7] Better, the lake Balaton, as is indicated by the subjoined mention of the province Valeria.[8] That new province corresponds to the northern part of the previous Pannonia Inferior. When was Valeria created? Diocletian went to Pannonia in 294 and conducted a campaign against the Iazyges.

---

[1] Lactantius, *De mort. persec.* 9. 2.   [2] Lactantius 11. 1 ff.
[3] W. Ensslin, P–W XIV. 2517.   [4] Procopius, *De aed.* 4. 4.
[5] C. Patsch, *Wiener S-B* CCVIII (1928), Abh. 2, 12. Florentianum is the modern Florentin: in Bulgaria, a dozen miles short of the Yugoslav frontier. See further H. Vetters, o.c. 11; M. Mirković, *Rimski gradovi na Dunavu u Gornjoj Meziji* (1968), 94.
[6] *Anon. Val.* 4. 9.
[7] H. R. Graf, *Übersicht der antiken Geographie von Pannonien* (1936), 27.
[8] A. Mócsy, P–W, Supp. IX. 525. The name 'Pelso', so it appears, could be assigned to either lake.

Galerius took over in the next year.[1] He settled the vanquished Carpi in Pannonia, as emerges from another passage in Victor (without his name): 'caesi Marcomanni Carporumque natio translata omnis in nostrum solum, cuius fere pars iam tum ab Aureliano erat' (39. 43). Mentioning Aurelian, the notice is doubly valuable. The other epitomators have nothing about the Carpi anywhere. Ammianus reports their presence in Roman provinces, at Sopianae in Valeria (XXVIII. 1. 5), and also in Moesia (XXVII. 5. 5).

The creation of Valeria should therefore fall in the vicinity of 294. That the province took its name from the wife of Galerius (and daughter of Diocletian), no other source records save Ammianus (XIX. 11. 4).

Victor brings the beneficent activities of Galerius (forests cut down in Pannonia and the draining of a lake) into close proximity with his decease. Both history and chronology have been compressed and confused. Galerius invaded Italy in 307, but only got as far as Interamna. His alleged siege of Rome (in Victor) results from conflation with the siege conducted, and given up, by Severus in the previous year (noted in Victor 40. 6). The death of Galerius occurred four years after his invasion of Italy, in the spring of 311, after that long and loathsome malady which Lactantius retails with holy relish—but not before the persecutor had seen the error of his ways and promulgated an edict of toleration.[2]

What appeals to Aurelius Victor in this instance is not the detail of chronology or warfare. It is the activity of Galerius in Pannonia, clearing the forests and draining the lake Pelso. In comment he is moved to digress on the qualities of emperors and their reputation, exhibiting his characteristic obsession with polite studies—'quare compertum est eruditionem elegantiam comitatem praesertim principibus necessarias esse' (40. 13).

13. The usurper in Africa in 308, (L. Domitius) Alexander. Victor is positive about the origin of this elderly and unprepossessing character—'agrestibus ac Pannoniis parentibus vecordior' (40. 17). For the *Epitome* he is a Phrygian (40. 20). The discrepancy is flagrant and noteworthy.[3]

14. The marshes near Cibalae. Mentioning the battle in which Constantine defeated Licinius in 314, the *Epitome* contributes a precise detail: 'apud Cibalas iuxta paludem Hiulcam' (41. 5). The word is nowhere else attested. Clearly the Volcaean Marshes where a Roman army of five legions under the command of two consular legates fought a great battle against the insurgents in A.D. 7.[4]

---

[1] For the campaigns of Galerius, W. Ensslin, P–W XIV. 2519 ff.; A. Alföldi, *Arch. ért.* II (1941), 53 f.　　　　　　[2] Lactantius 33 ff.

[3] Below, p. 229.　　　　　[4] Dio LV. 32. 3, cf. Velleius II. 112. 4.

Cibalae (Vinkovci) is situated on the narrow neck of firm ground that separates the low and swampy tracts on either side, northwards towards Mursa and the mouth of the Dravus, southwards to the Savus. Zosimus reports that it was five stades in breadth.[1] He has a full narration of Constantine's battle.[2] Cibalae also comes into the struggle between Constantius and the usurper Magnentius in 351.[3]

Fourteen items, therefore. Taken in isolation, no one of them amounts to much. Taken together, the cumulation is impressive. For the evaluation, however, extreme caution is to be enjoined. Sirmium is on conspicuous show with the village Budalia, and with the palace constructed on the site where Maximianus was born. Now Sirmium, on the high road of empire, was the residence of court and rulers, it witnessed the passage of armies and of officials. And anyone might know that there were marshes near Sirmium and near Cibalae, brought into notice through a battle—or even by the murder of an emperor when superintending the drainage.

Moreover, the postulate is hazardous that each and every notice about Danubian affairs should go back to a single source. There are discrepancies. For example, between Eutropius and the author of the *Epitome*, touching the regions Aurelian and Galerius came from. The KG might have registered variants; but it is not legitimate to argue from an assumption of that order.

The three epitomators exhibit divergences everywhere. Eutropius, much the shortest, adds little of his own. The *Epitome* can draw on independent information. Observe at an earlier stage, the account of Nerva, who gets as much space as Trajan.[4] Victor stands out from the others. He has stylistic pretensions, which he supports by an infusion of Sallustian language; and his operations on the basic source can be detected when items from Eutropius or the *Epitome* are called up for comparison. Victor is also a thinker. He frequently puts on parade his own reflections about state and society.[5]

One of the best-known specimens carries an allusion to his own origin—African, of humble and rustic extraction, but ennobled through devotion

---

[1] Zosimus II. 18. 2: στενὴ δὲ ὁδὸς ᾗ ἐπὶ τὴν πόλιν ἀνάγει, σταδίων πέντε τὸ εὖρος ἔχουσα, ἧς τὸ πολὺ μέρος ἐπέχει λίμνη βαθεῖα.

[2] There is an excellent account in Seeck, *Geschichte des Untergangs der antiken Welt* 14 (1921), 159 ff. [3] Zosimus II. 48. 3. [4] Above, p. 103.

[5] For his opinions, A. Alföldi, *A Conflict of Ideas in the Late Roman Empire* (1952), 112 ff.; C. G. Starr, *Am. Hist. Rev.* LXI (1956), 574 ff.

to literature (20. 5). It comes in his account of the African ruler, to whom he devotes more space than to Trajan or Marcus.

Diocletian and Constantine receive a fairly full treatment. Victor there evokes an incident concerning Tripolis in the time of Septimius Severus (41. 20); and he reports the rebuilding of Cirta (which had suffered damage in the rebellion of Alexander) and its new name, Constantina (41. 28).

Victor had not neglected that usurper, proclaimed at Carthage in 308.[1] He describes how Alexander was defeated by Rufius Volusianus the *praefectus praetorio*, how Carthage, 'terrarum decus', was sacked after the victory by order of Maxentius (40. 18 f.). Victor calls Alexander a Pannonian (40. 17). The particular may derive from local knowledge or a personal opinion. Those transactions had occurred only fifty years previously; and the usurper held Africa for several years, ample space to make him remembered.[2]

The *Epitome*, however, states 'Phryx origine, ingenio timidus, inferior adversus laborem vitio senectae aetatis' (40. 20). Likewise Zosimus in a closely parallel sentence.[3]

There is a further factor that comes into the general count. Victor acquired familiarity with Sirmium and the neighbourhood. Julian, arriving there in 361, met this exemplary person, 'scriptorem historicum . . . virum sobrietatis gratia aemulandum', so Ammianus describes him (XXI. 10. 6). Not long after, Julian honoured him with a bronze statue and the governorship of Pannonia Secunda.

The superscription of the *Caesares* declares a work carried down as far as the year 360. Further, by the reference near the end, 'Constantius annos tres atque viginti augustum imperium regens' (42. 20), the author proclaims that he is writing before September 9, 360: Constantius died on November 3, 361. It is rather unusual to find a historian or a biographer narrating the actions of a ruler before his death, right up to the year of composition. Victor is complimentary to Constantius, but the remarks on his ministers with which the work closes are very outspoken

---

[1] For L. Domitius Alexander, see O. Seeck, P–W I. 1445; P. Romanelli, *Storia delle Provincie Romane dell'Africa* (1959), 533 ff.; T. Kotula, *Klio* XL (1962), 159 ff. The duration of his rule is not quite clear, cf. T. Kotula, ib. 160; M. Leglay.

[2] It is strange indeed that the HA should know of him and name him in an invocation of Constantine—'his addendi sunt Licinius, Severus, Alexander atque Maxentius, quorum omnium ius in dicionem tuam venit' (*Elag.* 35. 6).

[3] Zosimus II. 12. 3: Ἀλεξάνδρῳ, Φρυγί τε ὄντι τὸ γένος καὶ δειλῷ καὶ ἀτόλμῳ καὶ πρὸς πάντα πόνον ὀκνοῦντι καὶ προσέτι γεγηρακότι. It is argued by T. Kotula that all the accounts of this usurper go back to a common source, a biography of Constantine (o.c. 161; 168 ff.).

(42. 24 f.). Perhaps there is artifice, the *Caesares* being composed a little later.

That hypothesis would have to play down the bronze statue—and it is a superfluity. To demonstrate the KG it is enough to establish details, for example about Sirmium, which happen to be absent from Victor. He lacks the name Budalia, which is supplied by Eutropius and by the *Epitome*. By contrast, those two when registering the murder of Probus, have nothing to say about the marshes near Sirmium. That item is in Victor, and also in the HA. But the HA has the iron tower, not in Victor. Yet Victor, it might be added, perhaps implies autopsy by the phrase 'urbem . . . quae palustri solo hiemalibus corrumpitur' (37. 4).

Again, it is the *Epitome* which alone furnishes the remarkable details about the birthplaces of two emperors. First, Maximianus, with the palace near Sirmium indicating the site, 'etiam nunc' (40. 10). Second, Galerius, in Dacia Ripensis, at Romulianum, which he named after his mother. The author states that Galerius was also buried there (40. 16).

A negative criterion can be brought in to give some support (not much). It is worth asking whether Victor and the *Epitome* show any marked interest in Danubian matters subsequent to the death of Constantine.

For Victor, the search is not likely to be remunerative, since his account of 337–60 is extremely compressed. Of Vetranio, who was 'litterarum prorsus expers et ingenio stolidior' he is content to say 'ortus Moesiae superioris locis squalidioribus' (41. 26); and he does not bother to mention the Battle of Mursa (in 351).

That was a great and murderous contest, so the *Epitome* states (42. 4).[1] That treatise can report the origin of Jovianus—'incola agri Singidonensis provinciae Pannoniae' (44. 1). One would wish to have the name of that place in the territory of Singidunum—which city belonged in fact to Moesia Superior, not to Pannonia. Further, in an author writing soon after 395 it is no surprise to learn something about Gratianus, the parent of Valentinian: he was 'mediocri stirpe ortus apud Cibalas, Funarius appellatus est' (45. 2).[2]

To sum up. The KG, as divined through the epitomators, discloses scraps of precise knowledge about Sirmium and about Dacia Ripensis. Did the author perhaps, like certain emperors, derive his origin from those

---

[1] cf. Zosimus II. 51. 1.

[2] Very close to Ammianus—'natus apud Cibalas Pannoniae oppidum Gratianus maior ignobili stirpe, cognominatus est a pueritia prima Funarius' (xxx. 7. 2). Each follows with the explanation: five soldiers had not been strong enough to pull a rope away from the youth.

regions? That does not follow. He might have held some post in the
Danubian lands, military or civilian, as did Aurelius Victor.

To the official class belonged two other epitomators coeval with Victor.
The dry Eutropius had been with Julian in his Persian expedition, such
is his own unexpected disclosure (x. 16. 1). Odd details in the sequel
build him up as a recognizable character.[1] He dedicated his *Breviarium*
to the Emperor Valens *c.* 370.

Next Festus, who also drew on the KG. To be identified as the notorious
Festus of Tridentum, on ample show in the pages of Ammianus.[2] The
composition of his *Breviarium* falls in 369 or 370.[3]

The epitomators show the practice of bringing their productions down
to a date close to the time of writing. Thus Victor and Eutropius (the
latter terminated with 364). Nor, it seems, did the author of the *Epitome*
wait for long after 395. He expands his treatment with Theodosius at the
end. Similarly, to judge by what Victor has to tell about Diocletian and
Constantine, the author of the KG gave much more amplitude than to
earlier periods. Victor's technique in this portion resembles history rather
than biography.[4]

The subject, it is true, determined that treatment, and the information
available. By contrast, the emperors in the middle years of the third
century, from Decius to Carus and Carinus. Under Constantine, deep
ignorance prevailed. Who in that harsh and untutored society had the
science or the incentive to seek on coins and inscriptions the exact name
of a ruler or the identity of his consort?

To dispel the darkness, no Latin biographer could be conjured up
from that generation. The last of them on authentic record is Marius
Maximus, writing under Severus Alexander. It fell to the HA to compensate the dearth by inventing a whole crop of writers—and by creating
six more to adorn the age of Diocletian and Constantine, four of whom
honour those rulers with loyal and affectionate dedications.

The KG reflects that general ignorance. It was able, it is true, to furnish
facts about the extraction of some of the Danubian emperors; but there
is no sign that it had pronounced upon the local origins of Claudius.

The KG fell a prey to sundry errors or delusions, for example the
'interregnum' of six or seven months after the death of Aurelian.[5] The

---

[1] J. F. Matthews, *Historia* XVI (1967), 484 f.

[2] On whom, O. Seeck, P–W VI. 2256 f. Identity with the epitomator, however, was
established by A. Garroni, *Bull. com.* XLII (1916), 123 ff.

[3] J. W. Eadie in his edition (1967), 4 ff.

[4] The *Epitome*, however, divides the matter according to rulers and usurpers.

[5] Below, p. 237.

epitomators who compiled from it added more, from their own haste and nescience Both Victor (27. 1) and Eutropius (IX. 2. 1 f.) conflate the second and the third Gordian. The KG may have avoided that confusion.[1] At least, the *Epitome* distinguishes three rulers of the name; and it states, correctly, that the boy was a grandson of the old proconsul, 'nepos Gordiani ex filia' (27. 1).[2]

Some of the errors transmitted by the KG help to indicate its date. It asserted that Septimius Severus defeated Didius Julianus in battle at the Pons Mulvius (Victor 19. 4; Eutropius VIII. 17). That reflects a famous engagement of the year 312.[3]

There was a further cause of obscuration: idle gossip among the ignorant or governmental fraud. Constantine in the year 310 made a useful discovery: he was related in some way or other to the Emperor Claudius. It was probably taken up by the KG. Eutropius has 'Constantius per filiam nepos Claudi traditur' (IX. 22. 1). The HA preferred to produce a more elaborate version, with corroborative names: 'Crispus', a brother of Claudius, had a daughter, 'Claudia', who married the Dardanian noble 'Eutropius', hence Constantine as grandnephew (*Claud.* 13. 2).[4]

A link with another good emperor, Probus, may have gained currency among the uncritical. The *Epitome* comes out with the horticultural parent of that emperor, 'Dalmatius' by name (37. 1). There is a chance that he is genuine—but a strong doubt.[5] The name evokes the half-brother of Constantine and his homonymous son.[6] If Claudius could be an ancestor of the dynasty, why not Probus, his peer in arms and in all excellence?

To equip Probus with a father, the HA has recourse to the contrary device—the unobtrusive name. 'Maximus' was his father, 'ut quidam in litteras rettulerunt' (*Prob.* 3. 2). And, since the HA, unlike the KG, had a lively fantasy together with the need to fill up space, 'Maximus' follows

---

[1] The KG is generally held responsible. Against which, cf. Hohl, *Klio* XI (1911), 194 ff.; XXVII (1934), 154 f. He pointed out that the Chronographer of the Year 354, presumably drawing on that source, registers a third Gordian.

[2] However, the *Epitome* might have had a Greek source. The HA was able to learn the truth—'hic natus est, ut plures adserunt, ex filia Gordiani' (*Gord.* 22. 4). See further above, p. 84.

[3] As emphasized in *Ammianus and the Historia Augusta* (1968), 106.

[4] Above, p. 204.

[5] Accepted by A. Stein, P–W IV. 2455; and not impugned in *PIR*², D 2. G. Vitucci opines that he is more likely to be a minor official than a gardener (o.c. 4).

[6] On whom, O. Seeck, P–W IV. 2455 f. There would be no call to bring in Valerius Dalmatius, a high official *c*. 400, commemorated in verse on a bronze tablet found between Sopianae and Mursa, the one or the other his *patria* (*ILS* 8987).

a military career, centurion and then tribune, ending with death in Egypt (but wife, son, and daughter survived). It is further intimated ('multi dicunt') that Probus was related to Claudius. The author remembers having read in an 'ephemeris' that Probus was buried by his sister, Claudia by name (3. 4).

'Dalmatius' as the parent of Probus (whenever created) suggests devices of retrojection such as appealed to the HA. One should look for other parallels. Eutropius describes the extraction of Diocletian as follows: 'Dalmatia oriundum, virum obscurissime natum, adeo ut a plerisque scribae filius, a nonnullis Anullini senatoris libertinus fuisse credatur' (IX. 22. 2). That might be taken without discomfort to be the version of the KG.[1] The name 'Anullinus' is plausible: there was a contemporary family of Annii Anullini.[2]

Victor offers no detail; but the *Epitome*, after mentioning Anullinus, proceeds 'matre pariter atque oppido nomine Dioclea, quorum vocabulis, donec imperium sumeret, Diocles appellatus' (39. 1). Now there was certainly an allegation current that Diocletian was originally called Diocles: Lactantius bears witness.[3] But a woman and a town both called Dioclea, that strains belief. It is a perversion of the known city Doclea, near the south-eastern edge of the province Dalmatia.[4]

All that can be known for certain about the origin of Diocletian is that he came from Dalmatia. The rest is, inference, fable, fiction. The additional 'information' which the *Epitome* supplies, going beyond Eutropius and of a different order, excites a suspicion.

Diocletian elected Salonae in Dalmatia for his retreat and built a palace on the shore, close to that city. When Maximianus and Galerius urged him to come back, he rebuked them with a quiet answer: 'utinam Salonae possetis visere olera nostris manibus instituta.' This story, which enjoyed enormous notoriety in the sequel, is vouched for by the *Epitome* (39. 6). The invention is pleasing; and the residence of Diocletian at Salonae encouraged the easy persuasion that he was born there.[5]

Suspicion is sharpened by another notice in the *Epitome*. It comes out with the notion that Claudius was the son of a Gordian: 'plerique putant

---

[1] Also, but without any variant, Anullinus occurs in the *Epitome* (39. 1). Zonaras likewise has the item and the name (XII. 31).

[2] *PIR*², A 632 (Annius Anullinus, the consul of 295, *praefectus urbi* in 306/7 and again in 312).   [3] Lactantius 9. 11, etc.

[4] It is another matter that the mother of Galerius should bear the same name as a city north of the Danube, viz. Romula, in the old Dacia Malvensis (i.e. in Oltenia).

[5] As in Zonaras XII. 32.

Gordiano satum, dum adulescens a muliere institueretur ad uxorem'
(34. 2). Claudius was born c. 214.[1] Which Gordian, therefore, is the parent?
Scholarship should not be baffled. The thing becomes possible, nay
attractive. The son of the proconsul was born in 192, according to the HA
(*Gord.* 15. 2).

This Gordian was noted for the habits of a voluptuary—twenty-two
acknowledged concubines, by each of whom he had three or four sons
(*Gord.* 19. 3). By the same token, however, a grave doubt might intrude
whether for his preparation for life he would delay until the late age of
twenty-two.[2]

This fable about the parentage of Claudius ought not to be discarded
or neglected. It can be turned to serious employ. Along with the senator
'Aurelius' (Aurelian's father was his 'colonus'), 'Dalmatius', the parent
of Probus, and 'Dioclea' (both a woman and a town), all three only in
the *Epitome*, it brings one into the congenial ambit of the HA, and raises
an important question: the origin and date of these fictions.

Two alternatives offer. First, the three items in the *Epitome* were
taken from the KG. That work certainly carried gossip or inventions of
the Constantinian age, for example Gallienus sending the 'insignia
imperii' to Claudius, then at Ticinum, and the 'devotio' of Claudius.[3]
It was therefore a predecessor of the HA in credulity—and perhaps in
deceit. As for one particular, 'Dioclea' the mother of the Emperor,
there is no warrant that it occurred in the KG. But the KG might have
admitted variants, as appears from what Eutropius reported about the
extraction of Diocletian (IX. 19. 2).

Second, these items are the peculiar property of the *Epitome*. If so,
they reproduce (whether or no inventions of the author himself) a
notable feature of the time: fraudulent scholarship brought to play on
the origins of emperors. Again, the methods of the HA, which now
finds either a predecessor or a companion, albeit rudimentary.[4] That

---

[1] *PIR*[2], A 1626.

[2] Gordian II as the subject of the fiction was assumed by P. Damerau, *Klio*, Beiheft
XXXIII (1934), 41 f. The boy Gordian was surely indicated, chronology being irrelevant
to the fable.

[3] Above, p. 203. The *Epitome* furnishes names to corroborate both incidents. For the
former, 'Gallonius Basilius', for the latter 'Pomponius Bassus'. Now 'Pomponius Bassus'
can be equated with an eminent personage of the time (above, p. 203). No evidence avails to
establish 'Gallonius Basilius', or to discredit him. The *nomen* had an appeal for the author
of the HA. Observe 'Gallonius Avitus', whom Aurelian instructed to make provision for
the Gothic princesses established at Perinthus, and notably for 'Hunila' (*Quadr. tyr.* 15. 6 f.).

[4] The *Epitome* adduces a genuine name in a fraudulent context—and perhaps invents
a name (see the preceding note).

masterpiece belongs in the close vicinity of 395. Scholars have duly looked for traces of the influence of one work on the other. They have not been ascertained. Naturally enough, if the two compositions are closely contemporary.

A consequence of some interest emerges. In the preceding pages a case was presented. Most of the precise Danubian notices in the three epitomators derive (it was argued) from the KG.[1] A distinction must now be drawn, segregating those which appear only in the *Epitome*. Two of them indeed are suspect: 'Dalmatius', the father of Probus, and 'Dioclea', the mother of Diocletian. But there is the pair of items with local precision, viz. the palace attesting the natal soil of Maximianus near Sirmium, 'etiam nunc' (40. 10), and Romulianum in Dacia Ripensis, where Galerius was both born and buried (40. 16). Sound method demands the segregation, and a doubt may subsist. None the less, these two notices appear to be something different from the inventions in the HA.

The *Epitome*, for all its exiguity, is a perplexing document. A number of peculiarities have already emerged. The *Epitome* brings up intricate questions of sources and interrelations.[2] Furthermore, it carries items that go back to a Greek writer, as is proved by some close parallels with Zosimus.[3] That touches a whole imbroglio of problems. Among them, the sources used by Ammianus (in the lost books), and by Zosimus.[4] To sort out those problems and state them in brief and firm formulation would not be an easy task, or enviable.

Trouble enough, if the HA did not come in. Herodian terminated with the fate of Pupienus and Balbinus in the summer of 238. The author now had to face once again the difficulty which had arisen when two Latin biographers fell out, first *Ignotus*, then Marius Maximus. This time the refuge and remedy was Dexippus.

The Greek historian was used for the account of Gordian III. He is named once only (*Gord.* 23. 1), but several signs are indicative, notably the consular dates assigned to four years in the reign.[5] After Gordian III, the author added a supplement, *Maximus et Balbinus*. In that volume, Dexippus happens to be named no fewer than five times.[6] And there is

---

[1] Enmann opined that the KG had an especial interest in Gaul (o.c. 435).
[2] For the sources of the *Epitome*, E. Hohl, *Klio* XI (1911), 192 ff.; 206 ff.; 227 ff.
[3] On which, W. Hartke, *Klio*, Beiheft XLV (1940), 49 ff.
[4] For Zosimus, see L. Mendelssohn in his edition (1887), xxxvi ff.
[5] Above, p. 170.   [6] *Max. et Balb.* 1. 2; 15. 5; 16. 4, 5, 6.

a piece from Dexippus that has always been recognized, viz. the Gothic invasion and the sack of Histria (16. 3).[1]

Recourse was also had to Dexippus for the reign of Gallienus—that heroic and exemplary Athenian himself came into the story (*Gall.* 13. 4). Hence signs of a Greek source, such as Goths designated as 'Scythae' and as coming from the Maeotis, or valuable sections, notably the conspiracy of the generals in 268.[2] The *Vita* carries four consular datings (261, 262, 264, 265), there is another (258) in *Tyranni triginta* (9. 1), and the last of them (270) occurs in the *Vita Claudii* (11. 3).

Dexippus ended at 270, that is clear. There were other Greek sources for the history of this age.[3] One of them, detected in Zosimus and in Zonaras, supplied almost all the facts (they are few) in the *Vita Taciti*.

---

[1] The event is antedated.   [2] Above, p. 210.

[3] For the Greek sources in the late *Vitae* of the HA, E. Hohl, o.c. 189 ff.; W. Hartke, o.c. 20 ff. For the *Vita Claudii*, P. Damerau, *Klio*, Beiheft xxxiii (1934), 8 ff.; A. Alföldi, *CAH* ix (1939), 721 ff.; for the *Vita Aureliani*, W. H. Fisher, *JRS* xix (1929), 126 ff.

XV · THE EMPEROR CLAUDIUS TACITUS

I. FOR THE HISTORY of this reign (it lasted for no more than six or seven months) Zosimus and Zonaras furnish brief accounts that are concordant and valuable.[1] Neither saw anything abnormal or portentous in the accession of Tacitus. Zonaras conveys the essentia facts: Tacitus was proclaimed by the troops, in absence; he was in Campania at the time; he went to Rome as a private citizen for his investiture (XII. 28).

The Latin sources import confusion.[2] Eutropius, it is true, discloses no harm. He says that Tacitus was 'bene moratus et rei publicae gerendae idoneus' (IX. 16). The *Epitome* has the phrase 'egregie moratus' (36. 2); but, referring to the murder of his predecessor Aurelian (who was killed near Perinthus late in the year 275), it comes out with the statement 'hoc tempore septem mensibus interregni species evenit' (35. 10).

Victor enlarges on the topic. The soldiers sent an embassy to Rome requesting the Senate to choose an emperor, 'suopte arbitratu'. The Senate referred the matter back. Hence a contest in 'pudor ac modestia' on either side, which novel phenomenon inspires Victor to reflect upon the singular prestige of Aurelian. He was comparable to the Founder of Rome—'soli quasi Romulo interregni species obvenit, longe vero gloriosior' (35. 12). Finally, the Senate chose an emperor in the person of Tacitus—'igitur tandem senatus mense circiter post Aureliani interitum sexto' (36. 1). Hence rejoicing because the Senate had recovered the 'legendi ius principis', but not for long or to a good outcome (36. 2).

Something has gone badly wrong. Aurelian perished in October or November of 275, and the reign of Tacitus cannot be prolonged beyond June of the next year.[3] An interval of six to seven months before the accession of Tacitus did not exist.

The source of the misconception was seen long ago. An actual interval (quite short, see below) is conflated with the duration of Tacitus' reign (six or seven months). The KG transmitted the error: the phrase 'interregni species' occurs both in Victor and in the *Epitome* (35. 12; 35. 10).

---

[1] Zosimus I. 63; Zonaras XII. 28.

[2] For the *Vita*, the long investigation by Hohl retains a classic validity (*Klio* XI (1911), 178 ff.; 284 ff.). For the facts about Tacitus himself, *PIR²*, C 1036.

[3] *PIR²*, D 135, cf. C 1036.

The error was due to compression and inadvertence. It was fostered, or rather engendered, by the notion that Tacitus and Florianus, brief reigns, were a brief interlude between Aurelian and Probus. That is reflected in the HA. They were 'quasi quidam interreges' (*Tac.* 14. 5).[1]

11. The HA followed the KG.[2] Better, Aurelius Victor, who had developed the engaging theme. Under this incentive, the author embarks on an elaborate romance, with full documentation after his fashion.

It starts in the *Vita Aureliani*. The army made appeal to the Senate, not once but three times. And so for six months the Roman world had no emperor—or change of governor in any province, save that 'Faltonius Probus' took the place of 'Arellius Fuscus' as proconsul of Asia (*Aur.* 40. 4).[3]

It is a pleasure, so the author says ('non iniucundum est') to insert the dispatch which the army sent (41. 1). When it arrived, the Senate met in the 'Curia Pompiliana' under the presidency of the consul 'Aurelius Gordianus' (41. 3). He passed the word to 'Aurelius Tacitus' (as the person is here designated). Tacitus descanted upon the military glory of Aurelian, proposed the vote of divine honours, but referred the selection of an emperor to the army. However, after envoys had been sent 'iterum atque iterum', Tacitus himself was chosen (41. 15).

The *Vita Taciti* leads off with a long disquisition on the nature of the 'interregnum' from the death of Romulus onwards, with erudite detail about curule magistrates and tribunes of the plebs, not omitting a scholar's honest admission on a controversial point—'video mihi posse obici' (1. 4). Verbose remarks follow about the miraculous and edifying situation—'eadem posteris humani generis stupenda moderatio, ut discant qui regna cupiunt non raptum ire imperia sed mereri' (2. 3). Finally, the interchange between army and Senate: 'dum id saepius fit, sextus peractus est mensis' (2. 6).

The high assembly again met in the 'Curia Pompiliana' on September 25.[4] It heard an oration from the consul 'Velius Cornificius Gordianus' (3. 2).[5] The Senate acclaimed Tacitus: 'princeps senatus recte Augustus

---

[1] Hohl, o.c. 284; 316.   [2] Groag, P–W v. 1349; Hohl, o.c. 284.

[3] For the names, above, pp. 6; 8.

[4] The 'Curia Pompiliana' (also in *Aur.* 41. 3), taking its name from King Numa, is a suitable addition to the topography of Rome. Compare the 'Campus Iovis' (*Pesc.* 12. 4).

[5] Like 'Aurelius Gordianus' (*Aur.* 41. 3), this consul shows that the author, dealing with Tacitus, had in mind his own portrayal of an earlier ruler endowed with the tastes of a scholar: old Gordian is a kind of Antonine ruler. In this place 'Cornificius' is appropriate: Cornificia was a daughter of Marcus. There is no point in adducing (as some do) the

creatur', and so on. Tacitus pleads age and incapacity for military exercises (3. 5 f.). The senators insist with acclamations, each twenty or thirty times repeated. Thus 'et Traianus ad imperium senex venit', and they quote 'incanaque menta regis Romani' (5. 1).[1]

The day was carried by a long and eloquent exhortation from 'Maecius Faltonius Nicomachus' (6. 1–9).[2] Then they all proceeded to the Campus Martius where the Prefect of the City, 'Aelius Cesettianus', spoke (7. 2 f.). Tacitus is presented next to the troops, with remarks from the Prefect of the Guard, 'Moesius Gallicanus' (8. 4).

The new emperor makes a brief statement to the 'sanctissimi commilitones'. He begins by repeating the senatorial acclamation about Trajan and asserts a comparison in his own favour: 'sed ille ab uno delectus est' (8. 5).

III. So far 'interregnum' and accession. Two more rubrics follow, viz. the programmatic speech in summary, with comments from the author (9), and a list, miscellaneous, of governmental measures (10). To round off the portrayal of an emperor chosen by the Senate, the character and habits of Tacitus are curiously delineated (11); and documents are appended to demonstrate that Rome has been brought back 'in antiquum statum' (18 f.).

The happy senators exclaimed 'ecquis melius quam litteratus imperat?' (3. 4). The author responds with alacrity to the congenial theme. He had already depicted Gordian as a venerable scholar whose days were passed in communion with the classics, himself an author of remarkable fecundity.[3]

Tacitus was temperate and frugal in his manner of life. Detail is vouchsafed. He was devoted to lettuce and 'amariores cibos'; he would not serve up a pheasant save at family or official festivals.[4] He liked the 'venationes', and, avoiding excessive use of the bath, he kept his vigour unimpaired in old age. He could decipher the tiniest letters in a manuscript, he would read or write something every night, save on the second day of the month (11. 8).

'[G]ordianus' on a list of eminent donors belonging to this age—or to the next (*CIL* VI. 37118). Emperors excepted, all characters in this *Vita* are patently fictitious: eight persons and one authority, viz. the biographer 'Suetonius Optatianus' (11. 7).

[1] *Aen.* VI. 809 f. (Numa). Previously employed in the 'Sors Vergiliana' vouchsafed to Hadrian (*Hadr.* 2. 8).

[2] For the name, above, p. 12. The three elements thus combined furnish one of the clearest clues to the age in which the HA was composed.

[3] Above, p. 101. Cf. also p. 238, n. 5.

[4] Similarly another old and frugal emperor 'fasianum nunquam privato convivio comedit' (*Pert.* 12. 6).

Moreover, honouring as an ancestor 'Cornelium Tacitum, scriptorem historiae Augustae', the Emperor ordained that his image should be set up in all libraries; and, 'ne lectorum incuria deperiret', each year ten copies of his writings should be made (10. 3).

For further personal details, they are numerous, the reader is advised to consult 'Suetonium Optatianum, qui eius vitam adfatim scripsit' (11. 7). For the restoration of the Senate to power and authority, dispatches testify which the high assembly sent to nine great cities of the Empire (18). Those which Carthage and Treveri received are quoted.

Also private letters. 'Autronius Tiberianus' writes in exultation to his parent, and so does 'Claudius Sapilianus' to his uncle. The latter utters a forecast: since we can now make emperors, we can preclude them—'possumus et prohibere'. He terminates with a quotation from Terence, 'dictum sapienti sat est' (19. 5).

Details are furnished about the Senate's revived authority. For example, 'nos recepimus ius proconsulare, redierunt ad praefectum urbi appellationes omnium potestatum et omnium dignitatum.' Thus 'Autronius Tiberianus' (19. 2), enlarging a little on the dispatch to Carthage (18. 3).

The details need not detain. A second 'senatorial restoration' occurred about eight months later, enjoined in his turn by the excellent Probus. Here the author is more specific—and yet at the same time vague.[1] The whole thing must be discarded.[2] To the context of these fantasies belongs the censorship with comprehensive powers, as announced by the Emperor Decius (*Val.* 6. 3 f.).[3] Probus said nothing about the *praefectus urbi*. In the definition of Decius, the censor shall have no jurisdiction over the *praefectus urbi*, *consules ordinarii*, *rex sacrorum*—or the senior of the Vestal Virgins, 'si tamen incorrupta manebit', so the Emperor scrupulously adds (*Val.* 6. 6).

---

[1] *Prob.* 13. 1: 'permisit patribus ut ex magnorum iudicum appellationibus ipsi cognoscerent, proconsules crearent, legatos (ex) consulibus darent, ius praetorium praesidibus darent, leges quas Probus ederet senatus consultis propriis consecrarent.'

[2] Attempts were made to rescue and employ this stuff. Thus L. Homo, *Rev. hist.* cxxxviii (1921), 40 ff. See the sceptical (but lengthy) discussion in G. Vitucci, *L'imperatore Probo* (1952), 87 ff. Hope revived with the inscription of Caesonius Ovinius Bassus, published by G. Barbieri in *Akte des IV. int. Kong. für gr. u. lat. Epigraphik* (1964), 41, whence *AE* 1964, 223. Probus appointed this consular 'ad pre[side]ndum iud(icio) mag(no)' (l. 12). Hence a firm argument (Barbieri, ib. 44 ff.) for the authenticity of *Probus* 13. 1, which mentions 'iudices magni'. Relevance, and a partial rehabilitation of the HA, is conceded by A. Chastagnol, *Bonner Historia-Augusta-Colloquium 1966/7* (1968), 67 ff. That is not the end of the matter. Inspection of the photograph suggests that 'lud.' should be read, not 'iud.', hence some kind of 'ludi magni' are in cause. See T. D. Barnes, *CQ²* xx (1970), 198 ff. For a new inscription of the consular, S. Panciera, *Epigraphica* xxix (1967), 19 ff.

[3] For the fictitious episode, above, p. 215.

Composing the *Vita Taciti*, the author could take a hint from Victor. That epitomator spread himself on the 'interregnum' (35. 9–14); and he stated it as a fact that the Senate had 'recovered the right to choose an emperor' (36. 1). A little later, in comment on the assassination of Probus, he asserts: 'abhinc militaris potentia convaluit.' From this point onward the Senate forfeited 'imperium creandique ius principis'. For that deplorable turn, Victor suggests various generalized explanations, blaming the Senate (37. 5).

Victor is the victim of a delusion. He proceeds to reinforce his opinion. Such was the modest comportment of the legions that the Senate in the reign of Tacitus would have been able to get back the 'militia' which it had recently lost: 'quippe amissa Gallieni edicto refici militia potuit' (37. 6).[1] A significant passage. Victor is referring to the exclusion of senators from military command. That was a process, not an act, still less something ordained by an 'edictum Gallieni'. The passage has produced controversy, misconceptions, and even a mistranslation of the word 'potuit'.[2]

Victor embellished Tacitus, but he was not able to adduce any positive measures of policy. Nor do the Greek sources single out anything for especial praise. Julian in his *Caesares* was totally unaware of this exemplary prince.

iv. Gibbon, in comment on the 'amazing period of tranquil anarchy' that ensued after the murder of Aurelian, describes it as 'one of the best attested but most improbable events in the history of mankind'. The historian was deceived by rhetoric and fantasy, by documentation and dates. A scholar in the present age can still give credit to six months of negotiation between army and Senate.[3] And a number of the minor felicities of invention pass without challenge.[4]

The fabrications have their modest utility. They illustrate aspects of life in the author's own time. Thus the importance of the *praefectus urbi*

---

[1] For 'amissa' Baynes preferred the 'amisso' of the *Codex Bruxellensis* (*JRS* xv (1925), 198 = *Byzantine and Other Essays* (1955), 177). It does not make much difference to the interpretation, since an unreal condition is postulated ('potuit').

[2] L. Homo argued that the 'edictum Gallieni' had actually been revoked by Tacitus (o.c. 45 ff.). Similarly a number of scholars, including A. Stein, *Der römische Ritterstand* (1927), 449. Observe how the potential form 'potuit' gets translated. Thus P. Lambrechts, 'le service militaire perdu (pour le Sénat) par l'édit de Gallien put être réintroduit' (*La Composition du Sénat romain de Septime Sévère à Dioclétien* (1937), 97).

[3] H. Mattingly, *CAH* xii (1939), 310: 'for some six months, from about April to September 275, embassies passed to and fro.'

[4] Below, p. 276.

or the copying of manuscripts: about the year 400 the eminent Symmachus supervised a revision of the text of Livy.[1]

v. Apart from fiction, what remains of this *Vita*?[2] The HA took a few facts from the KG and from Victor. More significant, the source of Zosimus and of Zonaras. It is drawn upon briefly in two places. First, the accession of Tacitus: he was in Campania, and he came to Rome as a 'privatus' (7. 5 f.). Second, Tacitus punished the assassins of Aurelian and he defeated a great invasion of barbarians who had come 'a Maeotide' (13. 1–3). Further, he perished 'insidiis militaribus', or, as others say, by disease (13. 5).[3]

About the first passage, the author makes an engaging admission. Tacitus was absent, in Campania, when made emperor, so 'plerique' affirm. The author proceeds 'verum est, nec dissimulare possum' (7. 5). His candour demolishes the whole preceding narration.

The *Vita Taciti* is about three quarters as long as the *Vita Probi*: about six months against six years. Its content of fact does not defy close calculation. A narrative of the reign, bringing in a few facts from the other sources (e.g. Tacitus' death at Tyana) and comment on the coinage, could (and should) be restricted to brief compass.[4] Few modern accounts fail to admit or discuss items in the HA that are patent fictions.

vi. According to the historian Tacitus, the fall of Nero published a great secret: 'posse principem alibi quam Romae fieri'. Towards the end of the year 275 the world contemplated a paradox—an emperor could be made at Rome, apparently.

How great was the anomaly? For some time emperors had been proclaimed in the camps before being acknowledged by the Senate. Now Tacitus was the candidate of the army, if the Greek source is to be trusted.[5] But he was not with the troops, or anywhere in their vicinity; and he came from Campania to Rome for his investiture.

An interval therefore occurred after the death of Aurelian, with no

---

[1] Symmachus, *Epp.* IX. 30.

[2] Scarcely anything, cf. Hohl's summary of the actual sources (o.c. 316 f.).

[3] For the Greek source, Hohl, o.c. 189 f.; for the decease of Tacitus, ib. 308 f. He fell victim to a military conspiracy (Zosimus I. 63. 1 f.; Zonaras XII. 28). In the KG it was a natural death (Eutropius IX. 16), at Tyana (Victor 36. 2), or at Tarsus from fever (*Epit.* 36. 2). It was Florianus who perished at Tarsus, killed by the troops (Victor 37. 1, cf. *Tac.* 14. 2 and the other sources enumerated in *PIR²*, A 649).

[4] As Mattingly affirms, the coinage of Tacitus and of Florianus 'has a life and colour of its own' (*CAH* XII (1939), 313).

[5] Zonaras XII. 28: τὸ στρατιωτικὸν δὲ αὐτὸν ἀνηγόρευσε καὶ ἀπόντα.

emperor. The Latin sources prolong it, to an incredible duration. Victor and the HA promulgate a further and a fatal misconception: Tacitus not merely owed his investiture to the Senate, he was chosen by the Senate. Not likely. That kind of impracticable and pernicious fancy had captivated the credulous in an earlier season. Trajan (so many asserted) was proposing to leave the choice of emperor to the Senate.[1]

Days or weeks might in fact elapse before the candidate became available. There is useful parallel, ninety years later. Jovian died at Dadastana. The army proceeded to Nicaea, where the generals took counsel together. Their choice fell upon Valentinian, who had stayed behind at Ancyra, 'diebusque decem nullus imperii tenuit gubernacula.' Thus Ammianus (xxvi. 1. 4). Zosimus employs the Greek term designating an 'interregnum'.[2]

As related by Ammianus, the transaction discloses real history. That is, debate, dissent, and rival candidates. The name of the tribune Aequitius was canvassed, but the 'potiorum auctoritas' went against him—he was 'asper et subagrestis'. Some slight consideration was given to Januarius, a relative of the deceased emperor, but unanimity emerged for Valentinian. One thing in his favour was his absence. Finally, to counter the danger that the 'armatorum mobilitas saepe versabilis' might overturn the decision, prudent steps were taken by Aequitius and by Leo, 'ut Pannonii fautoresque designati principis' (xxvi. 1. 6).

Aurelian was killed near Perinthus when on the way to a campaign against the Persians. Notoriety thus accrued to Caenophrurium, a post eighteen miles east of Perinthus on the road to Selymbria and Byzantium.[3] The affair was an accident. A minor official forged a paper showing Aurelian's intention to put some of the officers to death.[4]

Only one of them stands on record, Mucapor, who dealt the blow: the name is clamantly Thracian. He is mentioned by Victor (36. 2) and by the HA (*Aur.* 35. 5), which cleverly brought him in beforehand as recipient of a missive from the Emperor (26. 2). The author, though

---

[1] *Hadr.* 4. 9 (above, p. 126). Not but that the improbable could occur: Maximus and Balbinus were selected by the Senate (or by a committee of it, cf. above, p. 166).

[2] Zosimus III. 36. 3 (ἀναρχία).

[3] *It. Ant.* 137. 3. Caenophrurium was probably in the KG (Jerome's Chronicle has it). Not in Victor or the *Epitome*. Eutropius furnishes a valuable detail along with the name— 'interfectus est in itineris medio quod inter Constantinopolim et Heracleam est, stratae veteris' (IX. 15. 2). The 'strata vetus' is presumably the Egnatia, with Caenophrurium on it, shortly before the point at which the Egnatia was joined by the road coming from Serdica and Hadrianopolis.

[4] For the official called Eros (*PIR²*, E 90), whom the HA converts into 'Mnesteus' (*Aur.* 36. 4), see Hohl, o.c. 285 ff.

professedly a modest compiler of imperial biographies, is alert to a historical matter of central importance, namely the composition of the military oligarchy: as witness the eight dignitaries in Valerian's council at Byzantium (*Aur.* 13. 1) or the eleven generals whom Probus trained (*Prob.* 22. 3). This time inadvertence or the appeal of more congenial themes has spared the credulous—and defrauded his admirers.

VII. Curiosity might ask whether any survived of the company (mainly Danubian) that formed the conspiracy against Gallienus seven years before.[1] Other military men might come to mind, such as Julius Marcellinus and Aurelius Marcellinus, who together built the walls of Verona in 265.[2] The former was Prefect of Egypt in 271, the latter is probably Marcellinus the consul of 275.[3] Or again, persons soon on high notoriety such as Probus and his Guard Prefect M. Aurelius Carus; and also Aper who held that office under Numerian, the son of Carus.[4] Or for that matter, Saturninus, a friend of Probus, who made a proclamation in Syria and perished there, at Apamea.[5]

Probus excites attention, perhaps at this moment inconveniently absent in the eastern lands, but ready at once to rise against Florianus, the ephemeral successor of Tacitus. The HA credits Probus with a great command —but consigned to him by Tacitus (*Prob.* 7. 4).

In the Latin sources the generals have no voice. It is the army that speaks. Thus Victor, 'milites amisso principe legatos statim Romam destinant uti suopte arbitratu patres imperatorem deligerent' (35. 9). And the HA quotes the anonymous dispatch headed 'felices ac fortes exercitus' (*Aur.* 41. 1). The HA, however, discerns the implausibility and is impelled to offer an explanation by no means idle. It enlarges upon the mistake made by the 'militares' who murdered Aurelian—as a class they are credulous, angry, and often drunk, and in general void of sagacity (*Tac.* 2. 4). They came to their senses, but the army rejected them; and, 'odio praesentium', the army decided to make appeal to the Senate (2. 5).

In emergency the generals at Mediolanum in 268 had been able to agree upon one of their fellow conspirators. This time the conclave was diffident or discordant—and a candidate not present carried a clear premium. Intrigue and negotiation among senatorial factions after the removal of a ruler tend to throw up an elderly and innocuous candidate,

---

[1] Above, p. 210.   [2] *ILS* 544.   [3] *PIR*[2], J 403; A 1546.
[4] Aper (*PIR*[2], A 909) might be the same person as L. Flavius Aper (F 207).
[5] For the facts about the usurper C. Julius Saturninus, see A. Stein, P–W II A. 213 ff.; *PIR*[2], J 546.

if possible without a son, and sometimes in the design of filling a gap, until a stronger claimant can be imposed. Thus Nerva after the end of the Flavian dynasty. And the pair of emperors produced in 238, Maximus and Balbinus, will suitably be recorded.

When the military have the arbitrament, the result will be different. Tacitus was a 'senex'. The KG may have transmitted the fact—but it happens not to be in the epitomators. Zonaras assigns him the age of seventy-five, which might be a long way out.[1] The moral quality of Tacitus is briefly extolled: 'bene moratus' or 'egregie moratus' (Eutropius and the *Epitome*). And Victor says that he was 'mitis' (36. 1). No hint survives anywhere of any previous occupations. Tacitus comes on show as a senior consular, indeed he is designated in the HA as 'princeps senatus'.[2] His colleague in the consulship of 273, Julius Placidianus, should not escape notice. Under Claudius in 269 he held command of an army corps stationed in Narbonensis;[3] and soon after he became *praefectus praetorio*.[4]

There is no warrant for the notion that Tacitus was merely a blameless old senator. By training and affinity he may have stood close to the generals of Aurelian. When the military select an emperor, their choice is not likely to light upon a civilian. After the death of Jovian they looked for somebody 'diu exploratum et gravem' (Ammianus XXVI. 1. 3).

According to Victor, Tacitus punished with death and torture the assassins, especially Mucapor (36. 2); and the HA states that he executed all of them, 'bonos malosve' (*Tac.* 13. 1). A little later, however, it emerges that some survived, to be dealt with by Probus in a more gentle fashion, along with those who had murdered Tacitus (*Prob.* 13. 2 f.).[5] Which matter may be left as it is.

VIII. This emperor stands in isolation in the HA. No kin, or friend or ally, save only Florianus.[6] The HA asserts that Florianus was his brother, seven times; but in one place he is only a half-brother (*Tac.* 17. 4). An

[1] Zonaras XII. 28.
[2] The meaning of 'princeps senatus' (*Tac.* 4. 3) emerges from what had been stated a little before, 'Tacitus qui erat primae sententiae consularis' (4. 1). Cf. Mommsen, *Staatsrecht* III (1888), 976; Chastagnol, *La Préfecture de Rome sous le Bas-Empire* (1960), 70. For the latter term, cf. the description of Pomponius Bassus (*Epit.* 34. 3): in Victor's account, without the name, there is a hint of 'princeps senatus' (34. 4). In addition to Tacitus, the HA presents Valerian as 'princeps senatus', in 238 (*Gord.* 9. 7), and likewise an anonymous senator (*Val.* 5. 4). In any event, it is not an official title but a descriptive term. Yet, even as such, presumably anachronistic for the third century.   [3] *ILS* 569.   [4] *PIR*[2], J 468.
[5] Both categories are also registered by Zosimus (1. 65. 1) and by Zonaras (XII. 29).
[6] *PIR*[2], A 649.

error, it may be assumed, and attributable to Aurelius Victor (36. 2).[1]
Neither had any idea of their nomenclature, viz. 'M. Claudius Tacitus' and
'M. Annius Florianus'; and the former was introduced as 'Aurelius Tacitus'
(*Aur.* 41. 4). The Greek source showed no awareness of this pertinent
relationship.[2] Instead, something to be accepted and valued: Florianus
was the Emperor's *praefectus praetorio*.[3]

That source also discloses Maximinus, a kinsman of Tacitus, whom he
appointed to a command in Syria, with no good result.[4] Given the
military man Julius Placidianus, who had shared the *fasces* with Tacitus
in 273, there might be a temptation to look for other allies. But Aemilianus, the Emperor's colleague in 276, is only a name, and nothing can be
done with the two *praefecti urbi*, viz. Postumius Suagrus in 275 and his
successor the year after, Ovinius Pacatianus.[5] The basis is lacking for any
sort of rational speculation.

The origin of Tacitus might engage a passing thought. The HA allo-
cates no separate rubric, as it did for Claudius, Aurelian, Probus, Carus.
The large and lavish senatorial theme engrossed the inventive efforts of
the author—and there was probably nothing at all in the sources to build
upon or diversify.

A digression towards the end of the *Vita* offers compensation more than
ample. Two colossal statues of the brothers stood at their cenotaph at
Interamna, on their own property: made of marble and thirty feet high
(15. 1). The statues were struck by lightning. Whereupon *haruspices*,
being consulted, announced the future glory of their descendants: a ruler
who would hold dominion over the world to its known limits, 'qua
Oceano ambitur', who also and finally, 'senatui reddat imperium' (15. 2).
The prophecy, however, is not to be fulfilled until a thousand years have
passed (15. 3; 16. 4).[6]

The amusing fable (it contains other choice details) empowers the
municipal pride of Terni to claim among its citizens both an emperor
of Rome and a historian. Why did the fancy of the author light upon

---

[1] That was affirmed by Hohl, o.c. 310 f. Further, 'dubitare possis, fuerintne ulla parentela
coniuncti' (*PIR²*, A 649.)   [2] Both Zosimus and Zonaras present a detailed narration.

[3] Zonaras XII. 29.   [4] Zosimus I. 63. 2; Zonaras XII. 28.

[5] Known only from the Chronographer of the Year 354. Among eminent senators of the
time were Flavius Antiochianus (*cos. II* 270), *praefectus urbi* in 269 and 270, also in 272 (*PIR²*,
F 203), and Pomponius Bassus (*cos. II* 271). For the latter, above, p. 203.

[6] On this prophecy see further *Ammianus and the Historia Augusta* (1968), 140 f. The
author makes fun of the *haruspices*. They next appear when interpreting the thunderbolt
that struck a statue of Probus in the territory of Verona (*Prob.* 24. 2 f.). Great glory was
portended to his descendants. Few have failed to see the allusion to the illustrious Probus
—and to his sons, the consular pair of 395 (above, p. 11).

Interamna? His general conception would lead to Italy rather than the Balkans as the *patria* of a senator who was also a scholar; and it is hazardous to suppose that his curious erudition knew of some link between Interamna and the consular historian. An answer may not be forthcoming until that season arrives when it can be ascertained why he situated near Bononia the funeral monument of the usurper 'Censorinus', with the inscription 'felix omnia, infelicissimus imperator' (*Tyr. trig.* 33. 4).

For the emperor occupying the brief interlude between Aurelian and Probus, the Danube is a better guess. Local and regional affinities are liable to be overplayed in any age, it is true. And the case of Carus is a warning. Some suppose that he came from Narona on the coast of Dalmatia.[1] That is dead against the evidence of the KG, entailing the postulate of an original corruption of the text. The KG patently exhibited Narbo.[2] Paradoxical, it is true, for one of the military emperors. Narbo had exhibited nobody of any consequence since its first and last attested senator, an obscure person in the time of Hadrian.[3]

Nothing precludes the hypothesis that Tacitus was a known and eligible character to generals and officers at Caenophrurium. The phrase of Ammianus, 'Pannonii fautoresque designati principis' might be applicable.[4] When Tacitus acceded to the power, the Danubian armies, so prolific of pretenders during the previous thirty years, made no stir. The new Emperor himself, after no long delay, marched out to fight the Goths in Asia Minor, and had won a victory before he was assassinated at Tyana in the early summer of 276.

The Latin sources were not well enough informed to deny him a career with the armies; and Zosimus and Zonaras show no sign that he was a civilian. Tacitus, if the truth could be known, was perhaps one of the Danubian military. He was extracted from his retirement in Campania by the call of duty and the recognition of old friends. If so, a veritable link between Aurelian and Probus. The series of the military emperors was tighter than the writers knew.

[1] Thus Henze, 'richtig Narona' (P-W ii. 2456), citing *CIL* iii, p. 291, which has nothing to say. Mattingly has 'probably' (*CAH* xii (1939), 321). For Rostovtseff, 'another Danubian' (*SEHRE*[2] (1957), 447), with appeal in the footnote to P. Bianchi, *Studi sull'imperatore M. Aurelio Caro* (1911).

[2] For the *testimonia*, *PIR*[2], A 1475. Whatever be thought of the consensus in the Latin sources (derivative), Zonaras called him a Gaul (xii. 30).

[3] *ILS* 1048 (L. Aemilius Honoratus). However, some senatorial Cominii may come from Narbo, cf. *Historia* xiv (1965), 360.

[4] As has been shown (Ch. XIV), most of the Danubian emperors derive from two vital zones: the region of Sirmium and Dacia Ripensis.

XVI · LITERARY TALENT

1. 'WHAT REWARD may we expect for delivering Rome from a monster?' was the question asked by Maximus, in a moment of freedom and confidence. Balbinus answered it without hesitation, 'The love of the Senate, of the people, and of all mankind.' 'Alas!' replied his more penetrating colleague, 'Alas! I dread the hatred of the soldiers, and the fatal effect of their resentment.'

Thus Gibbon. He was paraphrasing a passage which had been added to the text of the HA a few years after the Editio Princeps of 1475.[1] The artful interpolator began with the phrase 'nec reticendum est', and he duly cited an authority—'ut Herodianus dicit'.

The same scholar was also inspired to emulate a typical device of the HA, the fraudulent catalogue of names. The *Vita Alexandri* registered the eight members of that emperor's *consilium*, from 'Fabius Sabinus', described as 'Cato temporis sui', down to 'Quintilius Marcellus, quo meliorem ne historiae quidem continent' (*Alex.* 68. 1). The list includes the two masters of legal science, Ulpian and Paul: none of the others stands for any character in the history of the time.[2]

The interpolator, raking the annals of jurisprudence, adds no fewer than thirteen names. He begins with Pomponius, 'legum peritissimus', and ends with Tryphoninus, bringing in Celsus and Proculus on the way, but missing, for example, Masurius Sabinus. All of them, he affirms, derived instruction from Papinian, and all were friends of Severus Alexander. He subjoins testimony—'ut scribunt Acholius et Marius Maximus'.

These artifices declare a kindred spirit. The quotation from Herodian was his own invention. It would have pleased him to know that 'Acholius', whom he found in the HA, is a bogus authority. Scholars in the epoch of the Renaissance understood the seductions of literary or erudite imposture. To them the HA was not the enigma it subsequently became. Muretus has an ironical and percipient remark about one of the 'six biographers':

magna huius, quisquis est, Vopisci felicitas: nemo unquam tam curiose in ipsius mendacia inquiret.[3]

---

[1] It was put in after *Max. et Balb.* 15. 7. For the edition printed by Riccius at Venice in 1489 see Hohl, *Klio* XIII (1913), 415 ff.

[2] For 'Catilius Severus' (*PIR²*, C 557), below, p. 279.

[3] Muretus, *Oratio xi.*

11. The search for facts leaves little leisure for the study of 'invention',
in either sense of the term. The biographies have seldom elicited praise
for any literary qualities. Marred both by abridgement and by additions,
the main *Vitae* down to Caracalla are unlovely products; the treatment in
the *Elagabalus* and the *Alexander* is untidy and diversely repellent; and
fatigue grows with the next section, where the events of the year 238 are
retold several times. The repetitive perplexities of 'Capitolinus' about the
identity between Maximus and Pupienus seem to betray a general incompetence; and some readers, if persisting so far, may lack the fortitude
to go on after the gap between the years 244 and 260.

Investigation into the language of the HA acquired, it is true, a
notable incentive after the year 1889. It became necessary to find
differences of vocabulary and diction, to devise criteria for isolating
and defining as many as possible of the 'six biographers'. Much effort
was expended.

It was a further benefit if distinct literary personalities emerged, each
with his own habits and predilections. Why not? A student of literature
has recently coaxed them up again, with embellishment. Spartianus was
sober and intelligent: not the man to forge documents. Lampridius,
whom Constantine esteemed, perhaps went a shade too far in deference
towards the august patron; further, he is prone to moralizing and the
scabrous. Capitolinus has no critical sense, but he can conduct an argument—until rhetoric takes over. Pollio is deficient in historical scruple.
He also lacks the *bonhomie* of Vopiscus, but he has a feeling for drama
and shows a keen interest in works of art. He is a vigorous and sincere
patriot. Vulcatius Gallicanus (with only one *Vita* to his credit) is the least
distinctive member of the group.[1]

From the outset, 'Vopiscus' had his fanciers. When the age of innocence
was about to end, he received a candid appreciation. Vopiscus, given the
unpropitious season when he wrote, exhibited unusual intelligence,
taste, and learning—and a healthy sense of humour.[2] Other tributes soon
followed to the literary quality of Vopiscus (he was perhaps the 'Constantinian editor');[3] but nothing seems to have been made of the humour.
However, a helpful doctrine formed: Vopiscus improved upon Pollio,

---

[1] H. Bardon, *Le Crépuscule des Césars. Scènes et visages de l'Histoire Auguste* (1964),
17 f.

[2] F. Rühl, *Rh. Mus.* XLIII (1888), 597: 'so viel Geschmack, so viel echte Bildung und so
viel gesunden Humor'.

[3] E. Wölfflin, *Bayerische S-B* 1891, Abh. 4, 480 ff., cf. 511; E. Klebs, *Rh. Mus.* XLVII
(1892), 37 ff.; 50 f.

by imitation (that was the way to dispose of suspicious resemblances).[1] Nor should his integrity be called in question.[2]

Loving care equipped each of the 'six biographers' with an identity. And they formed a group, not just a collection, so it was often assumed. On one showing, a company of loyal and zealous courtiers.[3] And the idea of collaboration could not fail to slip in—several of them if not all six. Perhaps 'Vopiscus', helped by one or two friends, touched up a manuscript and continued it.[4] Or again, 'un groupe de rhéteurs', commissioned by a nobleman to execute an urgent task of propaganda. They signed with spurious names, not corresponding to the actual share each had in the project.[5]

To explain the genesis of the HA (on any theory) recourse must be had to the historical imagination. However, no one of the six happens to assert that he is writing in collaboration.[6] Even if he did, sound method would prescribe a doubt, and careful scrutiny.

The attributions of several *Vitae* exhibit plain discrepancies. Attempts were made to sort them out. Labour in vain, so Mommsen opined.[7] His authority, eagerly enlisted wherever possible in the conservative cause, tended to be traversed in this instance.

Mommsen was emboldened to discard one of the six, viz. 'Vulcatius Gallicanus'. Of no more validity, so he pronounced, than any of the persons addressed in the fabricated missives of emperors.[8] Mommsen failed to pursue to the end the logic of his own argument. So did the *epigoni*.

If one of the biographers goes, can any stand? Some scholars reduce the total, generally evading precision of name or number. One recent theory, however (stated rather than argued), keeps three: one to write the *Vitae* down to Severus Alexander inclusive, when Pollio might be supposed to take over, to be continued by the unimpeachable Vopiscus.[9]

Belief in some sort of plurality takes a long time to die.[10] It may derive

---

[1] E. Wölfflin, o.c. 510; H. Peter, *Die Scriptores Historiae Augustae* (1892), 171 ff.; Ch. Lécrivain, *Études sur l'Histoire Auguste* (1904), 392 f.

[2] L. C. Purser, *Hermathena* xv (1909), 55: 'it is difficult to think that Vopiscus was a conscious deceiver.'   [3] H. Peter, o.c. 7 ff.

[4] N. H. Baynes, *The Historia Augusta* (1926), 147 (a reluctant hypothesis, 'merely an attempt to answer friendly criticism').

[5] H. Stern, *Date et destinataire de l'Histoire Auguste* (1953), 98. With appeal to Wölfflin and to Klebs he held that they were six in number.   [6] Above, p. 52.

[7] Mommsen, *Ges. Schr.* VII (1908), 317 f.

[8] Mommsen, o.c. 318.

[9] L. Pareti, *Storia di Roma* VI (1961), 331 f.

[10] Thus A. Momigliano, *JRS* XLIV (1954), 131 = *Secondo Contributo* (1960), 143: 'there is now a general agreement that they were more than one.'

some feeble sustenance among the untutored from the standard term 'Scriptores Historiae Augustae', and the persistent citation of the six names in works of reference. Confronted by the imbroglio, Gibbon made a sagacious choice. He decided to quote the biographies 'without distinction under the general and well-known title of the *Augustan History*'.

III. As in the beginning Dessau divined and decreed, a single literary personality is in cause, varying his manner as he compiles or as he indulges in free composition.[1] The verdict stands, albeit long disputed or evaded.

The impostor conceived the genial idea of passing himself off as a collection of six biographers. That he was able to create an illusion of plurality invites sundry reflections on authors and scholars in any age. On the lowest count, this man deserved credit for his talent. A wrong calls for redress. It will be instructive as well as equitable to examine in summary fashion his performance as a writer.

He was not an elegant exponent. His normal language is flat and monotonous. But uneven, and significantly so. For this author is erudite, a fancier of words, and a collector. Hence many rarities, or even inventions, to the profit of the lexicographer.[2] Two contrasted types of vocabulary may here suffice. First, when depicting the measures of a military disciplinarian, he brings in technical terms redolent of the camps.[3] Second, archaism, preciosity, and flowery words.[4]

The Suetonian genre, dealing in rubrics and the accumulation of small details, offered no encouragement to narrative. None the less, this biographer, when translating and abridging a historical source, can tell a story in sequence, for example the march of Maximinus from Sirmium to Aquileia, and the siege of that city (*Maximin.* 21 ff.).

He is better on the small episode. Notably the act of usurpation, vividly depicted. Thus Regalianus: 'capitali enim ioco regna promeruit.' The thing started from the folly of a pedant who began 'grammaticaliter' to decline 'rex, regis, regi, Regilianus' (*Tyr. trig.* 10. 5). Again, Aemilianus in Egypt. This proclamation issued casually from an angry incident, the natives being notoriously 'furiosi ac dementes' (22. 1 ff.). Appropriate detail is supplied.

One of the prime exhibits is the three days' insurgent Marius, 'vir

---

[1] *Hermes* XXVII (1892), 603.
[2] H. Paucker, *De latinitate scriptorum hist. Aug.* (Dorpat, 1879).
[3] Thus 'buccellatum' (*Pesc.* 10. 4); 'papilio' (11. 1); 'stellatura' (3. 8).
[4] For a brief selection, R. Syme, *Ammianus and the Historia Augusta* (1968), 130.

quidem strenuus' (*Tyr. trig.* 8. 3).[1] Victor or the KG gave the fact that
Marius had originally been an 'opifex ferrarius'.[2] The HA develops the
theme, with an erudite reference to the archetypal smith of ancient legend:
many called him 'Mamurius', some 'Veturius'. Suitable evidence attests
his bodily strength; and he addresses the soldiers in a plain man's vigorous
harangue. The martial smith proudly and neatly adduces his former trade
and the weapons of war, more than once; and he utters the hope that
through his victories 'omnis Alamannia omnisque Germania' shall know
that the Roman People is veritably a 'ferrata gens' (8. 11).

Aurelius Victor made explicit the parallel with the plebeian hero of the
Republic: no wonder, so it was said 'ioculariter', that a man of the same
trade and name and stock should attempt to repair the fabric of empire
(33. 11).[3] The author of the HA was more subtle. He indicated C. Marius
by allusion only, disdaining the obvious. His hero, leading off with 'scio,
commilitones', echoes the Sallustian 'scio ego, Quirites'.[4] And whereas
the speaker in Sallust calls up for detrimental comparison the lazy
luxurious *nobilitas*, the smith Marius exploits instead the wastrel Gallienus
—wine and flowers, women and taverns (8. 10).

To build up a character, the author proceeds by the accumulation of
small details in the fashion of Suetonius. For example, his portrayal of the
Emperor Tacitus. The result is often flat and lifeless: some of the military
rulers, such as Claudius and Probus, are almost interchangeable. The author
is not tempted to go beneath the surface, as is the habit of the Latin historians, bringing up fear, ambition, and anger, or exposing hypocrisy.
But there is a striking exception towards the end. Diocletian left a strong
imprint on the tradition for sagacity and craft, enhanced by his action in
abdicating.[5] The HA responds. Diocletian had always been possessed by
'imperii cupiditas': when he heard the Dryad's prediction in Gaul, 'ut
erat altus, risit et tacuit' (*Car.* 15. 1). There is something more, a brief

---

[1] Marius perished 'post biduum' (Victor 33. 12), or 'secundo die' (Eutropius IX. 9. 2).
The HA has 'tertia die'. But the coins of Imp. Caesar M. Aurelius Marius are very numerous (*PIR*[2], A 1555).

[2] In Victor he is 'ferri quondam opifex' (33. 9), in the curt Eutropius merely 'opifex'
(IX. 9. 2).					[3] No other source alleges that C. Marius was a smith.

[4] *Jug.* 85. 1. Further, this usurper was 'strenuus', a favourite adjective of Sallust (14 times).
Elsewhere in the HA for Pescennius, suitably (*Pesc.* 4. 1); and compare 'Saturninus', an
exemplary general and reluctant usurper—'cum multa strenue in imperio fecisset' (*Tyr.
trig.* 23. 4).

[5] Diocletian abdicated 'ubi fato intestinas clades et quasi fragorem quendam impendere
comperit status Romani' (Victor 39. 48). As for his character, 'moratus callide fuit, sagax
praeterea et admodum subtilis ingenii et qui severitatem suam aliena invidia vellet explere'
(Eutropius IX. 26. 1).

venture in psychology. Diocletian was 'consilii semper alti, nonnumquam tamen ferreae frontis, sed prudentia et nimia pervicacia motus inquieti pectoris comprimentis' (13. 1).

Nor should the skill be neglected that brings out sharp and dramatic contrasts between emperor and emperor. Against Maximinus, a savage and a soldier, he constructs the figure of Gordian, an old senator of cultivated tastes. Various devices are enlisted to parade him as an Antonine ruler. Further, the author has borrowed features (it may be suspected) from some contemporary paragon among the aristocracy, such as Petronius Probus.[1]

Military heroes offered little variety. Between Aurelian and Probus the author neatly sandwiches a scholarly senator, built up with curious detail. A piece of imaginative reconstruction, with no warrant in any source.

iv. Well-earned fatigue attendant upon the events of 238 seems to have dissuaded curiosity about the portrayal of Maximus and Balbinus, to whom the author of the HA decided to devote a whole *Vita*, after he had carried the narrative forward to the death of the third Gordian in 244. The essentials of their brief reign (about three months) had already been recounted.

When the two Gordians were proclaimed in Africa, the Senate took vigorous action, appointing twenty commissioners of consular rank to direct the war against Maximinus. Maximus and Balbinus were among their number. After the catastrophe in Africa they acceded to the imperial power.

The Latin sources were meagre. The HA drew on the fluent and copious narration of Herodian. Also on Dexippus.[2] Neither was wholly adequate. Herodian failed to notice the twenty consulars; and Dexippus put them after the end of the two Gordiani.[3] Nor had either much to offer about the extraction, character, and careers of the two rulers.

Herodian has the following statements.[4] Both were aristocrats, but Balbinus appealed to a superior pedigree and a second consulship. Balbinus had governed with credit a number of provinces. But Maximus held many military commands and had been an excellent *praefectus urbi*; further, as emerges, governor of one of the two Germanies.

Such (it appears) were the sole personal details about the pair to be

---

[1] R. Syme, o.c. 161. [2] Above, pp. 235 f.

[3] *Maximin.* 32. 3 (a note towards the end of the *Vita*). It cannot be taken as certain that the HA is accurate in reporting Dexippus.

[4] Herodian VII. 10. 4, etc. See above, pp. 171 ff.

got from the Greek historian. There is a chance that the KG assigned low
birth to Maximus. That is predicated of both emperors by Eutropius
in brief statement—'obscurissimo genere' (IX. 2. 1).

However that may be, the HA proceeds to draw contrasted pictures
of *novus homo* and aristocrat. Maximus had for parent a smith or, as others
say, a wheelwright (*Max. et Balb.* 5. 1). The mother, called 'Prima', gave
him four sons and four daughters, all of whom died young. Maximus
was brought up in the house of his uncle 'Pinarius'.[1] Of education, only
the rudiments—he was ever intent on 'virtus militaris', he owed his
rearing and sustenance to a lady called 'Pescennia Marcellina' (5. 7).[2]

Various posts in the career of Maximus are enumerated, down to a
command in Illyricum, when he defeated the Sarmatae, and another on
the Rhine, with victories over the Germans (5. 9). Then, an exemplary
Prefect of the City.

The next rubric describes his habits and character. Maximus was 'cibi
avidus, vini parcissimus', and so on (6. 1). In manner he was stern and
grim, 'ita ut et tristis cognomen acciperet', in feature 'gravissimus et
retorridus'. But despite his severity a just man, never 'vel inhumanus vel
inclemens' at the issue of any transaction. He was ready to pardon, he
never gave way to anger (6. 3). He avoided intrigue, and he relied on his
own power of judgement: 'neque aliis potius quam sibi credidit.'

Balbinus, however, was 'nobilissimus et iterum consul, rector pro-
vinciarum infinitarum' (7. 1). Seven provinces are registered, beginning
with Asia and Africa. By the amiable virtues of 'bonitas', 'sanctitas',
and 'verecundia' he won enormous affection. The family was of the most
ancient—he derived his descent from the historian Balbus Cornelius
Theophanes, to whom Pompeius gave the Roman citizenship (7. 3).[3]
As for his habits, 'in voluptatibus nimius', encouraged by great wealth,
which he increased through inheritances.

Thus 'vini, cibi, rei veneriae avidus, vestitu cultus' (8. 6). But he was an
orator of renown and first in rank among the poets of the age.

So far the comparison. In conclusion the author modestly stated that
'nonnulli' have thought of matching Maximus and Balbinus, as Sallust
did Cato and Caesar; and he instances three pairs of suitably contrasted
adjectives (7. 8).[4]

The author has been to some pains. He achieves a vivid study in

---

[1] On 'Pinarius', above, p. 177.
[2] The author has not forgotten the valour of Niger.
[3] For the source of this item, above, p. 5.
[4] For 'nihil largientem' cf. 'nihil largiundo' (*Cat.* 54. 3).

contrasts—already foreshadowed in precise remarks when the two rulers are introduced at an early point in the *Vita* (2. 1; 7 f.). Intervening in the senatorial debate, the senior statesman 'Vectius Sabinus' declares the need and purpose of creating two emperors—'unus qui res domesticas, alter qui bellicas curet' (2. 5). Nominating Maximus and Balbinus, the orator explains their complementary qualities. In the one, merit has exalted 'novitas'; the other began with benefit of birth, to which has accrued 'lenitas morum' and 'vitae sanctimonia' (2. 7).

Partnership in the supreme power, the idea was not novel; and a division of function between a civilian ruler at Rome and a warden of the armies had much in its favour, at least as a temporary measure. This time the arrangement arose from facts, not doctrine or pretext. The Senate's war against Maximinus imposed it.

The author of the HA grasped the idea and gave it a firm formulation. There is no hint in the vague and verbose narration of Herodian. It is irony that the sheer effort of imagination in the HA should show up and condemn the pretensions of a Greek rhetorician passing himself off as a writer of history.

It is also paradox that political insight should be discovered in the HA. Alluding to the dissension arising between Maximus and Balbinus, the author produces an aphorism in the manner of the Latin historians— 'discordiae, sed tacitae et quae intelligerentur potius quam viderentur' (14. 1). He would have gained comfort and cause for quiet merriment had he known the coin legends. Maximus advertises the 'amor mutuus' and 'caritas mutua' of the two Augusti. His colleague responds with 'fides mutua' and 'pietas mutua'.[1]

v. Structure and coherence are elementary virtues in any expositor, be he humble or pretentious. On surface inspection, they are far to seek in the HA.[2] Several of the earlier *Vitae* in the main series are defaced by abridgement, distorted by insertions or appendages. And the author, when he has a free hand, prolongs a biography which seemed to have reached its due termination. The same sort of incompetence is on show in later sections. After the decease of Tacitus and Florianus, a lengthy supplement is subjoined (*Tac.* 15–19).

None the less, there are guiding ideas in the work, conveyed by a variety of devices. The author hit upon the 'nomen Antoninorum', but

[1] R. A. G. Carson, *BMC, R. Emp.* VI (1962), 103.
[2] The author was dubbed 'der erbärmliche Stümper' by Hohl, *Misc. Ac. Berol.* II. 1 (1950), 291.

his employment of the theme is both clumsy and repetitive without advantage; and it entails mendacity about the nomenclature of emperors.[1] The splendid surprise comes later. As has been demonstrated, the author binds together emperor and emperor in a long sequence from Decius to Carus, and beyond, to Diocletian.[2]

It is a palmary exploit. No historian or author of fiction could have contrived the thing better. Curiosity turns to other devices used by novelists. One of them, most potent for creating the illusion of verisimilitude, is the recurrent character. The HA invents some thirty-four historians or biographers. Few of these 'authorities' are cited more than once.[3] But 'Junius Cordus' crops up for repeated employ in five books.

At a later stage the author perceived that he could exploit the reminiscences of his grandfather, more than once.[4] In the space of a few years, this worthy had garnered a precious store. He was in Palestine when the soldiers proclaimed Saturninus, and would often recount the words of the sad and reluctant usurper (*Quadr. tyr.* 9. 4). He seems to have made the acquaintance of the Gothic princess 'Hunila', established in Thrace, whom Aurelian consigned for wife to Bonosus, 'femina singularis exempli' (15. 4). Diocletian disclosed to none other (save Maximianus) the prediction made by the Dryad in Gaul (*Car.* 15. 1). The grandfather (it is to be presumed) had also participated in the Persian expedition of Carus. He was present with the army when Diocletian killed Aper, and he reported the Virgilian quotation that consecrated the act (13. 3).

VI. In the historians of antiquity, intent on facts and narration (as was proper), opinion or doctrine is conveyed by preface or orations. More in the latter. Prefaces tend to be brief, telling little beyond the conventional assertion of accuracy and integrity. The speeches furnish the significant clues to writers as diverse as Thucydides and Tacitus.

Continuing Suetonius, Marius Maximus imported an innovation. He inserted several speeches. The HA responds and multiplies. Its senatorial eloquence repays inspection and deserves a friendly appraisal.

When the Senate made war on Maximinus, a scene was re-enacted that annals and literature had rendered famous in the distant past, not once but twice. The senior statesman Marcius Philippus incited the high assembly to take action against the insurgent Lepidus. Forty-four years later Cicero mustered his eloquence for the contest with Antonius, the

---

[1] Above, Ch. V.   [2] Above, Ch. XIII.
[3] R. Syme, o.c. 203.
[4] A device perhaps taken from Suetonius, cf. R. Syme, o.c. 101 f.

proconsul of Cisalpine Gaul. Cicero was fully conscious of the precedent and parallel.[1]

Cicero begins an oration with complaint about the delays to action:

Parvis de rebus sed fortasse necessariis consulimur, patres conscripti. de Appia via et de Moneta consul, de Lupercis tribunus plebis refert (*Phil.* VII. 1).

In the HA the first speaker after the death of the Gordians has been announced makes a protest: 'minora vos sollicitant.' He goes on to specify public buildings under construction or repair: temples, a basilica, the Baths of Titus, an amphitheatre (*Max. et Balb.* 1. 3 f.).

This speaker calls for action. Then 'Vectius Sabinus ex familia Ulpiorum' intervenes, to enlarge upon the emergency, interpret the proposal, and put forward the two names (2. 1–8).

The oration is vigorous and well constructed. One of its forcible phrases might suggest Sallust in the speech of Philippus, viz. 'vos sedendo et consultando diem teritis' (2. 4).[2]

Delay to take action is also castigated in a later *Vita* where 'Ulpius Silanus' is the orator. He begins 'sero nimis, p.c., de rei p. salute consulimur' (*Aur.* 19. 3). One should compare the exordium of Cicero's *Third Philippic*: 'serius omnino, patres conscripti, quam tempus rei publicae postulabat, aliquando tamen convocati sumus.'

The author is aware of the classical models, but is not a slavish imitator. He has been able to reproduce the dignity and energy of high debate, with statesmen on show whose eloquence recalled the ancient days.

The long and solemn oration of 'Maecius Faltonius Nicomachus' falls into place (*Tac.* 6). And minor felicities reveal a composer with a subtle ear for propriety of discourse. An emperor in a dispatch to the Senate adopts the exordium of a senator, 'recte atque ordine'; and, addressing those 'qui et estis mundi principes et semper fuistis et in vestris posteris eritis', he refers to 'clementia vestra' (*Prob.* 11. 2).[3]

The glory of the Republic and the majesty of empire annex a potent testimony from aliens. In three epistles the vassal princes issue a warning to the Persian monarch (*Val.* 1–3). Sapor must not fancy that he has gained any advantage by having made captive a Roman emperor. The argument is reinforced by a notable aphorism—'Romani enim graviores tunc sunt quando vincuntur' (2. 1). For this congenial exercise the author could

---

[1] R. Syme, *Sallust* (1964), 220 f.

[2] That is, the tone and manner of *Hist.* I. 77, not any specific phrase.

[3] In Sallust the consul Lepidus, addressing the People, leads off with 'clementia et probitas vestra' (*Hist.* I. 55. 1).

draw general inspiration from the famous letter in Sallust, sent by Mithridates to the Parthian.[1]

VII. Next, prefaces. To explain what he is about, the author is eager and voluble. The four main programmatic statements are significant documents.[2] The first is the preface to the *Vita Macrini*. The subject is good biography against bad, the latter exemplified by the inept 'Junius Cordus', who filled volumes with trivial items, reporting of any emperor, as though he were Trajan or Pius or Marcus, 'quotiens processerit, quando cibos variaverit et quando vestem mutaverit et quos quando promoverit' (1. 4). The serious biographer confines himself to 'digna memoratu'.[3]

The exordium of the *Vita Aureliani* conveys an urbane interchange between 'Vopiscus' and the Prefect of the City.[4] From biography ('Trebellius Pollio' is both criticized and defended) the discourse moves forward to history, the four classic exponents being named: Livy, Sallust, Tacitus, Trogus. 'Vopiscus' shall write without fear, having for companions in mendacity the paladins of 'historica eloquentia' (2. 2).

The *Probus* brings up the four names. Also a brief catalogue of six exemplary writers of biography,

Marium Maximum, Suetonium Tranquillum, Fabium Marcellinum, Gargilium Martialem, Iulium Capitolinum, Aelium Lampridium (2. 7).

They wrote, 'non tam diserte quam vere'. The author here pronounces against the 'eloquium celsius' of historians (2. 6). Facts not style, that is the thing (1. 6).[5]

Finally the *Quadrigae tyrannorum*. 'Trebellius Pollio' earns warm praise for his 'diligentia' and his 'cura' (1. 3), while Marius Maximus comes in for stern denunciation: careless and verbose and a composer of 'mythistorica volumina' (1. 2). The author then proceeds to furnish an object lesson in the technique of verification. He reminds his friend 'Bassus' of the debate they once held with four other fanciers: the usurper Firmus was in question, the evidence of coins being adduced (2. 1 f.).

The argument set out in the four prefaces advances by a logical progression to assert the primacy of biography over history and demonstrate

---

[1] *Hist.* IV. 69, cf. R. Syme o.c. (1968), 42.

[2] Of less consequence are the remarks in the secondary *Vitae* (above, p. 55).

[3] Compare Ammianus, noting trivial details, and continuing 'et similia plurima, praeceptis historiae dissonantia, discurrere per negotiorum celsitudines adsuetae, non humilium minutias indagare causarum' (XXVI. 1. 1).

[4] Above, p. 17.

[5] Observe the close verbal parallel in *Tyr. trig.* 33. 8.

the erudition and candour of the good biographer. The attack on the high style of historians may inspire a pertinent reflection.[1]

VIII. It is a pleasing sight in any age to contemplate a writer developing his resources as he goes on, and gaining in audacity. Various other signs confirm.

He can take a hint from some source and exploit it to the utmost. Aurelius Victor, it may be conjectured, was the starting-point for the list of eleven generals formed in the school of Probus. A single statement of Victor about the smith who was a usurper inspired a Sallustian vignette. Further, from the notion that the emperor Maximus was a *novus homo* the author went on to shape a full-size confrontation between two rulers.

The KG reported a statement made by Probus after his victories— armies would soon become superfluous.[2] Whereupon the HA divagates into ingenious declamation. No soldiers, hence no imposts, no requisitions, no manufacturing of weapons, and so forth (*Prob.* 23. 2 ff.). In fact, an 'aureum saeculum'. That nation of the military, which now plagues the Commonwealth with civil strife, would be diverted into useful occupations: 'araret, studiis incumberet, erudiretur artibus, navigaret.' There is a solemn lesson for the present time: 'eant nunc, qui ad civilia bella milites parant, in germanorum necem armant dexteras fratrum, . . .' (23. 5).

The discovery of mistakes in predecessors engendered critical sense in the author—or at least confidence in his own discernment. The earlier part of the work showed familiarity with the expression 'duo Gordiani, pater et filius'.[3] Realizing now that there were three Gordians, he blames 'quidam imperiti scriptores' for their error (*Gord.* 2. 1).[4] Another piece of 'scriptorum imperitia' held the boy Gordian to be Prefect of the Guard (*Max. et Balb.* 15. 6)—that is, Aurelius Victor (27. 1) The Latin sources also alleged that Pupienus had killed Maximinus at Aquileia (15. 4).[5]

Further, annoyed by the perplexity into which he had fallen because the Maximus of the Greek writers was Pupienus in the Latins, the author denounces the 'imperitia vel usurpatio' of the authorities (*Max. et Balb.* 15. 5). Indeed, he will parade as a historian in his own right. Inserting elsewhere an imperial missive, he states 'ut alios annalium scriptores fecisse video' (*Aur.* 17. 1). It is no surprise that towards the end he can

---

[1] That is, the History of Ammianus (in part at least) had been given to the world.

[2] Victor 37. 3; Eutropius IX. 17. 3.

[3] *Diad.* 6. 3, etc. Above, p. 84.

[4] Perhaps Victor rather than the KG. For the imbroglio about the Gordiani see further above, p. 232.   [5] Victor 27. 4; Eutropius IX. 11.

come out with a panoramic survey of all Rome's history from Romulus to Carus (*Car.* 2 f.).

This author has a subject: good emperors, the Senate, the Roman tradition. He is not deficient in the sense of design.[1] On the contrary, consummate skill in connecting and interweaving; and he insists on using usurpers as well as emperors to further his purposes.

That device was a novelty. Not so the doctrines that emerge.[2] The contrary would surprise. Political thought among the Romans, even when, as with Tacitus, it reflected the facts and necessities of a historical situation (or predicament), cannot assert much claim to depth or originality.

Nor was strict consistency at a premium. The HA commends adoption against birth and parades a noisy affection for emperors chosen by the Senate. At the same time, it acclaims Claudius as the ancestor of a dynasty. Which has been the cause of perplexity to some scholars.[3] The author would discover no embarrassment. The poet Claudian celebrates a prince nurtured in the purple: 'patrio felix adolescis in ostro.'[4] In another panegyric on Honorius the poet duly pays homage to the line of the 'adoptive emperors'.[5]

IX. The HA discloses a literary personality. He turns out to be a writer of great skill and versatility, alert and audacious. A number of his signal exploits have already been put on show.

He professes to be a conscientious biographer, and he reinforces the claim by a wealth of documentation. Also by providing variants and scholarly dubitations. He is never at a loss for a plausible and corroborative detail. Care for learning is evinced by quotations from the classics or by neat allusions. It is also manifest in characters he admires. Severus Alexander was a scholar as well as a soldier: and he liked to have men of letters about him, especially historians (*Alex.* 16. 3). In climax, a descendant of Tacitus is chosen emperor by the Senate: who better (*Tac.* 3. 4)?

Such is the *persona*. But, it will be objected, the fellow is an impostor. The best part of his achievement, and the larger, is pure fiction.

Imposture was a challenge to literary talent. The author had to forge evidence for authentication. This he did in various ways, first of all by the dedications to Diocletian and Constantine. And it was expedient to avoid flagrant anachronism (mere absurdity would not have worried him).

[1] Baynes, o.c. 110.
[2] At need Marius Maximus and the imperial panegyrics might help.
[3] Thus Baynes, o.c. 57 (above, p. 207).　　　[4] *De IV cons. Hon.* 125.
[5] *De VI cons. Hon.* 417 ff., quoted above, p. 93.

For all his cleverness, he was not always alert to damaging discrepancy about the time of writing. To the author of the *Vita Claudii*, Constantius is still Caesar (*Claud.* 1. 1 etc.). That is, before May 1, 305, when he became Augustus, Diocletian abdicating. In the next *Vita*, 'est quidem iam Constantius imperator (*Aur.* 44. 5). That is 305/6, a close dating ostensibly (if 'Vopiscus' was familiar with the precise chronology). Further, Diocletian is described in the vicinity as 'iam privatus' in the report of the conversation he had with the author's father (43. 2). So far so good. Here and henceforth to the end the author carefully eschews any mention of Constantine.[1]

But Constantine had previously figured as the dedicant of four of the main *Vitae* composed by 'Lampridius' and by 'Capitolinus'.[2] And two of them carry corroboratory allusions. The latter author knows that Licinius has become emperor (*Gord.* 34. 5), whereas 'Lampridius' ingenuously assures Constantine that he will furnish a veracious account of his defeated rivals (Licinius among them), not passing over their good qualities (*Elag.* 35. 6). Licinius was overthrown in 324.

'Lampridius' and 'Capitolinus' are registered among the six good biographers in the *Probus* (2. 7). 'Vopiscus' therefore reckons them as predecessors in the noble art. What then is the remedy? The answer is, none. The author ran into trouble, and any who try to rescue him are in an even worse case.[3]

The author descants upon the Claudian ancestry of Constantius, whom he salutes as the destined progenitor of a line of Augusti (*Claud.* 10. 7). He did not know that the ancestry was only discovered and published when four years had elapsed after the death of Constantius. Had he known, he could have slipped through the way of escape favoured by some scholars in the modern age: Constantius or his son disclosed the great secret in advance, by special indulgence towards a loyal adherent and friend of the family.[4]

The author would not worry. He is immune from care or repining. It is his habit to create doubt and perplexity. After quoting a decree of the Senate (with its exact repository in the Bibliotheca Ulpia), he later says that he could not trace the document (*Tac.* 8. 1; *Prob.* 7. 1).

This genial impostor likes to display versatility. He can essay a splendid

---

[1] Instead, the Tetrarchy, as notably in *Car.* 9. 3; 18. 3 f., with much about Diocletian in that *Vita*, and a separate reference to Constantius (17. 6).

[2] Namely *Elag.*, *Alex.*, *Maximin.*, *Gord.*

[3] The two damaging names were dismissed as interpolations by Peter (in his edition 1884), and by Klebs, o.c. 518.

[4] Above, p. 204.

pastiche of senatorial eloquence, and he goes in for parody of erudite technique. In fact, a humorist of no mean order.

Many of the jokes are trivial and vulgar, to be sure. But wit and 'urbanitas' bring off some notable effects, such as the dialogue between 'Vopiscus' and the jesting Prefect. The scene is in fact laid at the *Hilaria*, a carnival with masks and impersonation. Further, the author developed a gift for bathos and the subversive. Hence the portrayal of usurpation as comedy no less than folly: the culmination is the *Quadrigae tyrannorum*. Or observe the long and solemn pageantry at the *decennalia* of Gallienus. The emperor interrupts it, clamouring for dinner and diversions—'ecquid habemus in prandio?' (*Gall.* 9. 3).

XVII · FICTION AND CREDULITY

A ROGUE SCHOLAR saw the fun to be got from erudition. His achievement stands out when once the belief is discarded that the HA is nothing more than incompetent and dishonest biography. An attempt might be made to put him in some literary genre, or at least in the vicinity.

The task is not easy. There is the question of category: fictional history or historical fiction. Two aids are lacking. No comprehensive study exists, dealing either with fraud and impersonation or with the historical novel. Vast and exciting themes, from the remote beginnings to the latest repercussions.

1. From researches in Persian archives, Ctesias, the royal doctor, was able to reproduce long periods of oriental history. For example, a whole sequence of monarchs in Media, leading off with 'Arbaces'.[1] The exploits of Ctesias encouraged Xenophon to compose the edifying romance about Cyrus not long after.

Ctesias assigned plausible names to his characters. Thus 'Artaeus', King of Media, who duly conducts a campaign against the Cadusii.[2] Some are lifted from contemporary transactions. Arbaces was one of the four generals who commanded the Persian host at the battle of Cunaxa.[3] Ctesias was there.[4] Xenophon was also present on that day. He registers Abrocomas along with Arbaces.[5] In the *Cyropaedia*, 'Abradates' and 'Panthea' enact a sentimental episode.[6] Centuries later 'Abrocomes' and 'Anthea' turn up as the pair of lovers in the romance composed by Xenophon of Ephesus, himself a pseudonym.[7] Tricks played with names, and also the deformation of names, will come as no surprise to any who care to inspect the HA.

---

[1] Diodorus II. 32. 4.

[2] ib. 33. 1 ff. The Cadusii (the later Gelae) tend to survive as a name in obsolete contexts —or in historical fiction. For Cadusii in the HA, cf. R. Syme, *Ammianus and the Historia Augusta* (1968), 35; 42.   [3] Xenophon, *Anab*. I. 7. 12.

[4] Plutarch, *Artax*. 11, etc.   [5] *Anab*. I. 7. 12.

[6] For other invented names in that work see H. R. Breitenbach, P–W IX A. 1712 ff.

[7] This 'Xenophon' is patently a pseudonym, cf. R. Kudlien, P–W IX A. 2058 f. For the choice of names, ib. 2069.

The Hellenistic age indulged in a proliferation of fabrications. Thus imaginative biography, letters written by statesmen or sages, exotic and Utopian romance, erudite mystifications. There was no abatement later in the Roman imperial period. As witness Ptolemaeus Chennus in the time of Trajan or the unknown author who translated from the Phoenician document the narration of Dictys (it was found in his tomb in Crete).[1]

From the outset, the annals of Rome were vitiated by 'Graecia mendax'. That phrase of Juvenal was not coined to impugn the most pernicious of audacities: the satirist might have adverted upon the national performance. The first native historian was Fabius Pictor, a Roman senator who wrote in Greek. Two specimens may suffice to illustrate the use of corroborative detail. Tarquinius Superbus spent forty talents on the construction of the Capitoline temple; and Coriolanus averred that exile bears harder on a man when he grows old.[2]

Such is the suitable exordium. In the last age Rome rediscovered erudition and dug up forgotten writings from the old empire. At the same time, prose fiction enjoyed enormous favour. The romance about Alexander (the pseudo-Callisthenes) was translated, about 330; Dictys the Cretan probably towards the end of the century; while the Phrygian Dares (who related the other side of the war at Troy) may belong somewhat later.[3]

Alexander and the Tale of Troy, those are the themes of predilection in the Middle Ages. To round off brief indications, a word may go to a masterpiece of the twelfth century: the *Historiae Regum Britanniae* composed by Geoffrey of Monmouth. His technique calls for appraisal.

Arviragus, a British prince, after leading resistance against the invasion, came to terms with Claudius Caesar and married his daughter. But he raised rebellion, and he fought in an indecisive campaign against Vespasian. His fame resounded through Europe, and no king was more celebrated at Rome (IV. 12–16). Juvenal testifies.[4]

This ingenious contriver also puts to good employ Asclepiodotus, the general of Constantius. Originally a duke of Cornwall, Asclepiodotus defeated Allectus, and also 'Livius Gallus, Allecti collega'. Liberating the island, he assumed the diadem and reigned for ten years, promoting justice and repressing brigandage. In the end, he was killed by Coel of Colchester. Coel in his turn was suppressed by the Roman senator

---

[1] For the former, A. Dihle, P–W XXIII. 1862.   [2] Livy I. 55. 8; II. 40. 10.

[3] For Dictys and Dares cf. brief remarks in R. Syme, o.c. 123 ff.

[4] Geoffrey cites (with one verbal error) Juvenal IV. 126 f.: 'regem aliquem capies aut de temone Britanno / excidet Arviragus.'

Constantius, who then married his daughter Helena: a lovely girl devoted to liberal studies (v. 4–6).

To enliven and certify his fluent narration, Geoffrey needed a multitude of characters. Where he got the names can often be divined. A number reflect his reading of late Republican history. Micipsa becomes a Babylonian, Bocchus a king of the Medes; and Sertorius is a ruler in Libya (x. 8).

Geoffrey comes out with new combinations of *nomen* and *cognomen*, often incongruous and thereby revealing. Thus the Roman senators Petreius Cotta, Marcellus Mucius, and Marius Lepidus (x. 4; 8).[1] And some may suspect that Q. Milvius Catulus (x. 1), who falls in battle along with Marius Lepidus (x. 9), derived his *nomen* from the famous bridge outside Rome where Q. Lutatius Catulus defeated a Lepidus.[2] Grotesque and comic inventions abound, such as Ferrex and Pollex, the sons of Gorboduc (ii. 16).[3]

To throw together the real and the fictitious is an old device of verisimilitude and deceit, as exhibited in the HA and in recent practitioners of the novel. Blended catalogues come in useful.[4] And a name often supplies a clue to source or date.[5]

Thus Geoffrey invents Anacletus, a treacherous Greek in the days of Brutus the Trojan (i. 5). Which reflects the pope of unsavoury repute in the author's own time. Further, Geoffrey was able to allude to one of his own predecessors in fictional history. He has Nennius kill the Roman tribune Labienus when Caesar invades the island (iv. 3). The name 'Labienus' was taken from Orosius, where it is a mistake for 'Laberius' in Julius Caesar.[6]

Geoffrey is erudite, citing Juvenal or referring to Apuleius (vi. 8). Likewise alert and scrupulous. There was a learned lady of high birth, Marcia, who composed the *Lex Marciana*. King Alfred came upon the document and translated it into Anglo-Saxon, calling it erroneously the 'Law of Mercia' (iii. 13).

---

[1] For this type in the HA, cf. 'Ablavius Murena' (above, p. 216); 'Fabia Orestilla' (above, p. 169).

[2] Florus ii. 11. 6. For the invention, cf. 'Mulvius Gallicanus' (above, p. 217). The form 'Milvius' occurs in manuscripts (e.g. some of Ammianus xxvii. 3. 9) and is retained in modern texts of Victor (19. 4; 40. 23). As a Latin *gentilicium* it is probably not on record.

[3] For comic names in the HA, R. Syme, o.c. 173 f.

[4] Thus H. G. Wells, *Ann Veronica* (1909), 143: 'the giant leaders of the Fabian Society. . . Bernard Shaw and Toomer and Dr. Tumpany'. Inventing a poet Canalis, Balzac registered him with Lamartine, Hugo, and others, several times.

[5] In the *Greenmantle* of John Buchan (1916), Hilda von Einem derives patently from the man who became Prussian Minister for War in 1902.

[6] Orosius vi. 9. 5, from *BG* v. 15. 5.

A candid author disclaims style and originality. The man who in a library at Athens came upon the manuscript of Dares the Phrygian states that it was written 'vere et simpliciter', and he confines himself to making a faithful translation.[1] Geoffrey was also modest—'agresti tamen stylo propriisque calamis contentus'. Preoccupation with style, he says, fatigues the reader and impedes the understanding of history. With this profession Geoffrey proposes to render into Latin that 'Britannici sermonis librum vetustissimum' which he got from his friend Walter the Archdeacon (I. 1).

The various artifices of Geoffrey encourage a look backwards to notable performers such as the author of the HA, Fulgentius the bishop of Ruspe, or the lunatic grammarian Virgilius of Tolosa.[2] Also forwards to erudite rogues in Italy of the Renaissance like Annius of Viterbo, who fabricated whole tracts of history, with proper documentation.[3] Nor were antiquarian studies immune, in a later age.[4]

The author of the HA exhibits an original choice. Not the remote, the exotic, the legendary. He deals with recent imperial history, coming down to a century before his own time. The product is a blend of influences old and new: scholiastic lore and the collection of 'curiosa', bogus letters and panegyrical eloquence, lives of pagan sages. How might the literary genre be defined? The author furnishes a clue. He denounces the 'mythistoriae' of the execrable 'Junius Cordus' and the 'mythistorica volumina' composed by Marius Maximus.[5]

II. It was not literature that led to revelation. The discovery that shook the 'templa serena' of classical scholarship in the year 1889 arose by good fortune from a necessary task of assessing names and persons. Dessau was at work on Volume II of the *Prosopographia Imperii Romani*.[6] The enterprise had other by-products. Klebs was in charge of the first volume (A–C). In 1888 he came out with a study of Avidius Cassius, which demolished the *Vita* of that pretender; and a paper in the next year showed up the fraudulent genealogy of Constantius.[7]

---

[1] Dares in his preface (a letter from Cornelius Nepos to Sallustius Crispus).

[2] R. Syme, o.c. 125.

[3] Parallels were duly adduced by Dessau, *Hermes* XXVII (1892), 572 ff. For an alert and sympathetic appraisal of erudite imposture see C. Mitchell, 'Archaeology and Romance in Renaissance Italy', in *Italian Renaissance Studies* (ed. E. F. Jacob, 1960), 455 ff.

[4] As witness Charles Bertram who in 1757 published the *Itinerarium* of 'Richard of Winchester': not shown up until 1866. See the article in *DNB*.   [5] Above, p. 76.

[6] Above, p. 7. He had made his début with a suitable subject, *De sodalibus et flaminibus augustalibus* (Diss. Berlin, 1877).

[7] E. Klebs, *Rh. Mus.* XLIII (1888), 321 ff.; *Hist. Zeitschr.* LXI (1889), 213 ff.

But Klebs could not (or would not) see that his argument overturned the ostensible date of the *Vita Claudii*. Further, in certain contributions to *PIR*, Vol. I, he retailed information about emperors without giving the slightest sign that it should be held suspect: thus on Gordianus and on Pupienus.[1] Some small fry he condemned, it is true: three persons called 'Celsus', and the consul 'Celsus Aelianus'.[2] But no note of warning accompanies, for example, 'Annius Cornicula', who praised Gallienus, 'Annius Severus', the father-in-law of Gordian, 'Aurelius Verus', who wrote a life of Trajan, 'Aurelius Festivus', the freedman of the Emperor Aurelian.[3]

Volumes I and II of the *Prosopographia* were published in 1897, Volume III in the next year. Another great enterprise, Pauly–Wissowa, had entered the field in 1894. Several of the articles on emperors conveyed antiquated knowledge. Various fables were admitted for Severus Alexander; and the HA's genealogy of Gordian was published on a stemma.[4] Credit was also given to the Claudian ancestry of Constantius.[5] Even Stein in the third volume (1899) kept far too much of the *Vita Taciti*, including the long 'interregnum' after the death of Aurelian and the 'senatorial policy' of Tacitus.[6] Groag, however, in his exemplary article on Aurelian, reduced the 'interregnum' to a month and a half.[7]

In the meantime the impact of the new learning on the facts of imperial history had been blunted or diverted by other preoccupations. The need was urgent to confront or elude the conclusions of Dessau about date and authorship. Mommsen was impelled to a quick response, among other reasons because in the *Staatsrecht* he had given credit to sundry assertions of the HA. While making notable concessions to Dessau, he tried to save what he could by postulating two editors, one in the late years of Constantine, the other under Theodosius.[8] That was not good enough for Klebs. He took an obdurate stand on the 'traditional date'.[9] So did the veteran Peter.[10]

The authority was impressive, likewise the learning and dexterity of argumentation. Other support accrued.[11] It seemed that the baneful

---

[1] *PIR*[1], A 664; C 929.   [2] *PIR*[1], C 533–5; 541.

[3] *PIR*[1], A 480; 529; 1313; 1248.   [4] P. v. Rohden, P–W I. 2619 f.

[5] Henze, P–W II. 2458.

[6] A. Stein, P–W III. 2872 ff. He even spoke of 'der Sieg des Senatsidee' (ib. 2876).

[7] E. Groag, P–W v. 1358; 1403 f.

[8] Mommsen, *Hermes* XXV (1890), 273 = *Ges. Schr.* VII (1909), 344.

[9] E. Klebs, *Rh. Mus.* XLV (1890), 436 ff.; XLVII (1892), 1 ff.; 515 ff. For his first article Klebs was able to use the proofs of Mommsen's paper in *Hermes*.

[10] H. Peter, *Die Scriptores Historiae Augustae* (1892), 242 ff.

[11] Thus G. De Sanctis, *Rivista di storia antica* I (1896), 90 ff.

influences of Dessau had been at least neutralized, and in the early years of the century inquiry took another direction, to concentrate upon the dissection of the earlier *Vitae*. Valuable results were achieved, notably for the *Commodus*.[1] But the dichotomy between good history and bad biography issued in the unhappy postulate of a great annalist writing in the reign of Severus Alexander.[2]

The later *Vitae* fell under some neglect. Conservative critics, it is true, had recognized the existence of large masses of fiction; and Peter produced a masterly exposure of *Tyranni triginta*.[3]

But there was much more than they fancied. In 1911 Hohl demonstrated the tiny residuum of fact in the *Vita Taciti*. His arguments, adducing suspicious parallels in other *Vitae* (including some in the earlier portion), also bore upon authorship.[4] Nor was Hohl indifferent to the question of the HA's design and purpose.[5]

Purpose and date received a novel and notable stimulus from Baynes in 1926. His ingenious thesis engrossed attention. Whatever its fate, it showed how fraudulent is the biography of Severus Alexander. But it diverted curiosity from other pieces of fiction—and from the general literary problem of the HA.

III. Allusion has been made in these pages more than once to the significance of the *Vita Taciti*. It was strange that through the years nobody seemed drawn to the *Quadrigae tyrannorum*, that other masterpiece in the mature manner which the author artfully inserted between the high themes of Probus and Carus as a variegated study in comic effects.

The preface, after praising 'Trebellius Pollio' for the diligence and accuracy he displayed in the *Thirty Tyrants*, discusses the technique of authentication and ends with a tribute to the writer's own candour— he had previously been in error when describing Firmus as nothing better than a petty brigand (2. 3, cf. *Aur.* 32. 2). All four rose against Aurelian, it is there stated: Firmus, Saturninus, Proculus, Bonosus (1. 4). The narration shows that to be true only for Firmus.

Firmus, insurgent in Egypt, finds mention in no other extant author.[6] The KG had the other three, hence brief mention already in the *Vita*

---

[1] J. M. Heer, *Philol.*, Supp. IX (1904), 1 ff. Heer's paper itself was published in 1901.
[2] Above, p. 34.
[3] H. Peter, *Abh. der phil.-hist. Kl. der K. sächsischen Ges. der Wiss.* XXVII (1909), 179 ff.
[4] E. Hohl, *Klio* XI (1911), 298 ff.; 319 ff.
[5] Hohl, *Neue Jahrbücher* XXXIII (1914), 698 ff.; *Hermes* LV (1920), 296 ff.
[6] Trouble at Alexandria under Aurelian is briefly alluded to by Ammianus (XXII. 16. 15) and by Zosimus (I. 61. 1).

Probi.[1] About one of them, Saturninus, more was to be got from a Greek writer (the source of Zosimus and Zonaras), including the notice that he was proclaimed in Syria and killed at Apamea.[2] The HA happens to refer to 'Onesimus, scriptor vitae Probi' (*Quadr. tyr.* 14. 4, cf. 13. 1)— which is short of proof that he existed (cf. *Prob.* 1. 3). But facts would only be an embarrassment to this artist.

The HA takes Saturninus to Egypt and puts his proclamation later, in Palestine, with suitable embellishments.[3] As for Proculus and Bonosus, it suppresses the fact (recorded previously in the *Vita Probi*) that they raised rebellion together at Agrippina. They are disjoined, totally. Proculus makes a proclamation at Lugdunum (13. 1), whereas Bonosus is left on the Rhine (15. 1).[4]

The narration is vivid, precise, and copious. Not all scholars have been able to resist the seduction of the picturesque details vouchsafed about the extraction and habits of the four usurpers. Even Firmus retains credit as a merchant prince with wide commercial activities.[5] Serious attention goes to the campaigns of Proculus and Bonosus; and Proculus, alleged a brigand from Albingaunum in Liguria, is allowed to keep that *patria*.[6] Likewise 'Samso' for his wife, with no discomfort felt.[7] Indeed, a standard work of reference recounts with apparent approbation most of what the HA has to say about Proculus.[8]

Others, however, are ready to maintain that nothing in the *Quadrigae tyrannorum* can pass for authentic save the bare names of the four usurpers. A question of method and principle is involved. When a piece of writing comes under suspicion, the defence is prone to assume authenticity unless or until absolute proof can be provided. Thus for Pseudo-Sallust.[9] By the nature of the case, proof of that order may not be available. It might not even be needed.[10]

As concerns the HA, when this or that item is confidently pronounced

---

[1] *Prob.* 18. 4. For the KG, cf. Victor 37. 3; Eutropius IX. 17. 1; *Epit.* 37. 2.

[2] *PIR*[2], J 546.

[3] Above, p. 18.

[4] For these three usurpers in relation to the scanty known facts, cf. R. Syme, o.c. 55 f.

[5] H. Mattingly, *CAH* XII (1939), 305. For the fictions about Firmus, above, p. 18.

[6] C. Jullian, *Histoire de la Gaule* IV (1913), 610 f.

[7] H. Mattingly, *CAH* XII (1939), 316. For 'Samso', above, p. 26.

[8] R. Hanslik, P-W XXIII. 75 f.: with errors, and with omission of *Epit.* 37. 2.

[9] K. Vretska, *C. Sallustius Crispus. Invektive und Episteln* I (1961), 15.

[10] Jacoby's treatment of Pseudo-Plutarch, *Parallela Minora* affords instruction and guidance (*Abh. zur gr. Geschichtsschreibung* (1956), 359 ff., reprinted from *Mnem.*[3] VIII (1940), 73 ff.). He enounced a principle: 'der Gesamteindruck entscheidet' (ib. 415); and, for any single item, the onus of proof lies on the defenders (ib. 363).

to be spurious, the sceptical (and the credulous) will properly ask for reasons, either general or particular. Taken as a whole, the HA exudes fraud. Therefore, so it might seem, nothing deserves to be accepted that is not confirmed by independent testimony.

That formulation is narrow and misleading. Distinctions must be drawn. For the lives of the emperors from Hadrian to Caracalla inclusive, the basic source was excellent. Numerous facts and names can be recovered, lacking other attestation, and not requiring it. Though uncertainty must subsist about a few items, the main result passes muster. In the later *Vitae*, despite the overwhelming mass of fiction, here and there, after proper inspection, valuable information emerges, even though the sources cannot always be defined or named.

For detecting fakes in the realm of the fine arts, no general rules can be prescribed, so it has been said.[1] As for the HA, the odour and context of a passage is often enough. There is something more. If the habits of the impostor are catalogued, and the emergence step by step of his fabrications, items not otherwise questionable fall into line.

Zeal in a good cause may go too far. Some persons in the earlier *Vitae* were impugned through a failure to regard source and context. Of the later fabrications not many, once detected, have had to be redeemed in the sequel. Of the Thirty Tyrants, Peter scouted 'Celsus', insurgent in Africa with aid from the proconsul 'Vibius Passienus' and the woman 'Galliena' (*Tyr. trig.* 29).[2] But he was also impelled to discard Aemilianus, the pretender in Egypt (22. 1 ff.).[3] That Aemilianus, however, had a mention in the KG (cf. *Epit.* 32. 4); and he is now certified as L. Mussius Aemilianus.[4] Peter further conceived strong doubts about Piso, who *inter alia* was 'Frugi dictus' and had a statue at Rome still to be seen (21. 1; 5 f.).[5] Piso, lacking warrant as a pretender, will keep his existence— as a general of Gallienus, for he occurs elsewhere in a good narrational context.[6]

The process of subversive inquiry incriminates ever more particulars. For example, names in a catalogue of senators killed by Septimius Severus,

---

[1] O. Kurz, *Fakes* (ed. 2, 1967), vi. He has useful remarks about fakes that lack models (303 ff.); the betraying symptoms of the period of fabrication (317); personal ambition and the delight in deceit (319).

[2] Peter, o.c. 219. See above, p. 7. Further, J. Schwartz, *Ant. class.* xxxiii (1964), 419 ff.

[3] Peter, o.c. 216.

[4] A. Stein, *Die Präfekten von Ägypten* (1950), 143 ff.; 227 ff.

[5] Peter, o.c. 215 f. In 1965 I incautiously assumed that this Piso never existed (above, p. 6). The fraudulent details seemed to discredit him. Compare 'Calpurnia' a little further on (32. 5 f.).

[6] *Gall.* 2. 1 ff. Compare, for Aemilianus, *Gall.* 4. 1; 5. 6; 9. 1.

among them six Pescennii.[1] Before that point, only one such forgery
is on clear record in the main *Vitae*, viz. the jurist 'Diabolenus' (*Pius*
12. 1).[2] But 'Apollonius Syrus Platonicus' deserves no credit, who reported an oracular response from the shrine of Juppiter Nicephorius
(*Hadr.* 2. 9).[3] Other sources do not attribute prophecy to the famous
temple at Antioch. The preceding notice carried a consultation of 'sortes
Vergilianae': a cherished device of the erudite impostor.[4]

iv. The historian Sallust saw ambition and contentiousness as the primor-
dial 'vitium humani ingenii'. That independent spirit would not have been
loath to censure the habit of deference and the will to believe. Some scholars
approach the HA in the hope and design of saving as much as possible.
Documents, it is suggested, may derive from pamphlets; and the letters
addressed to Sapor by the oriental princes (*Val.* 1–3) might be propaganda
circulated by the Roman government after the capture of Valerian by the
Persians.[5] Again, references to the Bibliotheca Ulpia and to the 'libri
lintei' should inspire confidence; and the reports of proceedings in the
Senate are authentic, on the whole. It was easy to verify and control.[6]

The summons to consult archives or authorities was also easy. Tertullian
knew that.[7] The art of apologists in eking out the 'scanty and suspicious
materials of ecclesiastical history' will afford instruction and entertainment.
Two devices are to be recommended. First, a statement is plausible, it
cannot be controverted. Second, a dubious document may be 'good in
parts'.[8]

Both devices are on show in the study of the HA. First, the plausible.
The author had some good sources for the middle of the third century
(i.e. Greek sources), if he cared to use them. But his true bent is invention,
and he can carry off some master-strokes. For example, he puts a group
of Gothic ladies at Perinthus (*Quadr. tyr.* 15. 6). A neglected fact can be
dug up: the station called Gothi on the road outside that city.[9] It is

---

[1] *Sev.* 13, cf. E. Birley, *Bonner Historia-Augusta-Colloquium 1964/5* (1966), 37. Of the
forty-two names, thirty-two are vindicated by G. Alföldy, ib. *1968/9* (1970), 4 f.

[2] *Pius* 12. 1, cf. above, p. 38.

[3] 'Apollonius' is not impugned in *PIR²*, A 928.

[4] Dessau, *Hermes* XXVII (1892), 582 ff.

[5] H. Bardon, *Le Crépuscule des Césars. Scènes et visages de l'Histoire Auguste* (1964), 26.

[6] ib.: 'le contrôle était aisé.'

[7] Tertullian, *Apol.* XXI. 19 (on an alleged eclipse of the sun): 'et tamen eum mundi casum
in arcanis vestris habetis.' Again, for those who raised doubts about the parentage of Christ—
'sed et census constat actos sub Augusto tunc in Iudaea per Sentium Saturninum apud quos
genus eius inquirere potuissent' (*Adv. Marcionem* IV. 19. 10).

[8] That is, the argument of the 'Curate's Egg'.   [9] R. Syme, o.c. 37.

valuable, but it lends no support for the engaging story about 'Hunila', the Gothic bride of Bonosus, and her dowry.[1]

The author was erudite and ingenious. To take a palmary example. The Emperor Gordian belonged to a cultivated stratum of high society: he had married a descendant of Herodes Atticus, and Philostratus dedicated the *Vitae Sophistarum* to his son.[2] Gordian might have been an orator or even a writer. No warrant, however, for any item in the catalogue of his works (*Gord.* 3. 2 f.). Again, the son of the old proconsul. He might have owned a library. The HA presents him with 62,000 volumes (18. 2).

All fiction. It was a felicitous device to parade the venerable Gordian as a literary gentleman, in sharp contrast to Maximinus. And not implausible. But the author did not find the notion in Herodian, his sole source of any compass for these transactions.

When invention is so pervasive and multifarious, a liar may tell the truth unawares. A clear distinction has to be drawn. The plausible is not the same thing as the authentic.

There are pertinent instances. The Emperor Diocletian in one of his laws made appeal to Marcus Aurelius, styling him 'divus Marcus pater noster religiosissimus imperator'.[3]

The HA also exhibits Diocletian as one who revered the memory of Marcus. A passage in the *Vita Marci* (19. 12) is explicit, and exuberant:

deusque etiam nunc habetur, ut vobis ipsis, sacratissime imperator Diocletiane, et semper visum est et videtur, qui eum inter numina vestra non ut ceteros sed specialiter veneramini ac saepe dicitis vos vita et clementia tales esse cupere qualis fuit Marcus.

A parallel, who can doubt? What, if anything, it indicates, that is another question.

The two passages have recently been brought into confrontation. Not to show a fortuitous coincidence between fiction and fact. On the contrary. The 'small detail', it is argued, suggests that the notice in the HA may be both authentic and contemporary.[4] That is to say, this passage conveys a genuine date and situation.

One must stop, and hesitate—and object. The dedications or invocations of Diocletian and of Constantine are all of a piece. If one might be authentic, why not any other? The consequences are delirious. Constantine

---

[1] 'Hunila', like 'Samso' (the Jewish Hercules) bears a masculine name. Not so exotic were the heirlooms conveyed to the Roman senator 'Toxotius' by his aristocratic bride 'Junia Fadilla' (*Maximin.* 27. 6 ff.).　　　[2] Above, p. 167.　　　[3] *Cod. Just.* v. 17. 5.

[4] A. D. E. Cameron, *CR²* XVIII (1968), 17 f. The item had been registered without consequences by Momigliano, *Secondo Contributo* (1960), 123.

compelled the author against his will to compose the life of Elagabalus (*Elag.* 35. 1). Constantine knew his Marius Maximus (*Alex.* 65. 4). He was aware of the evil regiment of court eunuchs, having once been subject to them—'qui talibus serviit' (67. 1). Further, the Emperor will not take it amiss if the biographer, speaking about his defeated rivals, pays honest tribute to their quality, 'ut nihil eorum virtuti derogetur' (*Elag.* 35. 6).

The dedications stand or fall together. That is, they fall. They are merely a device of the author, to insinuate both date and authenticity. And it was a device he hit upon during the process of composition, like the labels of authorship. Their occurrence in the main *Vitae* in the sequence from Hadrian to Caracalla furnishes a clue. Three times, in passages added after the original compilation of those *Vitae*.[1]

Those phenomena should have been registered before assigning any validity to the invocation of Diocletian in the *Vita Marci*. This passage, and the others, are patent accretions in the composition (but not to be assumed subsequent by any long interval of time).

According to the HA, Diocletian paid especial reverence to Marcus. Why not? For parallel one should observe how another emperor regards the 'sanctum illud nomen Antoninorum'. It is Constantine, in due deference: 'quod tu, Constantine sacratissime, ita veneraris ut Marcum et Pium inter Constantios Claudiosque, velut maiores tuos, aureos formaveris adoptans virtutes veterum tuis moribus congruentes et tibi amicas caras' (*Elag.* 2. 4).

A question of historical method is involved. Suppose some inscription or papyrus to turn up, which showed Constantine paying homage to any one of the Antonine emperors. What would follow? It would not avail to suggest that the HA in that instance might be either authentic or contemporary. Bare assertions in the HA cannot be segregated and commended to earnest attention merely because they happen to be plausible or correspond with sporadic facts on casual record.

Here as elsewhere, chance and coincidence will be allowed for. Another specimen may briefly be put on record. Severus Alexander was ashamed of being called a Syrian. Especially because various terms of opprobrium had been applied (*Alex.* 28. 7),

maxime quod quodam tempore festo, ut solent, Antiochenses, Aegyptii, Alexandrini lacessiverant conviciolis, et Syrum archisynagogum eum vocantes et archiereum.

Alexander as a 'Syrus archisynagogus', the notion is amusing. He is also

[1] Above, p. 72.

made to invoke the god of Gaza in the Roman Senate, combined with a reminiscence of Cicero (17. 4),

O Marna, o Juppiter, o di inmortales, Arabianus non solum vivit, verum etiam in senatum venit.

Another joke.

However, close relevance has been detected in 'archisynagogus'. Alexander was born at Arca in Syria. An inscription disclosed the fact that there was at Rome a synagogue of Jews from Arca.[1] A fact of some interest, no doubt. It deserved to be registered, and soberly estimated. But it would not confer authenticity on the notice in the HA about an anonymous festival which congregated, at some place not specified, Antiochenes, Alexandrians, and Egyptians, each exercising their notorious licence (familiar from literature) at the expense of Alexander, whom they deride as a chief of the synagogue and as a priest.[2]

Plain fiction once again. It is therefore superfluous to point out that the Roman synagogue may never have existed. The inscription is preserved in manuscript. Two copies. The one gives 'the synagogue of Arca', the other 'the city of Arca'. The latter version deserves the preference.[3]

For one reason or another an authentic document may mislead. The spurious had for a long time been the greater menace. In the early and genial epoch of classical scholarship, forged inscriptions (like other forms of erudite pastiche) were a normal phenomenon.[4] Some of them won credence, and kept it for a season. One notorious example is the *senatus consultum* found beside the river Rubicon: it forbade the entry of an army into Italy.[5] Antonius Augustinus showed it up, the Archbishop of Tarragona: a scholar familiar with inscriptions.[6]

The Rubicon Decree, so it happens, was on attestation in a literary source some time before it was inscribed on a stone.[7] With the progress of epigraphic science, mere forgeries have forfeited their appeal (for fabricators or for the credulous). A fresh danger now supervenes.

[1] Published by G. B. Frey, *Bull. com.* LVIII (1930), Supp. I, 97 (whence *AE* 1933, 102). Frey argued that the synagogue was built by Severus Alexander (ib. 104), hence a confirmation of the HA.

[2] Frey's notion was taken up and developed by Momigliano in the article 'Severus Alexander Archisynagogus. Una conferma alla Historia Augusta', *Athenaeum* XII (1934), 151 ff. Further, H. Bengtson incautiously assumed that the name of the Emperor and the title 'archisynagogus' actually stood on the inscription (*Grundriss der römischen Geschichte* I (1967), 365).

[3] For the detail see the careful discussion of H. J. Leon, *The Jews of Ancient Rome* (1960), 163 ff. The document is reproduced as no. 501 in his collection.

[4] Dessau, *Hermes* XXVII (1892), 574 f.   [5] *CIL* XI. *30.

[6] C. Mitchell, o.c. 457 f.   [7] By Omnibonus in 1475, in comment on Lucan I. 185.

Inscriptions are taken up with alacrity and much erudition, to confirm, to supplement (and perhaps to confute) the testimony of the written sources. For example, an imperial edict emanating from Palestine. It forbids the violation of tombs.[1] Hence related (so it seemed) to notable transactions of the year 33 (if that is the year)—but perhaps belonging to the time of Augustus or of Hadrian.

All of which is relevant to the HA, to various attempts which have been made to corroborate some of its most questionable allegations. So far no document has emerged to confirm a revival of the Senate's authority under the Emperor Claudius Tacitus. However, for a cognate theme, an inscription recently discovered brought evidence (at first sight) that might support an item in the 'senatorial policy' of Probus.[2] It turns out to be a total delusion.[3] Again, a *rhetor* called Maecius Faustinus appears on an inscription at Corinth and is hailed with delight as the paternal grandfather of the Emperor Gordian.[4]

The HA conveys a multitude of pertinent inventions. Probus, the son of a centurion (*Prob.* 3. 2), who can confute? Maximinus may well have given anxious care to the education of his son. The idea is tenable—but does nothing to certify any of the boy's teachers.[5] Balbinus is credited with the governorships of seven provinces, beginning with Asia and Africa (*Max. et Balb.* 7. 2).[6] It is possible that this eminent senator had been proconsul of either Asia or Africa.[7] Yet, if an inscription proved it, that would not in fact rehabilitate the passage in the HA. The author lacked precise knowledge about any provincial command of Balbinus.

Among the counsellors of Severus Alexander is registered 'Catilius Severus, cognatus eius, vir omnium doctissimus' (*Alex.* 68. 1). A Catilius Severus happens to be attested in the time of Caracalla. Identity has been promptly assumed.[8] That is premature, or rather illicit. The 'Catilius Severus' of the HA owes his existence to Catilius Severus, the aged kinsman of an earlier ruler (*Marcus* 1. 10). Compare the author's practice when he reproduces Baebius Macer and Lollius Urbicus.[9]

The HA presents 'Junius Balbus' as the consular husband of 'Maecia Faustina', old Gordian's daughter (*Gord.* 4. 2). The discovery of a contemporary homonym in the senatorial order, or of a high equestrian official in the previous generation, would not avail to accredit him.[10] He is of one piece with 'Junius Severus' whom Commodus sends to

---

[1] *SEG* VIII. 13.   [2] *AE* 1964, 223.   [3] Above, p. 240.
[4] Above, p. 169.   [5] Above, p. 183.   [6] For Asia, above, p. 172.
[7] But not likely, were the post supposed to fall subsequent to his second consulship in 213.
[8] *PIR²*, C 557: 'sine dubio'.   [9] Above, p. 4.   [10] Above, p. 169.

Britain, to replace a dangerous governor (*Clod. Alb.* 14. 1). The nomen-clature is drab and indistinctive. For a good reason. Like the novelist, this author when devising names for his characters opts for contrasted categories to the one end of deception. The ordinary name may elude suspicion, while the rare and striking also conveys authenticity.

v. Second, the pretext of 'good in parts', or partially forged, or dubious yet conveying some useful truth or 'tradition'. The ancestry of the Emperor Tacitus may be allowed to recede, silently, but the rest of the fable is too attractive to forfeit, namely the copying of the historian's works under official injunction (*Tac.* 10. 3).[1] Much of the long letter instructing 'Zosimio' to furnish supplies and equipment (*Claud.* 14) can be salvaged, as valuable evidence for regulations obtaining in the time of Constantine.[2] The 'Letter of Hadrian' (*Quadr. tyr.* 8), when purged of the references to Christians, will stand as a document of unique significance.[3] Again, something or other may emerge from the epistle in which the young Gordian blames his mother and her evil counsellors, 'Gaudianus', 'Reverendus', and 'Montanus' (*Gord.* 25. 3).[4]

Therefore it is no surprise that the fable of Alexander's domestic chapel should persist, with or without some hint of dubiety.[5] In it stood Apollonius, and further (so a writer of the time stated) Christus, Abraham, Orpheus, and other 'animae sanctiores' (*Alex.* 29. 2).

With no note of warning, or explicit defence, inventions of the HA (a variety of types) keep their habitation in works of learning. A number of specimens cropped up in the remarks on Maximinus and Tacitus. In epilogue a brief selection may be added.

The domestic policy of Tacitus (non-existent as far as facts go) receives ample space, and commendation.[6] And some of the small items are noted: he was against defacing the coinage (*Tac.* 9. 3).[7] That he forbade men to wear silk (10. 4) is passed over, it is true. But Tacitus gave a hundred

---

[1] It is accepted by R. P. Oliver, *TAPA* lxxxii (1951), 260 f.; D. R. Dudley, *The World of Tacitus* (1968), 17; L. D. Reynolds and N. G. Wilson, *Scribes and Scholars* (1968), 28.

[2] C. E. Van Sickle, *Ant. class.* xxiii (1954), 45 ff. For one damaging item, cf. above, p. 216.

[3] Thus Carcopino, cf. above, p. 19. Recently a scholar who argues that Hadrian visited Egypt in 134 as well as in 130 is disposed for that reason to accept Carcopino's thesis (J. Follet, *Rev. phil.* xlii (1968), 60 f.).

[4] P. W. Townsend, *YCS* xiv (1955), 87: 'though open to suspicion of forgery, the letter may none the less reflect a tradition of Gordian's relations with the Christians.'

[5] Qualified with 'maybe' by W. H. C. Frend, *Martyrdom and Persecution in the Early Church* (1965), 329. But there is no hint of doubt in E. R. Dodds, *Pagan and Christian in an Age of Anxiety* (1965), 107.

[6] M. Besnier, *L'Empire romain de l'avènement des Sévères au concile de Nicée* (1937), 266 ff.

[7] H. Mattingly, *CAH* xii (1939), 312.

columns of Numidian marble to the city of Ostia (10. 5). That fact is used as valid testimony both for economic history and for urban embellishment.[1]

The personality and habits of Pescennius Niger and Clodius Albinus, as portrayed in the HA, recur in a sober and scientific assessment of their coinage.[2] Nor do the family and extraction of emperors fail to appeal. Gordian is an especial favourite; and his daughter passes muster along with her husband 'Junius Balbus'.[3] And 'Varius Macrinus' stands unimpugned, a relative of Severus Alexander who wins a victory in Illyricum (*Alex*. 58. 1).[4] Likewise the aristocrat 'Ovinius Camillus', who conspired against Alexander (48. 1 ff.).[5] More serious, the army reforms ordained by that prince are accorded credit.[6] Further, the campaign of Probus in Isauria is accepted, along with the measures (plausible enough) which he took to maintain order in that region (*Prob*. 16. 4 ff.).[7] It will be observed that the other Isaurian passage, introduced by the non-existent usurper 'Trebellianus' (*Tyr. trig*. 26), is likewise spurious, suggesting the fourth century not the third.[8] Finally, three of the bogus *suffecti* of the year 238 are allowed to stand, viz. 'Junius Silanus' (*Maximin*. 16. 1); 'Claudius Julianus' (*Max. et Balb*. 17. 2); 'Celsus Aelianus' (ib.).[9]

VI. Purged of figments, the annals of the third century would become dull and arid and exiguous in long tracts. Such was the record, before the HA stepped in to expand and embellish.

The inventive fancy of the author also brought enrichment to the annals of Latin literature. The HA cites about thirty-four biographers or historians not otherwise on attestation.[10] A clear clue to its nature, and a question not to be evaded, but highly remunerative.

A small problem obtrudes, which would have delighted a 'curiosus' like the author himself, namely precise total and definition. 'Acholius'

---

[1] R. M. Haywood in *An Economic Survey of Ancient Rome* IV (1938), 117; R. Meiggs, *Roman Ostia* (1960), 89. The former scholar also registers the columns in the palace of the Gordiani at Praeneste (*Gord*. 32. 2).   [2] *BMC, R. Emp*. V (1950), lxxxv; cix f.

[3] W. Ensslin, *CAH* XII (1939), 79.

[4] Not questioned by Barbieri, *Albo*, no. 1179.

[5] M. Besnier, o.c. 96. On him cf. above, p. 96.   [6] M. Besnier, o.c. 99.

[7] Rostovtseff, *SEHRE*[2] (1957), 737; 740; D. Magie, *Roman Rule in Asia Minor* (1950), 720 f.   [8] J. Rouget, *Rev. ét. anc*. LXVIII (1966), 282 ff.; R. Syme, o.c. 47 ff.

[9] P. W. Townsend, o.c. 92. After conflating 'Claudius Julianus 'and 'Celsus Aelianus', he states that the person is identical with Ap. Claudius Julianus (*cos. II* 224 and *praefectus urbi*). Further, in the same context 'Vectius Sabinus' (*Max. et Balb*. 2. 1) is held to be a *suffectus* of 238—and 'a man of consular standing to whom the jurist Ulpian dedicated some of his books'. For this grotesque error (*Elag*. 16. 2) see above, p. 120.

[10] For the list, Schanz–Hosius, *Gesch. der r. Lit*. III[3] (1922), 87 f.

generally receives a single entry.[1] Better, two writers, since one is an official under Valerian (*Aur.* 12. 4), whereas the other appears to be a contemporary of Severus Alexander.[2] Asclepiodotus, the general of Constantius, who is cited for a pair of anecdotes (*Aur.* 44. 2 f.), should be regarded as a person rather than an author.[3] 'Gargilius' (*Alex.* 37. 9), later termed 'Gargilius Martialis' (*Prob.* 2. 7), has borrowed the nomenclature of an excellent Roman knight who wrote on agriculture.[4] In this context he is a different character, a bogus biographer.

Six of these 'authorities' wrote in Greek and are registered without misgivings (and with long stretches of quotation) in the standard collection of the fragments.[5] One of them is called 'Onesimus'. Now Onesimus of Cyprus (or of Sparta) is on record, a *rhetor* who wrote about Constantine.[6] Hence the 'Onesimus' in the HA might be conceded genuine —in one sense of the term only. There is no warrant for the belief that the HA, when it cites 'Onesimus', is drawing on the attested author of that name. The items suffice.[7]

'Junius Cordus' is the archetype of the deleterious biographer, denounced by the HA. Mommsen unmasked him, but he still deceives.[8] As for the others, Peter registered them all.[9] Some scholars opt for a selection.[10] It is idle to enumerate, or to assess the criteria for adjudicating upon phantoms.

Recently a plea has been entered in defence of the whole company. Contemporaries, it is urged, would not have been taken in. It is not fair to tax them with stupidity. The work was composed for the 'aristocratie intellectuelle'.[11]

The argument has a double edge. It cuts into the aristocracy of the intellect in other ages. A plethora of authors and their works encumbers the pages of literary history. A few examples may suffice.

---

[1] *PIR*², A 36.

[2] *Alex.* 14. 6; 48. 7; 64. 5.   [3] Above, p. 213.

[4] *PIR*², G 82. For his military career and exploits, *ILS* 2767 (Auzia).

[5] Jacoby, *FGrH* 213–18. Namely Callicrates of Tyre, Theoclius, Nicomachus, Onesimus, Fabius Ceryllianus, Claudius Eusthenius. The last of these is taken seriously by W. Seston, *Dioclétien et la Tetrarchie* I (1946), 18 ff.; *RAC* III (1957), 1036.

[6] Known only from Suidas, cf. Jacoby, ad loc.; W. Stegemann, P–W XVIII. 406.

[7] *Quadr. tyr.* 13. 1; 14. 4; *Car.* 4. 2; 7. 3; 16. 2; 17. 6. Amalgamating the two, Stegemann says 'wir lernen O. aus diesen Zitaten als einen Geschichtsschreiber kennen, der nach Originalität strebt' (o.c. 407). According to Kroll in the same volume, 'Schwindelzitate' (468).   [8] Above, p. 76.

[9] Peter, *HRR* II (1906), 120; 129 ff.

[10] Fifteen were kept by Ch. Lécrivain, *Études sur l'Histoire Auguste* (1904), 401 f.

[11] H. Bardon, o.c. 21. Indeed, as he says, the Prefect of the City was a patron. For Bardon's standpoint see further *La Littérature latine inconnue* II (1956), 274.

As has been shown, the HA produces sons for Julius Titianus, (Terentius) Scaurinus, and Serenus Sammonicus.[1] These creatures should be dislodged from the works of reference. The latest of such figments is 'Aurelius Apollinaris', who composed in iambic verse a poem about the exploits of Carus, to be outshone, 'veluti radio solis', by Numerianus, that emperor's son. The prince had also defeated the poet Nemesianus.[2]

Emperors or pretenders not only foster letters, they are adroit performers. Severus Alexander duly composed biographies of good emperors (*Alex.* 27. 8). As adornments of his literary circle are evoked, for example, the orator 'Catilius Severus' and the eminent jurist 'Aelius Gordianus'.[3] To be sure, those names are certified in the list of his counsellors (68. 1).

To this happy season belongs the library of 62,000 volumes owned by 'Serenus Sammonicus' and bequeathed to the younger Gordian, a former pupil (*Gord.* 18. 2).[4] The productive epoch of old Gordian fell much earlier —when only a boy he wrote the epic poem (30 books) on Pius and Marcus. Space can be found for the catalogue of his varied and voluminous writings (3. 1 ff.).[5]

A sombre but comforting verdict may be pronounced. Nothing that the HA relates about authors and writings subsequent to Marius Maximus deserves credit, except for the reference to the poems of Nemesianus of Carthage.[6]

The HA ought to have been studied as a whole, for its own sake: language and style, the structure, the literary genre (half-way between biography and romance). Little has been done. The HA tends to be used as a repertory of odd facts. It is also a treasure-house of fable. Students of Latin literature might have discovered a welcome enrichment of their domain.[7] There would be melancholy instruction in sorting out reasons for the paradox. It is enough to observe some of the consequences.

---

[1] Above, p. 10.

[2] *Car.* 11. 2. Stein (*PIR*², A 1453) drew attention to the earlier collocation of the two names: the brothers Apollinaris and Nemesianus were tribunes in the Guard (*Carac.* 6. 7), their *gentilicium* being 'Aurelius' (Dio LXXVIII. 5. 2). The authentic poet M. Aurelius Nemesianus, from Carthage, is styled 'Olympius Nemesianus' in *Car.* 11. 2. There is no reason to doubt the 'Olympius', cf. *PIR*², A 1562.

[3] E. K. Rand, *CAH* XII (1939), 589 (cf. above, p. 275).

[4] ib. 613. Also accepted by Kind, P–W II A. 1675; and, according to E. H. Clift, 'it is not unlikely that the collection was dissipated or destroyed' (*Latin Pseudepigrapha* (1945), 33).

[5] E. K. Rand, o.c. 589.

[6] *Car.* 11. 2, cf. above, n. 2.

[7] And there would have been no need for the anthology presented in this chapter.

A false picture of literary productivity obtains. The bleak and barren years of the third century are endowed with an efflorescence of authorship. Another unpropitious epoch, that of Diocletian and Constantine, engenders a school of biographers (six or fewer than six)—that is, when the 'traditional date' of the HA is accepted and commended. By contrast, the renaissance in the late years of the fourth century, with life and letters in close and vigorous symbiosis, is denied a congenial masterpiece of erudition and fraud.

XVIII · EPILOGUE

THE HISTORIA AUGUSTA is the only Latin source of any compass for a long tract in the annals of imperial Rome, from the death of Trajan to the accession of Diocletian. The task that confronts historians is clear and imperative. Their duty is to seclude fact from fiction and use the facts.

That does not always happen. Authorship and date obtrude, the strife persists. For its own sake, so it might seem on an unfriendly interpretation. An enigma, once recognized as such, acquires a seductive appeal for the erudite and the ingenious. The long debate that began in 1889 affords manifold instruction. And the 'history of the problem' becomes a subject in its own right. Doxologies form, the bibliography piles up. Hence fatigue and distaste.

It was pertinent to ask what is the main point at issue. At the outset a strong protest was uttered against the question of authorship: six fools or three, what does it matter?[1] Others in the sequel went on to wider verdicts, affirming that after all the labour spent on the HA the gain for history was negligible.[2] However, it was premature to underestimate the study of sources in this instance; and the whole investigation has in fact changed the face of the history.

The controversy brought up confident pronouncements. Hohl stated that for the future only Dessau's thesis would make the running.[3] By contrast, most of the arguments of Dessau had quickly been refuted (it was held).[4] And further, the late dating of the HA was inadmissible.[5]

---

[1] O. Seeck, *Rh. Mus.* XLIX (1894), 209. Seeck, as befitted a historian of late Antiquity, derived comfort from Dessau's dating, and enthusiasm, advancing the date further than was expedient or probable (*Jahrbücher für cl. Phil.* XXXVI (1890), 609 ff.).

[2] B. W. Henderson, *The Life and Principate of the Emperor Hadrian* (1923), 275: 'the time and labour spent upon the Augustan History in general and upon the "Life" of Hadrian in particular are overwhelming, and their results, so far as any practical use for history goes, are precisely nil.' Quoted by Baynes, with gentle irony, in his preface. For a grievous error of Henderson, caused by neglect of structure and sources, see above, p. 114.

[3] E. Hohl, *Bursians Jahresberichte* CLXXI (1915), 129.

[4] A. Momigliano, *Secondo Contributo* (1960), 114: 'it can be said that De Sanctis's article of 1896 succeeded in exploding the majority of Dessau's and Seeck's original arguments.' The article appeared in *Rivista di storia antica* I (1896), 90 ff.

[5] Thus D. Magie called the late dating 'untenable' (Loeb edition, Vol. II (1924), xxx).

The ranks of the conservative cause advertised no defections. On the other side, while none who had advocated a post-Constantinian date relapsed, notable shifts of allegiance occurred.[1] Reserve or scepticism therefore seemed to have a strong stance. Why not give up authorship and date—and turn to some of the neglected themes of imperial history?

Yet the HA abides as a classic problem, not to be evaded: it concerns criteria of evidence, literary as well as historical. Recent years have witnessed a revival of interest, a recrudescence. Not all may like it.

The method of approach is cardinal. It will be expedient to turn aside from the 'history of the problem', to break up, for the moment, the nexus between authorship, purpose, and date. The HA is a literary product. The primary task is to investigate its structure and genesis.[2] Inquiry should adopt a certain order of progression, starting from the work itself and going on to type and purpose. The date comes last. The thesis can be briefly stated.

I. *Composition*

1. Structure and sources. The early series of biographies of emperors down to Caracalla (nine in all) discloses a basic source that has been abridged—and added to. On the criterion of source and structure the cut comes before the *Vita Macrini*, which indicates a new turn by its programmatic preface. The historical transactions, however, ran continuous from the assassination of Caracalla through the brief reign of Macrinus to the accession of Elagabalus. The author might have waited until he completed the *Vita Alexandri* before turning back to compose the 'secondary *Vitae*' of princes and pretenders—and to revise the 'Nine *Vitae*'. That alternative does not impair the main thesis.[3]

2. Stages of composition. How many have to be reckoned with? The question is infested with complications, hardly to be resolved in entirety.[4] That need not detain. The author may, or may not, have paused to take brief breathing-space before he wrote the 'secondary *Vitae*' and made his revisions—or, for that matter, at some later stage. One thing is clear and needs to be said. No internal necessity entails anywhere in the HA intervals of years, decades, generations.

3. Authorship. As Dessau discerned, the same habits and devices obtain all through, sporadic in the earlier *Vitae*, accumulating when the author

---

[1] Above all, in the accessions to the theory of Baynes (among them Hohl, cf. above, p. 99). For the detail, A. Chastagnol, *Historia* IV (1955), 180.

[2] A task neglected by historians, so Hohl affirmed in his last contribution (*Wiener Studien* LXXI (1958), 152).   [3] Above, p. 87.

[4] For a definition of the stages, above, p. 52.

indulges in free composition. The labels of the first four biographers were carelessly affixed. Indeed an afterthought, so it may be conjectured.[1] They have no more validity than the dedications to emperors: of which the three that occur in the 'Nine *Vitae*' belong (it appears) to the revision.[2] Later on 'Vopiscus' cleverly testifies to three of his predecessors; but no one of the ostensible six anywhere claims to be writing in collaboration.[3] Nor is anything saved if the total be reduced to five, to three, to two.

4. The design. An original feature, which the HA proclaims with pride, is to furnish biographies of princes and pretenders: an innovation on Suetonius and on Marius Maximus. Those 'secondary *Vitae*' present striking resemblances of manner and content to later (and largely fictional) biographies of emperors.[4] Hardly therefore an afterthought, but central to the design; and they confirm the postulate of the single author.

5. The workmanship. Harsh verdicts are pronounced. For two reasons, viz. hasty and careless composition in the early *Vitae*, incompetence and error elsewhere. As a result, genuine talent has been denied or ignored. It exists, it comes out with peculiar force in three particulars: senatorial orations, dramatic contrasts, and the use of links for binding emperor to emperor in a long sequence. Furthermore, the writer gains as he goes on, in skill and also in humour.

II. *Purpose and type*

1. Forgery or imposture? 'Fälschung' and 'der Fälscher' have been in common currency.[5] A question of definitions arises. The HA is dishonest. It proposes to furnish sober and accurate history. The performance contradicts: the HA adduces a plethora of faked documents and bogus authorities. The thing was deliberate.[6] Therefore the HA is a fraud, whatever the date at which it purports to have been written—quite apart from the labels of the 'six', the imperial dedications, and the various devices for corroboration.

The term 'forgery' (so it has been suggested) ought to be held applicable only if the HA can be proved subsequent to the death of Constantine.[7]

---

[1] Above, p. 75.   [2] Above, p. 72.
[3] The contrary was recently stated by Momigliano, in 1963 (quoted above, p. 53).
[4] Above, p. 67.
[5] Those terms were discountenanced long ago by Hohl, *Neue Jahrbücher* XXXIII (1914), 706. He had to raise protest again, with the added comment 'die HA ist doch kein Geschichtswerk, sondern ein Stück Unterhaltungsliteratur' (*Bursians Jahresberichte* CCLVI (1937), 141).
[6] It is therefore a pity to eliminate from the estimation any category of the bogus or even of the suspect.   [7] Momigliano, o.c. 111.

The limitation, enjoined for the purpose of a subtle argument, is a paradox. Forgery is no less forgery if it happens to be contemporary.[1]

'Forgery' carries some connotation of profit or criminal conduct—and, in the strict sense perhaps, actual and personal handicraft. It may suitably be extended to cover the production of spurious documents or texts emended for some direct advantage in political or religious fraud.

Mere impersonation of the dead or the non-existent is another matter, lightly held in most ages, and not liable to legal penalty or even to much reprobation. The question (it appears) has been wrongly put. A different formulation is needed: how far is the HA a serious effort of deceit? The writer towards the end slips in some delicious avowals, such as the exordium to the *Vita Aureliani*. The missing preface of the whole work might have been just such another piece of elegant play, leaving no doubt even in the minds of the obtuse.

Not 'forgery', therefore. Rather 'imposture' or 'impersonation'.

2. Purpose. The Suetonian biographies carried much curious detail about the Caesars, of a kind disdained by historians. The HA follows suit. But, unlike Suetonius, it admitted orations and expounded at some length doctrines about emperors and Senate. And usurpers contribute, being brought in for reinforcement—but also for literary contrasts and even for comedy.

That edification should blend with entertainment is no surprise. The novel bears witness, in any age. It often conveys a coherent body of doctrine about state and society, the opinions being those of the superior type of plain man, who eschews paradox or fanaticism.[2] Assessment demands caution—and no cause to believe the true and ultimate purpose to be didactic or doctrinaire. Balzac professed that he was defending the cause of throne and altar. The work should be allowed to speak, not the author.

The political opinions advertised in the HA are conventional and traditional. As when a novel is in cause, it would be beside the point to impugn the sincerity of the writer. And, at the same time, premature to assume propaganda as the design behind the writing.

3. The literary genre. In the novel with a historical setting, the leading characters tend to be fictitious, on the edge of great events or even close to them. In the *Cyropaedia*, however, the main persons are authentic, and the bare framework. For the rest, narration, speeches, and a host

---

[1] Before or after 337, that has been asserted the 'basic question' about the HA, the 'vital point' (Momigliano, o.c. 116).

[2] As in the historical novels of G. A. Henty and J. Buchan.

of minor actors. A romance with a plain didactic purpose, it may be described as 'fictional history'. Similarly, the *Vita Alexandri*.[1] The components of the HA have already been indicated. Given the sheer bulk of fabrication and the nature of the artifices, the term 'mythistoria' may not be misleading.[2]

4. The writer. Not a drab and tedious compiler. As is suitable, he delights in his inventive role. More might be said in this context about the motives of literary and artistic fraud; and it is pertinent to adduce the forgers of inscriptions.[3]

Some would compare him to a journalist. The notion is not unhelpful. His erudition commends a friendlier label. Rather a scholar or a librarian.[4]

III. *The date*

Various criteria have been applied.[5] It is an economy if the use of an extant writer can be established beyond question. Dessau adduced Aurelius Victor, as embedded in a passage of the *Vita Severi*.[6] Not an interpolation, but woven into the text of the biography.[7]

Though an epitomator, both hasty and ignorant, Victor is a writer with a distinct personality. When his ideas or his errors recur in the HA, the case acquires singular cogency. For example, the HA reflects, though it does not share, Victor's fancy that the jurist Salvius Julianus and the Emperor Didius Julianus were one and the same person.[8] There are other items.[9] Further, it becomes permissible to surmise that Victor inspired the portrayal of the usurper Marius or the 'interregnum' after the death of Aurelian.[10] Finally, the HA has Severus Alexander meditating a legal enactment which, in Victor, was ordained by Philip: the same type of comment accompanies each passage.[11]

For a long time faith and hope found a way out: the HA drew upon the

---

[1] Ensslin, however, adducing a verdict of Hohl, described the *Vita Alexandri* as a 'historical novel' (*CAH* XII (1939), 59).

[2] The Greek novel was usefully discussed by F. Altheim, *Literatur und Gegenwart im ausgehenden Altertum* I (1948), 36 ff. But he produced no clear definitions. And historical fiction was dismissed from his theme, explicitly, by B. E. Perry, *The Ancient Romances* (1967).   [3] Above, p. 274.

[4] R. Syme, *Ammianus and the Historia Augusta* (1968), 183 ff.; 197 f.

[5] Summarized, o.c. 214 ff.

[6] Dessau, *Hermes* XXIV (1889), 363 ff. (on *Sev.* 17. 5–19. 3).

[7] As was properly conceded by Leo, *Die griechisch-römische Biographie* (1901), 286 f.; 302 f.   [8] Above, p. 123.

[9] Above, pp. 81; 123; 148; 238; 252.   [10] Above, pp. 252; 238.

[11] *Alex.* 24. 4 derives from Victor 28. 7. That was established, only recently, by A. Chastagnol, *Bonner Historia-Augusta-Colloquium 1964/5* (1966), 54 ff.; *Rev. phil.* XLI (1967), 95 f.

source of Victor, viz. the KG.[1] It will not work any more. For Enmann, the KG, antecedent to the HA, had to terminate with the accession of Diocletian: the traditional date of the HA had not yet been disputed. Otherwise (it may be conjectured) Enmann would have been happy to carry the KG a long way beyond the year 284.[2]

Aurelius Victor displaces the HA and puts it subsequent to the year 360. Other writers therefore come into play. In the first instance, the historian Ammianus Marcellinus. Sundry items have been adduced.[3] To cut short and concentrate: three episodes standing close together in Book xv of his History inspire (it is argued) three figments in *Quadrigae tyrannorum*.[4] Ammianus, it is generally held, published his History down to Book xxv in the year 392.

If the influence of Ammianus is conceded, various conclusions follow. First, the literary incentive. It was double and diverse—to assert modest and veracious biography against the high style and pretensions of a historian, and to outdo Marius Maximus. The latter author was probably a recent discovery. Outside the HA he finds mention twice only, in Ammianus and in the *scholia* to Juvenal.[5]

Second, the impact of events. A composer of fiction cannot always escape it, even if he takes care. There is no sign that the author of *Quadrigae tyrannorum* was at any pains. That book, it may be surmised, reflects recent transactions in Egypt and in Gaul: the destruction of the Serapeum in 391, the proclamation of Eugenius in 392.[6]

Third, political opinions. The writer is a pagan, devoted to tradition and the Roman Senate. The set purpose of composing propaganda in defence of the good old cause has often been discovered and declared. Certain themes that he developed with gusto may be accorded some contemporary relevance. Thus declamation against civil war, the call for merit against birth in the selection of emperors, the danger of having children for rulers. Further, covert criticism of Theodosius might be

---

[1] Discussing the passage in the *Vita Severi*, Momigliano admitted that '*prima facie* the *Historia Augusta* is shown to be later than Aurelius Victor' (o.c. 118). The formulation, in a careful writer, conveys doubt or a latent antithesis. Momigliano invoked, as was legitimate, the common source. But he ruled out other passages that might point to Victor—'in other cases the *Historia Augusta* and Aurelius Victor undoubtedly depend on a common source' (o.c. 117).   [2] Above, p. 221.   [3] Summarized in R. Syme, o.c. 69.

[4] R. Syme, o.c. 70. Namely the fatal banquet of Africanus (Ammianus xv. 3. 7); the usurpation of Silvanus the Frank (5. 16); the description of the Gallic 'virago' (12. 1). The pendants in *Quadrigae tyrannorum* are the drinking cups which 'Africanus' should not abuse (8. 10); the spouse of the usurper Proculus, 'Vituriga', who is called an 'uxor virago' (12. 3); the fabricated Frankish origin of Proculus (13. 4).   [5] Above, p. 45.

[6] For the Serapeum, above, p. 28. For the events in Gaul, R. Syme, o.c. 76 f.

suspected. Fiction can be didactic. That explains, in part, the *Vita Taciti* or the *Vita Probi*. Not, however, *Quadrigae tyrannorum*.[1]

The attitude which the HA adopts toward the new faith now acquiring dominance is reserved or ambiguous, so it seems. It is on the defensive— or even putting in an unobtrusive plea for tolerance. The notion carries a certain seduction.[2] Yet Christianity, it is clear, was not among the main preoccupations of the HA.[3] All in all, an earnest political design is not disclosed.

Fourth, the milieu. Extreme positions are adopted. The HA has been described as propaganda directed towards a popular audience.[4] On the other side, and more frequently, a man of birth and station is detected, belonging to the 'circle of Symmachus'.[5]

Inspection of the HA as a whole should reveal the reading public it presupposes. Clearly a milieu that appreciated learning and would not miss abstruse allusions to the classics. The author's attainments cannot be disputed. Perhaps the danger subsists of rating his social station too low. For what it may be worth, 'Pollio' and 'Vopiscus' allege that they have aristocratic friends.[6] A scholiast's erudition and tastes do not exclude a decayed aristocrat.[7]

Fifth, a by-product. Once the approximate period emerges, a large number of items in writers of the time can be put on show, not to confirm the date, but for comparison. Hence a clearer understanding of life and letters towards the end of the fourth century.

A date in the vicinity of 395 becomes easy and attractive.[8] It was a momentous year. Theodosius died on January 17, the Empire to be divided between boy-princes, with dissension apparent between the two courts. Further, the Goths soon seceded in the Balkan lands, the Huns came through the Caucasus.

The year was also memorable in the annals of Latin literature, with Claudian emergent; and Ammianus was bringing to completion the

---

[1] The four usurpers are brought in for an artistic reason (to separate Probus and Carus). And, more than that, for comedy and for a display of scholarly technique. The *Quadrigae* (generally neglected) is cardinal for the understanding of the HA.

[2] Hence admitted above, p. 16. It can stand in a modified form. The author was against fanaticism (observe his portrayal of Egyptians), and devoid of any pronounced religious beliefs.   [3] Thus, and firmly, Momigliano, o.c. 129 ff.

[4] N. H. Baynes, *The Historia Augusta* (1926), 57.

[5] Thus, among others, W. Hartke, *Römische Kinderkaiser* (1951), 413; A. Chastagnol, *Bonner Historia-Augusta-Colloquium 1963* (1964), 67.

[6] R. Syme, o.c. 192 f.   [7] R. Syme, o.c. 197 f.

[8] The date advocated by Alföldi and by Chastagnol (above, p. 16, n. 2). For Chastagnol the limits are the years 394 and 398.

supplement to his History (Books XXVI–XXXI). The HA comes out with a prophecy of the glory that will accrue to the descendants of the Emperor Probus.[1] Petronius Probus had been the pride and peak of the Roman aristocracy: his sons share the *fasces* in 395. Dessau assigned the HA to the reign of Theodosius. When some thirty years had elapsed after his audacious exploit, he proffered a brief remark, almost casually: the last decade of the fourth century.[2]

The present disquisition advances along the lines laid down by Dessau; and its conclusion is no novelty. The enduring controversy, with so many hypotheses defended or demolished, deters undue confidence. By the same token, courage and clarity are requisite. The time has passed for anxious debate about small or sporadic particulars. A candid and rational inquiry should formulate a general theory about the character and genesis of the HA.

By its very nature, fiction about the past is under compulsion to insinuate authenticity through the manufacture of corroborative detail. One type of artifice explains how the original manuscript came into the hands of its sponsor, editor, or translator. Hence discoveries made in a library, a temple, or even a sepulchre. For the HA, the loss of the preface has robbed posterity of delightful revelations.

For the rest, the four biographers from 'Spartianus' to 'Capitolinus' invoke Diocletian, then Constantine. A tetrad of writers was not inappropriate. The grammarian Messius Arusianus had a *quadriga* of classical authors; and the HA itself produces four Roman historians who stand nowhere else in collocation.[3]

When the work embarked on the emperors from Gallienus to Carus, it had advanced a long way towards the ostensible time of writing. Hence the fatal temptation (with the enhancement of audacity and joy in creation) to fabricate more and more evidence for authenticity. There are a number of allusions to Constantius and to the Tetrarchy. Constantius appears at an early stage as 'Caesar' (*Gall.* 7. 2), and several times in the sequel; and towards the end Diocletian is much on show.

That earlier *Vitae*, with the son of Constantius as emperor, indicated a later date, the author had forgotten—or rather did not care.[4] He now had fresh scope for invention, with other attractive devices, such as the

---

[1] *Prob.* 24. 2 f. The significance was seized by Dessau, *Hermes* XXIV (1889), 355 ff. Mommsen could not deny it (*Ges. Schr.* (1909), 345 f.). The bogus prophecy was played down, with subtle arguments, by Momigliano (o.c. 121 f.).

[2] Dessau, *Woch. für kl. Phil.* 1918, 393.

[3] R. Syme, o.c. 99; 126 f. Cf. 169 (four Augustan *rhetores*).

[4] Above, p. 261.

tales of a grandfather. The new development is conveyed by two more biographers: first 'Pollio', then 'Vopiscus', who dedicate their production to friends.

If the various devices are accorded credence, and combined with the plurality of authors, the result is an imbroglio. To resolve it, Peter came out with a complicated hypothesis: composition of the *Vitae* at intervals through a stretch of time, with 'Capitolinus' reverting to authorship at the end and editing the collection about the year 330.[1]

Mommsen, clinging to the dedications, segregated a 'Diocletianic series' and a 'Constantinian series', with an editor. But he was constrained to postulate a second editor in the reign of Theodosius. He felt and admitted the force of certain arguments adduced by Dessau.

Meanwhile, the signs that point to a single author and a late date keep on accumulating. Is there a way of escape?

An argument might be put out that those items avail to date only the passages in question, nothing else.[2] That entails a corollary: pervasive interpolation or the hand of an editor in many sections of the HA where the structure betrays no trace of any tampering.[3] Editing and revision are manifest, it is true—in the earlier *Vitae*. But, as has been shown, no known fact, no internal necessity imposes a significant efflux of time separating those operations from the original compilation.[4]

Should a general theory be propounded that the HA took shape gradually through long years, its formulation will have to fall back on elaborate explanations.[5] No objection—if the facts demand it. The precedent and authority of Mommsen might be invoked. But Mommsen's theory was a shield, not a sword.

[1] Peter, *Die Scriptores Historiae Augustae* (1892), 49. Closely similar, Lécrivain, *Études sur l'Histoire Auguste* (1904), 27; 395 ff. Coincidence does not help the hypothesis.

[2] That argument or plea was recently adduced by Momigliano: 'one or two passages may point to a post-Constantinian date either for the whole collection or at least for the passages themselves' (*The Conflict between Paganism and Christianity in the Fourth Century* (1963), 96). Similarly A. D. E. Cameron, deprecating influences from Ammianus: 'this argument, even if accepted, cannot be regarded as proof that the *H.A.* as a whole was written at this period: only that certain elements in it were' (*CR* xviii[2] (1968), 20).

[3] For example, items in *Quadrigae tyrannorum*. Or, for that matter, 'Toxotius' (*Maximin.* 27. 6), or 'Maecius Faltonius Nicomachus' (*Tac.* 5. 3).

[4] To be sure, the contrary has been stated in a general verdict about the composition of the HA: 'the *Historia Augusta* as we have it was not all written at the same time, . . . and no theory that it was merits serious consideration' (A. D. E. Cameron, o.c. 18).

[5] A theory of this type was recently formulated by H. Bardon, *Le Crépuscule des Césars. Scènes et visages de l'Histoire Auguste* (1964), 326. In his scheme 'Vopiscus' is writing 'peu après 305' (ib. 312). But 'Vopiscus' is also a contemporary of the Emperor Constantius II (ib. 34), which puts him in the period 337–60. The author of the HA got involved in a difficulty of the same order (above, p. 261).

If the above sequence of argumentation, which takes its inception from the literary problem, is found acceptable, the author of the HA regains his congenial niche in a society that took delight in Juvenal and Marius Maximus. He fits in without discomfort. To write something better than mere compilation presupposes a reading public. It is there. The HA may incite to various study or speculation about the author and his time. As he said, 'curiositas nil recusat.'[1]

[1] *Aur.* 10. 1.

BIBLIOGRAPHY

SINCE the present book (which was given to the Press in April of 1969) is a sequel and companion to *Ammianus and the Historia Augusta* (1968), the appended list is restricted to the titles of periodical articles and the like not there registered.

Two more volumes of the *Bonner Historia-Augusta-Colloquium* have now appeared, containing the papers delivered in 1966 and 1967 (1968) and in 1968 and 1969 (1970): twelve and twenty items respectively. Furthermore, by A. Chastagnol, *Recherches sur l'Histoire Auguste* (Bonn, 1970). The first of its three substantial chapters, entitled 'Les recherches sur l'Histoire Auguste de 1963 à 1969', continues the survey he published in 1964.

In epilogue it may be relevant to note the following reviews of *Ammianus and the Historia Augusta*: A. Chastagnol, *Rev. phil.* xliii (1969), 268–74; J. Crocis, *Rev. ét. lat.* xlvi (1968), 510–15; É. Demougeot, *Rev. ét. anc.* lxxi (1969), 203–8; A. H. M. Jones, *JTS*, N.S. xx (1969), 320–1; A. Momigliano, *EHR* lxxxiv (1969), 566–9; P. Petit, *Ant. class.* xxxviii (1969), 265–7; G. Sabbah, *Latomus* xxviii (1969), 224–7.

ALFÖLDI, A. 'The numbering of the victories of the Emperor Gallienus and of the loyalty of his legions.' *Num. Chron.*⁵ ix (1929), 218. Reprinted (in German) in *Studien zur Geschichte der Weltkrise der 3. Jahrhunderts nach Christus* (1967), 73.
—— 'Epigraphica IV.' *Arch. ért.* ii (1941), 40.
ALFÖLDY, G. 'Septimius Severus und der Senat.' *Bonner Jahrbücher* clxviii (1968), 112.
ANDERSON, J. G. C. 'Trajan and the Quinquennium Neronis.' *JRS* i (1911), 178.

BANG, M. 'Die militärische Laufbahn des Kaisers Maximinus.' *Hermes* xli (1906), 300.
BARBIERI, G. 'Sulle falsificazioni della Vita di Pertinace negli Scriptores historiae Augustae.' *Stud. it. fil. class.* xiii (1936), 183.
—— 'Nota sull'imperatore Decio.' *Omagiu lui Constantin Daicoviciu* (1960), 11.
—— 'Nuove iscrizioni campane'. *Akte des IV. int. Kong. für gr. u. lat. Epigraphik* (1964), 40.
BARNES, T. D. 'The family and career of Septimius Severus.' *Historia* xvi (1967), 87.
—— 'Philostratus and Gordian.' *Latomus* xxvii (1968), 581.
—— 'Pre-Decian *Acta Martyrum*.' *JTS*, N.S. xix (1968), 509.
—— 'The lost Kaisergeschichte and the Latin historical tradition.' *Bonner Historia-Augusta-Colloquium 1968/69* (1970), 13.
—— 'Three notes on the *Vita Probi*.' *CQ*² xx (1970), 198.
BAYNES, N. H. 'Two notes on the reforms of Diocletian and Constantine.' *JRS* xv (1925), 196. Reprinted in *Byzantine and other essays* (1955), 173.
BENARIO, H. W. 'The date of the *Feriale Duranum*.' *Historia* xi (1962), 192.
BIRLEY, A. R. 'Two names in the Historia Augusta.' *Historia* xv (1966), 249.
—— 'The duration of provincial commands under Antoninus Pius.' *Corolla Memoriae Erich Swoboda Dedicata* (1966), 43.
—— 'The Roman governors of Britain.' *Epigraphische Studien* iv (1967), 63.
—— 'The Augustan history.' *Latin Biography* (ed. T. A. Dorey, 1967), 113.

BIRLEY, A. R. 'Some teachers of M. Aurelius.' *Bonner Historia-Augusta-Colloquium 1966/67* (1968), 39.
—— 'The Coups d'État of the year 193.' *Bonner Jahrbücher* clxix (1969), 247.
BIRLEY, E. 'The governors of Numidia, A.D. 193–268.' *JRS* xl (1950), 60.
—— 'Some Militaria in the Historia Augusta.' *Bonner Historia-Augusta-Colloquium 1966/67* (1968), 43.

CALDER, W. M. 'Corrigenda et Addenda.' *CR* xxvii (1913), 11.
CAMERON, A. D. E. 'Three notes on the *Historia Augusta*.' *CR*, N.S. xviii (1968), 17.
CANTARELLA, R. 'Le ultime parole di Nerone morente.' *Il mondo classico* i (1931), 53.
CARSON, R. A. G. 'The coinage and chronology of A.D. 238.' *Am. Num. Soc.*, Centennial Volume (1958), 181.
CHASTAGNOL, A. 'Emprunts de l'*Histoire Auguste* aux *Caesares* d'Aurelius Victor.' *Rev. phil.* xli (1967), 85.
—— A propos du 'iudicium magnum' de l'empereur Probus.' *Bonner Historia-Augusta-Colloquium 1966/67* (1968), 67.
—— 'L'Histoire Auguste et le rang des préfets du prétoire.' *Recherches sur l'Histoire Auguste* (1970), 39.
CLARKE, G. W. 'Some victims of the persecution of Maximinus Thrax.' *Historia* xv (1966), 445.
CROOK, J. A. 'Suetonius *ab epistulis*.' *Proc. Camb. Phil. Soc.* iv, 1956/7 (1958), 18.

DE SANCTIS, G. 'Gli S. H. A.' *Rivista di storia antica* i (1896), 90.
DOMASZEWSKI, A. v. 'Der Truppensold der Kaiserzeit.' *Neue Heidelberger Jahrbücher* x (1900), 218.

FINK, R. O. 'Lucius Seius Caesar, Socer Augusti.' *AJP* lx (1939), 326.
—— A. S. HOEY, and W. F. SNYDER. 'The Feriale Duranum.' *Yale Classical Studies* vii (1940), 11.
FITZ, J. 'Legati Augusti pro praetore Pannoniae Inferioris.' *Act. Ant. Ac. Sc. Hung.* xi (1963), 245.
FOLLET, J. 'Hadrien en Égypte et en Judée.' *Rev. phil.* xlii (1968), 54.
FREY, G. B. 'Una comunità giudaica d'Arca del Libano a Roma, nel III secolo, secondo una iscrizione inedita.' *Bull. Com.* lviii (1930), Supp. I, 97.

GABBA, E. 'Sulla *Storia romana* di Cassio Dione.' *Riv. stor. it.* lxvii (1955), 289.
GEROV, B. 'L'aspect ethnique et linguistique dans la région entre le Danube et les Balkans à l'époque romaine(Iᵉʳ–IIIᵉ siècles).' *Studi urbinati*, N.S. (1959), 173.
—— 'Zur Identität des Imperators Decius mit dem Statthalter C. Messius Q. Decius Valerinus.' *Klio* xxxix (1961), 222.
—— La carriera militare di Marciano, generale di Gallieno.' *Athenaeum* xliii (1965), 333.
—— 'Epigraphische Beiträge zur Geschichte des mösischen Limes in vorclaudischer Zeit.' *Act. Ant. Ac. Sc. Hung.* xv (1967), 85.
GILLIAM, J. F. 'The *Dux Ripae* at Dura.' *TAPA* lxxii (1941), 157.
—— 'The governors of Syria Coele from Severus to Diocletian.' *AJP* lxxix (1958), 225.
—— 'On the *Divi* under the Severi.' *Hommages Renard* ii (1969), 284.
GUEY, J. 'Communication sur la date de naissance de l'empereur Septime-Sévère, d'après son horoscope.' *Bull. Soc. nat. ant. France* (1956), 33.

HELM, R. 'Hieronymus und Eutrop.' *Rh. Mus.* lxxvi (1927), 138; 254.

HOHL, E. 'Beiträge zur Textgeschichte der Historia Augusta.' *Klio* xiii (1913), 258; 387.

—— 'Das Ende Caracallas.' *Misc. Ac. Berol.* ii. i (1950), 276.

—— 'Kaiser Commodus und Herodian.' *Berliner S-B* 1954, Abh. 1.

—— 'Kaiser Pertinax und die Thronbesteigung seines Nachfolgers im Lichte der Herodiankritik.' *Berliner S-B* 1956, Abh. 2.

HOMO, L. 'Les privilèges administratifs du Sénat sous l'Empire et leur disparition graduelle an cours du IIIᵉ siècle.' *Rev. hist.* cxxxviii (1921), 40.

HONORÉ, A. M. 'The Severan lawyers. A preliminary survey.' *Studia et Documenta Historiae et Juris* xxviii (1962), 162.

INSTINSKY, H. U. 'Das angebliche Legionskommando in der militärischen Laufbahn der Kaiser Maximinus, Claudius Goticus und Aurelianus.' *Klio* xxxiv (1942), 118.

JACOBY, F. 'Die Überlieferung von Ps. Plutarchs Parallela Minora und die Schwindel-autoren.' *Mnem.*³ viii (1940), 73. Reprinted in *Abh. zur gr. Geschichtsschreibung* (1956), 359.

KLEBS, E. 'Das dynastische Element in der Geschichtschreibung der römischen Kaiserzeit.' *Hist. Zeitschr*, N.F. xxv (1889), 213.

KOTULA, T. 'En marge de l'usurpation africaine de L. Domitius Alexander.' *Klio* xl (1962), 159.

LAMBRECHTS, P. 'L'empereur Lucius Verus. Essai de réhabilitation.' *Ant. class.* iii (1934), 173.

LEPPER, F. A. 'Some reflections on the "Quinquennium Neronis".' *JRS* xlvii (1957), 95.

LIFSCHITZ, B. 'Beiträge zur palästinischen Epigraphik.' *Zeitschrift des deutschen Palästina-Vereins* lxxviii (1962), 64.

LIPPOLD, A. 'Der Kaiser Maximinus Thrax und der römische Senat.' *Bonner Historia-Augusta-Colloquium 1966/67* (1968), 73.

—— 'Herrscherideal und Traditionsverbundenheit im Panegyricus des Pacatus.' *Historia* xvii (1968), 228.

MATTINGLY, H. 'The reign of Macrinus.' *Studies Presented to D. M. Robinson* (1953), 962.

MIHAILOV, G. 'Contributions à l'histoire de Thrace et de Mésie.' *Klio* xxxvii (1959), 226.

MITCHELL, C. 'Archaeology and Romance in Renaissance Italy.' *Italian and Renaissance Studies* (ed. E. F. Jacob, 1960), 455.

MODRZEJEWSKI, J. and T. ZAWADZKI. 'La date de la mort d'Ulpien et la préfecture du prétoire au début du règne d'Alexandre Sévère.' *Rev. hist. de droit français et étranger* xlv (1967), 565.

MOMIGLIANO, A. 'Severus Alexander Archisynagogus. Una conferma alla Historia Augusta.' *Athenaeum* xii (1934), 151.

MOREAU, J. 'Nachträge zum Reallexikon für Antike und Christentum (RAC). Constantius I, Constantinus II, Constantius II, Constans.' *Jahrbuch für Antike und Christentum* ii (1959), 158.

Moreau, J. 'Krise und Verfall: das dritte Jahrhundert n. Chr. als historisches Problem.' *Scripta Minora* (1964), 26. Reprinted from *Heidelberger Jahrbücher* v (1961), 128.

Murray, O. 'The "quinquennium Neronis" and the Stoics.' *Historia* xiv (1965), 41.

Nesselhauf, H. 'Publicum portorii Illyrici utriusque et ripae Thraciae.' *Epigraphica* i (1939), 331.

—— 'Die Legionen Mösiens unter Claudius und Nero.' *Laureae Aquincenses* ii (1941), 40.

—— 'Die Vita Commodi und die Acta Urbis.' *Bonner Historia-Augusta-Colloquium 1964/65* (1966), 127.

Oliver, J. H. 'The Ancestry of Gordian I.' *AJP* lxxxix (1968), 345.

Panciera, S. 'Miscellanea storico-epigrafica III.' *Epigraphica* xxix (1967), 19.

Pflaum, H.-G. 'Deux carrières équestres de Lambèse et de Zama.' *Libyca* iii (1955), 123.

—— 'Les gendres de Marc-Aurèle.' *Journal des Savants*, 1961, 28.

Piganiol, A. 'L'état actuel de la Question Constantinienne 1939/1949.' *Historia* i (1950), 82.

Pöschl, Fr. 'Erläuterungen zur Vita Antonini Pii in der Historia Augusta.' *Wiener Studien* lxvi (1953), 178.

Préaux, C. 'Sur le déclin de l'empire au IIIᵉ siècle de notre ère.' *Chronique d'Égypte* xxxi (1941), 123.

Ritterling, E. 'Zum römischen Heerwesen des ausgehenden dritten Jahrhunderts.' *Festschrift Hirschfeld* (1903), 345.

Rougé, J. 'L'Histoire Auguste et l'Isaurie au IVᵉ siècle.' *Rev. ét. anc.* lxviii (1966), 282.

Rühl, F. 'Die Zeit des Vopiscus.' *Rh. Mus.* xliii (1888), 597.

Starcky, J., and C. M. Bennet. 'Découvertes récentes au sanctuaire du Qasr à Petra, III.' *Syria* xlv (1968), 41.

Stein, A. 'Ἐπίσκεψις. *Charisteria Rzach* (1930), 176.

Syme, R. 'Missing senators.' *Historia* iv (1955), 52.

—— 'Missing persons.' *Historia* v (1956), 204.

—— 'The Jurist Neratius Priscus.' *Hermes* lxxxv (1957), 480.

—— 'Antonine relatives: Ceionii and Vettuleni.' *Athenaeum* xxxv (1957), 306.

—— 'Consulates in absence.' *JRS* xlviii (1958), 1.

—— 'Pliny's less successful friends.' *Historia* ix (1960), 362.

—— 'Les proconsuls d'Afrique sous Hadrien.' *Rev. ét. anc.* lxvii (1965), 342.

—— 'Governors of Pannonia Inferior.' *Historia* xiv (1965), 342.

—— 'Hadrian in Moesia.' *Arheološki vestnik* xix (1968), 101.

—— 'The Ummidii.' *Historia* xvii (1968), 72.

—— 'Not Marius Maximus.' *Hermes* xcvi (1968), 494.

—— 'Three Jurists.' *Bonner Historia-Augusta-Colloquium 1968/69* (1970), 309.

Toutain, J. 'Réflexions sur une monnaie romaine.' *Mélanges Bidez-Cumont.* Coll. Latomus ii (1949), 331.

Townend, G. B. 'The Post *ab epistulis* in the Second Century.' *Historia* x (1961), 375.

Townsend, P. W. 'The revolution of A.D. 238. The leaders and their aims.' *Yale Classical Studies* xiv (1955), 49.

TROPEA, G. 'Antonini Nomen negli S. H. A.' *Rivista di storia antica* iv (1899), 233.

VELKOV, V. 'Ratiaria. Eine römische Stadt in Bulgarien.' *Eirene* v (1966), 155.

WAGENER, C. 'Eutropius. Jahresbericht.' *Philologus* xlv (1886), 509.
WERNER, R. 'Der historische Wert der Pertinaxvita in den Scriptores Historiae Augustae.' *Klio* xxvi (1933), 283.
WHITE, P. 'The authorship of the *Historia Augusta*.' *JRS* lvii (1967), 115.

INDEX

'Ablavius Murena', 216.
Abraham, 26, 276.
'Acholius', 96, 120, 248, 277–8.
Aedinius Julianus, M., 151–2, 153, 157.
'Aelii', 74.
Aelius Aristides, 161.
'Aelius Bassianus', 62.
Aelius Caesar, in HA, origin, 69; called 'Verus', 19, 40, 80; tastes and pastimes, 62–4.
'Aelius Celsus', 74.
'Aelius Cesettianus', 239.
'Aelius Corduenus', 74.
'Aelius Cordus', see 'Junius Cordus'.
Aelius Donatus, 7.
'Aelius Gordianus', 170, 279.
'Aelius Lampridius', 73–5, 249, 261; praised by 'Vopiscus', 47, 258.
'Aelius Spartianus', 73–4, 249.
Aelius Triccianus, 118, 190.
'Aelius Xiphidius', 8, 12, 216.
Aemilianus, usurper in Egypt, 28, 251, 270.
Aemilius Aemilianus, 202, 219.
'Aemilius Parthenianus', 55, 59, 61.
Aequitius, tribune, in Ammianus, 243.
Africa, 35, 50, 163, 165; proconsuls of, 137, 145, 157–8; senators from, 140–1, 164; Italian *nomina* attested, 141, 143.
Aiacius Modestus Crescentianus, Q. (*cos. II* 228), 139, 140, 143, 158.
Alani, 182.
Albini, in false genealogies, 62.
Alexander the Great, 96, 98, 103–104, 127, 155, 162.
Alexander, usurper in Africa, 227, 229.
Alexandria, 20, 28, 35, 268; wit of Alexandrians, 273–4.
Alfenus Senecio, L. (*cos. c.* 197), 136, 138, 139, 140.
Ambrose, influence on Theodosius, 24.
Ammianus Marcellinus, 192, 203, 227, 230, 258, 287–8; historical *exempla*, 92, 102, 199; views on Roman aristocracy, 15, 47, 85, 94; on Trajan, 106; on Marius

Maximus, 45, 47; influence on HA, 19, 26, 28–9, 76, 259, 286.
Anacletus, Pope, in Geoffrey, 265.
Ancharius, Q., in Cicero, 6.
'Ancharius', 'Quintus', 5–6, 8.
Anicii, 11.
Anicius Faustus, Q., consular, 139.
'Annibalianus', 213.
Annii Anullini, 233.
'Annius Cornicula', 267.
'Annius Fuscus', 4, 7.
'Annius Severus', 4, 101, 169, 267.
Annius of Viterbo, 266.
Antinous, 115.
Antiochenes, their wit, 26, 273–4.
Antiochianus, *praefectus praetorio*, 119.
Antonii, senatorial, 167.
Antonines, their occurrence in late writers, 89–93; invented descendants of the dynasty, 4, 10, 69; history of the name 'Antoninus', 78–80; elaboration of the name by HA, 80–8, 273.
Antoninus, usurper under Severus Alexander, 79, 159.
'Antoninus Gallus', 216.
Antoninus Pius: nomenclature, 4, 37, 78; his life and reign in HA, 36–41; City Prefects, 39; reputation in late antiquity, 89, 91–2.
Antonius Augustinus, Archbishop of Tarragona, 274.
Antony, the Egyptian hermit, 15.
Aper, Praetorian Prefect, 219, 244.
Apicius, his cookery book, 62.
'Apollonius Syrus Platonicus', 72, 114, 271.
Apollonius of Tyana, 26, 276.
Apollonius, teacher of Marcus, 40.
Aquileia, 50, 165.
Aradii, from Africa, 140.
'Aradio', 9, 140.
Arca, birthplace of Severus Alexander, 274.
Arcadius, 104.
'Arellius Fuscus', 6, 9, 238.
Aristomachus, tribune, 119.